P9-CMX-676

NOSTRADAMUS

ALSO BY STÉPHANE GERSON

Nostradamus, *The Prophecies,*
edited with Richard Sieburth (trans. Sieburth)

*Why France? American Historians Reflect on an
Enduring Fascination,*
edited with Laura Lee Downs

*The Pride of Place:
Local Memories and Political Culture
in Nineteenth-Century France*

NOSTRADAMUS

❧❦❧

*How an Obscure Renaissance
Astrologer Became the Modern
Prophet of Doom*

Stéphane Gerson

ST. MARTIN'S PRESS
NEW YORK

www.stmartins.com

Design by Kathryn Parise

The Library of Congress has cataloged the print edition as follows:

Gerson, Stéphane.
  Nostradamus : how an obscure Renaissance astrologer became the modern prophet of doom / Stephane Gerson.
       pages cm.
   ISBN 978-0-312-61368-6 (hardcover)
   ISBN 978-1-250-01756-7 (e-book)
   1. Nostradamus, 1503–1566.   2. Nostradamus, 1503–1566— Prophecies.   3. Twentieth century—Forecasts.   4. Prophecies (Occultism)   I. Title.
   BF1815.N8G47 2012
   133.3092—dc23

                                                          2012031001

First Edition: November 2012

10 9 8 7 6 5 4 3 2 1

For Julian, with love

In memory of Owen, who saw things others did not

Contents

❦

I want a form that's large enough to swim in,
And talk on any subject that I choose,
From natural scenery to men and women,
Myself, the arts, the European news.
                    —W. H. Auden,
                        "Letter to Lord Byron"

The Nostradamus age was there
Cities destroyed—joy driven out.
                    —Jean Cocteau,
                        "Broken Poem for Picasso"

Preface

꠶

In the wake of 9/11, politicians offered reassurance, firefighters became heroes, and newscasters pulled on-air marathons. The rest of us simply tried to grasp what had happened and imagine what might follow. Enter Nostradamus. Within hours, rumors circulated that he had predicted it all. One widely distributed e-mail contained a prophetic text that spoke of a city burning, a third big war beginning while a great leader succumbed, and two brothers torn apart by chaos. Another evoked a great king of terror and disaster during the year of the new century and nine months. "The sky will burn at forty-five degrees and fire shall engulf the world." September was of course the ninth month of the year and New York City's latitude is forty-one degrees. The message was clear: Nostradamus had foretold the attacks and warned the United States.

By September 12, these e-mails had spread across the country. One hundred of 120 students in one southern California high school received at least one. Several talk shows mentioned Nostradamus and propelled his name to the top of search engines, ahead of Osama bin Laden. Snopes.com debunked these messages as hoaxes, which was true only to a point. A Canadian student had written the prediction about two brothers, but the references to the great king of terror and the burning sky came from actual Nostradamian quatrains. Another email began circulating with the following words: "Fire at the earth's core / Shall set the New City all quake." People debated whether the great leader was George W. Bush and whether New York was indeed the big city in flames. On Brooklyn stoops, teenagers waved the quatrains while telling passers-by that "this guy, Nostradamus" had seen it coming.[1]

Within four days, Nostradamus's *Prophecies* had jumped to the top of Amazon's best sellers list. Five other books about him cracked the top twenty-five. "It's one of those morbid business realities that in times like this people turn to relevant products," explained a company spokeswoman. In one Barnes & Noble store in Brooklyn, twenty customers asked for Nostradamus in a single day. Joanna Jusino, a thirty-two-year-old New Yorker, told a journalist that she had ordered the *Prophecies* to know what to expect in the weeks to come. Booksellers restocked as fast as they could. The same happened in Hungary, where the *Prophecies* became a number-one best seller. In England, the *Times* remarked that Nostradamus was becoming more popular than books on sex. In Singapore, too, people pondered a prediction that seemed to have portrayed the attacks with such accuracy. "We were even discussing how it could be a sign that it was the end of the world," explained one media executive. This was no fringe movement. In the midst of global distress, Nostradamus infiltrated mainstream culture.[2]

I could not help but watch in awe. My wife and I lived a few blocks from the World Trade Center at the time, and we evacuated our apartment while the towers burned. Holed up in a hotel room with our sons during the weeks that followed, we nursed our anguish as best we could while time itself grew still and furious. Like others, we participated in candlelight vigils and took in the impromptu memorials at Union Square. Nostradamus was something else: a mysterious lure, an emotional pull that drew so many people to scintillating words that came from another era and yet had never seemed more relevant. I did not consult Nostradamus that September, but I remembered that these predictions had entered my life once before. It happened in Brussels, where I grew up, during the early 1980s. I was fifteen or sixteen, and every magazine seemed to contain an article on his predictions and Soviet missiles flattening Western Europe. "Maximum Danger: Summer 1984!" blared the French weekly *Paris-Match*. Strong stuff. I was petrified and mesmerized and did not know what to make of this. But I kept on reading—without telling anyone.

When the quatrains resurfaced after 9/11, I could thus recall their force.

Mostly, I was struck by their prevalence in our own times. Others paid attention as well. Norm Magnusson, a Manhattan-based artist, nailed a copy of the *Prophecies* to a twelve-foot-high wood beam and called the piece *The Feeling We're Entering an Era of Prophecies.* It was part of a series on America and the world after 9/11. This sculpture expressed one take on the matter—Nostradamus as talisman—but it did not limit itself to that. "These paroxysms of prescience usually leave me flat," Magnusson wrote in his artist's note, "but this time they resonated just a bit. Maybe we were entering a foretold era. I didn't believe it, but this time, I didn't just write it off."[3]

I did not write it off either, although like so many people I could barely associate a face with the name. There is a wonderful scene in the first *Sopranos* episode to air after 9/11 in which mafiosos Tony Soprano and Bobby Bacala catch up over dinner. At one point, Bobby remarks that Quasimodo had predicted the attacks. Tony looks up and replies that he is confusing Nostradamus with the fictional hunchback of Notre-Dame. "Oh, right, Notre Damus," says Bobby—at which point Tony interjects that Notre-Dame and Nostradamus are altogether different. Bobby is puzzled and Tony knows little more. Neither do we. All of us have heard of Nostradamus; a few among us are aware that he lived a long time ago. But that is pretty much it. If asked what Nostradamus brings to mind, we might speak of "tabloids, crazy people on the street, and other rather strange phenomena in our culture." This is one of the answers I received after posing the question to a class of college students not long ago.[4]

Nostradamus does draw us into a strange universe, full of ghosts, eerie prophets, and ominous forecasts. The strangest thing of all, however, is that Nostradamus and his predictions have become an enduring facet of the modern West. (*Modern* refers to the era that came into being during the Renaissance. Historians further distinguish between early and late modern periods, with the French Revolution as the dividing line.) It is rare for a book to speak to successive generations about their world, across national borders, languages, and cultural or political divides. The Bible has had such an afterlife, even if many religions dismiss it entirely. The plays of Shakespeare have had one as well. And so have Nostradamus's *Prophecies,* a remarkable feat for a work that was written in Old French and obtained little religious or literary recognition in its time and afterward.

I was not drawn to Nostradamus by the prospect of determining whether the quatrains had really rested on extrasensory experience or precognitive information. I would not be the one to determine whether the "fire at the earth's core" truly referred to the burning towers. Instead, I wanted to know where these predictions came from and how they had made it this far. I wanted to understand why they have mattered and continue to matter to all kinds of people. I wanted to recover the humanity and the multiple facets of a phenomenon that has become so diffuse and received such scorn that only a caricature remains. And I wanted to figure out what all of this says about the society that hosts Nostradamus. So it all began.

⁓ΘᏀ⤜

One of the joys of writing about such a topic is that people love to talk about it. Over the years, I have heard countless stories. A Puerto Rican student spoke about her grandmother, a devout Catholic who was obsessed with these predictions. A San Antonio retiree confessed that she once rescheduled a trip to California because Nostradamus had predicted an earthquake. A Los Angeles librarian told me that she cherished her aunt's dog-eared copy of the *Prophecies*. And numerous residents of Salon-de-Provence, the town that the seer made his own, sat down for interviews about Nostradamus's presence (or absence) there. I am indebted to all of them, and to numerous other people, for trusting me with their tales and recollections.

Others have listened to my ideas and voiced their own as well. Students in my course Apocalypse Now? The Lure of Nostradamus asked probing questions that took us into new directions. Special thanks to Anastasia Belinskaya, Marion Cohn, Dean Linnard, Amanda Mayo, Antonio Urias, and Xiaoying Zhang. Many friends and colleagues have provided suggestions, references, and rich conversation. It is a pleasure to thank Charles Affron, Olivier Berthe, Vicki Caron, Arnaud Coulombel, Steven Englund, Aude Fauvel, my mother Francine Gerson and my late father Bernie Gerson, Josh Gilbert, Denis Hollier, Tony Judt, Dominique Kalifa, Brigitte Lane, Bettina Lerner, Chantal Liaroutzos, Tod Lippy, Judith Lyon-Caen, Norm Magnusson, Dominique Martin, Gordon Neavill, Jacques Revel, Emmanuelle Saada, Maurice Samuels, Steven Sawyer, John Siciliano, David K. Smith, Marie-Eve Thérenty, and Laura van Straaten. I am also grateful for the opportunities to present this work at Columbia University, Cornell University, the Institute of French Studies (NYU), the Nineteenth-Century French Studies Conference, the Remarque Institute (NYU), the Society for French Historical Studies, the Sorbonne, SUNY Albany, Tufts University, and Yale University.

A book of this scope necessarily builds on the work of others. While I acknowledge my debts in the notes, I wish to make special mention of the scholars of the Renaissance and early modern era who have contributed so much to our understanding of Nostradamus and his words: Robert Benazra, Pierre Brind'Amour, Anna Carlstedt, Bernard Chevignard, Denis Crouzet, Hervé Drévillon, Claude-Gilbert Dubois, Patrice Guinard, Edgar Leroy, and Bruno Petey-Girard. Michel Chomarat took me on a memorable walking tour of Nostradamus's Lyon and granted me full access to his remarkable collection on the man and his afterlife. The second leading Nostradamian collector of modern times, Daniel Ruzo de los Heros, died years ago, but his heirs auctioned off much of his library in 2007. I am grateful to Tobias Abeloff, Early Printed Books specialist at the Swann Auction Galleries in New York, for allowing me to consult these precious items, some of which had been presumed lost forever.

My research was supported in part by grants from the American Historical Association, the American Philosophical Society, the NYU Research Challenge Fund Program, and the Remarque Institute. It was made considerably easier by the help provided by librarians and archivists in countless institutions. I am beholden to Jean-Paul Laroche (Bibliothèque municipale de Lyon), Françoise Pelé and Guy Bonvicini (Archives municipales de Salon-de-Provence), Jacqueline Allemand (Maison Nostradamus), and Barbara Hall (Margaret Herrick Library). In France, I also wish to thank the staffs of the Archives départementales des Bouches-du-Rhône, the Archives Nationales, the Bibliothèque de l'Arsenal, the Bibliothèque Mazarine, the Bibliothèque Méjanes, the Bibliothèque Nationale de France, the Chambre de Commerce et d'Industrie Marseille Provence, the Institut Catholique de Paris, and the Institut de France. Elsewhere, thank you to the staff of the British Library, the libraries of Columbia, Cornell, and Harvard universities, the Houghton Library, the Huntington Library, the Newberry Library, the New York Public Library, and NYU's interlibrary loan office. Ned Comstock (USC Cinematic Arts Library), Frédéric Maguet (Musée des Civilisations de l'Europe et de la

Méditerranée), Emilienne Molina (Bibliothèque municipale d'Avignon), and Pascale Vignaud (Bibliothèque municipale de La Rochelle) kindly sent me copies of documents and images.

Françoise Wyss-Mercier shared documents and photographs from her personal collection on Salon-de-Provence's historical pageants. Patricia Jeanbaptiste forwarded a copy of her master's thesis. My colleague John Hamilton, my student Lisa Kitagawa, and my brother-in-law Tiziano Recchi provided translations of Latin, Japanese, and Italian sources. Steven Crumb and Joshua Jordan translated some French documents. Four fine research assistants—Suzanna Denison, Kari Evanson, Mary-Elizabeth O'Neill, and Rachel Wimpee—helped locate and transcribe sources; Grace Stephenson assisted with the bibliography. Heartfelt thanks to all of them—and to *Esopus* magazine for allowing me to reprint excerpts from my "Searching for Nostradamus: Tracking the Man, the Legend, and the Name Across Five Centuries."

Several friends and colleagues have devoted considerable time and attention to this project. Dan Ain, James Smith Allen, Herrick Chapman, Mitch Horowitz, Suzanne A. Kaufman, and Anne-Marie Thiesse read parts of the book and provided helpful feedback. I am deeply indebted to four scholars who were generous enough to comment on the entire manuscript. Richard Sieburth provided a stimulating response to an early draft. Steven Crumb and Frédéric Viguier pushed me to clarify certain claims and draw new connections. Paul Cohen did the same, and also drew from his encyclopedic knowledge to help me broaden my scope. I am also grateful to Julia Serebrinsky for her sensitive input on the epilogue. While all of them have made this a better book, its shortcomings are mine alone. Tim Bent, Daniel Goldberg, Jon Karp, Cindy Karter, and Paul Katz gave vital advice regarding trade publishing. The path from manuscript to publication would have been much rockier without the steady hands and warm support of my agent Steve Hanselman. It has been a delight to work with Michael Flamini, Vicki Lame, and the entire team at St. Martin's Press.

My deepest appreciations are at home. My son Julian has grown up with stories about Nostradamus and kept an eye out for relevant docudramas on late-night cable. He is a savvy conversationalist and an unusually sensitive person who accepted and perhaps even understood my fixation with these prophecies. It is difficult to express what my wife Alison has given me these past years. It goes far beyond the book, but when it came to this, she provided all of the encouragement and advice that I needed. She was willing to discuss facets of this story even when there were more urgent things to contemplate. She also gave the manuscript an astute read, capped by a memorable edit session in Arizona. Alison is a force and a wonder, and I am incredibly lucky to have her in my life.

Introduction

✦

S omeone once wrote that, inch per printed inch, the most quoted Frenchman in history was neither Voltaire nor Charles de Gaulle, but Nostradamus. I cannot vouch for this, but the claim feels true as one begins to delve
into the reams of material surrounding these predictions. It is a lot to take in,
but a few things quickly become clear. First, there is indeed a man behind the
name: a Frenchman of Jewish descent named Michel de Nostredame who
was born in Provence in 1503 and died there in 1566. He was a true Renaissance polymath: a plague doctor, a botanist, an avid traveler and letter writer,
an astrologer who made mathematical calculations and wrote horoscopes for
clients across Europe, and a publishing maven who produced countless
almanacs for a competitive market. He was also the author of the *Prophecies,*
a collection of prophetic verse that first came out in 1555. In his day and for
a long time afterward, Europeans knew exactly who this Nostredame was.
They felt the power of his ferocious predictions.[1]

I also realized fairly quickly that the astrologer has left hundreds of predictions but no consensus regarding their meaning or import. During his lifetime and afterward, his words have fascinated and flummoxed the West. There
have clearly been moments of shining visibility—typically linked to national
and international crises—and others during which Nostradamus has receded
into the background. The cocktail has always contained equal parts fascination,

consternation, and discomfort. Legitimacy has been an issue from the start. But Nostradamus has never fully vanished, which is odd since most Renaissance soothsayers, and there were many, are now forgotten. Alongside the man, there has been a long-lasting phenomenon: to distinguish between them, I refer to the first as Nostredame and to the second as Nostradamus. Nostredame wove rich relationships with people and cultural realms and, intentionally or not, set into motion forces that have played out across centuries.

But biography does not explain everything: Nostredame did not single-handedly shape his posterity. We must thus look beyond his intentions and the question of what he *really* sought to accomplish and instead consider the power of his words. These words acquired a singular force during his lifetime. Afterward, they were parsed again and again—during the Wars of Religion and other early modern conflicts, the Great Fire of London and England's Glorious Revolution, the French Revolution and Napoleonic Empire, the age of romanticism and mass culture in the nineteenth century, nearly every conflict between the U.S. Civil War and the cold war, and the anxious closing decades of the twentieth century. Readers have ranged from kings and queens to businessmen and lawyers, from peasants and artisans to journalists and students. Men and women have plunged into this universe with awe and uncertainty, curiosity and apprehension, glee and irony. Some have done so in the midst of cataclysms, while others have parsed the predictions in calmer times. Some have simply dipped in, while others have devoted days and nights to unraveling these mysteries. This does not mean that a majority of the population has been drawn toward the predictions, or that people have read them in a consistent and resolute fashion. But Nostradamus clearly draws us into the maelstrom of social and political life, into a universe in which the Apocalypse is present, but not the only thing. Wonder, politics, entertainment, and the quest for meaning lie at the heart of this story.

The next thing that became apparent is that Nostradamus's commentators have by and large fallen into two camps over the centuries. In one corner stand the enthusiasts, captivated by predictions that, with the right lens, promise to illuminate the course of the world. In the opposite corner are the skeptics, the cynics, the debunkers who took aim during the Renaissance and have never let Nostradamus out of their sight. Six days after 9/11, an American journalist complained that "the kooks are coming out of the woodwork." This language is typical. Intellectuals and scholars, too, are wary of a phenomenon that reeks of astrology and magic. Nostradamus has long been seen as either an imminent casualty of secular progress or a nefarious remnant of times past. In the 1970s, NYU offered a continuing education course on Witchcraft, Magic, and Astrology. Its instructor (one Owen Rachleff) was the author of several books on astrology and parapsychology. He apparently sought to warn impressionable young minds about the perils of the occult, which included Nostradamus. It is easy today to find serious studies of astrology or our perceptions of time that either exclude this charlatan or mention him only to illustrate the inconsistency of the human mind.[2]

This stance softened somewhat in the 1990s, when scholars began questioning the notion that science, rationality, and secularism had displaced wonder, spirituality, and mystery in the modern West. As they punctured holes in this story of disenchantment, they rediscovered prophets, astrologers, spiritualists, magicians, and occultists who in reality had been hiding in plain sight. Historians of science had already been examining astrology as a specific form of knowledge. Renaissance specialists now began paying attention to Nostradamus's almanacs and melancholy poems. But unease continues to surround a mode of thinking that seems so foreign, especially for scholars who study recent times. The word *Nostradamus* has a way of eliciting blank stares and incredulous questions in certain circles. I vividly remember a dinner party at which a historian found my object of research so perplexing that he stared at me in silence for long seconds. Unable to muster a response, he simply looked the other way and began a conversation with somebody else. I have in all honesty received plenty of support from colleagues, but never did I better grasp the meaning of guilt by association than on that evening. Such encounters capture the way in which Nostradamus became a kind of detritus, consigned to what the critic Walter Benjamin called "the refuse of history."[3]

And yet, Nostradamus continues to loom in the West. The specter of a figure who lived so long ago has maintained a presence in our collective imagination. To ask why is to examine how we have determined what is reasonable, rational, and permissible at different points in history. It is also to examine our relationships to fear and horror, to uncertainty and loss and massive collective crises. These relationships are constantly changing, but they are also indebted to what happened in earlier centuries. The similarities are sometimes striking. The past thus beckons as a foreign land that must be studied in its own terms, and as a strangely familiar one that leaves us with unfocused but recognizable images.

The most common explanation for Nostradamus's lasting appeal is that his arcane predictions could mean anything. The English priest Herbert Thurston makes the point as well as anyone in his 1915 book *The War & the Prophets*. Nostradamus, he explains, is a "masterpiece of Delphic ambiguity" (a reference to the Greek Oracle of Delphi) whose success rests on the sheer number of quatrains and the *Prophecies'* dearth of categorical statements and references to specific times and places. This makes it easy to uncover startling coincidences and impossible to claim that the prophet was mistaken. Nostradamus, Thurston concludes, "provides an ingenious system of divination in which the misses can never be recorded and only the hits come to the surface."[4]

Thurston is right on one point: there is a machine at work and we will have to figure out how it works. But there have been other predictions of the sort, and most have vanished. The machine alone does not explain why Nostradamus has appeared and receded from view and then returned again and again. It says nothing about Nostradamus as a political instrument, a cultural framework, a dramatic imprint of its world, a response to personal or collective crises, or a means of imparting meaning to external circumstances. We will not understand much about this phenomenon by falling back on what some call the Barnum effect, named after the showman P. T. Barnum (give a little bit of something to everyone), or the notion that the vaguer the statement, the more people recognize themselves in it.[5]

The main idea that runs through this book is that the man and the phenomenon are creatures of the modern West rather than aberrations or vestiges from some antediluvian era. They captured some of its central volitions and ambivalences during the Renaissance and have continued doing so during the centuries that followed—largely because the Nostradamus phenomenon inhabits what might be called the in-between. The historian Tony Judt spoke of *edge people* whose multiple identities, communities, and allegiances bump against one another. There is something of the edge person in Michel de Nostredame, the man who traveled from one realm to another, took it all in, digested it, maintained his distance throughout, and then incorporated this world into predictive or prophetic quatrains.[6]

Nostredame the man was sandwiched between the astronomer Nicolaus Copernicus and the philosopher Giordano Bruno. The former placed the sun rather than the Earth at the center of the universe; the latter imagined that the universe could contain an infinite number of worlds that were similar to the earth. Both contributed to the process by which the notion of a closed, religious world faded behind a boundless and eventually godless cosmos. The Copernican revolution displaced humanity from the center of the world but also provided a rational purchase on the cosmos. Nostredame likewise came of age as several tectonic shifts shook the foundations of the West. The discovery of the Americas and its pagan inhabitants launched vast enterprises of exploration and conquest while challenging the boundaries of the known world and the conviction that Christ had spread the good word to all. The printing press opened up intellectual vistas and spread doctrines and ideas while allowing new forces to challenge the authority of dominant institutions. The Protestant Reformation's assault on Catholic dogma and clergy fed yearnings for renewed spirituality and social equality while cracking the confessional unity of states and principalities, some of which now included both Catholic and Protestant residents.[7]

Nostredame did not precipitate these sea changes, but his words embraced and concentrated the world that was coming into being, with its mix of the old and the new, its shifting forces and fault lines, its opportunities and its anxieties. They took in this overflowing multiplicity, made it visible and tangible, and gave it dramatic form without flattening out contradictions. There were other such cornucopian texts at that time, but this one had a tautness and yet also an elasticity, a sense of eternity and yet also an urgency of its own. At once empty and full of meaning, his inscrutable words have invited readers to decode, elucidate, and project their own concerns. They summon magical forces as well as logical deduction. They impart both knowledge about the world and the vertiginous feeling that nothing can be known. They feed optimism about human abilities and pessimism regarding human proclivities. They generate fear and desolation while tapping the past, reordering the present, outlining the future, and helping people respond to anxiety and collective crises. It is a welter of contradictions.

new ways of thinking about France as at once national and local, abstract and tangible, unified and diverse. Ensconced in the margins, the local infused the center, outlined blueprints for collective life, and helped shape what we might call modernity. It was hard to miss the paradox.

It is possible to tell a similar story about Nostradamus. Everything for which the phenomenon stands—not just magic or astrology but also apocalypticism, unreason, and popular culture—has been pushed to the margins of the rational, liberal West. While Nostradamus is usually portrayed as a rearguard force, I realized early on that, far from remaining immobile, far from speaking to narrow segments of the population alone, the phenomenon has continuously refashioned itself, reaching out to people from disparate backgrounds. Precarious as it may be, the edge also affords freedom and opportunities to cross boundaries. If Nostradamus inhabits our outer banks, then these are broad, open expanses in which people sometimes grow dependent or paralyzed and sometimes explore new domains and give coherence to their world.

Nostradamus resides on the edge in yet another way. Historians have examined the ways esteemed individuals such as George Washington and Victor Hugo entered collective memory. The premise is that social forces—national and ethnic communities, religious traditions, political schools—underpin this memory and that without such a foundation, a given figure will disappear. But no regime or political formation, no organized religion or intellectual school has made Nostradamus its own. No learned academy, no pantheon, no national commemorations have recognized the astrologer. No secular or religious canon has deemed the predictions fit for inclusion. This is a story without collective institutions. It is also one without moral lessons or heroic qualities, without legitimacy or founding myths. Nostredame is not Lincoln, the glorious leader whom every American generation refashions in its own image. He is not Billy the Kid, the historical figure who spawned a legend while remaining tethered to a particular era. He is not even Robin Hood, the noble bandit who despite his fictional origins became a Saxon hero in modern Britain and then suffused mass culture. It is no surprise that Tony Soprano and his brother-in-law Bobby knew so little about the man.[8]

Still, Nostradamus endures. The phenomenon takes us beyond conventions of virtue and heroism, into what we might call the crevices of memory.

There are no gatekeepers here, few norms and hierarchies, and little over-sight. This has opened up a space for individuals who entertain loose rela-tionships to collective memory. None have played a more important role than the news and entertainment media. From the Renaissance to the present, Nostradamus has surfed every media wave, from almanacs to newspapers to movies and the Internet. Each one has both publicized and reshaped the phenomenon while making the world at once more comforting and more intimidating, more approachable and more distant. This is also a story, there-fore, about editors, publishers, translators, interpreters, commentators, imita-tors, forgers, journalists, and others yet. These men and women took hold of the predictions, sometimes grappled with them, and rarely hesitated to alter them as they saw fit. Given Nostradamus's controversial nature, many of them likewise chose or ended up on the margins, conversing with one another across centuries and national borders, all of them part of an underground and yet open to the broader world. They may have failed to solidify the image of Nostredame and make him respectable, but they imparted Nostradamus to others and brought it into the mainstream. In this story, the margins of the modern West are not only margins. They are also one of its driving forces.

⁊⊚⊚̃

A few years ago, a new port of call appeared on Nostradamus's itinerary: De-cember 21, 2012. The 2012 prophecies now take countless forms, but most commentators begin with the notion that the Maya's Sacred Calendar (a 260-day count) and their Vague Year (a 365-day count) will converge on that fate-ful day. The date will also mark the end of two great cycles, which began respectively in 24000 and 3113 BCE. In recent years, media outlets and commentators have added Nostradamus to the mix. Some now say that, ac-cording to the Maya and Nostradamus, we should expect a cataclysmic event on that winter solstice. They announce a reversal of the earth's magnetic poles and a shift of its axis, a pulse of light emanating from a black hole at the center of our galaxy, or star flares that will disturb our electrical grid. Others speak of a change of cycle, the end of an era, and perhaps transformative change as human civilization enters a millennial era of ecological harmony.[9]

Whatever will come, the irrepressible Nostradamus tells us something about our times as well. It might be about loss and fright in an era of ever more salient risks and catastrophes (so it seems). Or it might be about something more subtle: forces that come together in ways that no one had anticipated, yearnings that seem to contradict one another, new ways of defining oneself and one's world. We will see.

Vertigo sets in, however, as one beholds this phenomenon over a half millennium. Jean Cocteau reportedly quipped that the only way to know a country is to stay there for either three hours or thirty years. I have spent considerable time in the company of Nostradamus, but three decades might not have sufficed to follow this story. There can be no illusions of exhaustivity, especially for someone like me, who is neither a lifelong aficionado nor a scholar of astrology or prophecy. Outsiders can contribute a new sensibility and ask different kinds of questions, but they also face a steep climb.

I thus decided at the outset to pay special attention to France, the country in which Nostredame first came into view and then remained most salient. Many of the insights that France provides have broader applications. But one must also look beyond the nation to grasp the phenomenon in its international and local dimensions, to understand how these predictions and the image of the man have circulated across space, and to retrieve its connotations—sometimes similar, sometimes not—in different parts of the world. This has required prolonged stays in Salon-de-Provence as well as incursions into Great Britain, Germany, Italy, the United States, and Japan.

Another early decision was to focus on both words and people: Nostredame himself, the interpreters and editors, the naysayers, and the men and women who have gravitated toward the predictions over the centuries. Determining how ordinary people related to written words in past eras is a challenging task given the dearth of sources. Historians of cultural reception, as it is called, must thus acknowledge that much will remain unknown and yet refuse to concede defeat. One of my strategies has been to comb archival catalogs for manuscript letters and diaries that mention Nostradamus (I found more than thirty). I also read a hundred travel accounts to Provence, paying special attention to what visitors wrote after visiting Nostredame's tomb in Salon. Even if they sometimes cribbed from guidebooks or other accounts, these travelers put enough of their own selves into these texts to provide insights. Midway through my research, new electronic databases provided a final and unexpected window. These tools raise complicated questions (how representative, for example, are the occurrences found on Google Books?). Still, the three dozen databases that I mined have made it possible to watch all kinds of people, both famous and unknown, connect with Nostradamus out of sight.

My last decision was to organize the book around episodes and individuals who capture key facets or turning points in this story. First comes the Renaissance, with Nostredame the doctor with a horoscope practice, the poet and almanac writer, the published prophet, and the controversial celebrity. After his death in 1566, we enter Nostradamus's afterlife in the company of his secretary and then jump from one historical moment to another. By following a blacksmith from Salon to the court of Louis XIV, we penetrate the early modern world of wonder and politics in which Nostradamus flourished. By sojourning in London during the Great Fire of 1666 and in Salon during the French Revolution, we grasp what his verses meant during natural and political crises. Public entertainment enters the story. In the nineteenth century, we meet a journalist, a priest, and a dime novelist who encapsulate Nostradamus's presence between lowbrow, highbrow, and mass cultures. During World War II, totalitarian and democratic propaganda machines turn the quatrains into tools of mass persuasion. And at the turn of the third millennium, gloom settles upon the West like the white powder that blanketed lower Manhattan on 9/11.

Each of these moments is at once a contained unit, a chapter in a broader story, and a launching pad for further reflection. While this book is steeped in considerable research, it is best seen as a blend between a historical essay and a map of a little-traveled expanse. It sprouted from sheer curiosity and will, I hope, speak to readers who are equally intrigued—and may even go on to explore facets of this phenomenon in greater depth than is possible here. Some questions are elided; others are only touched upon. This is neither a religious history of millenarianism nor an intellectual study of time, for instance. There is nothing about Scandinavia, South America, and other places in which Nostradamus has acquired a presence. I have come to accept this, even if these lines from Walt Whitman were never far as I wrote: "You road I enter upon and look around, I believe you are not all that is here, / I believe that much unseen is also here."

The unseen is everywhere when it comes to Nostradamus. We do not see the origins of the words. We do not perceive the powers on which they rest, or even the horizons to which they point. Nor do we necessarily discern the forces that push us in their direction. In the mid-1980s, I bid farewell to Nostradamus when I left Belgium for a bucolic American campus. Soon thereafter, the fall of the Berlin Wall lessened the threat of nuclear war and lowered anxieties. Why, then, had these predictions entered my life for a short but intense moment? And why had this fascination made me so uncomfortable that I kept it to myself? Such questions did not enter my mind when I began this book, at least not consciously. This seems odd in retrospect, but historians do not always ponder why they do what they do. Conversing with the dead in the archives, as one scholar put it, may be easier than looking into one's soul.

The vagaries of life can disrupt the most comfortable arrangements, however. As I wrote this book, my family was hit by a tragedy that made me feel all too viscerally those forces that we associate with Nostradamus. At first, I resisted broaching the matter in these pages, but I eventually had to acknowledge that, personal as it was, this experience became part of the broad story I set out to write. I could no longer dodge my own ambivalence. In life as in the archives, the dead sometimes take us to places that we can barely contemplate.

~❧~

Nostradamus's key book, the *Prophecies*, contains 942 four-line poems: the quatrains. They are divided into ten sections called *centuries*. In the pages that follow, I identify each quatrain according to its position in its original *centurie*: 4.50 thus refers to the fiftieth quatrain of the fourth *centurie*.

Quotations from Nostradamus's *Prophecies* come from the Penguin Classics edition, edited by Stéphane Gerson and Richard Sieburth, translated by Richard Sieburth, translation copyright © 2012. Used by permission of Penguin, a division of Penguin Group (USA) Inc.

Unless otherwise indicated, all French documents have been translated by the author. I have sometimes modernized the spelling of texts in Old English.

Chapter 1

꘏꘎

A Good Friend in
Renaissance Europe

Today we associate Nostradamus with New York, Paris, and other mega-cities whose demises are linked to his name. Back in the sixteenth century, however, people visited or wrote him in a small southern French town called Salon de Craux (later changed to Salon-de-Provence). Salon sits in the heart of the Crau, a windswept plateau that was so arid and desolate that some visitors likened it to a little Sahara. Thanks to a rich soil and a propitious location along trade routes, the town nonetheless flourished. In the summer, bishops and lords came to Salon for its shade and water, its meadows and fruit trees. Such charms must have won over Michel de Nostredame because he settled in Salon after years of travel across Europe. It was around 1547. He started a family, opened a practice, and spent the last twenty years of his life there. He now signed his letters and publications as a resident of "Salon de Craux, French Provence." French readers knew him as *Michel de Nostradame, Docteur en médecine, de Salon de Craux en Provence,* Italians as *Michele Nostradamo, Dottore in Medicina di Salon di Craux in Provenza.* The same was true in England and the Low Countries. Nostradamus could prove beguiling, enthralling, or puzzling. Elusive he was not.[1]

A couple of years after 9/11, I too came looking for Nostradamus in Salon. A terrible heat wave hit Europe that summer—seventy thousand people died—and Provence was sweltering. Whatever shade could be found in Salon provided meager relief. Except for overworked café waiters, everyone operated at half speed. Not that the town buzzed with activity during the rest of the year. A cruel observer might have said that the heat simply exacerbated Salon's torpor. Without an industrial base or landmark sights to attract investors and visitors, the vibrant market town has become a pit stop for Riviera-bound tourists. A tired castle hangs on a promontory in the medieval quarter, overlooking chapels and small houses painted in sad pastels. Farther out, single-family homes with red-tiled roofs and drab housing projects bake in the sun. Fighter jets from the local air base roar overhead during the day, but at night all is still. The old quarter belongs to cats and teens.

Nostradamus proved easy to find. His original home now houses a wax museum that tells his life story and conveys his vision of the cosmos. His tomb lies in a corner of the Saint-Laurent Church, not far from an altar. A street, a boulevard, and a public square bear his name. Walking around town, I came across a huge fresco of the man as well as two statues, one erected in 1867 and the other—an abstract metal sculpture—in 1999. I bought Nostradamus wine and candy in local shops. By chance, my visit coincided with the five hundredth anniversary of the astrologer's birth. The Tourist Office devoted its entire window display to local events. There was an exhibit, a traditional herb garden, and a conference on the man and his times. Whether any of the conference participants attended the town's Renaissance ball remains unclear, but no one could miss the four-day historical extravaganza that transformed Salon's old quarter into a Renaissance village. Dressed as lords, ladies, and artisans, hundreds of residents took part in a historical pageant that featured Michel de Nostredame and bore his name. These festivities, I later learned, have transported the town across time every summer since 1986. Most years, they reenact one of the key events in Salon's history: the visit of French King Charles IX and his formidable mother, Catherine de Médicis, in 1564.

This visit had taken place during precarious times for the Crown. The king had barely come of age, and factions competed for control of the royal council. Across France, rioters protested against taxes, municipal leaders flaunted their independence, and pamphleteers defined grounds of legitimate resistance. The French Wars of Religion had begun, and violence between Catholics and Protestants threatened public order and political unity. Catherine did what rulers often did in such situations: she took to the road. This tour of France, which lasted two years and covered twenty-seven hundred miles, was a massive undertaking. The royal party included thousands of ambassadors and councilors, messengers and tailors, Swiss guards and falconers. Carts of tableware, cooking utensils, and tapestries followed. Like a lumbering army, the court traipsed across the countryside. It was a long haul, but the new king needed to see and be seen.[2]

When the royal party reached Provence, Salon welcomed it with wooden arcades, scents of rosemary, and odes to the king's glory. Catherine settled in the old castle for the night and insisted upon meeting Nostredame. The astrologer was an esteemed resident of Salon by then, a learned man to whom burghers turned for an inscription on a new fountain or public compliments for distinguished visitors. More pertinently, he had acquired an international reputation. The sixty-year-old Nostredame slowly made the climb to the castle, leaning on his silver-handled cane. Once he had arrived, Catherine asked about the fate of France and her three young sons: Charles IX, the future Henri III, and Hercules. Nostredame reportedly assured her that peace would soon prevail. He also said that Charles would live to the age of ninety. "I pray to God that he spoke the truth," Catherine wrote shortly thereafter. She could not be certain, but was satisfied enough to present Nostredame with three hundred crowns and later appoint him Counselor and Physician in Ordinary to the King.[3]

Why Salon decided to reenact this encounter at the end of the twentieth century—and what this says about Nostradamus in our times—is a question for a later chapter. First comes a queen mother who deemed it essential to consult this renowned astrologer in the midst of a civil war. She made time for Nostredame, and others in Europe did so as well. A German law student declared that, of the many horoscope writers whom he had met, there was "but one Nostradamus, who alone is worth all the others." A Tyrolean mine owner named Hans Rosenberger likewise deemed him superior to other astrologers. Like countless contemporaries, all three were drawn to predictions and an individual with a reputation, an individual who circulated from one domain to another and provided them with what they needed. Nostredame was trustworthy before he became tantalizing. This is the first thing that I learned in Salon.[4]

❧❧❧

When Nostredame settled in this town, he was middle aged and mostly unknown in European astrological and political circles. But he had two things going for him: his background as a Renaissance humanist and his experiences as a physician.

Humanism was at its zenith in France. As an outlook on the terrestrial and celestial worlds and a way of being in the world, it imprinted leading schools of poetry, the court, and the Collège des Lecteurs Royaux, in which learned men taught Greek and Hebrew and later law or mathematics. Humanism came in many shapes and forms, but a capsule summary necessarily begins with the recovery of the Greek and Roman heritage and a conception of the individual as inherently good and free, the measure of all things. Individuals could reach their full potential and attain happiness on earth, rather than simply pine for the afterlife, as theologians insisted. Humanists accordingly embraced ambition and pride in human achievement, either material or spiritual. Engaged, creative reason could grasp the workings of nature, shape circumstances, and fashion itself. Self-perfection entailed learning, interpretation, dialogue, and a give-and-take with precedents and authorities. This explains the importance humanists granted to education, informal schools and libraries, rich epistolary relationships, and travel as a means of exchange and personal growth.

Humanism provides a key backdrop to Nostredame's biography. It must be said, however, that few reliable sources survive about his life. Besides a small collection of letters, we have his two prefaces to the *Prophecies,* his will, and some accounts by contemporaries, including his eldest son César. But not much more. The legend surrounding Nostradamus has grown so thick that biographers have a difficult time distinguishing what is true from what is invented. We do know, however, that Nostredame was born in 1503 into an educated and reasonably well-off family from the small town of Saint-Rémy-de-Provence, near Salon. Today, tourists flock to this old Roman colony for its antique ruins and the sensual landscapes that Vincent van Gogh immortalized centuries later. Back in the sixteenth century, the town was known for its flowers, vegetables, and olive oil.[5]

There were doctors and merchants on both sides of the family. Most of Nostredame's kin, at least the men, were literate. His paternal side included converted Jews, perhaps of Spanish origin, though we do not know for sure. His great-grandfather, a grain merchant and moneylender from Avignon, had converted to Christianity around 1453. His son, who had been a teenager at the time, followed suit a few years later and changed his name from Guy Gassonet to Pierre de Nostredame (or Notre-Dame). Guy's wife would not give up her faith, so the couple split up. Pierre then married Blanche de Sainte-Marie, who most likely came from a family of converts as well. Overtly Christian names such as Notre-Dame and Sainte-Marie were a perfect way of publicizing one's new devotion. The name Nostredame may have come from a local street, a chapel, or the parish in which Pierre was baptized. Jews had lived in Provence for close to a thousand years, but they still faced adversity. Anti-Semitic riots were rare by now, but ordinances instructed Jews to wear identifying marks while royal edicts commanded them to either convert or leave the region. Whenever an epidemic hit, some accused Jews of spreading the disease. Life was not easy for converts either, suspected as they were of engaging in secret cults. In 1512, for instance, King Louis XII levied a tax that applied to Provençal converts alone. Still, many of them entertained professional or social relationships with non-Jews and managed to carve a niche in this Christian world.[6]

One of the children of Pierre and Blanche, Jaume, began his career as a petty merchant and scribe and ended it as a notary and occasional moneylender. Around 1500, he left Avignon (a papal city) for Saint-Rémy. His letter of naturalization, signed by King François I, sealed his integration into France. Jaume then married one Reynière de Saint-Rémy, who reportedly brought a nice dowry to the marriage, with a house, fields, and an orchard. They had nine children. Little is known about the only girl, but the boys did well for themselves. Two became merchants and landowners, one was a prosecutor and poet, and a fourth served as a municipal councilor. As for the fifth—Michel—he chose medicine, a profession that attracted cultivated young men of certain means, many of them the sons or grandsons of doctors.[7]

An oft-repeated tale holds that Michel's maternal great-grandfather, himself a doctor, noticed the boy's intelligence and introduced him to medicine and astrology. Whether that was the case or not, the teenage Nostredame left home for Avignon to pursue classical studies ranging from grammar, rhetoric, and logic to arithmetic, geometry, music, and astronomy. He then traveled sixty miles to the southwest and studied medicine at the University of Montpellier, one of the most prestigious in France. But he cared little for this bookish, theoretical, lecture-heavy approach and did not refrain from voicing his opinion. He preferred collecting medicinal plants and preparing powders and concoctions. None of this sat well with the medical school's dean, who excluded him from the corporation for practicing the manual trade of apothecaries and for speaking ill of his teachers. The former was deemed inferior to medicine; the latter was forbidden. Nostredame thus spent most of the 1520s traveling in southern France, pursuing medical studies on his own. At the end of the decade, he returned to Montpellier. What happened then remains foggy, but the university's records indicate that master Michelet de Nostre-Dame paid his dues and joined the corporation of students in 1529. He probably obtained his medical degree at this time.[8]

By his late twenties, Nostredame could lay claim to the humanist's deep learning as well as the physician's training and prestige. He built a sizable library and interspersed his letters with references to Lucillius and other classical authors. Besides French, he mastered Latin, Greek, Italian, Hebrew, Spanish, and perhaps Arabic. He read widely—poetry, astrology, history—and worked on a French translation of the Greek physician Galen, the kind of literary endeavor that Renaissance writers took on to garner prestige. Later in life, he extolled self-understanding and denounced people who lacked not only knowledge but even the desire to know. This, he felt, was "a terrible evil in men of any estate." As for physicians, who diagnosed diseases and prescribed therapies, they remained scarce in Renaissance Europe. Few people could afford to consult them; fewer yet had acquired the habit of doing so. Arthritis or gallstones were deemed unavoidable. Still, the number of physicians was growing, and so was their stature as medical practitioners, natural historians, wise men, and sometimes community leaders.[9]

Nostredame's formative years thus straddled lines and boundaries. The Frenchman was a Provençal, born in a province that had but recently joined the French kingdom. The devout Catholic descended from recent Jewish converts. His family of middling merchants was close to the local elite, but not close enough to join the upper ranks of society. The humanist had trained in a prestigious university, but kept a distance from the dominant course of medical study. The physician, finally, was a constant traveler, seeking out new experiences and encounters. Nostredame was from the start a creature of the in-between, present in many spheres, in touch with different forms of knowledge, shuttling between cities and provinces and social groups.

⁓ఌ౿⁓

As soon as he graduated from medical school, Nostredame resumed his journeys. It was common for young doctors to follow Hippocrates's advice and travel for a few years before settling down, typically in their native city. Such journeys provided hands-on experience, access to leading professors, and valuable contacts. But they tested the most resolute of travelers. Men and horses moved slowly across a country that remained half barren, with dense forests, forbidding swamps, and arid plains in the south. Roads, if present, were narrow and poorly maintained. Downpours left mud pits in their wake. Frigid spells created ice floes that could carry away bridges. Cities charged tolls and closed their gates at night, leaving travelers to fend off thieves, the cold, and sometimes wild beasts outside their walls. As for local inns, they would have been more welcoming if guests did not have to share a bed with strangers of questionable mores.[10]

Nostredame proved more resilient than most. The lure of the road was apparently so strong that he remained an itinerant physician for more than a decade. He traveled across southwestern France in the mid-1530s. In the city of Agen, he befriended Julius Caesar Scaliger, the famed doctor, poet, and philologist known to some as a bottomless pit of erudition. Later, Nostredame was spotted in Bordeaux and Béziers, Carcassonne perhaps, Marseille, and northern Italy, too: Turin, Genoa, and Venice. In town after town, he met physicians and apothecaries, astrologers and city councilors—men who taught, learned from, and engaged with this curious and enterprising physician.[11]

Travelers were exposed to another danger: the plague. One outbreak followed another at this time, spreading faster in towns than in the countryside given the higher concentration of residents. Between 1451 and 1550, Provence alone suffered forty-three years of epidemics. Migrants carried the disease, and so did the bands of unwashed, lice-ridden soldiers that roamed across the continent. The mortality rate was lower than during the Great Plague of the fourteenth century, but the disease's stealth and horrible symptoms continued to induce panic. Some people even feared speaking its name. Divine punishment of human transgressions had long been the favored explanation, which is why so many communities organized processions and took collective vows. But some also interpreted the plague in medical terms. Following Galen, most physicians believed that a body's health rested on a delicate balance among the four humors: blood, phlegm, yellow bile, and black bile. A severe surfeit of any one humor—caused by the plague's toxic vapors, for instance—led to illness. Overcrowding, open-air sewers, stagnant water, and shallow graves hence posed health risks. Provençal cities began quarantining neighborhoods, setting up hospitals and disinfection services, and keeping foreigners at bay. They also hired doctors from the outside, though not always to cure patients since bloodlettings and purges had little effect. Physicians would also sit on the health boards that devised sanitary measures and oversaw palliative care.[12]

Nostredame had encountered the plague during his earlier travels and reportedly offered his services to various towns. In 1546, Aix-en-Provence called upon him. Nostredame penned a vivid description of the epidemic. Parents abandoned their children. Delirious residents threw themselves down wells. Cemeteries overflowed. While Nostredame grasped the plague's social devastation, his pamphlets lacked the probing theological reflections or the medical analyses found, for instance, in Claude Fabri's contemporaneous *Paradoxes of the Cure of the Plague*. They did, however, fuse religious, astrological, and medical explanations and regimens. The plague, as he saw it, owed as much to divine punishment of "sins and wickedness" as it did to changes in the positions of stellar bodies, which drew pestilential air into the body. Like the Swiss physician Paracelsus, Nostredame also believed that moral failings, melancholy, and excess of any kind left the body vulnerable to poisons suspended in the air. The treatment he prescribed entailed spiritual cleansing (or repentance), prophylactics, and a sensible lifestyle. He urged residents to perform good deeds, exercise, eat moderately, and sleep long nights. To protect themselves from the corrupt air, they were to cover their mouths and noses with a powder of his invention. Where others used garlic or goat urine, Nostredame ground green cypress, red roses, cloves, and other plants into patties that he dried in the shade.[13]

While his powder may well have proved effective, there is no evidence that it really did protect anyone from the plague. His key contribution may instead have been to enforce measures of public hygiene, though we lack definitive evidence here as well. What matters is that local residents believed that this dedicated physician had done some good and risked his life for strangers. Doctors could after all contract the plague or find themselves accused of spreading it. Many of them thus fled, either to save themselves or because they doubted that they could provide much help. Cowardice and incompetence could both harm a physician's standing. But Nostredame did not flee. His behavior during these years endowed him with a regional reputation for ingenuity, courage, and devotion to public welfare.[14]

One biographer has suggested that the young Nostredame learned to care for others by watching his father help people from all walks of life in his notarial practice. This is possible, though another event had changed his life: the death of his first wife and their two children in the late 1530s, apparently of the plague. Losing a child was a common occurrence at the time—so common, some historians argue, that parents would withhold affection in order to protect themselves. The assumption is that they grieved less acutely than we do in the West today. I wonder about this. People and societies certainly found ways of living with losses that seem unbearable in our own world. But one need only cross the Channel and watch Ben Johnson and Shakespeare mourn their young sons to realize that things are more complicated. Johnson composed a harrowing poem about his son. "My sin was too much hope of thee, loved boy," he wrote. "Seven years thou wert lent to me." Shakespeare included a grieving mother in *King John,* the first play that he wrote after his own son's death in 1596. "Grief fills the room of my absent child," she laments. "Lies in his bed, walks up and down with me." The pathways of loss are too personal to allow generalizations, and no sources have survived about the impact of these deaths on Nostredame. Still, the plague doctor had encountered human suffering up close. He, too, lived and slept and walked up and down with grief in tow.[15]

This experience did not turn Nostredame into a paragon of kindness and altruism. In some of his letters, he comes across as peremptory, thin-skinned, abrupt, and even caustic. In others, however, he seems modest, generous, and attentive. "When you receive my letter," he wrote a law student named Lorenz Tubbe in 1561, "I urge you not to keep me waiting too long for your answer. You know that nothing is more agreeable for me than to savor your eloquence as well as your wisdom." A contemporary who knew him well in his later years claimed to discern great humanity behind his nimble reasoning and severe demeanor. Retrospective character analysis is a dangerous sport and yet we may surmise that the man who had traveled across provinces and social divides grew sensitive to the pain of others and the uncertainties of everyday life. He could not shun crises.[16]

꙳

Nostredame spent several months in Aix-en-Provence. His medical and social skills earned him admiration from local residents and the gratitude of town leaders. Lyon then called upon him, followed by Salon shortly afterward. It is there that the esteemed physician faded behind the famed astrologer, that Nostredame gave way to Nostradamus, and that a little-known man morphed into an international phenomenon.

In Salon, Nostredame married a local widow, Anne Ponsarde Gemelle, who had inherited a respectable sum. The couple purchased a nice house near a mill, in a prosperous neighborhood that was home to Salon's leading merchants. Nostredame continued to travel, but his wanderlust abated around 1550. Approaching the age of fifty, he may have grown tired of these journeys and become enticed by the charms of sedentary life. He may have harbored unfulfilled aspirations that required concentrated work in his study. He may also have looked for ways of providing for his new family (Anne gave birth to six children between 1551 and 1561). Nostredame still practiced medicine, but small-town physicians did not have it easy. With a small base of potential patients, meager appointments, and surgeon-barbers as competitors, many struggled to make a living. Nostredame soon ventured into other domains.[17]

He began by marketing his medical expertise in a treatise that provided all kinds of prescriptions for a healthy life. In the spring, people should open a vein, vomit, and purge their bodies. In the winter, they should eat meat and avoid bathing and sluggishness. The man who also fancied himself an apothecary and continued to experiment with plants now wrote elaborate recipes for restorative jams and cosmetics. His readers learned to prepare teeth-whitening pastes and hair colorings by mincing lemons or cuttlefish bone. His love philter was so powerful, he told his readers, that placing a few drops in a woman's mouth while kissing her would trigger burning passion. Though Nostredame wrote little about alchemy, his treatise betrays sympathy for its combinations of minerals and metals. His most delicate balancing act, however, was to maintain his medical reputation while disclosing secrets that other physicians wished to keep within the corporation. The man of learning had read the classics and traveled great distances in search of plants and remedies. Yet he wrote in florid, accessible French, as if untrained readers could become as proficient as those who had pored over such recipes for years. Nostredame explained at one point that his book would prove useful but not miraculous. Do not expect to regain lost youth! he said. The learned physician who spoke a language of truth opened his trade to an uninitiated audience.[18]

Nostredame entered a second booming market, this one for astrological knowledge. Natural astrology perceived human beings as microcosms, or miniature versions of the universe. The celestial bodies governed various parts of the human body and mirrored character traits. The sun, for instance, was equivalent to the head and stood for ambition. Celestial bodies could exert a positive influence (Venus and the moon), or prove harmful (Mars and Saturn), or remain indifferent (Jupiter, Mercury, and the sun). Astrologers thus drew up horoscopes, or birth-chart commentaries, to grasp customers' strengths and weaknesses and identify the influences that presided over their destiny. It was a two-step process. First, astrologers mapped the positions of the celestial bodies at the time and place of the customer's birth and calculated their angular relationships to one another. The sky was divided into twelve houses, named after the zodiac signs, and each was linked to a specific domain, such as riches or friendship. The body in the first house, the ascendant, imprinted temperament and destiny. Astrologers used astrolabes to calculate the position of these celestial bodies and consulted tables of the phases of the moon (known as ephemerides). The second step, interpretation, involved fewer instruments but no less skill.[19]

Astrology had been part of the medical curriculum since the Middle

Ages, but Neoplatonism magnified its resonance. This current held that a divine soul permeated all domains of celestial and terrestrial life, from cosmic fluxes to occult sympathies. Standing at the center of the universe, man could contemplate this harmony, unravel its secrets, master nature, and partially steer his own destiny. Astrology was one way of accomplishing this. But uncertainty surrounded the relationship between macrocosm and microcosm and, hence, the nature of the astrologer's craft. Was astrology a divinely aided interpretation of warnings concealed in celestial events? Or was it a form of understanding rooted in natural science? Could apparent gatherings of two or more planets in a given location (they were called conjunctions) concentrate energy and explain universal history? Or did such explanations minimize the import of divine Providence?

Despite such debates, astrology retained its hold. Countless Europeans, including humanists, used it to understand their world and lessen its unpredictability. There were leading schools in cities such as Beauvais and Wittenberg. Thousands of treatises and handbooks were published across the continent. Paris alone numbered more than thirty thousand astrologers. On the shelves of his library, the archbishop of Avignon kept astrological treatises alongside his books on theology and law. Demand for horoscopes exploded. Neither a visionary nor a prophet, the astrologer was a learned savant with far-reaching insights and assumed goodwill. He could become eminent.[20]

By 1550, Nostredame was defining himself as an astrophile—one who loves the stars—and lauding this superior science. There was nothing more beautiful, he said, than scrutinizing the heavens for secrets of the cosmos and the shape of things to come. Nostredame reportedly did his scrutinizing from an observatory on an upper floor of his home. As a physician, he told patients that his diagnoses combined medicine, surgery, and horoscopes. By this time, medicine was beginning to separate itself from astrology. Some people were rejecting astral determinism, and they might have looked askance at Nostredame's methods. But he was no aberration. Plenty of physicians continued to take astrology into consideration when prescribing remedies or deciding when to schedule a medical intervention. It is unclear whether Nostredame viewed astrology as a component of medicine or rather believed that medicine contributed to an astrological practice that identified the causes of diseases and gauged whether patients were truthful. Still, his medical use of astrology is unlikely to have fazed many patients.[21]

Nostredame's horoscopes encompassed many concerns besides health. Some of his customers wondered about the fate of a commercial venture or the best profession for their son. Others asked when to begin a trip or launch a new enterprise. Still others sought insights that only a seer could provide, such as the name of the person who had stolen sacred objects from a local church or, more intimately, how to explain their sudden desires. A captain wanted to know about his next conquests; an Italian dignitary traveled to Salon to inquire about future plots against the duke of Florence. Customers were also concerned about broader political events, whether the impact of a forthcoming eclipse or France's fate during looming wars. The mine owner Rosenberger, one of Nostredame's most loyal customers, requested details about the calamities that threatened "our ill-fated Europe."[22]

Nostredame answered such queries because, in addition to studying planetary influences, he practiced judicial astrology, the art of making forecasts about wars or epidemics based on the position of the planets. The technique rested on a cyclical conception of time and the conviction that astral conjunctions, like eclipses or comets, affected terrestrial events. Having identified a past event, the astrologer determined its longitude and latitude, the prevailing conjunction, and its location in the firmament. He then calculated the recurrence of this conjunction and hence of similar events. Lesser conjunctions returned every 20 years, major ones every 240 years, great ones every 960 years. The most infrequent were also the most destructive. Nostredame thus linked a conjunction between Saturn and Jupiter in the house of Cancer to religious strife. Whether or not these calculations came true, Nostredame's dual status as a courageous physician and a practiced astrologer made him a legitimate guide. There were doubters, certainly, but Nostredame made sure that all saw him as a learned humanist. He dropped the names of ancient divinities and philosophers, he made references to mythology and history, and he sprinkled foreign words into his publications like raisins in a loaf of bread.[23]

Nostredame's practice grew increasingly successful. Some customers called on him personally while others had couriers deliver messages and payments. There were merchants from Lyon and patricians from Augsburg, a judge from Salon, the bishop of Apt, and the son of an adviser to a German prince. Prelates stopped by on their way to Marseille. Requests flowed in at such a furious pace that Nostredame struggled to keep up. He made this clear in letters that ring true even if they also sought to boost his honoraria. He told clients that he had finished horoscopes after "many nights of vigil," "at the price of long days and of enormous work, proportional to the importance of the subject." The process was indeed labor intensive. Nostredame calculated the positions of the ascendant and ephemerides using the tools of the trade, wrote out horoscopes by hand, had a secretary transcribe them, and then showed or sent them to his customers. Sometimes he provided several birth charts, each one following a different method: the Indian one, the Babylonian, and a mysterious third method that he never defined. In some cases, he added details gleaned from portraits or medallions provided by his customers. When he was done, Nostredame summarized his findings in a letter, sealed it in wax, and signed his name along the edge. One could not be too careful.[24]

Things did not always go smoothly. Nostredame sometimes used several astronomical tables at once, rushed through calculations, and made errors in drawing up houses or determining ascendants. He balked when German customers asked for horoscopes in Latin rather than in French, which they did not understand. Perhaps Nostredame did not like to be told what to do; perhaps his Latin was not as good as he claimed. Some customers complained about unanswered letters and tardy responses. A resident of Padua inquired in a follow-up letter what month it was whose twenty-third day would prove dangerous. Disorganized and forgetful as he could be, Nostredame nonetheless retained his allure as a horoscope writer until the end of his life. New customers kept coming while many of the old ones, even those who grumbled, remained loyal. The mine owner Rosenberger wrote Nostredame that he had consulted several astrologers at once—a common practice at the time—but that his horoscopes alone had proved reliable. "I await [them] with great impatience. I am eager to read them . . . in order to know what awaits me in the future."[25]

How, then, did Nostredame satisfy the likes of Rosenberger? The authority that he derived from his almanacs (more about which later) led customers to downplay or tolerate his limitations. This was the minor cost of doing business with a luminary. Rosenberger's personal acquaintance with Nostredame then confirmed that, as he had suspected, his astrologer was incomparable. So many of Nostredame's horoscopes had come true: the mine that burned down, the discovery of a new copper deposit, the onset of dropsy. There was also much to like in Nostredame's high degree of conviction, his passion, even. The man clearly took such matters seriously. He provided lengthy horoscopes (one of them included forty-two chapters) and answered requests with polish and courtesy. His letters to Daniel Rechlinger extolled this Viennese courtier's loyalty and integrity, his strong soul and noble heart. When another customer inquired impatiently about his horoscope, Nostredame firmly asked not to be disturbed until he had completed it. But he warmed up in his parting comment: "Your value shall increase in the future: your heart is in good shape, even though you are unaware of it."[26]

Nostredame's letters allow us to watch the astrologer forge relationships with customers. His psychological acumen jumps out. Ending missives on an encouraging note was a staple of his practice: "The stars promise you the greatest things." Nostredame seemed to understand what his customers needed or wanted and, more often than not, he provided it. What they needed and wanted was not a stream of favorable predictions. They expected truth—all of it, the good and the bad—and sufficient warning to chart the best course of action. A French doctor asked Nostredame to tell him everything in order to "profit from what is good and resist adversity with courage." Like other customers, he respected fate, but he also believed that human beings could parry the worst blows, if warned. Nostredame provided dark truths when his calculations led him toward them, but he couched them in comforting words and always included grounds of hope. The horoscope he sent to Prince Rudolf, son of the Holy Roman Emperor Maximilian II, spoke of enemies, illnesses, exile, and foreign captivity, but also of delights, inheritances, power, and authority. This, too, is what contemporaries expected from their personal astrologer, a person who today would be a family doctor, a financial adviser, and a therapist rolled into one.[27]

Nostredame also provided a path toward a satisfying existence. His counsel was simple and consistent: work hard, provoke your own good luck, prepare yourself for the peaks and valleys of life, and stay the course when adversity

hits. "Effort is the true seasoning of all things human," Nostredame wrote
Rosenberger. "Any pleasure and any joy are always supplied with some
sorrow. But the sorrow taken will be revealed profitable." When Rosenberger's silver mines seemed to have dried up, Nostredame counseled patience and perseverance. He then urged his customer to live in a wholesome
manner: "Take care of your health. Give yourself over to gaiety, joy and
light-heartedness. Avoid arguments, disputes, and torments." And drink
good wine with moderation. There was nothing dogmatic or judgmental
about his philosophy of life, which was applicable to all. Nostredame gently
furnished advice to which his customers were open. "I will continue to try,
with perseverance," Rosenberger promised Nostredame. "I will not let myself be cut down by these calamities which seem to have conspired against
me." Nostredame the physician, healer of minds and bodies, never strayed
far from the horoscope writer.[28]

Neither did the friend. Reading these letters, one is struck by their con-
tinual references to love and friendship. A bishop asked Nostredame to examine the stars on his behalf if he loved him. Another customer wrote from
Italy to obtain a horoscope as a testimony of love. The law student Tubbe
engaged in intricate rituals of friendship in letter after letter, soliciting affection from his dear Nostredame: "I am one of your true friends," he said—and
he showed it. Tubbe opened up to his astrologer, discussing his travels, opining on current events, and disclosing his lifelong quest for honor and glory.
He also offered to send new customers his way. These individuals sought
love and friendship from Nostredame, and he apparently needed the same.[29]

Here, too, humanism provides an important backdrop. Drawing inspiration from Aristotle, Cicero, and evangelical notions of charity, humanists
viewed friendship as the social glue of human community. Friendship was
a virtuous bond of equality and reciprocity between men of reason and virtue, men of similar stations who shared interests or professional goals. It also
constituted a higher form of love, which mirrored on earth the spiritual relationship between God and the faithful. Friendship thus entailed moral commitment, fellowship, and sometimes an emotional connection as well. Whether
friends were mere allies and associates or else entertained deeper feelings, they
elevated, protected, and provided for one another. These mutual obligations
governed social exchanges, enhanced careers, and sealed alliances in the

private and public realms alike. As tensions between Protestants and Catholics intensified and relations frayed, even within families and business partnerships, true friends became ever more indispensable.[30]

While Nostredame had his share of spats, acquaintances spoke of his good faith and generosity, of the advice and social introductions he gave to people he barely knew. He asked for reports on the health of his customers and conveyed his heartfelt sympathy before their misfortunes. "I sympathized, and still sympathize deep in my heart," he wrote Tubbe, "with the misfortunes that have been befalling our friend, Hans Rosenberger." He also told customers how much their letters meant to him and kept them apprised of the latest in his own life. Sometimes, he shared his "deepest thoughts," including his fear that his predictions might one day become useless. Nostredame reached out to customers just as he had to readers of his jam and cosmetics recipes. He told them that his horoscopes originated in his heart as much as his mind, and he showed them that a gifted astrologer could be compassionate and faithful. But it was not only about sentiments. Nostredame sent these friends information and insights that would have a bearing on their businesses or careers. In return, he obtained affection, reverence, favors, gifts, and invitations. These relationships were nothing if not quid pro quos. When an Avignon lawyer asked his "venerated friend" for a horoscope in 1562, he promised to pay him well and to remain forever obligated to Nostredame and his descendants. The horoscope was ready within the month. It told the lawyer to expect attacks on his reputation during the following summer. Afterward, the stars promised nothing but prosperity and good fortune. Nostredame was a good friend in all senses of the word.[31]

⁓❦⁓

And then came the queen mother, no ordinary friend. Orphaned very young, raised in Florence, Catherine de Médicis had married the French King Henri II in 1533, at the age of fourteen. Life at the court did not prove easy. In the courtesan Diane de Poitiers she faced a formidable rival for Henri's affection. Catherine devised a deft strategy. If she could not own her husband's heart, then she would win his mind and become his confidante. When Henri was away on long military campaigns, she wrote him often and fulfilled his requests. Those skills served Catherine well after Henri's untimely death in

1559. Thrust into the center of courtly life, she assumed key roles. It fell upon her to tutor the young king, govern the court, and protect the kingdom. She parlayed traditional female virtues—submissive spouse, bereft widow, devoted mother—into a position of power. All officials now reported to her; all dispatches passed by her desk.[32]

Catherine was both anxious about the future and enthralled by the divine harmony that astrology could discern. She reportedly invited leading European astrologers to join her atop her Colonne de l'Horoscope, a Doric column that still stands in Paris's first arrondissement, near the Halles. Catherine asked these astrologers to advise her on momentous decisions and lay out the destinies of her ten children. Other rulers did the same, of course. From Queen Elizabeth and margrave Johann of Küstrin to Philip II of Spain and Pope Urban VII, Protestants and Catholics alike consulted astrologers in preparation for campaigns and tournaments and other such matters. Horoscopes were a source of information and an instrument of rule. They were not quite commonplace, since some questioned their veracity, but widespread nonetheless (not unlike our own financial forecasts).[33]

In the 1980s, the organizers of Salon's historical pageants claimed that Catherine had cherished Nostredame as much as she did her most trusted political councilors. He was not a permanent presence in her entourage, but he did serve a similar function. In 1555, Catherine had invited him to the court to provide horoscopes of her children. He stayed a few weeks, fulfilled his obligations, predicted that the queen would see all of her sons accede to the throne (a frightening prospect for it implied that some would die), found some members of the court more welcoming than others, fell ill, and then made the long journey back to Salon. Royal chroniclers relate that, during the following years, Henri II commonly asked for predictions about upcoming battles. His courtiers read him only favorable ones, but several astrologers warned the king about a head wound around his fortieth birthday. Catherine obtained confirmation from Nostredame, then sought to safeguard her husband. She succeeded for a while—until 1559.[34]

That June, France and Spain sealed a long-awaited peace treaty by organizing two weddings between members of their royal families. The highlight was a grand jousting tournament that featured the fit forty-year-old Henri. The king announced that he would fight all challengers in order to provide an example of virtuous behavior. Paris's rue Saint-Antoine was closed off and decorated with triumphal arches and statues symbolizing the benefits of peace. Ladies watched from stands as the champions fought in embossed suits of armor and plumed helmets. Henri entered the competition on the third day, a hot afternoon. His daughter later reported that he did so despite the fact that Catherine had had a premonitory dream about his wounded eye the previous night. Henri wore black and white (the colors of Diane de Poitiers) and—this is true—rode a horse called Unfortunate (*le malheureux*). After defeating two opponents, he squared off against the young Gabriel de Lorges, count of Montgomery and lieutenant in the Scottish guard. The first round yielded no outcome. Catherine implored her husband to stop, but the king insisted that there be a victor. "I want my revenge," he cried, "for he has shaken me and almost unhorsed me." This time, the two riders collided violently. As their horses tumbled, their wooden lances shattered, and shards of the lieutenant's slipped through the king's visor. They pierced his right eye and entered his brain. Henri was taken to a nearby residence, where leading doctors and surgeons tended to him. Initial reports were hopeful, but the wound left him in agony. Ten days later, the king was dead.[35]

The contrite Montgomery secured forgiveness and retired to his estate, but Catherine was devastated. She wore black for the rest of her life and changed her emblem from a rainbow to a broken lance. Her husband's death was both a private sorrow and a disaster for the kingdom, which was burdened with debt. The heir to the throne, François II, was only fifteen. Members of the court alleged at once that Nostredame had predicted this misfortune in his 1559 almanac. "The Great One to be no more": this was the key verse. Others in France turned to quatrain 3.55, which spoke of a lord killing his friend, a befuddled court, and a troubled realm during "the year one eye over all France shall reign." In later years, people linked the king's death to quatrain 1.35, which remains to this day one of the most famous:

The young lion shall overcome the old	Le lyon jeune le vieux surmontera,
On the field of battle in single duel :	En champ bellique par singulier duelle :
He'll put out his eyes in his cage of gold,	Dans caige d'or les yeux luy crevera,
Winner taking all, then a death most cruel.	Deux classes une, puis mourir, mort cruelle.

Henry was the old lion; Montgomery the young one (both jousters had lions
as their emblems). The cage of gold stood for the king's gilded helmet. The
deux classes in the fourth line denoted the king's two wounds, above and below the eye. When François II fell ill and died in turn eighteen months after
his father, many members of the court summoned Nostradamus anew. Had
the astrologer not foretold that this monarch would die before the age of eighteen, that heresy would follow, and that the royal house would lose its two
youngest sons?[36]

The deaths of two monarchs created a deep crisis of political authority. In
France as elsewhere in Europe, attacks against Catholicism and a proliferation of creeds furthermore opened up a space for alternative sources of guidance. Nostredame benefited from this. People consulted his predictions for
intimations of the future as well as confirmation of unexpected events. In
France, Nostradamus was deemed to have foreseen a recent military victory.
In Germany, Rosenberger was convinced that the Frenchman had foreseen
the Wars of Religion. In England, diplomats and ambassadors discussed
quatrains about the accession of Queen Elizabeth and the marriage between
Mary Queen of Scots and the French heir. His predictions made it to the
court and into the homes of prominent elites. Some Puritans even complained that nobles were trusting Nostradamus more than they did God.[37]

People gave Nostredame credence because some of his predictions
seemed to have come true and because they deemed him reliable. The man
whom Catherine sought out in Salon was in one respect a seer whose intimations about political and religious affairs had been fulfilled. One Spanish
diplomat reported that Catherine placed Nostradamus in the company of the
Gospel writers John and Luke. But the queen mother was also visiting a
horoscope author whom she trusted. Nostredame had drawn on humanist
networks, medical knowledge, courage (or the impression of courage), empathy, astrological abilities, and reliability to establish his professional credibility. In the sixteenth century and for some time afterward, this proved
pivotal. As cities expanded and states extended their reach, doctors, secretaries, and diplomats became members of nascent professions. This was a
messy process, with vague norms and expectations of behavior that people
struggled to decipher, but Nostredame seemed to grasp them better than
most. Maybe it was his social background, or his varied experiences on and

off the road. As he traveled from one domain to another—medicine, horoscopes, politics—he accumulated knowledge, mastered practical arts such as
letter writing, and deftly managed relationships with ordinary customers
and princes alike. He learned the virtues of caution, nowhere more so than at
the court, a volatile world that could swiftly turn on a threatening individual.
An ill-timed or unrealized prediction could provoke a rapid fall. Nostredame
praised the royals in his publications and denounced their enemies. As a
royal astrologer, he fed Catherine's curiosity about princely alliances and
delivered sanguine news about France. His vision of "peace, love, union,
and concord" echoed all too clearly her own dreams for the kingdom. If
he voiced criticism, he directed it at French or Christian society rather
than the monarchy. It is no surprise that one of his friends congratulated
Nostredame for his "success at Court with the King, the Queen and other
dignitaries."[38]

And yet, the accommodating professional, the man who circulated in the
hallways of power and high intellectual reaches also challenged prevailing
ways of doing things when they went against his convictions. Nostredame
placed experimentation and the plants he collected above the abstract lectures of his Montpellier professors. He drew up birth charts according to an
idiosyncratic method. He disclosed pharmacological secrets to a general audience. And he preferred Salon to the courtly gatherings of Saint-Germain
or Blois. Ultimately, Nostredame charted his own singular course from his
Provençal base, reaching out to customers and readers from different backgrounds, erecting bridges between diverse worlds.

~⚌~

Michel de Nostredame was not a peerless astrologer who proved superior to
all competitors. He was not a cynical operative who sought worldly recom-
pense alone. And he certainly was not a bewitching visionary who inhabited
the margins of European society. The man was both simpler and more complicated. His motivations (to the extent that we can discern them) were mixed:
sincerity tinged with guile, empathy coupled with thirst for recognition, audacity tempered by prudence. Beyond that, Nostredame circulated between
the centers of power and their outermost reaches. At once a protected insider
and a freestanding outsider, at once an establishment figure and a maverick,

he followed the rules of the game while taking liberties with them. He operated at the crossroads of disparate domains, present in all yet confined to none.

As a master of the trade, Nostredame offered his contemporaries security and legitimate knowledge. As an inspired interloper, he promised adventure, freedom, and the thrill of unparalleled insight. And as a friend—a friend in life and on the page—he pledged to meet the expectations they harbored of their physicians and astrologers. He would listen and soothe anxieties and restore the order of a world that he knew from the inside out. So began the process by which Michel de Nostredame became *Michael Nostradamus, Doctour of Phisike, of Salon of Craux in Provance.*

Chapter 2

❦

The Power of Words

Plenty of people questioned Nostredame's literary talents in his lifetime, but no one could dispute the hold of his words on the collective imagination. "I believe well that we do not have anyone like you in all of Europe," wrote Hans Rosenberger in 1561. No astrologer combined with such dexterity "the admirable virtues necessary for the knowledge of the occult sciences as well as the mathematical ones." And no writer expressed this with greater vigor. One need only dip into his torrent of words—a crashing river rather than a flowing brook—to feel its formidable pull. Words cascade from line to line in an irresistible surge. "The coin of the realm shall be much descried," intones one line. "Peace, novelties, holy laws in decline." The current one feels is the energy of a voice that could measure and shape its world while submitting to its unyielding force. This was Nostredame's talent as a writer: the ability to see and sense everything and then distill it all in words that seared minds across the continent.[1]

Today, fortune-tellers flourish in the West, but most of us obtain our global predictions and prophecies secondhand, through magazines, Web sites, and tabloids. I got mine in *Paris-Match* in the 1980s. During the Renaissance, however, people went straight to the source. More often than not, this meant almanacs and prognostications—the fastest-growing medium in Europe. Nostredame began writing such annual publications in 1550 and continued doing so until his death sixteen years later. Bundling jagged words and world-images in far-reaching literary missives, he rose to the top of a highly competitive market, filled with doctors, surgeons, and astronomers.

Short and flimsy as they were, almanacs helped readers manage their lives. They always included a calendar, which made it possible to master present and future, and ephemerides. Readers considered the phases of the moon before timing key decisions, such as bleedings or commercial ventures. Almanac authors and publishers might then add a fair schedule (essential for traders) or weather forecasts (which alerted landowners and others to the risks of famine). Nostredame wrote at least one almanac each year and also penned prognostications about the year to come. Both genres tapped astrology, but almanacs resembled tables whereas prognostications took the form of prose narratives about weather patterns, epidemics, wars, and even the behavior of men with soft or bellicose temperaments. His prognostications began with the year's "general disposition" (for instance, unrest in Italy and pestilence across Europe) and then provided detailed forecasts for each season as well as each month.[2]

Nostredame gave readers what they expected. Here were predictions about set months alongside "perpetual" ones that encompassed hundreds of years. Here were comets and earthquakes and other omens announcing wondrous events. And here were conjunctions and calculations that showed, say, that Saturn's revolutions would cause an upheaval at the end of the eighteenth century. References to such revolutions could be found in other publications besides Nostredame's. Commentators have long sought to identify the sources from which he drew inspiration. They have drawn connections to classical authors such as Suetonius and historians such as Philippe de Commynes, to the fourth-century *Book of Prodigies* of Julius Obsequens, and to Richard Roussat's 1550 *Book on the State and Mutation of Time*. Nostredame probably consulted the *Mirabilis Liber,* a compendium of prophecies, mostly in Latin, that was first published in Paris in 1522 to buttress the supremacy of King François I over the Hapsburg Charles V. No doubt Nostredame also read almanacs. He neither came out of the blue nor broke with his intellectual world. Contemporaries knew where to place him.[3]

Nostredame, in turn, knew where to place his almanacs. He had the good fortune and also the good judgment to enter an editorial universe that was full of promise. Demand for printed matter, whether theological or secular, Latin or vernacular, was on the rise. This market was unregulated and unforgiving, however. Powerful dynasties of printers and publishers oversaw large workshops and sometimes controlled the entire process, from the purchase of paper to manuscript selection and the correction of proofs. Given the costs of print, storage, and distribution, they were always looking for new products. The most successful publishers understood what the market wanted and recognized a promising opportunity—such as the almanac— when they saw one. Demand was high, and publishers could streamline the process by reusing the same material and the same woodcuts in different editions. Some publishers specialized in the genre; others offered it alongside other products. All made sure that the peddlers who sold books and pamphlets in Renaissance cities were amply stocked.[4]

Nostredame developed close relationships with several publishers, but this required that he leave Salon. On several occasions throughout the 1550s, he closed his books, put his papers in order, bade his family good-bye, and started a 150-mile journey due north, toward the proud, bustling city of Lyon. Having spent time in Lyon in his youth and later as a plague doctor, Nostredame knew the city well. He had seen it build on its prime location near the Swiss and Italian borders to become one of the main commercial centers in Europe. Lyon may have lacked Paris's political power and universities, but it boasted rich banks, tax-exempt commercial fairs, and an enterprising merchant class. Credit was cheap. Spices and silk abounded. Trade routes flowed to the Low Countries, Italy, and the Mediterranean. Riding past the city's ramparts, down narrow streets and hidden passageways, Nostredame found himself in a cosmopolitan maelstrom, teeming with German traders, Flemish textile merchants, Florentine bankers, and hordes of artisans. Nostredame recognized familiar abbeys and orchards but also uncovered river quays, hospitals, and plazas that had not been there a few years earlier.[5]

Nostredame eventually crossed a bridge and entered the city's commercial heart, a narrow peninsula that lies between the Rhône and Saône rivers. His destination was the rue Mercière. Each trade had its neighborhood in Lyon, and this street, the most vibrant in town, belonged to printers and publishers. Lyon was now one of the leading publishing centers in Europe.

Professionals from Italy, Germany, and the Low Countries had settled there in the early 1500s, bringing with them expertise and ambition. By the middle of the century, thousands of printers, type makers, binders, ink suppliers, writers, translators, engravers, illustrators, copy editors, and booksellers toiled side by side. There were two hundred workshops, half of them in the narrow houses that lined the rue Mercière. The thumping of presses and the din of conversations filled the air at all hours. The town's publishers invented new formats and diversified their offerings, from aphorisms and emblem books to illustrated works, all of which were shipped to Antwerp, Venice, and countless other cities.[6]

By the time he arrived in Lyon, Nostredame would have completed his publications for the next year. He began work a year ahead, writing in the winter and spring, securing the requisite privileges in the early fall, and then handing in his manuscript in time for publication in October. It was imperative to launch them during Lyon's November fair and then make the most of the busy winter season. Nostredame seems to have handled this well. His correspondence contains no complaints about tardy or lackluster manuscripts. In Lyon, he made the rounds of publishers. He might start his day in the company of Benoît Rigaud, the peasant's son who had made a fortune by cornering the regional market for almanacs and broadsides (the ancestors of modern-day posters). In the afternoon, he might drop in on the prolific Macé Bonhomme, who published some of his books as well as almanacs. On another day, he might take a stroll with Antoine Volant, the onetime domino maker who once made a special journey to Salon to see him. And he certainly spent considerable time with Jean Brotot, the trusted bookseller who held his mail when he was away. Nostredame dealt with all of them because authors did not have exclusive contracts at this time. Instead, publishers secured the permission (*privilège*) to publish a given work for a year in a particular city or region. Several publishers could thus release different editions of the same work at the same time.

Publishers commonly inserted new material in manuscripts after accepting them; it might be a list of saints, a series of epigrams, or agricultural precepts. This was standard practice, and Nostredame complied, but he could also assert himself. He cut off publishers whom he deemed too self-interested and overruled timid ones. Some years, he wrote two or three almanacs and prognostications for the year ahead. Brotot doubted that the market could absorb so much Nostradamus: "Such is the fashion, dear Michel—brevity is appreciated." Brotot went on, "How do you suppose that the average reader will accept two separate prognostications without raising his eyebrows, especially coming from one and the same source?" Nostredame ignored the advice and forged ahead, with utter confidence in his own judgment.[7]

He may have felt that a single almanac was unlikely to yield significant dividends. Authors lost out (as did some publishers) in a system that allowed a book to rapidly fall into the public domain. Plagiarism, pirated editions, and illegal copying of almanacs were rife. Lyon's Jean Huguetan once had an associate travel sixty miles to Valence in order to purchase a copy of the latest Nostradamus almanac, which he would then publish himself. Authors could not count on reliable payments from their publishers, and the payments they did receive were generally modest. In England, almanac authors made around forty shillings per year (less than a thousand dollars today). Wealthy patrons hence played a key role in this economy. Authors inserted dithyrambic dedications in exchange for financial support or protection against criticism and official reprimands. Nostredame secured many such patrons. A full list would tax the reader's patience, but it included Catherine de Médicis, kings of France, several lords, and high-placed magistrates. He was especially solicitous of local dignitaries whose backing he might need, such as the governor of Provence.

Sales of Nostredame's almanacs did not enable him to quit writing horoscopes, but they brought him income and broad exposure. Other publishers spotted a successful product and began releasing almanacs under his name in Lyon and Paris. Foreigners soon came calling. Germans were the quickest, translating and publishing half a dozen of his works by century's end. Italians from Milan, Padua, and Rimini followed suit in 1556. They published twice as many, perhaps because Nostredame's travels had taken him to northern Italy. The English came next, with a *Prognostication of Maister Michel Nostradamus* in 1558. Several other translations followed in short succession. At least twenty English bookshops sold his almanacs by 1562. A few years later, publishers from Kampen and Antwerp translated a couple of his almanacs into

Dutch. This international presence was not exceptional, for Renaissance publishers knew what was happening in other countries. But these translations—whether authorized or not—were commissioned early, repeatedly, and over a wide expanse.[8]

French and foreign publishers thus helped mold the "Nostradamus" that was available for public consumption. Nostredame was not the sole protagonist in this story, but he did create a potent mixture of tradition and innovation, tapping divination and old forms of patronage while embracing modern technologies and aspirations. In the mid-1550s, a local engineer named Adam de Craponne came to him with an ambitious plan. He had designed a canal that would irrigate Salon and the barren Crau plateau with water from the Durance River, making it possible to cultivate olive trees and build flour mills. All he needed was funding to launch the venture. Nostredame loaned Craponne money on three occasions. The canal was inaugurated in 1559 and, as one agronomist put it in 1600, it "changed the appearance of the lands it irrigated." Nostredame had apparently grasped the potential of this technological innovation.[9]

Print likewise altered Renaissance Europe. It spread knowledge, fostered new ways of contemplating the world, and altered the ways people organized knowledge about this world. If Nostredame outperformed other almanac authors, it is in part because he managed his editorial ventures with dexterity. Despite starting late in life, he understood and accepted the rules of the market. Whether tapping several genres or cultivating professional relationships in Lyon, he displayed the same mix of audacity, obstinacy, and caution as in his astrological practice. Self-promotion did not faze him, either. "I would like you to be aware of my almanac for next year," he wrote Rosenberger in the fall of 1561. "I discuss in French, and according to my method, the numerous wonders as well as the no less numerous calamities that threaten our unfortunate Europe." The result was a massive output of vernacular publications that were easily reproducible and readily available, dependent on the author's authority and yet open to readers. Nostredame and his publications exemplified the media culture that was taking form in Western Europe.[10]

But editorial prowess is only part of this story. The man's prose and verse also captured the enigmatic power of words. During the Middle Ages, theologians and philosophers had endowed nouns, formulas, and incantations with therapeutic or magical powers. Words embodied hidden truths and divine ideas and the essence of things and people. Whether one understood them or not, they contained layers of meaning and might even modify the natural world. Determining where these powers came from proved more complicated. What some attributed to God or the devil, others linked to a natural origin, such as stars or modulated sounds. These debates continued in Nostredame's time, and so did enthusiasm for words that transcended the symbolic realm to become analogies of the cosmos. Some Christian humanists even agreed with the Jewish kabbalah that words could transmit divine revelation through not only what they said but also the order and numerical values of their letters.[11]

Renaissance poets, too, were enthused about the ability of words to overcome audiences. Cultivated people learned poetry in school because its rhymes and cadences facilitated memorization. Many then developed a lifelong taste. Kings, churchmen, doctors, lawyers, and others read and often composed poems. Humanists codified a genre that could convey common sense or indignation, a genre that could name the underlying essence of things, present and sometimes future. The Neoplatonists believed that poets could contemplate and render meaningful mysteries that befuddled ordinary mortals. A divine inspiration, or furor, elevated their soul beyond human understanding, toward ecstasy and apprehension of the universe's governing forces. This mattered more than adherence to poetic rules, said Nostredame. The poet who channeled celestial music often could not grasp what he conveyed. Endowed with mystical gifts and a sacred mission, he became a conduit of Truth. Carried afar by print and an increasingly standardized French language, his portentous words spoke to the ear, the mind, and the soul.[12]

So it was with Nostredame. He most likely read León Hebreo, Cornelius Agrippa, and Christian kabbalists whose works—many of them published or republished in Lyon around this time—illuminated the truths of sacred texts and recovered classical notions of dreams and divine emanation. His friend Jean de Vauzelles, a priest and doctor of laws who descended from an old family of notaries, contributed to the renewal of Hebrew studies in Lyon's humanist circles. There is no evidence that Nostredame consulted the kabbalah itself or secretly practiced Judaism. Still, Jewish traditions may well have left an imprint in his family. This might include a predilection for symbols and interpretation, respect for books (a sacred repository for a people deprived of power), and awe before the power of words. It is easy to make too much of such hypothetical filiations, but there is no reason to dismiss them either. It is equally easy to overlook Nostredame's ambitions as a poet. For centuries, literary scholars have done just that, relegating his writings to some prophetic dustbin and keeping his pedestrian verse out of their anthologies. Only in recent years have some critics argued that, without equaling the best Renaissance poets, Nostredame produced an original mélange of poetry and melancholy prophecy. True, he never wrote odes or sonnets or presented himself as a superlative poet. Still, he adorned all of his almanacs with four-line poems—called *présages*, or portents—which he claimed to compose out of natural instinct and poetic frenzy. He provided one portent for the whole year, one for each month, and sometimes a fourteenth one as a bonus of sorts for faithful readers. This was his signature as an almanac writer.[13]

᠆᠊ᅌᅙᅙᅌ᠊᠆

The point is not to rehabilitate Nostredame as a leading Renaissance poet: readers will come to their own conclusions about the quality of his verse. But he considered himself a poet and wanted to be seen as one, and this says a great deal about the way his words were written and received. It is partly for this reason that he traveled to Lyon, a city whose cultural ebullience matched its commercial energy. Proximity to John Calvin's Geneva opened Lyon to new religious movements. The Italian traders who had settled there in earlier decades had brought deep reverence for the Greco-Roman heritage and the verses of Petrarch. And the absence of a university or a leading law court (*parlement*) emboldened residents and visitors to broach all kinds of topics without fear of rebuke.

The workshops of the rue Mercière were full of learned, curious publishers who produced new editions of Boccaccio and published the leading mystic, hermetic, and Neoplatonist poets of the day. Wealthy families recited poetry in their homes, and so did successful artisans. The literary salons that convened in stately residences took verse most seriously. Poets traveled hundreds of miles to join the conversation. When Nostredame visited Lyon, the city's poetic school still loomed large in France (within years, the rival Pléiade would supplant it). The verses of Maurice Scève, Louise Labé, and others expressed feelings of love and conveyed their vision of the cosmos. They also shaped the poet's illustrious image.[14]

Nostredame did not belong to any school, but he joined the city's literary circles during his visits. He entertained close ties with Gabrielle Simeoni, a learned writer with whom he shared a publisher, and dedicated one of his prognostications to Jean de Vauzelles, who was an accomplished poet and translator. He also became a protégé of Guillaume de Gadagne, scion of Lyon's wealthiest family (one was *rich like Gadagne* in these parts of France). This banker and representative of the king surrounded himself with prominent artists and writers, and Nostredame made the cut. As Gadagne's houseguest in 1557, he must have attended his lavish receptions and mingled with members of Lyon's intellectual elite. Later that year, he dedicated a *Prognostication* to the hospitable Gadagne, who had introduced him to persons of "honor, conviction, nobility, and erudition." This most likely included poets.[15]

A single portent suffices to convey the pulse of Nostredame's poetry. These are the verses that had been linked to Henri II's death in 1559:

The great to be no more, rain in the crystal	Plus le grand n'estre, pluye, au char le cristal
Tumult moved, of all goods abundance.	Tumulte esmeu, de tous bien abondance
Cut up, hallowed, new, old, fateful	Razes, sacrez, neufs, vieux, espouvantal.
Chosen unthankful, death bewailed, joy, alliance	Esleu, ingrat, mort, plaint, joye, alliance.

It is a quatrain, a brief, condensed genre that was being rediscovered after centuries of neglect and now used in psalms, adages, courtly epigrams, and moral instruction. The original French conveys features that are lost in translation, including internal line breaks (or caesuras) that made readers pause after the fourth syllable and allowed the poet to create anticipation. The French also displays the ten-syllable lines (or decasyllables) that were then so common as well as the crossed *abab* rhyming pattern. Some poets were now composing alexandrines, poems with twelve-syllable lines, and alternating feminine and masculine rhymes (the former ended with a mute *e,* as in *la France*). Not Nostredame. In fact, he was not beholden to literary convention or fashion. Poets liked the quatrain because its simple rhyme patterns enabled them to focus on a single idea and convey weighty and even heroic or moral topics. Nostredame made it his preferred literary form but did not hesitate to move from one theme to another. His rhymes were sometimes considered mediocre because they involved the final syllable alone (*cristal* and *espouvantal*); or else syllables that were spelled the same way but pronounced differently (such as *cher* [pronounced share] and *boucher* [pronounced boohshay]). He also slipped in the odd eleven- or twelve-syllable line and occasionally followed the caesura with a word that began with a consonant rather than a vowel (see the first line). This went against usage.[16]

Still, the poet proved good enough to build on the quatrain's didactic foundation while subtly redirecting it toward the future and entering a long continuum of verse prophecy. Poetry did not merely endow his words with gravitas and an aura that other almanac writers lacked. It also provided a conduit into the order of the cosmos, the designs of nature, the immensity of God, and the tumult of the world. Ultimately, it all came back to words, both verse and prose. Nouns and adjectives flashed like lone strobe lights in his multi-hued universe, but they also tapped the others' energy. "Chosen unthankful, death bewailed, joy, alliance": who could tell whether these were placeholders in miniature narratives or pick-up sticks in a game of verbal Mikado? Perhaps it did not matter. Married with alliteration and consonance (*profanés, pillez, expoliés*), layered with detail and texture, his words flattened chaos and imposed order on time and space. They also intensified moods and foreboding, pulling the reader toward an inexpressible climax. "All dying by sword, fire, cannon, plague": Nostredame could show and tell at the same time.[17]

One computer analysis has identified eight thousand words in his vocabulary: more than the Old Testament, equal to Milton, half that of Shakespeare. Nostredame drew from Latin and Greek and sometimes the Provençal of southern France, but mostly he restricted himself to French. In the sixteenth century, Italian was the language of choice for commercial transactions and religious exchanges with Rome. Latin retained its primacy in learning, literature, prophecies, and letters between European humanists. Most residents of France spoke dialects, but French was gaining ground as a means of communication in cities and a prestigious literary form. A decade before Nostredame began writing almanacs, a royal ordinance had prescribed the use of French rather than Latin in all contracts, judicial acts, and official documents. This would guard against ambiguity. Nostredame did not mind ambiguity, but he found that French had qualities of expression that he could not find in Latin. "I have written out my work in French," he wrote a customer, "because it is nourished by the Gallic muses." French would also enable him to reach a larger urban readership, boost his sales, and perhaps bolster his legitimacy by obtaining widespread appeal. The language anchored his predictions within the everyday lives of readers while preserving their sacral aura.[18]

Some words surfaced again and again: *death* and *tumult, loss* and *conflict, king* and *alliance, old* and *new.* Like branches caught in the whirlpool, they swirled on the surface of a current that overflowed with discord, surprises, and reversals. Nostredame foretold the "adventures" of the year to come in tableaus of mesmerizing if unsettling beauty, full of heroic hatreds and high emotions. Conspirators schemed and staged nocturnal assaults. Some cities rose while others fell. Fire and water made sudden irruptions. Women fainted from joy. People were jailed and then escaped. Secret letters led to treason or deadly poisons. The flow of words often proved irresistible: "the unusual nocturnal sounds forebode a pestilential affliction." Elsewhere, one finds startling set pieces. In one of them, weeds grow knee-high in city streets while the sun bakes the land dry. Another announces a conflict between Europeans and Muslims. Factions would band against others, mutineers would return, barbarians would invade by land and sea, and then the jailers themselves would land in prison. And yet nothing would be settled. The prediction ended starkly, with deeper friendship among savage beasts than among human beings. These almanacs and prognostications were episodes in a human drama that kept promising an impossible denouement.[19]

Nostredame left nothing out. He piled it on. "Cut up, hallowed, new, old, fateful": there were hundreds of such lines. One thinks of the orderly series, the colonnades and rows of galleries that the Renaissance found so satisfying. Nostredame nonetheless stood out in his single-mindedness. "Snow, ice, great frost, winds, rains, fogs, cunning weather, and frequent rainfalls across the western regions." His series coupled adjectives and nouns, with or without articles. They owed as much to the notary's inventories as to the physician's diagnoses. His prognostications in fact recorded the plague's symptoms: inextinguishable thirst, dry mouth, vomiting, bowel movements, and yellowed skin. Alongside these enumerations came repetition. Many people, he said, would be "beaten, robbed, fleeced, & many temples desecrated, plundered, ransacked." There are repetitions of synonymous adjectives, repetitions of fragments in the same quatrain ("for forty years"), and repetitions that simply accentuate the sense of abundance ("many and various shipwrecks"). Even though Nostredame wrote repetitive sentences in some of his letters, it is difficult to escape the conclusion that this was a literary effect, a means of expressing the abundance of his world or averting the distressing possibility of emptiness—what contemporaries called *horror vacui*.[20]

Nostredame encompassed every facet of his world: military sieges and shipwrecks, plots and papal elections, endless rain, cattle lost, hunger and scabies, passages by land and sea, brothers knocked for a loop, dignitaries signing treaties and others engaging in public debates. All lives were connected; all human activities had an impact on one another. His prognostication for 1558 ended with the hope that God would grant *us* a year of peace, love, and harmony. Most other prognosticators wrote about the weather or comets rather than politics. When they did broach the topic, it was through terse, factual, general remarks about wars, rebellions, and the high and mighty. The Englishman Cornelys Scute thus devoted separate sections of his 1554 prognostication to the leading rulers of the day. Nostredame's purview was broader: namely, the collective destinies of cities, regions, nations, and Christendom. By making politics high and low a defining trait of his almanacs, Nostredame upheld the genre's traditional domains while adding another horizon. As discord between Catholics and Protestants intensified, poets found it difficult to confine themselves to the celestial realm. They were public figures, too. As such, they were expected to endorse parties, justify causes, denounce enemies, and provide alternatives to crisis. Nostredame's marriage of poetry and politics suggests that he had grasped this as well.[21]

⁂

Once he had settled matters with his publishers and renewed his ties with Lyon's intelligentsia, Nostredame packed up and headed home. He would be back soon enough to look after his next almanac or prognostication—the ephemeral publications that first drew attention to Nostradamus. Sales, earnings, and success mattered to him. But such ambitions did not compromise Nostredame's depictions of the cosmic and social orders. He continued to view himself as a guide and a friend. And the words always came first.

Nostredame was not the only one to string words into series or pictorial tableaus of abundance. Poets such as Maurice Scève and Pierre de Ronsard composed rhymes with greater skill. Only in the twentieth century was the stupefying, rule-free Nostradamus reclaimed as a model for a literature that freed itself from the shackles of middle-class convention. In 1966, the Swiss writer Blaise Cendrars told the *Paris Review* that he had been reading these predictions and admiring their linguistic virtuosity for forty years. "I gargle with them, I regale myself with them," he said. "As a great French poet, Nostradamus is one of the greatest."[22]

One literary critic has suggested that Nostredame was first and foremost a crib artist, whose mix of ancient and recent sources prefigured European avant-gardes. Nostredame's true literary talent resided, it is true, in his powers of creative amalgamation, but it went farther than that. The man seemed to have seen, read, and experienced everything. His journeys from one province and one world to another had introduced him to all kinds of people, languages, and moods. Some travelers simply march across new lands. Nostredame, in contrast, soaked everything in and then made these lands his own by tapping assorted literary strands and emotional registers. He was both a pathological hoarder who left nothing out and a diamond cutter who chiseled words into fine stones. Instead of inventing new literary forms, he stretched the boundaries of existing ones and then filled them with infinite possibilities. His prognostications bulged over with meandering sentences that were at once precise and nebulous. His lean almanacs melded the tangible and the evanescent. And his portents were crisp, nervous concentrates of the mundane and the arcane. Together, they created a literary world whose visceral intensity belonged to Nostradamus alone—or, rather, to Nostradamus and everyone else. The omnivorous writer gave his readers everything they could have expected. And more.[23]

Chapter 3

❦

Unfathomable Afflictions

There is one thing that Nostradamus has never provided: clarity. Whether first-time or repeat, readers rarely escape profound bewilderment. "I enjoy [the predictions] but I don't understand them," said Blaise Cendrars. Such feelings were already present during Michel de Nostredame's lifetime. The man lived in an age of mystifying prophecies, allegorical engravings, and analogical means of reasoning. Contemporaries expected to encounter symbolic depictions of the world and to parse signs for intimations of cosmic mysteries. And yet Nostredame still stood out. The prevailing opinion was that he wrote in "veiled terms, enigmas, and a disguised language," as one observer put it. His predictions seemed more cryptic than others, or else cryptic in ways and for reasons that others were not. This mix of density and opacity made all of the difference.[1]

A lawyer from Avignon was so puzzled by one horoscope in 1562 that he requested clarification: "If you could translate your answer into a language that is—I won't say utterly common, but at least a little clearer, perhaps I might understand something of what it says." Around the same time, Lorenz Tubbe wrote Nostredame about the catastrophe that he had predicted for the French town of Bourges. "What is it about?" Good question. So are the follow-ups. Did Nostredame have to be so cryptic? And so dark, too, with his "tears & shrieks & moans, vociferations, fright"? What does this say about the lure of Nostradamus in the late Renaissance and afterward?[2]

Over time, these questions came increasingly to revolve around his *Prophecies,* which first came out in 1555 and allowed Nostredame to join a line of prophetic figures who had been expressing themselves through print since the late fifteenth century. The book was a collection of quatrains, grouped in sets of one hundred. Each set was called a *centurie,* a term that has sometimes been used as the book's title (*The Centuries*). The first edition contained 353 quatrains and a preface to his oldest son César. Two years later, a second edition included seven *centuries,* two of them incomplete. In 1568, two years after Nostredame's death, a final edition added three full *centuries* and an epistle to King Henri II. All three editions were published in Lyon, although by different publishers. This final total of 942 quatrains is odd. Why, after all, did the book not include a thousand?

Nostredame may have intended it as such, or perhaps not, perhaps he ran out of time. Quatrains may have gone astray in publishers' workshops or—yet another possibility—he may have fit as many as he could in the sixteen-page sheets that publishers routinely used. It is not clear either why the last three *centuries* came out after his death. Some commentators believe that they had been part of a lost 1558 edition that bore the imprint of the eminent Jean de Tournes, publisher of Ovid and Dante and other illustrious authors. Others have suggested that the last three *centuries* and the epistle were composed by an unknown scribe after his death. It is true that some features, including the erratic use of commas and semicolons, change noticeably in the latter section of the book. But the rhythm, the tension, the tenor of the words are the same. And ultimately, conjectures about single or composite authorship will not take us very far. The key point is that most readers believed in his own time and later that Nostredame had penned the 942 quatrains.[3]

Nostredame was not the first to write *centuries* but by all appearances he was the only one to publish them alongside almanacs and prognostications. He thus provided predictions about the year or decade to come as well as long-term ones whose timing was vague. Whether in his horoscopes or his publications, Nostredame's calculations and visions rarely yielded utmost precision. He generally spoke of favorable or unfavorable configurations. The *Prophecies* included few dates: 1580 (a very strange age), 1607 (Arabs seize a king), 1609 (a papal election), 1700 (attacks from the east), 1703 (realms changing), 1727 (the capture of a Persian monarch), 1792 (a new age), 1999 (a king descending from the sky), and 3797 (the end of the world).[4]

The quatrain that seemed to refer to 1727 (3.77) condenses Nostredame's approach:

In the third clime comprehended by Aries,	Le tiers climat sous Aries comprins,
October seventeen twenty-seven :	L'an mil sept cens vingt & sept en Octobre :
King of Persia seized by the Egyptians :	Le roy de Perse par ceux d'Egypte prins :
Battle, death, defeat: the cross most disgraced.	Conflit, mort, perte: à la croix grand opprobre.

Nostredame continued to draw from astrology, linking future events to astral influences, inclinations of the sun, and conjunctions. But he now did so alongside prophecy. Astrologers provided interpretations of celestial signs according to a method. Prophets, in contrast, were elected by God to convey augurs to humanity. They typically proffered warnings or requested renewed devotion. Nostredame danced around his devotion to vatic arts. Many prophets and visionaries had come out of Provence during the late Middle Ages, men with names like Jean de Roquetaillade, but Nostredame did not position himself as their heir. Nor did he resemble familiar prophetic types: the lowly, unorthodox man, the pure figure who disregarded his body, or the divine envoy who interpreted Scripture to help a leader overcome adversity. Some prophets were educated scribes, not unlike Nostredame, but he renounced the prophet's title, name, or power. The secrets of God the Creator, he explained, remain closed to mere human beings. "If I have made mention of the term prophet," he wrote in his preface to the *Prophecies,* "far be it from me to arrogate a title this exalted, this sublime." A prophet, he added, "is properly speaking someone who sees distant things with the natural knowledge possessed by all creatures." And his *Prophecies,* he concluded, were written "in nebulous figures rather than palpably prophetic."[5]

Still, the book's title is not innocent. Nostredame combined facets of the

Jewish prophet who brought together past, present, and future; the Christian prophet who could accomplish nothing without divine power; and the melancholy Aristotelian prophet who could connect with the soul of the world. He may also have seen himself as a modern-day oracle who reactivated classical traditions. He liked to depict himself alone in his study at night, his mind cleansed and peaceful, open to messages inscribed in stars and to intimate encounters with a divine voice. Guided by "natural instinct & accompanied by poetic furor," overcome by prophetic inspiration, and dabbling in white magic (he wore laurel crowns and a sky-blue stone ring during these sessions), Nostredame composed what he called "nocturnal & prophetic calculations."[6]

In quatrain 3.77, one of these calculations revolved around the king of Persia's capture by Egyptians in 1727. (I have been unable to uncover any such event that year, though the Safavid ruler Tahmāsp II and the soldier of fortune Nadir Kuli did stop Afghan advances into Persia. Two years later, they pushed back the Ottomans as well). Nostredame often referred to such noteworthy but vaguely identified figures. Others include the king, the emperor, the Great Turk, the pope, the chief, the first personage, and the "ornament of his age." This king's capture is but one of the violent incidents depicted in the book, along with raids and expeditions, kidnappings and betrayals, and the battles and defeats mentioned in the fourth line. They are ubiquitous but seldom linked to specific events.[7]

As for the disgraced cross in the last line, it may well refer to Catholicism. While religion is a prevailing concern in the *Prophecies,* the book says little explicitly about Christian rites, mysteries, and the Holy Ghost—much less than other theological or prophetic works of that era, even if it refers more than once to the "divine word" and the "corporal substance of the spirit" (quatrains 3.2 and 8.99). This was probably a reference to the Catholic doctrine of transubstantiation of Christ's blood and body into the Eucharist, which Catholics were reaffirming in the face of Protestant attacks. The *Prophecies* were written while Catholic prelates convened at the Council of Trent to denounce Protestant heresies, reaffirm the central Church doctrine, and issue reform decrees. Quatrain 8.99 might have referred to the council and transubstantiation: "They shall change the site of the Holy See / Where the corporal substance of the spirit / Shall be restored & received as the true seat."[8]

Still, some contemporaries grew suspicious of Nostredame's religious convictions. Had he not attended a medical school with a notorious Protestant bent? Had he not befriended the dubious Julius Scaliger? And did rumors not accuse him of mocking the cult of the Virgin Mary? Some commentators raised the question in his lifetime, and others have regularly returned to it ever since, claiming that Nostredame found in Protestantism a mystical piety and an intimate relationship with God that Catholicism could not offer. After all, he distinguished "Christians" (i.e., Protestants) from "papists" (Catholics), and used *qui cum patre,* a supplication to the Holy Spirit that took liberties with the mystery of the Trinity. He expressed sympathy for "brothers & sisters captured here & there," a possible reference to oppressed Protestants. Founded as it is on a godly plan, divination also has affinities with Protestant doctrines of predestination. The case regarding Nostredame as a covert Protestant remains circumstantial, however, and it minimizes many things: Nostredame's public denunciations of sects and religious schisms; his references to a great emperor and the pope (two mainstays of Catholic prophecy); and his private reverence for the Virgin Mother. It also implies that the Catholic authorities were dim or permissive, neither of which was true. The devout Catherine and other Catholic leaders did not question his faith. Ultimately, we are left with a man who wrote horoscopes and predictions for Catholics and Protestants alike, who did not side with any camp, and who may well have sought to go beyond such cleavages. He was never reclaimed by Protestants as one of their own. And he requested to be buried in a Catholic church "as a good, true and faithful Christian."[9]

Nostredame knew how orthodoxy dealt with people who challenged its authority or creed. He understood the risks taken by alchemists who made mass irrelevant, by false prophets who dangled prospects of redemption outside the church's purview, and by judicial astrologers who presented astral bodies as first causes that determined everything, supplanted God, and left no room for free will and personal responsibility. Nostredame accordingly vowed to subordinate judicial astrology to the Holy Scripture but without interpreting Scripture in the manner of biblical prophets. If he foresaw dangers looming for Rome (which he did in some quatrains), he did not frame them as punishment for the clergy's corruption. He also denied venturing into a divine sphere in which human beings had no place, for this came close to demonology. He warned his son to avoid that "execrable magic that was long condemned by the Holy Scripture and the canons of the Church," for this would cloud his mind and drive his soul to perdition. Regardless of his beliefs, Nostredame moreover cultivated relationships with bishops, vice-legates, and even the pope, this "Atlas of our Christian civilization," to whom he dedicated at least one almanac. This is why he ran into few problems. Parisian magistrates inquired at one point about his activities, but they quickly dropped the matter. His *Prophecies* were neither burned in public squares nor included on the papal Index, the list of prohibited books that was issued by Paul IV in 1558.[10]

✦

To censor the *Prophecies* required that one understand them—and this was no easy task. Where, after all, was the third clime in the quatrain about the Persian king? Who would be defeated? Who would die? And could Nostredame not have been more precise regarding that cross?

Nostradamus's literary world is governed by discontinuity. Lines often end with periods, raising questions about their relationship to what precedes and follows. Many quatrains switch direction after the second line. Transitions escape easy detection. It is never clear when successive clauses or lines build on one another. The same holds true of successive quatrains in the *Prophecies*. Two or three in a row sometimes touch on similar themes, but most of them stand alone. There is no linear progression, no single narrative arc with finely sketched characters and a resolution. Nostredame's fragments and abrupt changes of course broke with the active verbs and declarative sentences of late medieval prophecy. They also shared little with the simple, transparent style that the Renaissance deemed appropriate for lowly topics. This was a world apart.[11]

Once again, it comes down to the words. French dominates, but one also finds Greek, Latin, Hebrew, Spanish, Italian, Provençal, and Celtic. Some words are abbreviated. *Narbon.* presumably stands for the town of Narbonne in southwestern France, but what about *Car.* and *Carcas.*? Perhaps the neighboring city of Carcassonne, perhaps not. Many words are anagrams or symbols. Commentators have suggested that the great *Chyren* designated King Henri or Henry (*Henryc* in Provençal). *Rapis* was Paris, the *Phoacean port*

Marseille, the *lion* a war chief, the *Castulon monarque* Emperor Charles V. *Snakes* stood for heretics. *Whites* and *reds* designated French magistrates who wore robes of that color. This is plausible but not more since Nostredame did not leave a glossary. And what about *the great wounded one, the big cape, the white feather,* and what he called *la grande grande*? Some words hang between opposite meanings (*resserer* could mean to lock or to unlock). Predictions likewise seem to posit one thing and its contrary. An unnamed monarchy would see its power increase and diminish in 1553; the summer of 1557 would be one of drought and floods. Strange things would happen, too. "Nourishing the rock the deep white clay / From a cleft below takes its milky birth" (quatrain 1.21). Contemporaries may have found it easier to figure this out than we do, five centuries later, but not always.[12]

Nostredame left so many words out. Sometimes, it is the subject of a sentence: "Dispatched without much resistance." Sometimes, it is an article, a preposition, or an adverb. "Battle, death, defeat" in the 1727 quatrain may be a chronological sequence—or not. Adjectives and qualifying clauses regularly end up far from the nouns they modify. This resembles Latin, except that Latin syntax and morphology compensate for loose word order and prevents such ambiguity. Take "For him great people without faith and law will die" (a literal translation of the third line of quatrain 2.9). Does it mean that people will die without faith and law? That, according to this person ("him"), they lacked faith and law? Or that a faithless, lawless individual will provoke the demise of this people? (In this case, we might follow a recent translator and render the line as "For this lawless one a great people dies.") It might be something else altogether—hard to tell. The words of Nostradamus hang together in some fashion, but, without the glue of punctuation, conjunctions, and conventional word order, they are unmoored. Like bumper cars, they collide and crash and tap into each other's kinetic force. New relationships are forged while old ones come to an end, in a process of perpetual renewal.[13]

Other poets and prognosticators used Latin constructions or elided articles, but none did so with Nostredame's resolve. Here, too, he piled it on. No wonder that people asked him for clarifications. When customers complained about indecipherable horoscopes, Nostredame blamed his poor handwriting. His secretaries were too harried to pore over his scribblings, or to mind their own handwriting while copying his manuscripts. Some filled in the blanks themselves, a move that seldom yielded clarity of meaning. His poor penman-ship had larger consequences yet in the world of print. Once a manuscript arrived in a workshop, a printer read it out to a typesetter, who then picked characters and composed sentences. This was done in haste, in order to pub-lish as much as possible and make the best use of a short supply of movable type. The perils are obvious: words could be mistaken for their homonyms; apostrophes and punctuation could disappear.[14]

Without original manuscripts at our disposal, it is difficult to ascertain how much his texts suffered from this process. But Nostredame lived far from the printing shops of Lyon. On at least one occasion, he lambasted a printer for mutilating his manuscript (these were his own words). Close readers have tracked minute variations between editions of his works. One has *tendues* (tense) where the other has *rendues* (returned); or *mois* (month) where the other has *moins* (less). Nostredame's eagerness to publish exacerbated the problem. This may explain why one surviving copy of the *Prophecies* is miss-ing two quatrains and another one, from the same publisher in 1557, is not. Contemporaries thus read editions that differed in small but significant ways from what Nostredame had written. There is no original version of the *Proph-ecies*. Pinning Nostradamus down has always been a hopeless task.[15]

Translation into English or Italian added another remove from this origi-nal. Foreign publishers picked and chose within the French editions while deciding what to translate. This came at a cost. The *Almanac for the Yere 1562*, for instance, consisted of portents that Nostredame had written for 1555. Elsewhere, commas vanished. In one portent, *le jeune meurt* ("the young one dies") became "the oldest died." All Renaissance translations were vulnerable to such alterations. Once authors turned in their manuscripts, they typically lost control. Without page proofs to correct, they could not prevent errors and unwanted modifications. Still, while no authors were safe, those who penned poetic or predictive works in which every word mattered had the most at stake.[16]

Some of Nostradamus's obscurity might thus be involuntary. The same is true of his stylistic predilections, his affection for Provençal place-names, and the demands of poetic meter (which led him to omit, invert, or truncate words). To this may be added fascination with the past. The humanist in him looked back to antiquity and Byzantium while the astrologer studied vast planetary cycles. His publications are full of references to Roman leaders, omens, and ceremonies. Nostredame may have sought out analogies between Roman and French history. After all, by publishing the *Prophecies,* Nostredame hoped to secure the recognition of patrons and educated elites. He may also have wanted to further impress readers with his learning and predictive abilities. While some of them recognized these references, others must have deemed them mystifying.[17]

But not everything was accidental. Nostredame also relished obscurity in his publications. He told Jean de Vauzelles that he had purposefully concealed the meaning of his almanacs under obscure words. Perhaps he sought to express the volatility of his era, the instability of the human condition, the hidden workings of the world, or the mysteries of the cosmos. In the late 1540s, after all, he wrote a long poetic rendering in French of the hieroglyphics of Horapollo (long unknown, it was found in a French library in 1967). The latter, a Greek treatise on Egyptian hieroglyphics, had been written in the fifth century AD near Alexandria, rediscovered in 1419, and published in 1505. Dozens of editions, translations, and commentaries followed, many of them by Neoplatonist humanists who, inspired by these lapidary signs, devised enigmas, anagrams, and other symbolic modes of expression. Hieroglyphics now surfaced in courtly festivals, princely entries into cities, and poems—part of a vibrant symbolic repertoire that would disclose its secrets to learned initiates.[18]

On a personal level, obscurity was the entry badge into a brotherhood of prognosticators who shared a command of mysterious languages and esoteric bodies of knowledge. Expertise led to authority. Nostredame's obscurity might also show that he grasped the danger of saying too much, or saying things too clearly, during volatile times. Self-protection was a necessity for sixteenth-century soothsayers, who had to placate secular rulers as well as religious authorities. From Flanders to England, statutes banned predictions and prophecies that threatened public order or the ruler's majesty. Some prognosticators thus refused to ascribe a binding status to their predictions. Others used coded words and kept out vital information. This is how Nostredame presented his situation. He had long kept silent, he said in the *Prophecies,* because his predictions were likely to incense powerful individuals. He would now speak out, but in "cryptic sentences" and "under a cloudy figure." In due time, people would realize that events had occurred as he had predicted. In due time, they would understand what he had meant to say. As religious and political crises intensified, however, Nostredame grew convinced that Christendom was moving toward a moment of reckoning in which everything, truth as much as evil deeds, would rise to the surface. "Will be discovered what has been hidden for so long." He returned repeatedly to this theme, promising imminent revelations regarding plots or conjurors. As a voice of truth, he could no longer keep quiet.[19]

Still, he had to protect the fragile sentiments of coarse readers who could neither grasp nor handle such news. He used coded warnings, he said, to avoid intimidating the populace. Truth would remain the preserve of the cognoscenti, capable of reading between the lines. Others would feed on illusions—for the time being perhaps. This was an ancient notion, found in oracular and hermetic traditions as well as in Renaissance commentaries on the book of Revelation, commonly seen as a puzzling moral allegory. It also permeated literary circles. Poets lived in elevated, allegorical worlds and safeguarded mysteries against the profane. Petrarch's poetry, a veil that aroused marvel before divine mystery, protected the ignorant while opening itself up to the learned and wise. Maurice Scève likewise conveyed truth to those pure, elevated souls who took the time to parse enigmatic verses. Some poets thus accepted that Nostredame could not express himself any other way. Others, however, felt that clarity was the poet's first virtue and the play of light and obscurity his modus operandi. Arcane words and verbal disorder could not reign unchallenged.[20]

⁓ᴏᴇ⁓

The matter remained unresolved, but one thing was plain to all: Nostradamus's uncompromising bleakness. "Battle, death, defeat," the last verse of the 1727 quatrain, could serve as the *Prophecies'* subtitle. Elsewhere, Nostredame spoke of fire and floods and so much bloodshed that rivers ran red. His contemporaries may have been inured to such language. Violence had after all suffused poetry since the Middle Ages, and unforeseen catastrophes filled the plays of Shakespeare a few decades later, revealing hardship behind apparent well-being. And yet Nostredame stood out here as well. The gentleman Guillaume de Marconville remarked that he alone among prognosticators foresaw both political and religious upheaval for 1563. Two decades later, a

pamphleteer brought gloomy tidings but deemed it necessary to insist that he
was no Nostradamus.[21]

This is because Nostredame drew readers into a harrowing world in
which "hunger, burning fever, fire and from blood smoke" make up the daily
lot. Animals are invariably ferocious, fields barren, wars great and deadly,
peace unlikely to hold. Enemies lurk and factions conspire. They also plot,
rearm, attack. Fires break out at sunrise, assaults are launched on the borders. Counting words can take us only so far, but it says something that *black*
and *night* outnumber *white* by three to one and that *death* is seven times
more present than *life*. The recurring words are *famine* and *plague, unrest*
and *calamity, tumult* and *oppression, sedition* and *plunder*. The West trem-
bles, said Nostredame. It lives in a state of perpetual emotion. Nothing can last
when appearances deceive and upheavals turn things upside down: "Everything will be changed, frustrated, transmuted, thwarted." The healthy fall
ill; the cheerful grow morose. Friends turn into enemies, harmony into
chaos. Everywhere, Nostredame saw doubt and "*doubte double*." The idea of
transformation was as central to people's daily experiences as it was to alchemy, with its modifications of grapes and metals. Here, it metastasized into
an all-encompassing "renovation of reigns and centuries."[22]

All was suffering, both physical and psychological. As a horoscope writer,
Nostredame was accustomed to probing the innermost reaches of the human
psyche. And what he found rarely proved appealing. Hidden rancor governed all relationships. The powerful trampled the weak. Friends betrayed
friends. Malice and perversity overcame loyalty and bred the illusion of virtue. War had long constituted the most heroic of topics for poets, but there
was no room for bravery or epic glory in this landscape. The century's adversity brought out the worst in people: "The good will be followed by the evil."
Inklings of hope surfaced here and there: a declining intensity of war and
disease in 1550, France spared invasions in 1555. Mere respites all. Expect
constant escalation and paroxysms of misery, said Nostredame. Troubles were
a hundred times worse than the previous year. The misfortunes that awaited
the planet were as devastating as Nero's fiery destruction of Rome. Historical
comparisons become indispensable when calamities have no equivalents in
human memory.[23]

Readers could not be blamed for taking this at face value in the sixteenth century. The European population doubled, causing inflation to jump and wages to stagnate. This pressure was especially strong in the countryside, where disastrous harvests and changes in agriculture and feudal relations left peasants freer but also more vulnerable. Thousands sold their landholdings and moved to towns. The price of grain practically quadrupled over the century. One witness reported in 1586 that peasants were eating bread made of acorns, roots, fern, brick, and sprinklings of flour. They were fortunate: others had nothing but grass. Coupled with high feudal dues and tax increases, famine was a recipe for riots, and there were plenty. Religious conflicts yielded new heights of bitterness and cruelty in the name of true faith. States raised quasi-permanent armies and now waged war during all seasons. Muskets, mines, and crossbows caused new kinds of wounds. Beyond the battlefields, soldiers and deserters marauded, plundered, destroyed crops, and sacked towns. It was no longer clear who protected whom.[24]

Provence was spared nothing, neither riots nor invasion by the armies of Emperor Charles V, neither repression of heretics nor religious conflicts of rare violence. It was in this crucible that Nostredame grew up and then lived his adult life. He saw it all firsthand: the suffering and the dying, the violence and the persecutions. In 1561, Catholic peasants rose up against Protestants, whom they viewed as threats to their traditions and community. In Salon, they roamed the streets and burned houses. When they accused Nostredame of harboring Protestant beliefs, he took refuge in Avignon with his family. (This, too, points toward his Catholicism. A Protestant fleeing a Catholic mob might have opted for the nearby Huguenot stronghold of Nîmes rather than the papal enclave of Avignon.) Nostredame waited for the governor to restore order before returning to Salon, but he could not shake his despondency before this course of events. He wrote bitterly to a customer about a "popular fury that is bordering on madness." The injustice and cruelty that he had witnessed further convinced him that he lived in wretched times. He went on: "Freedom is oppressed, religion corrupted. War imposes silence on the law, all are full of fear and see things turning to insatiable carnage, bloodshed, fire, in short—as you said—toward civil war. However, we are not at the end of our troubles and we have not yet reached the bottom."[25]

Nostradamus clearly partook in the eschatological mood that had spread across the continent and the British Isles. Eschatology, which refers to the last days of history and what lies beyond, includes several strands. The apocalyptic one revolves around a divine message announcing the final struggle between good and evil, the Last Judgment, and the advent of a celestial kindgom in which injustice will be redressed. The millennialist strand postulates the advent of a Golden Age of happiness. The kingdom of Christ and his saints will overturn sinful, worldly rule and last a thousand years (or some other time span), until the Last Judgment. The messianic strand, finally, announces the arrival of a messiah who will champion divine justice in the struggle between good and evil. Beyond their differences, all three share a vision of history as divinely predetermined and structured, gloom regarding an era that was mired in crisis, and belief in the impending triumph of good over evil.[26]

The Protestant Reformation contributed to eschatological thought. For one, it made the Gospels available to laypeople. Matthew 24:7 is among the better-known verses: "Nation shall rise against nation, and kingdom against kingdom: and there shall be famines and pestilences, and earthquakes." Countless Protestants also saw themselves as true believers who launched the final battle againt the papal Antichrist. The Reformation itself was seen as a sign that the Last Days had begun. It was not the only one. Unbaptised natives were found and then exterminated in the New World. Charles V sacked Rome in 1527. And the Turks advanced into the Balkans and threatened the Mediterranean. Europeans looked at this Ottoman Empire with fascination, dread, and repulsion. Turkish piety might provide a model for the regeneration of a true Christian kingdom, but these satanic legions could also devastate Europe. The prophecies that had proliferated since the siege of Constantinople in 1453 said as much. Nostredame rarely named the Ottomans in his publications, but he spoke often of barbarians and infidels from the Orient.[27]

Europeans of all social backgrounds thus made sense of their world through an eschatological prism. There was a surge of astrological prophecy, increasingly focused on the Last Judgment and the struggle against Satan. Even if many Christians contemplated their future with equanimity, this outlook permeated broad swathes of European society. One finds it in sermons and processions, in prophecies and commentaries on the book of Revelation (growing numbers of people now accepted that it referred to their era), and especially in almanacs. A Swiss medical student was stunned by the number of apocalyptic prophecies circulating around Montpellier in 1568. This outlook may well have found its purest expression in the prognostications and quatrains of Nostradamus, which were caught between apocalypticism and cyclical millennialism, but invariably and unmistakingly dark.[28]

～๑๑～

Some of Nostredame's publishers played up the darkness. In 1559, an English almanac that was attributed to Nostradamus included a portent about fear, pillages, and epidemics on its cover. An Italian publisher likewise announced "horrendous things to understand" on the title page of one of Michele Nostradame's prognostications. This helps explain the reports of Nostradamus-induced panic in London and Toulouse in the early 1560s. But these outbreaks were not that common. His bleak words did more than simply scare people.[29]

For one, Nostredame outlined peace and reconciliation alongside affliction. He had little taste for gore, bloody atrocities, and fear for the sake of fear. His *Prophecies* captured the twin dimensions of apocalypticism in ways others did not. The first story he told, a tragic account of looming cataclysms and suffering, is easy to spot. He conveyed pessimism about an era that succumbed to sin and human passions, warned about harsh retribution, and announced violent confrontation between believers and nonbelievers. Nostredame combined a vision of the struggle against the Antichrist with the classical notion of the four ages of humanity. Decline set in after a Golden Age of justice and happiness and led to ages of silver, bronze, and—most ominous of all—iron. Nostredame could not exclude the possibility that the age of iron had returned, heralding what he called the great chaos.[30]

And yet, unlike those prophets who obsessed about the world's end and provided its imminent date, Nostredame broached the topic intermittently; he had the *impression* that it approached; and he placed it in a distant future. He never engaged in scapegoating, though it was a frequent practice at the time. He also told a second story, this one about universal peace under a great monarch and people who overcame their ignorance or nastiness, acknowledged their faults, repented, and could thus reenter society. Omnipotent, stern, and sometimes angry, his God punished those who neglected divine laws. But He was more merciful than vengeful and did not allow human beings to suffer more than they could endure. One could placate God through duty and sincere devotion. Drawing from a prophetic tradition that told readers to accept the magnanimity of God and heed divine warnings, Nostredame conjured up dreadful visions before intimating that a compassionate God would "help the poor populace, and any human creatures who feared and loved Him." All was not lost. The historian Denis Crouzet has recently gone farther and depicted Nostredame as an evangelical humanist (in the tradition of Erasmus) who sought to open the hearts of his brethren to an all-powerful, sometimes angry, but loving God. The prophet's cryptic and dark words thus plunged readers into a haze of confusion that called not for elucidation but instead for awareness of one's weaknesses and for quiet awe before an unfathomable divine Mystery. There was nothing to understand besides the importance of faith in this benevolent deity. Whether or not one accepts this depiction of an evangelical Nostredame (few if any contemporaries viewed him as such), this is indeed the God that he outlined for his readers.[31]

If the words of Nostradamus did more than scare contemporaries, it is also because they slipped in time and space. We now associate this name with the future, but in the sixteenth century (and for some time after that), it straddled past, present, and future. After all, Nostredame wrote during an era in which the West's understanding of time was changing. As they looked back toward antiquity, humanists could discern the changes that had transformed the world during past centuries. Linear notions of a break with the past and constant advances were coming into focus. But humanists also uncovered commonalities among distant eras. Some things stayed the same, or resurfaced again and again. Civilizations could mirror one another across centuries. New conceptions of time thus coexisted with old ones. So it is with Nostredame, who once again brought it all together. His conjunctions hinged on a cyclical notion of time, in which past figures and political states returned at set intervals. Cycles of growth, renewal, and decline governed history. Nostradamus's prophecies also involved biblical time: the progressive unveiling of a hidden message, the ineluctability of the Apocalypse, and a future age that was free from the corruption of the material world. The Roman idea of Fortuna, or chance, with its unpredictable yet formidable disturbances, was present as well. Out of this overlay came a vision of time as cause and outcome of radical and sometimes violent changes. When Nostredame spoke of "transmutations of time," he endowed time with a dynamic energy and intimated that it was an active force of change, able to modify, improve, and obliterate. "From good to evil time will change." The past heralded, programmed, and provided signs of the present.[32]

The present and the future, too, were intertwined. "It is not easy for me to distinguish the present from the past, or the past from the future," Rosenberger wrote Nostredame after reading his latest horoscope. Time clearly moves in some quatrains, propelling readers into vast cycles and commotions. But it is a time without regular flow, a fleeting present that draws from the past and morphs into the future. Words are never limited to any one era. Countless lines are bathed in vague chronology: "Here is the month for evils so many as to be doubted." Others lack verbs and hence float above time, or else switch between present and past tenses. The following is typical: "Venom, cruel action, ambition replete, weak one injured." It is a prediction for September 1557 but also a comment on current affairs and a consideration on human passions and interactions. It is ultimately about people making choices, entering into conflicts, and suffering consequences. Nostredame is discussing the tragedy and comedy of life—present, future, and eternal.[33]

His geography, too, crossed boundaries. Editions of the *Prophecies* often included the following subtitle: *Represents Part of What Is Now Happening in France, in England, in Spain, and in Other Parts of the World.* Readers thus gained "world explanations" about the known continents—especially Europe. Crossing rivers and oceans, Nostredame took them on a vast journey from London to Algiers by way of the Balkans and Tuscany. Such references endowed his words with authority since divine visions are typically broad in scope. They also enabled readers from diverse locales to locate predictions about their city or country. This was especially true for the French, whose country is mentioned in 28 percent of the quatrains (Italy and Britain come next). The *Prophecies* refer to eighty-five French cities. France surfaces as a physical place and the home of what Nostredame called the French people. It also constitutes an anthropomorphic entity that he addressed directly: "France, if you pass beyond the Ligurian sea, / Within isles & seas you shall be enclosed." France, finally, was the state governed by a "Gallic monarch." Siding with this ruler, Nostredame forecast victories for the country, signaled threats, and warned against costly letdowns.[34]

By the sixteenth century, Europe had resonated for at least two centuries as a cultural entity, with shared saints and charters. Aristocrats, traders, and humanists met and corresponded with counterparts from other countries. Maps and historical accounts proliferated. Europeans could define themselves against American natives and eastern barbarians. Still, feelings of continental identity remained weak. While Nostredame's references to far-flung European cities may have spread a common geographical vocabulary, it is not clear that they deepened a shared sense of belonging. Would Bavarians empathize with populations facing rabid dogs in Liguria? Some people might relate to such perils and feel compassion, but they might just as easily view them as distant, inconsequential threats.[35]

The same held true for France. By addressing the country, speaking about it at length, and describing "folk from the vicinity of Tarn, Lot & Garonne" and other regions, Nostredame certainly brought France to life on the page. He enabled readers to visualize its cities and regions, to picture looming dangers, and to appreciate its glory. Nostredame exemplifies a growing interest in France's topography in the late Renaissance. Geographers and poets alike now provided tangible depictions of French regions, waterways, and mountains. They deployed rich images to contemplate this world and imprint the minds of their readers. Henri II requested maps of his provinces and Catherine de Médicis contemplated a vast cartography of the French territory. Nostredame drew from this geographical effervescence—picking place-names out of contemporary guidebooks—and also contributed to what the literary critic Tom Conley has elegantly termed "topographies of sensation and experience."[36]

Some might conclude that the *Prophecies* contributed to budding national sentiment, the sense of belonging to a community founded in a common language, territory, and shared character. To be sure, French was making inroads and the monarchy was broadening its powers. It incorporated provinces such as Brittany, granted itself exclusive rights to coin money and declare war, expanded its justice system and bureaucracy, and sought a cultural radiance that would surpass Italy's. Still, it struggled to collect taxes, put down peasant rebellions, and govern unruly nobles and provincial institutions. The country was far from unified, with its innumerable dialects, independent provinces, English enclaves, and papal possessions. Provinces and towns retained their own legal customs, fiscal regimes, and even weights and measures. It is not clear, therefore, that a strong sense of Frenchness was in place by this time, that new forms of nationhood were taking form, or that we can speak, as one scholar recently did, of "literary nationalism." Rather than abstract national sentiments, Nostredame's references to France were more likely to denote fidelity to a monarch whose maps, as a royal geographer put it, displayed the breadth, greatness, and might of the Gallic kingdom.[37]

Still, the words of Nostredame also imprinted space with meaning and anchored contemporaries in specific places while allowing them to contemplate expansive vistas. His readership included not only French men and women but also members of a literate French-speaking elite realm that spilled out beyond the kingdom's borders, toward Savoie and Lorraine, Geneva and Brussels. All of them could uncover France and much else as well in a literary work that belonged to a broader world and encompassed it, too. Nostredame, poet of the Gallic realm, cautiously celebrated the French dynasty while nourishing a vast topographical imagination.

In one respect, Nostredame provided a screen on which readers could uncover or project expanses that were distant in place or time. The images that fluttered on his pages offered a mesmerizing spectacle whose relationship to their lives was as real or tenuous as they wished it to be. In another respect, Nostredame furnished a mirror of his times. As they immersed themselves in his publications, readers could identify people, places, and events such as the Spanish victory over the French at Saint-Quentin in 1557. Many recognized depictions of the era's hardships and felt those major shifts that, from print and the Reformation to far-flung voyages and the new astronomy, altered their lives or the way they saw the world. All was in flux.

To some extent, so was Nostradamus, with these impenetrable words and fragmented prophecies. But his regular predictions also cushioned the confusion. Nostredame fashioned an organized, predictable universe in which occurrences were part of series, and series were linked to other series. His almanacs always resembled those of years past. His prognostications invariably followed the same month-by-month template. And the *Prophecies* were codified strings of one hundred quatrains, a premodern metric pattern that provided a pleasing sense of harmony. There were surprises and reversals in his world, but there were *always* such surprises and reversals, and they always took the same form. Readers could expect them in every *centurie* just as they could expect the same words, situations, and conflicts. Nostredame never deviated or disappointed. Like canvases in a series by Mondrian, individual quatrains drew from the same pictorial language and thematic palette and yet subtly departed from one another. The parts were autonomous, but the whole was greater than the parts. Everything held together.[38]

Everything was also full of meaning—so much so that readers could believe that something lay behind the words even if they could not make sense of individual quatrains. Nostredame's references to strange figures, plots, and collusions unveiled the workings of this chaotic world. He seemed to have inside knowledge of the hidden forces that governed people's lives. This is also part of the appeal of the book of Revelation, but other publications promised similar insights at this time. Chapbooks (or *canards*) were affordable, simply written booklets that related dramatic or sensational news items, such as crimes, floods, and earthquakes. *Histoires tragiques* were longer and stylistically more ambitious stories and tragedies. Like Nostredame, their authors used predictive or prophetic language to express a fascination with afflictions and depicted a climax of horror. All claimed to describe this tumultuous world truthfully, but dramatized it in a vivid language of violence, marvel, and fright. All also oscillated between distance and the likeness of shared pathos. The words of Nostradamus helped contemporaries sacralize their world and bolster connections with a divine realm, but that is not all they did. They also named the era's confusion, anchored it within a linguistic framework, gave it dramatic tension, and expressed what readers sensed but could not—or dared not—put into words. Opacity and darkness could prove meaningful for people who contemplated the present and the future with stupefaction.[39]

Attentive readers could also discern a just, harmonious moral order in these publications. This, too, proved meaningful. If things were dismal in the sixteenth century, Nostradamus seemed to say, it was because so many people were transgressing divine commandments, human laws, and moral norms. Counterfeiters, pillagers, thieves, rebels, and adulterers who participated in "extraordinary fornication" harmed men, women, and children. The danger came from those people who, as Nostredame repeated again and again, broke human and divine laws and disregarded the natural hierarchies that kept the social order standing. The late Renaissance made much of the notion that a great chain of being structured the universe. God resided at the top, above the celestial order. Below that, humanity served as a bridge toward the material realm. Then came the animal kingdom, plants, and rocks at the bottom. Monarchs and manual laborers were the bookends of a human hierarchy of dignity and authority, with aristocrats above ordinary folk, men above women, the old above the young. People were expected to accept the lot that they had been given at birth, obey their superiors, and remain loyal.[40]

But the Renaissance also provided new opportunities for social promotion. Print, trade, and the growth of cities nourished aspirations that challenged the status quo. Nostredame denounced ambition and the quest for riches. "Life is of more value than money or treasure," he wrote. At the top of society, he said, treason and disloyalty were sowing sedition. Lower down, insolence caused disrespect and riots. Religious sects further exacerbated discord by preying on the weak. The cross was disgraced, said the quatrain quoted earlier. In a world that pitted one social group against another, a world that neglected nurturing relationships, a world that was losing track of faith and law, "the yearning for hierarchy will not be vain at all." Such admonitions did not come out of nowhere. During times of change, prophets commonly reminded people of the moral content of ancient traditions. Chapbooks and *histoires tragiques* often ended with disquisitions on human passions and divine punishment. Other almanacs linked duplicity to mayhem during the Wars of Religion (1562–98) and later condemned threats to the social order. Nostredame channeled a disquiet that, ironically, responded to social and technological changes from which he benefited and to which he contributed. The contradictions of Nostradamus include the man's relationship to his own yearnings and behavior.[41]

This led him to fashion a universe that defined standards of conduct and spelled out the consequences of infractions. Stay in your place. Respect laws. Obey the church. Beware of sects. Nostradamus conveys the yearning for social order that saturated prophetic tracts as well as the conservative tenor of apocalypticism and horror tales, whose strict divides between good and evil tend to embrace tradition and erect moral absolutes. Nostredame the

establishment figure, the friend of princes and powerful aristocrats, denounced reform and resistance. In his epistle to Henri II, he admonished
towns, provinces, and countries that had abandoned their original ways in
pursuit of liberty. Eventually, he said, they would return to the right path.

This being said, mighty individuals could also fall or meet harsh fates in
Nostradamus's world. The high would be put low and the low put high:
"From all sides the great ones will be afflicted." They, too, were vulnerable.
Here is Nostredame the outsider, cautiously challenging protocols and privilege. The social hierarchy that he upheld had to rest on well-understood duties. If a mighty lord could hand out charity one day and find himself begging
for alms the next, it was partly due to the vagaries of fortune. More often, it
was because he had neglected his responsibilities. Those who suffered the
steepest falls had lied, betrayed, dishonored, and inflicted violence upon
others. They had placed personal gain above their duties toward their underlings or masters. The cruel knight, the disloyal councilor, the immoral
bishop, the wayward prince—all would receive their due. "For the great ones
every man for himself no joy."[42]

This is not to say that Nostredame was a firebrand or an evangelical
revolutionary. He did not link the return of a Golden Age to the demise of
the powerful. Instead, he used quatrains—a poetic genre that imparted
moral precepts—to convey a message of his own and point all readers toward
an ethical, virtuous plane in which justice and duty resided above rank and
privilege. Princes could deflect forthcoming travails by upholding such justice. As for common folk, their ignorance and savagery were all too obvious.
They, too, could succumb to passions and violence. Nostredame did not
hold warmer feelings for the rabble than others from his milieu. But God-
fearing human beings could have a dignity of their own. Oppression of the
populace sowed bitterness and launched new cycles of violence. On a deeper
level, it offended equity. Given his dealings with the meek and the powerful,
Nostredame could speak to both. Some Europeans thus read him and uncovered order and authority; others found the same order and justice. All
could derive comfort and meaning from a universe in which things happen
for a reason; a universe in which neglect, cruelty, excessive violence, abuses
of power—anything that denies people their humanity and threatens social

stability—are neither unnoticed nor free of consequences. This was a universe that contemporaries could somehow make their own.

～∞～

Nostradamus nowadays conjures up images of unremitting fear. During the Renaissance, things played out in more subtle ways. Some writers responded to calamities such as the plague by conceding that language could never convey the unspeakable. They wrote about what they could *not* express, or told readers that the only thing such disasters could teach them was that the world was meaningless. Nostredame, however, captured what contemporaries called matters of the times (*affaires du temps*) and placed them in broader cosmological and moral universes. His cryptic and ominous words tapped cosmic forces and pointed toward divine, eternal, and universal designs. At the same time, they embraced the breaks and misfortunes of the world in which people lived their lives; they told meaningful stories about what Nostredame called "a sinister age"; and they outlined paths of conduct and collective fates while accepting that there might never be full closure. Nostredame told readers that everything was linked, that everything came together, and yet that discontinuity governed the world. It was all there.[43]

As a writer, Nostredame was perpetually on the move, making his way from prose to poetry, prediction to prescription, depiction to exclamation, warning to precept. He was not necessarily the best at any one of these genres. But the man who journeyed across realms without fully belonging to any one could grasp them from the inside *and* from the outside. His words could convey the conflicting forces and aspirations that propelled the Renaissance world forward in chaotic and often disconcerting ways. His readers could recognize what was true and immediate, imagine what was distant yet plausible, and feel tremors that launched personal transformations.[44]

From our twenty-first-century vantage point, this is both foreign and familiar. We recognize the desire to delve into horror and keep it at bay. We understand why people sought to come to terms with changes that proved disorienting—or welcome and disorienting at the same time. And we discern yet other facets of a media culture that made distant expanses tangible as well as relevant. Rather than drawing readers into escapist realms, Nostredame expanded time and space and fostered a sense of being in the world. If we squint a little while parsing his words, we might even glimpse premises of the *Economist*, Oprah, and true crime. *The National Enquirer* or *Paris-Match*? Not so much.[45]

Chapter 4

꙳

Fame and Infamy

During the last months Michel de Nostredame's agony grew unbearable. Arthritic pain began in his hands, descended to his knees, and finally reached his feet. His joints swelled. Contemporaries called it dropsy, though today we might speak of arteriosclerosis. Composing horoscopes became an ordeal. During one stretch, he could not leave his bed for twenty-one straight days. Nostredame felt his strength decline. "May God allow me to live until then to describe the threats inscribed in the stars," he wrote in his 1565 almanac. In June 1566, he finalized his will with his notary and left instructions regarding the future of his children. The astrologer then made his final confession and devoted eight days to acts of contrition. On July 2, he died at the age of sixty-three. It was the day of the Feast of the Visitation of Notre-Dame.[1]

Nostredame was buried that very day. Funerals of well-to-do Catholics were now becoming theatrical affairs, with as many masses and priests as families could afford. Without belonging to Salon's upper crust, Nostredame was wealthy enough to bequeath a house and a respectable two thousand gold écus to his descendants. He also left donations to beggars and friars in order to speed the release of his soul from purgatory. The funeral procession unfolded "with full pomp and circumstances," reported his son César. His two executors, a burgher and a nobleman, led the party to the Church of the

Convent of Saint-François, home to Franciscan monks known as *Cordeliers*. Nostredame was buried inside the thirteenth-century church, against an inner wall. As he had requested, four candles surrounded his body.[2]

Most people were still buried in collective graves at this time, either in churchyards or cemeteries. Burial inside a church was reserved for high clerics, gentlemen, merchants, and intellectual luminaries. It was an honor that priests and monks sold, sometimes with zeal. In Salon, members of leading families usually asked to be buried in Saint-François. They did so for spiritual reasons and to secure an undisturbed resting place (cemeteries were also used for dances, markets, and animal grazing). Some also sought to display their social status and leave a permanent trace of their distinctive virtue. The rituals of death became a means of self-glorification for individuals, families, and dynasties.[3]

Nostredame's tomb lay near the church entrance and projected a foot from the wall. It contained a bust of the man in his later years, a small portrait, and his coat of arms. The epitaph, written by his widow, praised "the most famous Nostradamus who among men has deserved by the opinion of all to set down in writing with a quill almost divine the future events of the entire universe caused by the celestial influences." The encomium begins with fame and public acclaim rather than skills or inspiration. This, Anne Ponsarde seemed to say, was incontrovertible proof of powers that no other seer could match. Others agreed. Customers addressed their letters to the very famous Master Michel Nostradamus. A Hungarian wrote that "one name alone is on everybody's lips, that of Nostradamus, famous among all." An Italian marveled that his reputation spread so fast that the winds must have carried his name from France, flying gloriously above the peaks and cliffs of the Alps.[4]

Nostradamus was not the first celebrity in the West. In the literary realm alone, Dante and others had come before him. But no secular figure arguably proved more intriguing in Renaissance Europe, and none garnered more attention for his popularity. The mine owner Rosenberger wrote him that he had grown "aware of your celebrity a long time ago because your reputation was universally widespread." Nostradamus's superlative fame was itself becoming a source of awe. One could now become famous for being famous (though not only for that). But this fame also generated controversy. The factors that lay behind it—not merely the predictions but also the ubiquity and the disregard for boundaries—touched a nerve. The Nostradamus phenomenon captured these facets of modern culture, and this made all of the difference.[5]

⁓ᴏᴇ⁓

The fame began with the plague doctor's reputation. To sell a new collection of potions, one publisher told potential readers that Nostredame himself had invented some of them. He fully expected this imprimatur to boost sales. Building on medicine, astrology further magnified his fame. It was his "almost divine skill in wisely interpreting the future from the stars" that had made him so famous, explained one of his correspondents. Afterward, prophecies, visits to the French court, and his prediction regarding the death of Henri II brought his fame to yet another plane. Nostredame's publications were "praised to the skies throughout tripartite Gaul, admired by foreigners, eulogized by everyone," raved one of his horoscope customers. Like other facets of the phenomenon, Nostredame's celebrity was ultimately rooted in print and media culture.[6]

This fame benefited from rising literacy, especially in the higher reaches of society but also among urban artisans, tradesmen, and apothecaries. In England, roughly one man in ten and one woman in a hundred could read. And many chose almanacs or prognostications. Nostradamus's were read by lords and merchants, prelates and priests, diplomats and officers. A military aide consulted one during the Spanish siege of Saint-Quentin and was convinced that it predicted defeat for France. In Paris, a gentleman received a new shipment of his almanacs in 1554. The English Lord Lumley owned at least one, as did the French cardinal François de Tournon—a gift from a church chancellor. In Normandy, Gilles Picot de Gouberville had several in his library, along with books by Rabelais and Machiavelli. This lord, who lived off the revenues of his estate and dispensed justice in his seigneurial court, had probably bought them at a nearby fair.[7]

Evidence becomes skimpier as we descend the social ladder, but Nostredame apparently had considerable success. When a flood hit the French city of Nîmes in 1557, residents turned to a quatrain about an overflowing river. Two years later, an English ambassador reported that sailors accepted his predictions about imminent storms and shipwrecks. Around the same time, a French servant took three books with him as he left for England: one was religious, the other a work of popular entertainment, and the third a prognostication signed Nostradamus. According to one contemporary a few decades later, it was the common voice of the people that had brought a quatrain to the attention of the duke de Guise in 1588.[8]

Things were different in the countryside, where literacy lagged behind and printed matter remained scarce. Still, Nostradamus's words must have been present in some form. Plenty of rural folk traveled to towns, where they could purchase his publications at fairs. Sailors and soldiers could bring them home when visiting their native village. Servants working for the likes of Gouberville could peruse almanacs on his estate and then share with others what they had found. Word-of-mouth communication remained much more prevalent than private reading. People listened to wandering preachers and tale singers and attended public readings in alehouses or village squares. Friends and kin commonly read to one another, whether Bible selections, tales of adventure, or prophetic poems. It is likely that some read fragments of Nostradamus as well. His predictions, it is true, lack the daring deeds and climaxes of traditional tales. Unlike epics, they do not trace the exploits and adventures of a noble hero. They are difficult to sing. But they share features of oral storytelling: formulas and rich images, troves of clauses and adjectives, repetition, and multiple levels of meaning.[9]

Nostradamus thus circulated between the aristocratic library and the boisterous marketplace—or, more broadly, between a learned culture and the popular one of peasants and artisans. These cultures shared expectations and beliefs (in marvelous prodigies, for instance), but they also differed in their languages, their cultural horizons, and their relationships to print. The itinerant doctor Nostredame penned words that spoke to all, but in different ways. Some people consulted his predictions at home while others did so in taverns or under a tree. Some finished dense prognostications in one sitting while others struggled to make out a quatrain. Some were drawn to his political prophecies while others limited themselves to weather forecasts. Social background was a factor, but it did not determine everything. Gouberville instructed his men to sow wheat on a given day in 1558 because Nostradamus had predicted that it would yield ample crops. Like countless others, he read his almanacs and prognostications as a matter of course, or planning. Others turned to Nostradamus after natural catastrophes. There were several ways of consulting his predictions.[10]

Nostredame proved so successful that one Englishman declared in 1560 that he "reigned here so like a tyrant with his soothsayings that without the good luck of his prophecies it was thought that nothing could be brought to effect." By the end of the century, he had entered biographical dictionaries. The *Portraits of Several Illustrious Men,* for instance, included 144 French clerics, officers, poets, scholars—including Michel Nostradamus, royal doctor and great mathematician and astrologer. His portrait was sandwiched between a naturalist named Pierre Belon and the architect Guillaume Philander, two admirable men who soon fell into oblivion. This did not happen to the astrologer from Salon.[11]

⁓ʒᴄ⁓

Personal accomplishments had yielded renown and a reputation. Reputation endowed with widespread visibility generated fame. During the late Middle Ages, renown came to reward military prowess, and then learning, wisdom, eloquence, and probity as well. As merit and the judgment of public opinion acquired greater weight, all kinds of people launched careers that rested in part on sterling reputations. They did so in such domains as politics, education, learning, and religion. The Renaissance brought new media and new opportunities for advancement that made it easier to attain fame. Once the pursuit became more acceptable, artists and humanists embraced fame as a fair ambition, an incentive to accomplish great things, and a just reward for their accomplishments. We cannot speak yet of a celebrity culture, with unknowns shooting to prominence and followers seeking to know them intimately. Still, fame had its secular heroes—adventurers, mapmakers, artists. Authors likewise set themselves up as independent masters of their craft and sometimes as print celebrities. Erasmus did so. Christopher Marlowe did so. The Italian astrologer Girolamo Cardano did so as well (his discovery by a Nuremberg printer was, he said, "the beginning of my fame").[12]

The self-made Nostredame did the same thing. Here, too, agility trumped outright invention. His multiple editions, quick translations, and savvy use of patrons played their part. And the name! Nostredame had the acumen or good fortune to coin one that captured Europe's collective imagination. Even his critics spoke of his "sublime name." In the Middle Ages, reputations had revolved around a name (*nomen*) rather than achievements alone, as if names held magical power, as if words could act upon the world. (Psychologists call this nominal realism.) The scholar who sought renown thus had first to name himself. In the intellectual world of the Renaissance, humanists likewise coined names to obtain respect and stature. Most latinized their names in order to display their connection to the classical tradition. Nostredame used two distinct patronyms at once, which was unusual. By the mid-1550s, he was publishing his *Prophecies* and other publications as Michel de Nostre-dame (or Nostre-Dame) while signing almanacs and private letters as Michel Nostradamus. Predecessors and contemporaries included the epigram writer Jacobus Securivagus, the astrologer Regiomontanus (Johannes Müller von Königsberg), and countless others. Still, it was the name of Nostradamus that would resonate loudest across the continent. Was it its play on the Catholic Notre-Dame (Our Lady)? Its meter and sonority, equally euphonious in the main European languages? Or its plasticity, its ability to generate multiple expressions and word games? There is no way to tell, but the name took off.[13]

This name provided gravity and mystery, intrigue and playfulness (people everywhere used it as a toy, said one contemporary). It was also part of a public image. Nostredame began one prognostication with this epigraph from Ovid: "May the universe praise my name against those who have so often deemed me dead." Fashioning such an image for public consumption was a favorite activity of Renaissance authors and artists. Since human beings were malleable, it followed that eloquent words could shape individual personas. And given the competition among writers, artists, and prognosticators, it was becoming necessary to sing one's own praise, or at least to control the way one came across. Nostredame fashioned such an image as well. Intentionally or not, he became the first draftsman of his public persona.[14]

His prefaces and the woodcuts that adorned his publications portrayed a diligent astrologer at work in his study. He scrutinized the skies at night, made careful calculations, and uncovered hidden patterns. His workbench, the open tome and weighty books, the portable sphere and compass—all of this conveyed seriousness of purpose. Other astrologers used such woodcuts, which drew from medieval images of prognosticators and studious evangelists. Still, pictures and words came together perfectly in this case to outline a reputable man, rooted in a city and devoted to the "spirit of truth." This persona was familiar to contemporary readers, but Nostredame also stood out in his divine inspiration and his concern for others. By addressing his son in the preface to his *Prophecies,* he came across as paternal and protective—a father to all of his readers. Even when his predictions seemed incongruous, he had to trust his instincts, he said, and share what he had seen in order to benefit humankind. "A commiseration and piety is come upon me," he wrote in 1559. All of this distinguished Nostredame from swindlers, black magicians, and sorcerers, who riled up the crowds by playing upon fantastic things. Charlatans looked out for themselves, but this honest astrologer shielded ordinary folk from diseases, ignorance, and temptation.[15]

Nonetheless, Nostredame's voice could seem arrogant. It grew forceful when he lambasted those who dared to contradict him or when he warned the Gallic fleet to avoid Corsica: "Once captive, you'll believe me yet." A Parisian customer once warned the astrologer that he seemed to deem himself superior to others. This was but one facet of his persona. Nostredame also depicted himself as the greatest sinner in the world, implored God to grant him a pure soul, and acknowledged his limitations. Future afflictions troubled him as much as they would any ordinary person. More than once, he expressed consternation before dire turns of events. More than once, he acknowledged feeling sorrow, shame, or fear before the calamities that flowed from his pen: "The western planets predict some sinister accidents . . . so strange that tears come to my eyes as I hold my quill." Contemporaries could picture the astrologer in his study, tearing up while contemplating insights that he could not keep to himself. By admitting that he could err, Nostredame told his readers that he was as responsible as they were for God's ire. By emphasizing his humanity, he told them that he, too, was subject to the vicissitudes that afflicted them. All belonged to the same fragile community.[16]

Like the man, this persona straddled registers. Extraordinary yet flawed, confident yet tentative, coldly authoritative yet emotional, Nostradamus captured a range of human behavior. Readers could relate to and even identify with someone who shared their pain. They could also trust someone who transcended it. The extraordinary person who could tap all of these expectations deserved widespread fame.

⁕

Unless he did not. Success bred jealousy and scrutiny and all kinds of questions about Nostredame. Could he really predict the future? If so, where did he find inspiration? Was he an astrologer, a prophet, or both? A true prophet or an impostor? A good Christian or a satanic envoy? Had fame not rewarded a fraud, or worse?

After all, his predictions did not always come true. Many readers, it is true, could live with such errors. Belief was the prevailing disposition of mind, an effortless acceptance of otherworldly forces that escaped causes and possiblity. And no one, not even the divinely anointed, could be right every time. The French king's ability to cure *some* sick subjects by touching them was deemed miraculous. Nostredame's ability to predict *some* events and not others could likewise be deemed prophetic. But there were contemporaries who saw these mistakes as proof of serious shortcomings. The Anglican theologian Matthew Parker distanced himself from what he called fantastical hodgepodge (he also denied having hesitated before accepting the position of archbishop of Canterbury due to ominous Nostradamian warnings). Others reviled the "infection of these pestilential poisoned lying prophecies." His slightest error, Nostredame complained, aroused endless mockery. Two weeks before his death, he asked a lord to protect him against "the calumniators and mischief makers" who spoke ill of him.[17]

Nostredame was surrounded by a multitude of detractors. The first was Julius Scaliger, the Italian philologist who had welcomed the young man in Agen but reportedly grew envious and repudiated him as an ill-intentioned buffoon. Scaliger's diatribes remained private, but others made their views known. Prognosticators, poets, and clergymen—both Catholic and Protestant—used print to denounce Nostredame's almanacs and prophecies. The jurist and lord Antoine Couillart penned vitriolic pamphlets from his estate in central France. The doctor and prognosticator Laurent Videl published a *Declaration of the Abuses, Ignorance and Seditions of Michel Nostradamus* in 1558. Other French critics hid behind pseudonyms such as

Hercules le François. In England, a twenty-two-year-old Puritan polemicist named William Fulke denounced Nostredame in a vitriolic *Antiprognosticon*. The astrologer Francis Coxe faced charges of magic and sorcery, recanted, and then wrote *A Short Treatise Declaringe the Detestable Wickednesse, of Magicall Sciences* that starred the reprehensible Nostredame in 1561. All of these authors expressed their outrage in vivid, oftentimes violent terms. Nostradamus touched a nerve.[18]

This was because the seer who dipped into all divinatory methods and media was both ubiquitous and exceptional. Girolamo Cardano came under attack for his astrology, Merlin for prophecies, Albertus Magnus for magic, and the fictitious Matthieu Laensberg for almanacs that bore his name. Nostradamus, however, could embody all of this at once. By lambasting him, Hercules le François condemned all "sorcerers, charmers, diviners, bewitchers, magicians and enchanters." The name of Nostradamus thus provided a way of opining on the contentious matter of divination. Some of the questions at stake—regarding its relationship to divine providence, for instance— had proven more explosive during the Middle Ages than the Renaissance. Leading Catholics now accepted a natural astrology that affected the body and passions while leaving human will intact. Still, astrology and magic could reconfigure humanity's relationship with the cosmological world. Evangelicals went after judicial astrology while Calvinists denounced dark prophets who turned the faithful away from the mysteries of the Word, an omnipotent God, a redemptive Christ, and belief in predestination. It is a "foolish curiosity to judge according to the stars all that must happen to men," John Calvin wrote in 1549.[19]

Nostredame's lugubrious language and his suggestion that astral bodies determined human behavior threatened key tenets of grace, free will, moral autonomy, and efficacy of prayer. Grappling with divine secrets was folly and utter arrogance. Nostradamus thus came to embody *error*, a blasphemous assault against the majesty of God and public trust. The sorcerer communicated with demons, said the doctor Videl, and he infused his quatrains with "diabolical intentions." Some Catholics equated his predictions with the satanic designs of Protestants. A few years after his death, a French canon recounted a telling story. In 1560, he said, Nostredame had spent a few days in Lyon. One evening, during a dinner with eminent burghers, he walked to a window and contemplated a church. His fellow guests wanted to know what was on his mind. He replied with a prediction: enemies of Catholicism would try to destroy the edifice and fail, because God would protect the sacred structure. Two years later, the Church withstood a Protestant assault during the French Wars of Religion. Satan had clearly sent a warning through his favorite Nostradamus. The canon who recounted this story did not mention his Jewish origins, but others did. Scaliger, for one, disparaged his "Judaic ramblings" and accused him of practicing kabbalah. Nostradamus was not one of us.[20]

And yet he proved so popular. As the number of astrologers and published prognosticators exploded, rivalries heated up. Some of his competitors depicted Nostredame as a mediocre soothsayer whose inane imaginings and technical incompetence flouted the rules of astrology. Others denounced an ambitious man who benefited more than anyone else from his predictions. When Videl and others went after him, they sought not only to stop his climb but also to bolster principles and a craft and a social status that amateurs now threatened. There were simply too many newcomers talking "off the top of their heads about things in which they had never learned so much as a single letter," complained one German prognosticator. All of these attacks created a counterpersona of Nostradamus. As a seductive impostor, he led the pack of charlatans and prognosticators who were posing as doctors and astrologers. As a lunatic madman, he coined a jargon that challenged human deduction. As a savvy upstart, he attained a level of fame that challenged Christian humility and social hierarchies. And as a callous soothsayer, he held a firm grip over European psyches. His word seeped across Gaul, lamented Scaliger, and infiltrated the minds of princes and ordinary folk. This "sweet and delicious poison blinded and bewitched the wits of men," explained the astrologer Francis Coxe. His predictions fostered chimeras, heretical notions, and, in due time, disobedience and riots. Nostradamus did not only threaten the salvation of souls. He also imperiled the future of the republic, said Videl. The stakes were nothing less than the religious and social foundations of Europe.[21]

⚜

Critics were so incensed that they gave Nostredame new monikers. He became *Monstradamus, Monstradabus,* and the *"monstre d'abus."* These names played on the French word *abus* (breach of trust) and on monstrosity. Hercules le François loathed "this hideous monster" and his bewitching, twisted enigmas. Monsters had long fascinated Europeans, but they now seemed to be moving from the margins of society into the center. Reports about conjoined twins or bodies with multiple heads were so numerous that contemporaries struggled to keep track. They responded with wondrous delight in the variety of nature and horror before creatures that deviated from the norm. Like other marvels, monsters could transmit a divine warning about human corruption, call for repentance, and tap eschatological fears. The same was true of Nostradamus's portents. Monsters also defied the natural order's decorum and moral codes. As monstrosity became a form of invective in Europe, so did the ubiquitous creature Monstradamus.[22]

There was something yet more disturbing about monsters. They blurred boundaries—between human beings and beasts, humanity and divinity, the natural and the miraculous, and good and evil. They clouded what had to be kept distinct and melded what had to be kept apart. Monsters were *partially* different from ordinary human beings, and this made them yet more unpure. It was impossible to define or tolerate such liminal creatures. Boundaries between social groups, religious communities, and ways of knowing were essential, for they told people how the world was organized, what place they occupied within it, and how they should conduct themselves. But the changes that took place during the late Renaissance—the print media, the possibilities for social mobility, the confessional warfare, the new outlooks on the cosmos—made such social and conceptual boundaries increasingly porous. This was a source of opportunities in terms of careers and knowledge, no doubt, but also of deep-seated anxieties about stability and order.[23]

No one captured this more acutely than Nostredame, the man who reviled rapid change and yet benefited from it. The maverick circulated across realms without belonging exclusively to any one. The insider-outsider who neither embraced nor rejected dominant protocols resided between true astrology and a newfangled one, between art and commerce, between tradition and innovation. His predictions went beyond the limits of nature, said a French gentleman. The interloper who erected bridges between disparate places and domains showed all too clearly that older partitions no longer held. His accessible but mystifying language seemed to blur the line between divine perfection and human understanding, between the ordinary and the extraordinary. And the very grounds of understanding appeared to be in perpetual motion in his works. In the late 1550s, an anonymous poet denounced "this great liar Monstradabus." The following verses began to circulate around the same time: *"Nostra damus cum verba damus, nan fallere nostrum est, / Et cum verba damus nil nisi nostra damus"* (We give our own things when we give false things, for it is our lot to deceive, and when we give false things, we are only giving our own things). When *Nostra damus* was read as *Nostradamus,* the verses mocked the empty, deceitful nature of the astrologer's words: "We are only giving the words of Nostradamus." The prognosticator who sometimes recognized what was certain and sometimes imagined what was possible also voiced deeper uncertainty regarding truth and falsehood, authenticity and dissimulation.[24]

It was not just that, like classic prophets, Nostredame operated in the breach and relayed divine proclamations to ordinary mortals. The cryptic prognosticator who practiced his arts at the intersection of humanism and divination made his era's underlying contradictions and anxieties all too explicit. Targeting him hence provided a way of denouncing abstract threats, distancing oneself from offending forces, and affirming indispensable norms. Whereas some people believed in Nostradamus, Videl, Coxe, and others needed this transgressor to redraw boundaries and exorcise the fears that lurked outside and inside their own souls. By turning Nostradamus into Monstradamus, they began to restore the order of their world.

The debate heated up during the last decade of Nostredame's life. As skeptics grew more vocal, supporters came to his defense. One aristocratic writer and bibliographer from France accused detractors of confusing the astrologer with lowly forgers and imitators. The law student Tubbe promised Nostredame that he would fight his rivals, "these incompetent giants in the art of calculation who, as I have heard, are slandering you." And Ronsard vindicated a fellow Catholic poet whose prophecies had been confirmed by recent marvels. (Given his reliance on Catherine de Médicis's patronage and protection at the court, Ronsard had little to gain by criticizing her astrologer.) False accusations against Nostredame reflected poorly, Ronsard said, on Protestants and people who discounted God's warnings. "Poor France." This show of support inflamed Protestant pamphleteers. They inveighed yet

more passionately against a demonic impostor who was leading Europe
astray. "O crazed Ronsard, how dare you welcome the damned Nostredame,
approve his claims . . . when God denies them." Among the paradoxes that
Nostradamus displayed, let us include the fact that faith (Protestant, in this
case) could prove more cautious than reason.[25]

Nostredame may have welcomed the controversy. We will never know,
but he had seen the detractors coming. He had written in the *Prophecies* that
some people would take issue with his sweeping predictions. Once the attacks began, he defended himself against what he called misunderstandings,
exaggerations, and calumny. Then he counterpunched. He dismissed his
adversaries as ignorant asses whose minds were warped by envy, and devoted
an entire quatrain to what he called inept critics. "Let those who read these
lines consider them with care," he wrote. "Astrologers, Fools & Barbarians,
beware." Nostredame also secured new patrons to hold these detractors at
bay and recalibrated his persona. Some Renaissance elites were now fashioning personas that were in accord with social conventions. They did so
through their dress, writing, and other such means. This process often required an alien force, a competing authority that had to be discovered or invented and then overcome. By defining himself publicly in opposition to his
slanderers, Nostredame could come across as vulnerable or even a victim.
Whereas his critics maligned what they could not understand, he probed the
unknown. They insulted him, but this man of faith and common sense was
incapable of harming other human beings. Taking the high road, he asked
for forgiveness if he had unwittingly aggrieved anyone. All might still become friends one day, he said. Nostredame needed his detractors as much as
they needed him.[26]

⁓☙⁓

By the end of his life, Nostredame was bathed in fame and infamy. As an English astrologer put it a century later, "the Book hath procured him both a
good, and a *bad Fame.*" All of this endowed Nostredame and his predictions
with intrigue, drama, and aura. But it did so in a peculiar way. While his
death reportedly saddened some residents of Salon, there were no reports of
massive grief, no collective fervor or social movement born in its wake. Part
of the problem is that neither his persona nor his supporters could make

Nostredame appear virtuous or heroic. Christian virtues include charity, temperance, kindness, and humility. Classical virtue implies modest, often unrecognized devotion to the public good. As for heroes, they battle the mighty or dominant norms in the name of justice and freedom. By overcoming challenges and learning from misdeeds, they provide moral lessons or guidance. As Nostredame's plague years receded into the past, so did the courageous, self-sacrificing doctor. In his place, there remained the prudent or famous astrologer and prophet. But prudence does not translate into courage, and fame neither edifies nor teaches self-sacrifice. An essayist once identified twenty-two components of the hero's life story. Nostradamus's included three at most: he was chosen by God, his demise proved mysterious (more about this shortly), and none of his children succeeded him. His life story never yielded a myth, a symbolic narrative about humanity or the natural universe that helped people think through contradictions.[27]

Nostredame failed to generate a social movement for other reasons. The astrologer had been a personal adviser and a writer rather than a magnetic leader who sought to build a mass following. Mercurial and conservative, wary of sects and public opinion, he never tried to organize people around a common cause. Similarly, his legitimacy always rested on words. People interacted with Nostradamus through horoscopes and publications rather than prayer, intercession, or public gatherings. From the start, the phenomenon thus revolved around individual relationships rather than communal rites. There was no religious apparatus here, no institutions or sacraments, no explicit admonitions or pathways to salvation.

As a result, Nostredame never became a saintlike figure. I found no accounts of people praying to him for solace or assistance. Collective pilgrimage routes never converged around his tomb. Instead, people made their way to Salon on their own. Prior to the French Revolution, the monks of Saint-François would welcome visitors at the church's entrance and lead them on candlelit tours. They charged for this privilege and sometimes pushed copies of the *Prophecies* on the way out. Thomas Jefferson found these cicerones insufferable during his stopover in 1787—they "wish for your money and suppose you give it more willingly the more detail they provide," he wrote in his diary—but others went along over the years. French queen Marie de Médicis paid a call in 1602. The geographer Louis Coulon made a special trip from Aix forty years later and penned a description of the tomb in his guidebook to France. John Locke transcribed Nostredame's epitaph in his travel journal in 1676. Some visitors came for spiritual reasons; others paid homage to a fascinating author; and countless European travelers simply passed through Salon and found little else to see in a town that ranked far behind Avignon, the Pont du Gard, and other Provençal curiosities. Visitors hence made it to Saint-François from different directions, but all of them were very much aware of the astrologer who, as one of them put it, "has made Salon fashionable as his cradle, his home, and his burial ground."[28]

It was the fame again, the fame that drew people into his orbit and distinguished *il famoso Michele Nostradamo* from other astrologers and prophets, however well known. This fame revolved around a person whom people could situate in place and time. The soothsayer signed his prophecies; the venerable master adorned the covers of almanacs. Even detractors vowed to shake and needle the man whom they called *Michel*. Inside the church, explained one English traveler, a portrait by his son César represented him "exactly in his own proper Form and Dress." Biography prevailed. It anchored Nostradamus in the lives of Europeans and provided a tangible author with whom they could converse, either in person or in their imagination.[29]

But biography had company. There was also the name, which sometimes stood alone. In 1571, Nostredame was the only proper name to appear under *astrologer* and *prognostication* in a French collection of synonyms. And there were strange tales, which people began relating in hushed or incredulous tones after his death. Nostredame, they said, had forecast the exact day and hour of his passing. He may even have opened his crypt a day before expiring and asked a priest to perform the funeral service. His secretary told a slightly different story. As he bade his master good night on the eve of his passing, the old man took a sheet of paper and wrote, "my death is near." The next morning, the secretary found the astrologer's lifeless body slumped next to his bench. His thoughts, like those of others, went at once to one of Nostredame's last portents: "Will be found dead near the bed and bench."[30]

Chapter 5

※6·

The Nostradamian Underworld

Death could have marked the end of the story. It certainly did for other prognosticators and soothsayers. Besides historians, how many among us have heard of Guillaume de La Perrière, Simon Forman, or Joseph Grünpeck? All faded from view at some point after their passing. This did not happen to Michel de Nostredame.

Take Paris around 1610. The astrologer had been dead for five decades, and yet bookstalls carried innumerable publications bearing his name. There were pricey editions of the *Prophecies* and cheaper ones on flimsy paper. In public markets as well as in elegant residences, people looked up his predictions before princely marriages, during military expeditions, or after the deaths of prominent marshals. Around the main court of justice, striking lawyers denounced a magistrate's new regulations by quoting a quatrain predicting his defeat. On the Pont Neuf, the new stone bridge that teemed with comedians and tooth-pullers, hawkers sold songs about Nostradamus.

Some of these songs and predictions announced the assassination of King Henri IV. The French monarch had acceded to the throne in 1589, abjured Protestantism, and promulgated the Edict of Nantes, which ended the Wars of Religion by allowing Protestants and Catholics to live together in peace. But the monarch still had plenty of enemies. He survived several assassination attempts, and rumors of his death were rife. Nostradamian quatrains predicting his demise had circulated at the French court and elsewhere for years. One of them (a fake) seemed to announce something momentous for the "Great Celtic Lion" in his fifty-seventh year, which fell in 1610. As fate had it, a rabid Catholic stabbed the king to death that spring. A few contemporaries rejoiced, a few sought revenge, but most were in shock. In Paris, women cried and pulled their hair and prayed for the new king. Men took refuge in their homes or else grabbed swords and ran wildly in the streets while spewing profanities. The civil wars were about to resume! The final days had descended upon France! People turned to predictions, numerology, and Nostradamus, whose prophecies disclosed "all that is new in the world," as one chronicler put it. It was said that quatrain 7.17 had announced the king's untimely death:

The rare pity & mercy of this king	Le prince rare de pitié & clemence,
Whose death shall transform simply everything :	Viendra changer par mort grand cognoissance :
In times of great peace, the realm at ill ease,	Par grand repos le regne travaillé,
When the lord goes down to major defeat.	Lors que le grand tost sera estrillé.

For some, this was just too much. "There are many hollow brains, and minds fit only to receive anything that is extravagant," wrote the scholar Gabriel Naudé. "[They] think their pockets empty without these *Centuries,* which they idolize." But the appeal of the *Prophecies* could not be denied.[1]

Nostredame stood out. While his competitors held one or two pieces of the puzzle across the sixteenth century, he alone seemed to own the full set. La Perrière's *Considerations on the Four Worlds* (1552) provided four *centuries* of quatrains on the divine, angelic, celestial, and sensible realms but said nothing about the present world or the future. In England, Forman and John Dee grew famous as astrologers, yet neither one published much. Forman opened a successful horoscope practice but lacked medical credibility and ties to the court. Dee penned political predictions but his geometrical language required technical know-how. He also had the misfortune of landing in jail on charges of necromancy. In Italy, Girolamo Cardano understood the new media culture but did not fashion a poetic universe. In the Holy Roman Empire, finally, the humanist Grünpeck coupled astrology and eschatological prognostication but also interpreted biblical prophecies and glorified Emperor Maximilian I. As a court chaplain and the emperor's personal secretary, he linked his name to a specific religious tradition and a political party.[2]

The tantalizing but controversial Nostredame, however, roamed freely. Granted, he came across as a Catholic astrologer with ties to the court. One prominent royal biographer credited him with having told Catherine de Médicis that her three oldest sons would accede to the throne (which they did), and that the middle one, Charles IX, would rival Charlemagne. But Nostredame had not been a royal or papal propagandist. He had not hammered his ideological views and moral precepts into the minds of readers. Nor had he directed his *Prophecies* toward a single party or cause, or even Catholic circles alone. In the wake of his death, therefore, no religion, sect, or political faction affiliated itself with Nostradamus. None took it upon itself to maintain or disseminate the quatrains. They could easily have faded into oblivion, but Nostradamus did not vanish. Instead of belonging to no one, the quatrains belonged to everyone, opening themselves to people from various backgrounds and religions.[3]

Among them was a string of editors, compilers, interpreters, translators, forgers, and hacks—we might call them Nostradamian providers. "Nostradamus is a planet," a literary critic noted in 1834. "He has his satellites, and he acquires new ones as he advances in space and time." The metaphor is well-chosen. The phenomenon has indeed been a planetary system, filled with satellites that both reflect and intensify the radiance of the main celestial body. The people who orbit Nostradamus form neither a subculture nor a counterculture, with distinctive or subversive values. There was no harmonious community here, no consensus. Instead, ambitious, fiercely independent, freewheeling individuals have inhabited a cultural underworld that endures across time and space, just below the surface. They have embraced Nostradamus for different reasons. Sometimes, it is to imbue their world with meaning, sometimes it is to advance particular agendas, sometimes it is to improve their own lot, and sometimes it is a mix. Regardless, they have kept

Nostradamus's name alight in the predictive firmament and given it different hues. Cultural transmission and cultural transformation go hand in hand.[4]

⁓᠑ᡒ⁓

The first and brightest satellite was Nostredame's personal secretary, the man who reportedly bid him good night on the eve of his death. The son of a Burgundian gunsmith, Jean de Chevigny had apparently studied medicine and law before devoting himself to poetry and higher mysteries. He began corresponding with Nostredame as a young man and visited him in Salon in 1560. The astrologer calculated his horoscope and his brother's as well. Within a year, Chevigny was living in Salon and assisting Nostredame with his correspondence and paperwork. When an opportunity presented itself to work for the governor of Avignon in 1563, Chevigny demurred. He enjoyed his quiet but rewarding intellectual life alongside the man he once called "High Priest of Sun and Moon." Following Nostredame's death, he moved to Grenoble, composed poems, and worked on a history of the French Wars of Religion. He also spent years poring over his master's writings. In 1594, he published the first major book about Nostradamus: *The First Face of the French Janus.*[5]

There is a wrinkle to this story: the book's author was one Jean-Aimé de Chavigny. Most contemporaries believed that Chevigny had simply changed surnames. He may have discarded a name that smacked of lower origins, or added Aimé—the adored one—after falling in love. But some claimed that Chevigny and Chavigny were different individuals. Chavigny, a young man from eastern France, came upon the scene around 1580, after Chevigny's death, and claimed to be Nostredame's disciple. Either he had never met Chevigny, or else the older man took the younger one under his wing without imagining that he would usurp his identity. Some scholars have devoted years to this matter. The problem is that, without direct evidence, we are left with circumstantial arguments and two hypotheses that seem equally plausible and inconclusive. At any rate, the controversy endowed the phenomenon with another coat of mystery. Commentators could now debate not only what the predictions meant but also who this first provider really was. All of this bolstered the notion that, when it comes to Nostradamus, strange happenings rarely lag behind.[6]

Something else matters: a man whom we might as well call Chavigny became Nostradamus's leading booster. He took it upon himself to transmit his divine pronouncements and protect his legacy. Chavigny, who claimed to have collected all of his master's publications after his death, put together a manuscript of 6,338 numbered portents. Such is the genesis of his *French Janus*, which included a selection of portents drawn from Nostradamus's almanacs and of quatrains from the *Prophecies*. The original almanacs were hard to find after Nostredame's death, but the *Prophecies* grew increasingly popular. Publishers from Lyon, Paris, and Amsterdam had released close to a hundred French-language editions by 1700, many in small portable sizes. Sales numbers are elusive, but a French judge noted the book's incredible success in the 1620s. Outside France, however, this long, cryptic work discouraged translators. The first translation of quatrains from the *Prophecies* (a selection) seems to have occurred in Barcelona in 1641. I have located only one full translation of the book at this time. It came out in London in 1672, the work of one Theophilus de Garencières, a French-born apothecary who sought to deepen reverence for God by helping readers relate current events to Providence. Italian, German, and Dutch readers could consult either French editions of the *Prophecies* (plenty of educated people had the required linguistic skills) or translations of selected verses.[7]

Chavigny did not seek exhaustiveness. The man who knew Nostradamus better than anyone else felt entitled to select 267 key predictions and then reorder them, with utter disregard for his master's original plan. The Nostradamian provider was first of all an editor and a conveyor. He altered words to improve rhymes, eliminated references to specific months, and inserted exclamation marks. Chavigny's book was not static, and neither were other seventeenth-century editions of Nostradamus. Some of the changes made in those editions seem accidental. An *f* became an *s*; a *y* became an *i*. *Volant* (flying or stealing) became *voiant* (seeing). "*Le né sans fin*" (the born without end) became "*le né sang fin*" (the born blood end, or the born blood thin). Other changes, in contrast, were deliberate. To entice readers, publishers wrote their own subtitles—for instance, *The Marvelous Predictions of Master Michael Nostradamus* or *The True Centuries and Prophecies*. Like Chavigny, they also added prefaces and indexes and versions of a biographical sketch that first appeared in the *French Janus*. This "Brief Discourse on the Life of

M. Michel de Nostredame" owed as much to hagiographies of saints as to Plutarch's *Lives* and Nostredame's own persona. Here was the wise, hardworking humanist who slept only five hours a night. Here was the luminous prognosticator who devoted himself to public welfare. Here was the devout Catholic who abhorred vice. Chavigny's Nostradamus was a legitimate soothsayer, a moral guide, and a patriotic, devoted subject of the Gallic Crown.[8]

But there was a major change of inflexion. Nostradamus now came across as a self-proclaimed, unabashed prophet. This was a far cry from the man's attachment to astrology and his caution regarding prophetic matters. Chavigny placated theologians by defining prophets as prognosticators rather than unerring visionaries, but his convictions were plain. A benevolent God had tapped the virtuous Nostradamus to convey His will and warn of tribulations and scourges ahead. By quoting quatrains alongside Deuteronomy, Chavigny placed this seer within a Christian vatic tradition. His *French Janus* inaugurated a long-lasting depiction of Nostredame as an elect oracle who, like Isaiah, received supernatural impressions and disclosed divine mysteries. A French historian remarked in 1646 that Nostradamus was now seen as an incomparable prophet, an extraordinary genius, a mind full of profound reflections. By tapping the country's prophetic enthusiasm, these providers recast Nostradamus and opened up new readings of the quatrains.[9]

Some providers went further yet and assumed his voice or name. This was especially true in almanacs, which remained the leading medium in Western Europe. It was common for households to own only two publications: almanacs and a Bible. Even though Nostredame's own almanacs had vanished, new ones continued to use his name and predictions. It is in these publications that most ordinary Europeans encountered Nostradamus between the seventeenth and the nineteenth centuries. To succeed in the almanac market, publishers needed an imposing author, a "doctor in physyck and astronomie" who would make their publication seem ancient and reputable. If they could not hire such an author, they simply invented one. There are traces of thirty such authors in France, the most popular being Matthieu Laensberg and Nostradamus. According to one memoirist, no almanac could succeed without sporting the name of Nostradamus. Some publishers simply picked a few of the quatrains and claimed that they pertained to the years to come. In 1799, for instance, a Swiss almanac presented seven successive quatrains

of the ninth *centurie* as predictions for the years 1800–1806. This happened
again and again. Other publishers flat-out copied Nostredame's almanacs, or
combined material from his various publications. Counterfeit ones had surfaced across the continent for decades and continued to do so. In some cases,
publishers simply married Nostradamus's name with content that had nothing to do with him. There was a thin line between counterfeiting, forgery,
and outright invention.[10]

Some readers did not care who had penned their almanacs. An English
diplomat received one that was attributed to Nostradamus, assumed that it
was written by some monk, but shared it with an ambassador anyway. Others,
however, wanted the original. In 1563, the French diplomat Hubert Languet
had sent a friend a Nostradamus almanac that he had received from an acquaintance. But he added a caveat: "I think it has been falsified and fabricated by a greedy printer." Hans Rosenberger, too, had told Nostredame that
he hesitated to order his almanacs from Lyon because of local forgers. Aware
of this problem, Nostredame had certified in some almanacs that he was their
true author. Elsewhere, he warned readers that, without his handwritten
dedication, the publication that they held was the work of counterfeiters from
Paris, Avignon, or Toulouse.[11]

Chavigny was neither a forger nor a counterfeiter, but his *French Janus*
included several new quatrains. He claimed that they came from eleventh
and twelfth *centuries* that had until now remained hidden. These fake *centuries* entered many editions of the *Prophecies,* including Theophilus de
Garencières's translation. Some publishers slipped in other new quatrains
surreptitiously while others drew attention to their new find. In the 1620s,
for instance, editors of the *Prophecies* quietly inserted two quatrains at the
end of the seventh *centurie.* Throughout the seventeenth century, people
hence pondered and discussed predictions that, unbeknownst to them, had
been forged to illuminate current events. The much-discussed verse about
the "impetuous effort" (Henri IV) defeating "La Tour" (lord Henri de La
Tour d'Auvergne) in 1606? The two quatrains about the 1627 siege of La
Rochelle ("three times seven plus six") by the forces of Louis XIII ("seven
and six")? All of them fakes.[12]

The most significant addition to the Nostradamian corpus occurred around 1605, when editions of the *Prophecies* began to include fifty-eight six-line poems known as sixains. This is another mystifying story, involving a doctor and flour merchant named Vincent Seve. This devout man, a resident of Beaucaire in southwestern France, reportedly lived in a hidden cell within an abandoned quarry. He devoted his days to his two passions: the history of his native town and astrology. Seve claimed that, on the eve of his death, a nephew of Nostredame named Henry had entrusted him with his uncle's unpublished sixains. He kept quiet for a while but decided to make the sixains public upon realizing that they related to present happenings. It was his duty as a faithful subject to inform Henri IV of what awaited France in the new century. By the end of the year, the sixains had entered many editions of the *Prophecies* under the title of *Admirable Predictions for the Current Years of This Century*.[13]

Much of what we know about Seve comes from his own introduction to the sixains. I have uncovered no trace of a nephew named Henry, no record of a royal audience around 1605, no documents explaining how the sixains made it into print. While the sixains shared the quatrains' predilection for metaphors and place-names, they contain more complete sentences, dates, and references to events set in the early seventeenth century. All of this made them easier to decipher. They are also more sanguine than the quatrains and praise Henri IV's Bourbon dynasty (which acceded to the French throne after Nostredame's death) in ways that the quatrains never did. Everything suggests that the sixains were forgeries. Seve insisted, however, that they were authentic—Nostredame had simply written them with unusual clarity— and many contemporaries believed him. Pamphleteers depicted the sixains as another lost *centurie*, or else claimed that they completed the forty-two quatrains of the fourth *centurie*. In the 1690s, an aristocrat from Avignon was certain that Nostredame had composed these predictions shortly before dying—as a parting comment on the seventeenth century. The allure of the mysterious Nostredame, the appetite for anything odd or rare, and the loose conditions of publishing set the stage for yet another transformation of the entity known as Nostradamus.[14]

And what about this strange nephew? Nostredame had vowed never to teach his craft to his children. There were just too many ill-intentioned astrologers—and, no doubt, easier paths of social mobility. He apparently kept this promise since none of his six offspring followed in his footsteps. César was a poet, a painter, a historian, and a mayor of Salon; one of the other boys became an officer, the other one a monk; and we know little about the three girls. And yet all kinds of relatives and descendants were soon publishing predictions under Nostradamus's aegis. We know nothing about them, not even if there were actual people behind these pen names. But all believed that the Nostradamus patronymic would play in their favor. "I don't know who he is," Nostredame's (real) brother Jean wrote about one of these spurious relatives in 1570. "On my life and my honor, I swear that he borrows Nostredame's surname to grant his banter more authority." This happened to other renowned astrologers, but the famous Nostradamus drew once again more than his share. This is why, a century later, a polemicist could mock an astrologer as an "ancestor to the 2,480th degree of the ancestor fourth removed, on his mother's side, of Michael Nostradamus." Impostors joined the ranks of the Nostradamian providers.[15]

First up was Mi. de Nostradamus, an enigmatic figure who kept his relationship to Nostredame vague while writing prognostications in the 1560s and 1570s. Next came Michel Nostradamus the Younger, an author who claimed to be his son and published several prognostications (some of them with Nostredame's own publisher, Benoît Rigaud). This doctor had supposedly found portents in his father's study after his death, an improbable claim given that he could not have been older than thirteen when Nostredame published his first predictions. Official records bear no traces of him, and yet many believed in his existence in early modern Europe. By the early 1600s, a tall tale held that the younger Michel had been caught lighting a fire in the town of Pouzin in order to confirm Nostredame's prediction that it would burn down. A lord summoned him and asked whether he expected to suffer a misfortune. When he replied that he did not, the lord startled a horse, which kicked the deceitful soothsayer in the stomach and proved that he was a fraud.[16]

No tragic fate seems to have befallen the last two supposed relatives who came onto the scene in the late sixteenth century. The nephew Philip or Filippo Nostradamus wrote in prose and found publishers in England and Italy. Antoine Crespin dit Nostradamus—who claimed to be lord of Hauteville and a doctor from Marseille—opted for verse. Instead of composing his own predictions, however, he fashioned quatrains by cutting and pasting random lines from the *Prophecies*. This familial connection retained a purchase on the public imagination during the centuries that followed. A phony grandson published pamphlets in Paris in 1649; the author of a French Catholic almanac claimed to belong to the Nostradamus lineage in 1828. No doubt there were still others, all of them promising an intimate encounter with a man and an inspiration that seemed increasingly distant and yet very much part of their own world.[17]

⁓◦⦉⦊◦⁓

What, however, had Nostredame meant to say? The question was as urgent as ever after his death, and Chavigny did not elude it. If Nostredame was a prophet, then someone had to interpret his mysterious pronouncements. Chavigny realized that some of the quatrains did not match up with actual events and that some of the predictions had apparently not come true. One of them depicted 1555 as a safe year for the pope, and yet Julius III died that March. Chavigny did not conclude that the prophet had erred or uttered meaningless words. Instead, he accepted the claim that he had concealed his true message to protect himself as well as the populace. Ordinary people naturally struggled to decipher the quatrains, but Chavigny insisted that "a good speculator and interpreter" could uncover their hidden meaning. The Nostradamian provider, he said, was a hunting dog who would lead his masters—the readers—to their prey.[18]

But even a hunting dog needs to earn the trust of his masters. Chavigny's authority rested on three foundations. To begin, his close acquaintance with Nostredame had granted him unparalleled insights. Direct evidence after all carried considerable weight at this time. Tales about monstrous births and other extraordinary happenings often rested on eyewitness accounts. Having worked with Nostredame and taken care of him during his last days, Chavigny could claim quasi-familial familiarity with the man and his mind. Second, he had devoted considerable energy to studying, unraveling, and collating predictions that few people could truly understand. No one knew more about prophecy and history; no one read the quatrains more patiently; no one worked harder at linking past events with future ones. Like Nostredame, finally,

Chavigny committed himself to helping others and serving his kingdom by sharing a text that had been lost. As a witness, a learned scholar with unimpeachable work habits, and a man of virtue, Chavigny was a legitimate and irreplaceable go-between.[19]

Readers of the *French Janus* hence follow an interpreter who, like a practiced guide wielding his machete, leads his party across a thick semantic jungle. Chavigny surrounded each quatrain with copious annotations. Moving from one line to the next, he clarified anagrams and disentangled symbols. *Augé,* he explained, meant both escalation and ruin in one quatrain. The lion and the barking dog in another quatrain symbolized Henri IV and his enemy. Elsewhere, the terrestrial and sea legate designated a royal ambassador to the Council of Trent. When Nostredame wrote that "Germany shall see the birth of diverse sects / Quite like the paganism of ancient times" (3.76), he was expressing his displeasure with Protestants. Chavigny showed readers where Nostredame had inserted nonsensical quatrains to conceal the meaning of others and where he had written one date but really meant another. Nostredame had invented the game, but it fell upon Chavigny to set the rules. This he did with utter confidence.[20]

Chavigny launched something big. From now on, the Nostradamus phenomenon would revolve more and more around a dyad: the mystifying words and the experts who had the qualifications to clarify their meaning. A cottage industry of interpreters came into being. In 1620, to mention but one, an anonymous *Small Essay or Commentary on the Centuries of Master Michel Nostradamus* arranged forty quatrains into a story about the five preceding decades in French history. Like Chavigny, and nearly all of the interpreters who have surfaced since, the author picked freely from the *centuries*. Nostredame had never claimed that the quatrains depicted events in chronological order, so why not jump from one to another? The *Small Essay* showed readers that even the most chaotic events had a structure. Someone had seen it coming and someone could now figure it all out. Readers simply needed help. Publishers of the *Prophecies* obliged in the late seventeenth century. Editions now included introductions to Nostredame's anagrams, metaphors, and punctuation. They might explain his use of infinitives or point out that *saigne,* as he used the word, meant marshes as well as castration. One Amsterdam publisher promised that, with his crib sheet in hand, readers would see "clearly what our Prophet had hidden from us in obscure terms." They would grasp what had until then been unknown or poorly understood about the most remarkable events of their times.[21]

The interpreters who came after Chavigny could not claim a direct acquaintance with Nostredame, and most felt uncomfortable inventing a familial connection. Instead, many of them claimed to own the irrefutable key to the *Prophecies*. Some pointed toward their natural intuition and divine gifts. After a century of confusion, said the translator Garencières, God had summoned a person of "peculiar Genius"—none other than himself—to clarify the meaning of the quatrains. Others emphasized their command of astrology or political affairs. In 1710, a Normandy priest named Jean Le Roux declared that no one had yet fathomed Nostredame's peculiar mode of expression. Imagination had led rival interpreters astray. Le Roux's close philological study revealed, however, that Nostredame had mixed Latin grammar with French sentence structure. Grounded in meticulous study and a commitment to order and clarity (rational tenets that were central to the early Enlightenment), this insight enabled Le Roux to decode the quatrains. By the eighteenth century, many providers summoned numerology or cartomancy (the study of playing cards) while probing quatrains and professing, like Chavigny, to uncover a man whom no one else could fathom.[22]

Like Chavigny as well, many Nostradamian providers entertained grand designs. Chavigny was convinced that Nostradamus had offered meaningful depictions of the cosmos and an eventful period in French history. His pronouncements on the "century's corruption" convey a vision of the world in which subterraneous forces, recurring cycles, magical powers, and astral conjunctions came together in mysterious yet indisputable ways. By reorganizing quatrains in a sequence of his own making, he looked backward as well as forward, like the two-faced Roman god Janus, who beheld the past and the future. "The defining trait of prediction," he explained, "is not only to receive future events, but also to relate present and past ones." Chavigny began with history, whose edifying examples made it possible to distinguish good and evil, and asked readers to behold Nostredame's ability to depict the forces shaping European politics. Most of the *French Janus* pertained to the years 1555–1589, a period that ended with the Bourbons' ascent to the French throne. The French Wars of Religion loomed large in this chronology, along with schisms and peace treaties, negotiations and sieges. Chavigny was more cautious about future events, though he did see the end of times approaching.[23]

More than revelations, the *French Janus* hence provided confirmation of past events, drawing readers beneath the surface of things while painting a tableau of wondrous happenings. Some of the Nostradamian providers who followed tried their hand at forecasting during the seventeenth and eighteenth centuries, but most of them were equally prudent. Prediction was less prevalent than a safer, more meaningful framework that fused Europe's past, present, and future. This outlook would long prevail.

⁊ᴏᴄ⳩

Nostradamian providers did not only entertain lofty aspirations. By choice or circumstances, many of them plotted their course across the marketplace. Economic crises, censorship, and the decline of fairs hurt the publishing business during the seventeenth century, but the number of publications—especially for those in modern languages and small formats—continued to climb. The Nostradamus phenomenon retained the allure it had acquired during the Renaissance. Publishers were drawn to a trove of predictions that, like ephemeral media, spoke about the lives, hopes, and anxieties of readers high and low. The quatrains could always yield something different and hence feed a public hunger for novelty. New editions, selections, adaptations, and interpretations of the *Prophecies* could by now tap a tradition that went back decades or even a century and yet still seemed fresh and relevant. The quatrains also lent themselves admirably to different economies of publishing, sliding from almanacs and chapbooks to pamphlets, engravings, and books. Easy to adapt to new circumstances, easy to reinvent, repackage, and recycle again and again, Nostradamus continued to tap key dimensions of the era's media culture.[24]

Some years, two or three publishers would release their own editions of the *Prophecies*. To stand out from one another, they began providing reading guides, adding indexes, and drawing attention to their products' added value. "Of all the editions of the *Prophecies* of Michel Nostradamus," one of them intoned from Amsterdam in 1667, "I can affirm that there have been none more accurate than the one I am putting forth today, since it has been revised with great care according to the oldest and best editions." Chavigny had launched this in his *French Janus* when he shared a gushing letter from a lord. This nameless correspondent (perhaps a real person, perhaps not) had written that Nostradamus made no sense whatsoever without Chavigny's commentaries. Such tireless labor on behalf of others, he wrote Chavigny, would be "the source of your renown, since no one else before now has been able to penetrate such obscurities as you will have done."[25]

This early book blurb captures the way Nostradamian providers tried to parlay the prophet's fame into renown for themselves. In the sixteenth and seventeenth centuries, many people struggled to win recognition within traditional institutions or bodies of knowledge. Either their birth was common, or their education insufficient, or the circle of their acquaintances too narrow. Sometimes, it was all three. Failure to secure the acceptance or status to which they felt entitled could cause deep frustration. As they searched for alternative pathways toward success and perhaps recognition, some individuals stumbled upon astrology, a hybrid, loose domain whose rules were being questioned and redrawn. Here was an opening. The same held true of Nostradamus's predictions. At once astrological and prophetic, at once obtuse and free for the taking, at once esoteric and ubiquitous, they provided opportunities for people who sought to carve out a position or jump-start their careers. The Nostradamian provider could make something of himself and gain authority as an unparalleled guide, a benefactor of Christendom, and an intellectual presence.[26]

This was not easy, for one had to justify oneself and defend Nostradamus against detractors. Le Roux responded with force to the critics who defiled his great prophet. This stance could suit people who felt unfairly marginalized or else had few other options. Throughout the centuries, most Nostradamian providers have had profiles similar to the lowly secretary Chavigny, the obscure priest Le Roux, and the middling doctor Garencières. They either entered a new domain with little capital, or sought to rebound after a professional failure, or else aspired to a form of authority that was missing from their lives. In so doing, all of them joined an underworld, a community—or perhaps an industry—whose members borrowed from and sought to outdo one another across the centuries.[27]

To broaden our canvas, we might consider the *Prophecies* alongside the

Bible. Both books spawned feelings of transcendence and embraced tradition more than social change (even if the Bible fed demands for reform). Both took off with the invention of print and spawned multiple editions, with occasional changes in the text. Both could also inspire, fascinate, terrify, or plunge readers into perplexity. With its allegories, parables, and strange words, the Bible seemed "wrapped in wrinkles," declared an Anglican bishop in 1537. Contemporaries wondered whether the book of Revelation (controversial from the start, like the *Prophecies*) was a work of allegory, history, or prophecy. They could of course harbor similar questions regarding Nostradamus. For early Christian communities, Scripture had not been a fixed work, but an activity that took people from bewilderment to discussion to illumination. The Pharisee Jews had likewise placed the study of Torah (Midrash) at the center of their spirituality. Later, Europeans focused on select biblical passages and quotations, interpreted them in different ways, and read between the lines. But some of them needed help. Like the *Prophecies,* the Bible thus generated a bevy of commentaries, summaries, comparative alphabets, foldout maps, and scriptural aids that would guide readers.[28]

There is an important difference between the two books, however. The history of the Bible is that of a sacred text that, despite its varied origins, came under the hold of institutions and collective movements and helped found political and moral regimes. Henry VIII's Great Bible announced on its title page that it was published under royal authority. Over time, Puritans, Mormons, Unitarians, and others used their own translations to support their beliefs. The Bible was codified, controlled, and updated only after collective bodies had come to an agreement. It made its way into religious services and academic study groups (not to mention Western literature, thanks to its open-ended ethical questions and a potent blend of narrative and doctrine).

None of this was true of the *Prophecies,* which hovered between the profane and the sacred, between dependence on and independence from God. There were no institutional controls, no traditions or clergy decreeing who could parse Nostradamus's predictions and how. Instead, we find an open expanse and motley providers who, from the outskirts of the Western world, from the edges of what was deemed respectable, made Nostradamus accessible to people from different walks of life by playing on broader yearnings for freedom and authority. These editors and counterfeiters, these guides and interpreters injected doses of novelty and mystery that percolated into the latest media and kept the free-floating Nostradamus relevant and intriguing.

All of this activity drew more readers. But it also raised new questions. Around 1600, a French publisher issued a warning about the shams who usurped the name of Nostradamus. Decades later, the tutor of the young Louis XIV invoked Michel the Younger to denounce the guile of judicial astrologers. Chavigny, too, came under fire in the nineteenth century for having made arbitrary selections, vague annotations, and baseless interpretations. The accusations are harsh, but these providers did dice Nostradamus into digestible bites, they did turn the *Prophecies* inside out, and they did occasionally pen their own predictions. The quatrains remained, but they were not always intact and no longer alone between the covers of the *Prophecies*. A century after the astrologer's death, Thomas Hobbes complained that most of what now carried his name consisted of posthumous fabrications. This was an exaggeration, but the larger point is well-taken. The autonomous, open-ended Nostradamus did not merely invite different kinds of readings. It also absolved everyone from preserving the original text's integrity. Freedom from oversight was also freedom from responsibility. Anything was possible. Anything could be true. The Nostradamus phenomenon was at once democratic and deeply unstable.[29]

Chapter 6

✥

Wonder and Politics
at the Court of France

A ghost appeared in Salon in 1696. It startled a local blacksmith and then ordered him to travel to the court of Versailles and convey a message to Louis XIV. When I stumbled upon this episode, my initial reaction was to dismiss it as trivial. But the ghost kept surfacing. I ran into it while reading letters and periodicals and other sources that made it clear that, even if one has little taste for such apparitions, the core of the story was real.

Each encounter brought out another facet of a tale that grew odder and more intriguing. The public became enthralled by the ghost and the black-smith from Salon. Versailles opened its doors to a commoner who lacked rank, a title, or a patron—the court's leading currencies. Louis XIV granted this unlikely visitor a private audience and reprimanded courtiers who questioned the man's mental balance. Nostredame's relationship to the whole matter remained mysterious. Some accounts claimed that it was his ghost that had returned, others that he had predicted the visit in a quatrain. Regardless, no other episode put Nostradamus as squarely in the public eye at the turn of the eighteenth century.[1]

Anthropologists and historians have long understood that the most impenetrable features of distant cultures can provide rich entry points into ways of thinking that are radically different from our own. Something was clearly going on in Salon and Versailles, something that might explain why men and women from all reaches of society continued to deem Nostradamus meaning-ful 150 years after his death. The Nostradamian providers played their part, but they did not do it all. Nostradamus was also an object of wonder and a component of a political culture that ranged from high aristocratic circles to popular pamphlets. Its political legitimacy in the sixteenth and seventeenth centuries is difficult to comprehend today. But this episode also marked a moment of change. What some deemed admissible in terms of public behav-ior and politics, others now found unseemly. This, too, I came to realize, makes the episode revealing. The ghost traveled between worlds in more ways than one.

๛

It began as follows. The middle-aged blacksmith François Michel was leading a quiet life in Salon, which remained as tranquil and prosperous as in the Re-naissance. A plague epidemic would devastate the region in 1720, but at this time olive groves, orchards, sheep farms, and tanneries sustained Salon's five thousand residents. While Nostredame had few living relatives in town—one traveler spoke of two nieces in 1671—his tomb continued to attract visitors. Whether local residents paid their respects to the prophet is an open question. Whatever personal or collective devotions they engaged in have left no traces in the archives. There is no doubt, however, that this devout town took pride in its collegial church and its stagings of martyrdom scenes. Oratorian monks taught school, and it is probably from them that the blacksmith had learned to write French. A pious man, he lived near the Capuchin convent and be-longed to the *Pénitents blancs,* a Catholic confraternity devoted to prayer and charity. Contemporary accounts describe him as tall, robust, and reserved.[2]

They also concur that the ghost appeared in December 1696, around the Feast of the Immaculate Conception. It happened in the evening, under a full moon. Some claim that the blacksmith was tilling his parcel of land. Others relate that a voice summoned him to an isolated chapel. Out of nowhere, the ghost grabbed the man's shoulders and instructed him to relay a secret mes-sage to Louis XIV. The blacksmith was so shaken that he reportedly spent a week in bed, hoping that the ghost would relent. But the specter returned twice, growing more threatening each time. Michel eventually gave in. Fol-lowing the ghost's orders, he asked the king's representative in Provence—the *intendant*—for an invitation to the court. The official had doubts. Catholic orthodoxy governed France at this time. The king had recently expelled Protestants and now faced a surge of popular prophecy in some regions. Visionaries could sow trouble; calls for repentance could lead to resistance or open rebellion. The *intendant* thus requested a character check from Salon's authorities. It came back positive, but he still deferred the matter to his superior at the court, the secretary of state. After pondering the matter, the higher official summoned the blacksmith to the palace of Versailles.

Michel set off the following February. News of the apparition had quickly traveled beyond Salon. Countless people wanted to meet the man they took for a prophet and stopped him along the road. In Lyon, crowds almost suffocated him. The blacksmith's presence at the court heightened the excitement. It was highly unusual for such figures to circulate in this aristocratic world and unprecedented for them to meet privately with the king (nobles pined for such audiences, too). Michel's modest station and his sex played in his favor. Female visionaries were more worrisome than their male counterparts for they could abandon Christian humility and their social role as women while making claims to spiritual authority. Still, royal doors would not have opened if the blacksmith did not have something vital to reveal. Upon arriving in Versailles, the ghost returned and told him what to say to the king. The duke de Saint-Simon, whose journal is an unparalleled source regarding life at Versailles, reported that everyone at the court pondered the matter. The secretary of state and other officials tried to pry the blacksmith's secret. So did princes, ministers, and ladies, who spent hours in Michel's company. None of them succeeded. By the time the king granted him an audience in April, the affair had become an international sensation. The ghost and the blacksmith made their way into journals, broadsides, engravings, and songs. One French diplomat even took time off from peace negotiations in Holland to ask a lady at the court for the latest developments.

François Michel does not seem to have mentioned Nostradamus while in Versailles, but the prophet's name was all over the story in media and public opinion. Nostradamus is the ghost! The blacksmith and Nostredame share the same name! Michel is his descendant! In one popular song, Michel intoned that he had come from his province in the name of Nostradamus. Some members of the court began referring to Michel as Nostradamus. One marquis spoke of "this man, whom people said is the penultimate member of the race of Nostradamus." He was quoting quatrain 2.28, which people had been linking to the episode before he reached Versailles:

The next to last of the prophet's name	Le penultiesme du surnom du prophete,
Shall take Joveday as his day of relaxation :	Prendra Dial pour son jour & repos :
He shall wander far with his frenetic brain,	Loing vaguera par frenetique teste,
Delivering a great nation from taxation.	Et delivrant un grand peuple d'impos.

Who could this wanderer be if not the prophet from Provence? Some commentators read *Dial* in the second line as a reference to Diana, goddess of the hunt and the moon. This was the name of Michel's mother, they explained, and she was a distant relative of Nostredame. A chapbook coupled a song on the affair with two portents from his 1555 almanac. As the episode unfolded, the diplomat in Holland, the lady at the court, and others discussed the meanings of various quatrains. Outside these rarefied circles, too, people linked the ghost and the blacksmith to Nostradamus. But few did so with certainty, few had a clear sense of whose ghost this was, and absolutely no one besides the king knew what message François Michel had relayed from the netherworld. And that more than anything is what contemporaries yearned to find out.[3]

Nostredame's transformation into a ghost took place organically. Ghosts were a type of apparition, the souls of dead persons made visible to the living. They usually appeared in human guise, at night, and cloaked in the clothes they had worn or else the sheets in which they had been buried. While apparitions could take the form of angels or demons, ghosts intervened in worldly matters and communicated with their kin. It was commonly believed that the spirits of the dead hovered near their bodies for a month after passing. Belief in ghosts also owed much to the Catholic notion of purgatory. Trapped there until they attained the holiness necessary to enter heaven, souls would sometimes ask their descendants for help. In 1628, for example, the ghost of a chambermaid appeared before her niece in Dole, a city in the province of Franche-Comté, toward the east of France. After confessing her sins, the ghost implored the young woman to complete the three pilgrimages that she had neglected to undertake in her lifetime. By doing so, said the ghost, the niece would alleviate the pain of a poor soul who had already spent seventeen years in purgatory. In return, the ghost baptized the niece's unborn child and showed her a path to salvation.[4]

A powerful, merciful God could also send ghosts to repair injustice and moral infractions. Ghosts haunted inveterate sinners, enforced obligations toward ancestors, and warned of looming dangers. This does not mean that such apparitions had to be taken at face value. The devil could manipulate the senses while imagination could generate illusions. Protestant theologians furthermore denounced ghosts and the purgatory as Catholic superstitions. Since souls had been predestined for heaven or hell, God had no reason to allow them to return. Despite such misgivings, belief in ghosts endured within wide swathes of Christendom, a tangible connection to the afterlife for people who did not necessarily believe in saints or angels.

Ghosts were thus interstitial creatures who harbored divine as well as human qualities and circulated between the living and the departed, between past and future. It is no surprise that Nostradamus should have joined their ranks. The mysterious man who never revealed his true intents seemed to couple human attributes and paranormal powers while looking backward as well as forward in time. In 1634, the illustrious Spanish poet Francisco de Quevedo had portrayed Nostradamus as a ghostlike figure who denounced an era in which money trumped justice and holiness. Fifteen years later, a French chapbook related that Louis XIII's widow Anne of Austria had encountered a specter while reading the *Prophecies*. Elsewhere, writers depicted Nostredame as a visionary who discerned what remained invisible to ordinary people. In the *Astrological Visions of Michel Nostradamus* (1649), for instance, his disarticulated voice revealed the hidden workings of current affairs. The ghostly visit of Salon hence points toward a broader fascination— mixing curiosity and dread—with the afterlife and those supernatural forces that suffused the material world. That Nostradamus captured both sides of the encounter, that he came across as both ghost and clairvoyant, made perfect sense. It was commonly believed, moreover, that ghosts haunted the locality in which they had lived their lives. They infused it with their presence while tapping its distinctive spirit, the genius loci. The specter that startled the blacksmith would thus have come from Salon. Who else could it be besides the famous Nostradamus?[5]

This does not mean that Louis XIV necessarily perceived this ghost as Nostredame's, or even that he believed in the existence of ghosts. But it is possible that he approached the episode with the kind of wonderment that had surrounded Nostradamus since the Renaissance. The Middle Ages had bequeathed a notion of wonder understood as awe and stupefaction before comets, eclipses, deformed animals, and apparitions. At once novel, strange, and rare, these occurrences lacked natural causes and obvious explanations. And they mattered, especially if they coincided with human events such as wars, because they pointed toward deeper meanings and hidden forces that cut across cultural or moral boundaries. These occurrences could thus be seen as portents regarding political or apocalyptic events: a plague, an invasion, a victory, or even the coming of the Messiah.[6]

By the late seventeenth century, learned people were increasingly leaving wonder and portents to what they called the vulgar. They now collected ostrich eggs or investigated earthquakes as strange, unnatural events that resulted from chance meetings of natural causes. Still, wonder maintained a purchase during an age of religious crises, protracted conflicts, and civil wars. Publishers and booksellers continued to find it enticing and commercially promising. Pamphlets, broadsides, chapbooks, and even learned journals promised their readers accounts of events that were "remarkable," "unusual," "extraordinary," or "strange and certain." *A Declaration of a Strange and Wonderful Monster,* about a headless creature from Lancashire, was typical. Wonder still furnished a grid through which countless Europeans made sense of the cosmos and the odd, unpredictable occurrences that shaped their world. At the very least, it was a way of pondering such questions.[7]

With his prophecies, omens, and monstrous ubiquity, Nostradamus was perfectly at home in this world. Had the astrologer not promised to furnish "numerous wonders" in his almanacs? Chavigny had agreed: his marvelous predictions filled the world with awe and admiration, he said. Successive Nostradamian providers likewise invited readers to behold unparalleled words that unveiled past and future designs. Prior to the ghost's apparition, English interpretations of the quatrains foretold "many strange and wonderful things" for England, France, and Ireland. Chapbooks and broadsides invoked quatrains while describing the sudden appearance of a new island, a devastating flood, or some other portentous event. How strange and wondrous that things had come to pass as Nostradamus had predicted! In 1668, a French placard recounted a spectacular battle between massive squadrons of birds above the city of Dole. Partridges and owls fought it out for hours against a dark sky. Twenty thousand perished. A woodcut depicted farmers and fishermen collecting carcasses as the mêlée raged. The accompanying text urged readers to ponder this astonishing event and draw the requisite moral lesson. It then established its credentials as an omen by quoting lines from quatrain 1.100:

For days on end a gray bird shall be seen	Long temps au ciel sera veu gris oiseau,
In the skies of Tuscany & near Dole	Auprés de Dole & de Touscane terre

So many people were still sending her this prophecy a decade later that Madame de Sévigné, the renowned aristocrat, wrote her daughter about it. The combination of startling incident and evocative quatrain continued to amaze. Nostradamus made events such as this one yet more wondrous and astounding and authoritative. They overflowed with meaning.[8]

That is what happened in the 1690s when courtiers and ordinary folk discussed the strange François Michel and Nostradamus's predictions, when chapbooks portrayed the ghost as an omen and his message as "something extraordinary," and possibly when the king received this Provençal visitor. Astonishment, amazement, uncertainty, and (sometimes) dread surrounded a series of events and a quatrain that, as one song put it, told a wondrous tale about the terrestrial and cosmic worlds. If the episode became a sensation, if the Nostradamus phenomenon continued to resonate as widely as it did, it was in no small part because it both channeled and generated feelings of wonder.[9]

But this was only part of it. From the court to coffeehouses and marketplaces, politics surfaced everywhere in seventeenth-century Europe. People discussed the destiny of monarchs, the fate of dynastic successions, the makeup of alliances, and the outcome of wars. In some circles, these conversations could revolve around abstract questions of sovereignty, rights, or religious freedom, but they rarely bypassed a pressing matter: the affairs of France. With the largest population in Europe after Russia, rich agricultural resources, a strategic location, and the ambitious Louis XIV on the throne from 1643 until 1715, the country dominated continental politics. Whether or not we call it absolutist, the divine French monarchy asserted itself in unprecedented ways. It expanded and modernized its army and bureaucracy, turned royal councils into centers of decision making, and intervened more forcefully in the economy. It also defanged many aristocrats by immersing them in the codified, etiquette-heavy, hierarchical court of Versailles. Military victories and annexations further enhanced the country's size and prestige.

By the end of the century, however, Louis XIV found himself on the defensive. After expelling Protestants from France in 1685, he sought to guarantee his borders and national security. The result was the Nine Years War (1688–1697), a conflict that pitted France against England, the Dutch Netherlands, Hapsburg Austria, and other members of the League of Augsburg. Across the Channel, partisans of the new Protestant King William III despised a French monarch who deemed his power universal, sought religious uniformity, threatened the English economy by abusing tariffs and trade barriers, and backed the Stuarts in their efforts to reclaim the throne of England. Louis XIV had even welcomed Catholic King James II, who had been chased out of England during the Glorious Revolution in 1688, and allowed him to organize a court in exile at the Château of Saint-Germain-en-Laye. Louis obtained early victories in the Nine Years War, but he soon found himself fighting on multiple military fronts. Enemy armies won several battles, bombarded French ports, and threatened invasion. This war of attrition took up nearly three-quarters of the country's public revenue. Faced with massive debt and a famine that killed a tenth of the French population, Louis tabled large campaigns and explored terms of peace. The ghost thus appeared in Salon at the end of a war whose outcome was both decisive and uncertain. This is the backdrop against which every apparition or omen was now examined in France.[10]

There were other reasons why contemporaries would have assumed that this episode carried political overtones. For one, royal audiences were nothing if not political rituals. Furthermore, apparitions often conveyed political messages. Ghosts were known to issue divine warnings about assassination attempts and the like. It was also common for playwrights and polemicists to broadcast political views through ghosts or imaginary dialogues between specters. More to our point, some contemporaries did so via Nostradamus, a natural choice given that the phenomenon had never strayed far from politics since the sixteenth century. While the astrologer's own designs had remained discreet, successive generations turned his predictions into an all-purpose political device. Every crisis brought him to the fore.

This began during the French Wars of Religion (1562–1598), when Catholics and Protestants both turned to prophecy, interpreted some quatrains, and coined others. Chavigny depicted Nostredame as a die-hard Catholic who denounced foreign plots and sects. In his view, the *Prophecies* confirmed an ancient myth about a divinely chosen Gallic king, a descendant of the Greeks and Romans, who would subjugate all Christian rulers, create a new empire, lead European countries on a victorious campaign against infidels (whom he would baptize by force), seize the Holy Land, and usher in a peaceful millennium that would precede the final apocalyptic battle. This Great Monarch, endowed with good fortune, strength, wisdom, and magnanimity, was Henri IV. Chavigny inaugurated a long line of Catholic apologists who have drawn from Nostradamus to extol a universal ruler who would govern a unified Christendom. Henri IV's assassination postponed such dreams, but it drew Nostradamus deeper into politics. This was the first major event since the death of valiant Henri II in 1559 that people linked to the quatrains. A year later, a French gentleman contended that Nostredame had predicted Protestant decadence, Jesuit resurgence, and enduring strength for the kingdom. France was not resuming its civil war, but Nostradamus retained its political appeal.[11]

This allure endured three decades later when Henri's successor, Louis XIII, died of natural causes. With the child Louis XIV too young to rule, Anne of Austria and her chief minister, Cardinal Mazarin, governed France. These were tumultuous years, marked by peasant revolts, tax riots, and aristocratic attempts to bolster their prerogatives. Tensions culminated with the Fronde, a series of rebellious movements led by French judges and discontented princes who objected to the monarchy's heavy hand. Around 1650,

France was submerged by pamphlets on such issues as taxation and representative institutions. Many of these *mazarinades* (so named because they denounced Mazarin) took the form of horoscopes and prophecies. Nostradamus surfaced in at least sixty. His quatrains, it was said, announced an ominous fate for the "unfit cardinal" who had plunged France into turmoil. Some warned readers that Paris would be destroyed unless they followed Nostredame's injunctions, reformed their ways, and made the right political choice. Others found in his predictions a reassuring portrayal of universal peace and fair taxation following Mazarin's demise. Twenty-five editions of the *Prophecies* came out between 1644 and 1650, some of them containing two new quatrains against the "Sicilian *Nizaram*" (an anagram of Mazarin) who would drown in the mire of civil war:

When Innocent shall hold the place of Peter,	Quant Innocent tiendra le lieu de Pierre,
The Sicilian Nizaram shall see himself	Le Nizaram Cicilien se verra
In great honors, but after that shall fall	En grands honneurs, mais après il cherra
Into the quagmire of a civil war.	Dans le bourbier d'une civille guerre.

The first line referred to the pontificate of Pope Innocent X, the others to Mazarin's demise following the war that he had caused.[12]

Political upheaval brought out Nostradamus in Britain as well. Events followed in dramatic succession: civil war between monarchists and parliamentarians, the beheading of King Charles I outside Whitehall in 1649 and the establishment of the Commonwealth of England, war against the Dutch in 1652, and the Protectorate under Oliver Cromwell. More than half a million people died between 1638 and 1652. All of this boosted prophetic traditions that had flourished in Protestant countries since the Reformation. Britain's advent as a leading power, coming as it did after the Thirty Years' War and uprisings on the continent, seemed to confirm a pre-apocalyptic shift, the imminent defeat of the Catholic Antichrist, and a thousand-year kingdom of peace. Such millenarian expectations had been heightened earlier in the century by the Rosicrucians, a purported secret society whose members called for universal reformation and promised to reveal secrets in their manifestos. Levellers, Diggers, Anabaptists, Ranters, and still others awaited the final denouement. "These are days of shaking," said one preacher, "and this shaking is universal."[13]

Monarchists and parliamentarians now collected, interpreted, rewrote, and published biblical and nonbiblical prophecies. They turned to the book of Revelation, the book of Daniel, and prophecies attributed to two lay figures who may or may not have existed in the fifteenth and sixteenth centuries: the Yorkshire soothsayer Mother Shipton and Robert Nixon, an idiot plowman from Cheshire. People also consulted Nostradamus. The famed astrologer William Lilly, who sided with parliament and predicted that kings would never again rule England, found signs as well as justification of Charles I's beheading while parsing the *Prophecies*. "The senate of London its king shall slay": this line from quatrain 9.49 was closely read in the wake of the king's death. A mysterious Merlin Ambrosius invoked it in 1651 while denouncing the Fifth Monarchists, a group that expected Jesus or a king from Scotland to establish a new millennial kingdom. This did not stop the Fifth Monarchist preacher John Rogers from summoning Nostradamus in his own account of universal history. Quatrain 5.99—"When an old Britannic chief shall rule Rome"—announced the English occupation of Rome and the city's reformation. The prophet from Salon provided all parties with rhetorical ammunition.[14]

Nostradamus resonated when the foundations of legitimate rule and the contours of political community escaped consensus. Other soothsayers inhabited the political realm, but Nostradamus made it so easy for moderates as well as radicals to establish their authority and puncture their opponents', and prove that God was on their side. The quatrains were ideally suited for early modern polemics. They could summon astrology as well as prophecy, these two bridges between political and universal orders. Their language also lent itself so well to the word games, anagrams, and linguistic excess that polemicists often favored. The concealed meanings and dearth of dates practically invited contemporaries to select, adapt, and reinterpret predictions to suit the needs of the day. Pamphleteers could pick a single quatrain, or three, or a dozen, and draw upbeat or alarming accounts—whatever they preferred. These quatrains kept on yielding new meanings and yet, as Nostredame himself receded into the past, they could also appear antique and venerable. One Englishman spoke of "predictions, or prophecies of one of an ancient date."

Nostradamus had entered an ancient prophetic tradition that had long proved its political credentials. Like saints and pious hermits, the famous Renaissance prophet could play the role of august voice piece for various religious and political currents.[15]

His predictions were thus available as a political device within and outside France. In the 1650s, Holy Roman Emperor Leopold I received a quatrain foretelling the impending end of the Austrian house. A few decades later, a Dutch economist rejected the notion that a worldly ruler could free the Church. He added that Nostradamus had indicated that William of Orange, ruler of the Netherlands, was not the long-awaited savior. Tracing Nostradamus's presence across the continent, or even his absence in countries like Russia, lies beyond the scope of this book. Still, his popularity in Britain shows that the quatrains led a multinational political life. This rich prophetic world had space for quatrains that included many more references to London than to Moscow. Many residents of the isles also kept abreast of continental affairs; and the country's political life remained turbulent at the end of the century. His quatrains were invoked in the 1670s to discredit the Popish Plot, a scheme by which Catholics would supposedly depose the current government and kill King Charles II. A decade later, some believed that Nostredame had announced that a legitimate heir of Charles II would accede to the thrones of England, Scotland, Ireland, and France. And during the Glorious Revolution, he was quoted to confirm that William III, the House of Lords, and the Commons deserved to wield power.[16]

The quatrains led separate lives in different countries. The Fronde and the English Civil War were both national crises during which one country's turn to Nostradamus made foreigners curious without generating equivalent uses abroad. Throughout the century, the French and the English selected different quatrains and pondered events that had more urgency at home than abroad. Of the twenty-three events discussed in a French-language edition of the *Prophecies* in 1667, nineteen pertained to France and four to England. A year later, the placard about the birds of Dole also seemed laden with political intent in France. Dole and Franche-Comté had passed from Hapsburg to French and back to Hapsburg hands in 1668. These were rough times for local residents. While the French destroyed enemy fortifications and emptied local coffers, the Hapsburgs overhauled the province's institutions and governed by repression. The placard told readers that the birds represented France, conquering entire provinces under the august leadership of an invincible monarch.[17]

Nostradamus was so versatile, however, that rival countries could also enlist him against one another. This happened in the 1680s and 1690s, when France, Britain, and the Low Countries battled for glory as much as land and security. Nostradamus was conscripted in a war fought not only on battlefields but also through pamphlets, medals, and engravings. In England, his quatrains announced naval defeats and other terrible tidings for the cruel, bellicose French state: "Peace and plenty shall not be long praised in his [Louis XIV's] reign . . . Death shall be brought" to France. In the Low Countries, French Protestant refugees marshaled quatrains to predict a fatal illness for Louis XIV and plagues for his decadent kingdom. William would crush the papists, they said. In France, Nostradamus indicated that the glorious Sun King would triumph over this impious alliance. One 1690 almanac even invoked the ghost of Nostradamus. The stern, white-clad specter warned William and his Protestant advisers that a "spectacle of horror" awaited them. Nostradamus hence contributed to political invectives as well as processes of state building and budding national identification that sometimes carried messianic tinges.[18]

This remained truer in France than elsewhere. An English traveler passing through Salon in 1673 visited the tomb of the "famous French Prophet, whose verses the Frenchmen esteem as oracles." Whether or not the French population saw him as such, some English pamphleteers felt compelled to justify their affinity for this Catholic from an enemy country—this "prophet of their own." Only in France did people dedicate interpretations of the quatrains to their dear country. Only in France, likewise, did Nostradamus fulfill yet another political role. Subjects who sought a promotion, a favor, or simply goodwill from the king or other eminent individuals commonly sang their praise in odes, anagrams, and madrigals. Some also used divination to uncover good things ahead for the persons whom they praised, or else to confirm their glory. Hyperbole was in fashion, and Nostradamus could deliver. In Rouen, an editor of the *Prophecies* included a sixain about a king who could expect "A triumphant reign, a fertile descendance, / An immortal glory, and honors without end." Placing the monarchy in a providential design reinforced its sacral nature. Some subjects hoped that it would do wonders for them as well. The priest Jean Espitalier had lost his position after officiating at the wedding of a courtier and a lady for whom the king had little consideration. To get back in his good graces, he composed a Nostradamus sonnet that foresaw the king's victory over William. Espitalier claimed that an old innkeeper from Salon had given him this sonnet thirty years earlier. In 1698, he forwarded it to Louis XIV and published it along with his "indispensable remarks to understand the thoughts of Nostradamus." This priest, too, hoped that Nostradamus would make him indispensable once again.[19]

When the ghost appeared in Salon, specters and Nostradamus were as firmly ensconced in the realm of politics as in the culture of wonder. This is why contemporaries were both awed by these events and convinced that the blacksmith was a political player. What, however, was the purpose of a mission that, as one pamphlet put it, "is thought to be ordered by Nostradamus"? Speculation ran wild.[20]

Few contemporaries believed that Michel had warned about looming threats. Given his fragile position, Louis XIV would presumably have been more receptive to such premonitions now than in earlier decades, but no one liked to bring a monarch unhappy tidings. Only in later years did some contemporaries claim that the blacksmith had foretold the terrible week of 1712, when the king lost three members of his family. Likewise, no one suggested that Michel had spoken of the Apocalypse. Michel Nostradamus the Younger, Chavigny, and other providers had drawn Nostradamus in this direction, but this was but one strand among many at this time—not the leading one. Nostradamus did not automatically conjure up visions of world's end. Apocalyptic language was in fact on the decline in Catholic countries. The Counterreformation had condemned it, and threats of Turkish invasions, bubonic plague, and famine waned at the end of the seventeenth century.

Might François Michel have curried a personal favor, then? This, too, was unlikely for a small-town blacksmith who, by all appearances, was both humble and selfless. But he may well have expressed veneration for the monarchy by providing useful information about future events or echoing royal propaganda. This was a prevailing view of the episode. According to one chapbook, Michel had promised the king military triumphs and favorable peace terms the following year. One of the popular songs about these events said the same thing: victory and peace, "that is assured." According to another chapbook, the ghost had told Michel that France would be blessed with such great fortune that people would talk about it for two hundred years. No wonder that the king seemed so pleased by the audience.[21]

All of this is plausible. Michel would most likely have discussed matters relating to France and its monarchy, or perhaps the monarch alone, or perhaps his doomed enemies. To champion, reassure, encourage, and bring what an English commentator of Nostradamus called "good and joyful news": this was the name of the game. Michel may even have gone farther and disclosed information about specific events. The duke de Saint-Simon and others were convinced that the whole thing was a conspiracy by Madame de Maintenon, the mistress whom Louis XIV had secretly wedded in 1683. To convince the king to make this marriage public, her entourage asked a Salon priest to draw the blacksmith into a field where a man covered by a sheet awaited, ready to relay God's ire before this state of affairs. This version stretches the imagination, but anything was possible and contemporaries could not be blamed for believing this, or assuming (as some did) that the blacksmith had exposed a plot against French military operations. Visions and apparitions were often strategic interventions in political affairs, and Nostradamus could play that role as well. A few years earlier, a schemer had sent the English ambassador to the Netherlands a handwritten note to persuade him that William deserved the English Crown. It contained a spurious Nostradamus quatrain ("In glory and goodness sovereign shall shine") and the interpretation that served his political goals.[22]

The aim of this handwritten note was to act upon events, not merely to make sense of them. Such was the final, and potentially most important, political dimension of the ghost-and-blacksmith episode. Commentators parsed with care the last line of quatrain 2.28, which declared that the prophet's descendant would "deliver a great nation from taxation." Surely, they thought, this referred to the new taxes that the monarchy was levying to finance the Nine Years War. None proved more contentious than the capitation, a progressive poll tax that divided the French population into twenty-two classes, each of which was required to pay according to its means. The clergy soon obtained an immunity, however, and nobles never paid their full due. The rumor spread that the blacksmith had asked Louis XIV to eliminate this unjust and highly unpopular tax. (The Crown did so at the end of 1697, after the war had ended, but this suspension was temporary). Popular media connected the ghost's message and Nostradamus's quatrain with this explosive issue. The blacksmith, they reported, had promised that his audience would benefit the French population. Such expectations may well account for some of the fervor that surrounded Michel on his way to Versailles.[23]

All of this remains murky, but the political overtones were hard to miss. Around the same time, a French satirical publication also featured the ghost of Nostredame. The quickest road to wealth nowadays, this specter explained, is to become a royal tax collector and take one's cut of the returns. These kinds of claims alarmed officials. Throughout the seventeenth century, agents of the state had kept watch on subversive interpretations of Nostradamus. Jean-Baptiste Colbert, the official who would become controller general of finances, was convinced that opponents of the monarchy were using the quatrains to foment sedition. This was no idle threat. Urban and rural revolts were endemic, and many of them rejected new forms of taxation. Colbert responded with brute force to such uprisings. He ordered offenders to be hanged or broken at the wheel and sometimes imposed collective punishments. Communities lost their freedoms, their fairs, and even their walls and bells. Some officials had likewise burned tracts invoking Nostradamus and sentenced their authors to the gallows. This time, the lieutenant general of police forbade the publication of a pamphlet that linked the ghost story to quatrain 2.28. Ultimately, the contents of the royal audience—which neither the king nor the blacksmith ever disclosed—matters less than the ways contemporaries imagined it.[24]

⁓✌︎⁓

After fulfilling the ghost's instructions, François Michel wasted little time at the court. People stopped him as he made his way back to Provence, but he was exhausted and hurried home. No more ghosts, no more apparitions. Over the years, his wife sold the chandeliers, platters, rings, and necklaces that members of the court had given him in the hope that he would talk. The modest blacksmith died in 1726, leaving his descendants a small house, an

orchard, and even some debts. Until the end, he had resisted prying questions. The wondrous mystery endured and so did the conviction that this
affair, like so many others involving Nostradamus, had been political. In
1697 as in earlier decades, these confirmations and predictions remained
available for all types of public and private uses, equally enticing whether
one sought to buttress or, on the contrary, to contest the authorities.[25]

And yet, there were cracks in the edifice. While Louis XIV listened to the
blacksmith, the French monarchy never associated itself publicly with these
visions or the quatrains. Nor did any political faction latch on to the episode.
Nostradamus surfaced throughout the political realm and provided ways
of contemplating and acting upon events, but as an occasional expedient, a
polemical device. It lacked permanence, a label, enduring followers, theoretical underpinnings, and the sanction of leading figures. The phenomenon's
foundations—manifold dimensions, obscure words, a basis in media culture,
nonexclusive affiliation—were also its weaknesses.

Legitimacy was furthermore becoming a problem. Pamphleteers would
not have tapped Nostradamus if it did not seem credible and summon precedents, fame, and astrological or vatic templates. In 1670, an English agent in
France had felt comfortable marshaling a quatrain to convince his secretary
of state that a French peasant revolt would come to naught. "Troops regroup
& legion turn about" was the key line (quatrain 4.12). But precedents hinged
on fickle interpretations; fame provided a devalued political currency; and
ghost stories were coming under growing scrutiny, especially in the upper
reaches of society. Astrology and prophetic insights likewise seemed increasingly fanciful. After contributing to the radiance of the Sun King, astrology
was losing its standing at the court. Scientific visions of a mechanistic universe punctured holes in its vast ambitions. Official edicts now targeted astrologers, sorcerers, magicians, and poisoners for their lies and plots. Soon
enough, Europeans would debate what was most ridiculous: reliance on
dreams, belief in apparitions, or faith in astrology? Soon enough, they would
dismiss Nostradamus and the blacksmith's vision as so many fairy tales.[26]

The blacksmith's visit elicited a fair share of skepticism in its own time.
The philosopher Pierre Bayle complained that it rested on hearsay rather
than proven facts. The poet Palamède Tronc de Coudoulet warned against
the perils of deception. The French diplomat who was negotiating peace terms

in Holland agreed that it was but "fodder for conversation on the vain curiosity of men, who seek in vain to discern the future." And the *Gazette of Amsterdam* wondered how people could believe in Nostradamus and other such chimeras in an enlightened century. The episode thus captured a transitional moment during which men and women both accepted and dismissed astrology, ghosts, and Nostradamus—all of them part of the mainstream and yet increasingly relegated to the margins of society. The episode was at once a high point in the political history of Nostradamus and the end of a chapter. This may be the strangest thing about the whole matter.[27]

The change was made manifest four years after the apparition. In 1701, two of Louis XIV's grandsons made an overnight stop in Salon. The municipal authorities welcomed them in the customary fashion with a solemn procession, victory trophies, and fireworks. They also hung a banner that proclaimed, "Nostradamus to the princes, grandsons of a hero: welcome. I have known you for a hundred and fifty years." Another banner presented six quatrains that had foreseen this visit and the main political crisis of the day: the future succession to the Spanish throne. A similar scene played out in the town of Beaucaire, thirty-fives miles to the west, when the king dispatched one of his top marshals to quash Protestant insurgents in 1704. Town elders welcomed this war hero by reciting sixain 43, which spoke of mutinies and sieges and the restoration of peace: "They will be greatly relieved, / When he shall make his entrance into Beaucaire." Both Salon and Beaucaire marshaled Nostradamus—the man and the quatrains—to express their loyalty and seal collective relationships with the Crown. Both deemed him acceptable as a political device, a means of legitimation, and a public language of praise.[28]

And yet, something was amiss. The marshal mocked the sixain privately as obsequious drivel. He would have said so publicly, but his diplomatic acumen prevailed. In Salon, the king's grandsons asked neither to meet François Michel nor to visit Michel de Nostredame's tomb. This surprised their hosts. After all, Louis XIII and Louis XIV had both paid the astrologer their respects during their visits to Salon decades earlier. This time, however, the princes moved on.

Chapter 7

☙⚜❧

Amazing Bones:
A Revolutionary Desecration

A century later, in the midst of the French Revolution, visitors of a different ilk came looking for Nostradamus in Salon. They cared less about
ghosts, however, than about skulls and bones.

These visitors belonged to the National Guard, a volunteer urban militia
that enforced law and order and sometimes defended the nation against its
enemies. In the spring of 1791, when violence escalated in the Comtat Venais-
sin, a papal enclave around Avignon, neighboring cities sent in guardsmen.
This included a regiment from the port of Marseille, made up of artisans,
shopkeepers, and some affluent citizens as well. On its way home from Avignon, the regiment halted in Salon. A few guardsmen—we do not know
how many—headed at some point to the Church of Saint-François. They
were neither inquiring about vespers nor saluting the dead. The National Assembly had abolished monastic orders a year earlier, and Salon had closed
the church's cemetery around the same time. No, the guardsmen were paying
a visit to the town's most famous resident.[1]

Nostredame's home was now in private hands and barely identifiable. No
local families carried his name. His last descendant was a dim-witted beggar
whom locals called the prophet. His crypt was accordingly the only place to
feel Nostradamus's presence. But the guardsmen spent little time pondering
such connections. Instead, they broke the tomb open, exhumed the remains,

and spread them across the church floor. Local residents later declared that the men were inebriated, and that one of them drank from the prophet's skull. Some accounts held that this profane guardsman perished days later, either ensnared in an ambush, hung by rioters, or executed after stealing silverware. Tales rapidly outnumbered facts.

Nostradamus once again takes us to a strange place in history. I have long studied and taught the French Revolution and yet had never encountered this odd episode. Like the ghost story, this incident appears inconsequential at first glance and grows more intriguing the more one pays attention. Why did these men hound Nostredame more than two centuries after his death? Had his predictions not vanished or become irrelevant, along with the ghost story, as France embraced reason and progress? Why, in other words, did Nostradamus warrent attention in the midst of this most modern of revolutions?

After all, the eighteenth century witnessed the apex of the Enlightenment. According to the long-prevailing view, rational ideas percolated from the salons, cafés, and academies of Paris and London, or even Bordeaux and Manchester. Philosophical essays and encyclopedias extolled freethinking individuals who combined sensations into original ideas, bore natural rights, and could both improve themselves and better their society. This worldview sprang from the Reformation, with its ideals of industriousness and success, and the Scientific Revolution, which embraced evidence and reason to grasp and master the natural world. It then gained strength as capitalism, bureaucratic states, and scientific institutions grew more prominent. There was no need for sacral rituals and enchantment in this modern universe: no supernatural agents or magical forces, no hidden symbols for higher minds to uncover, no miracles, no awe before divine intervention in human affairs. If astrology and the like survived during the eighteenth century, it was on the fringes, in the fumes of occult subcultures, as remnants of a primitive, magical spirit that preyed upon irrational fears.[2]

Nostradamus was thus fated to recede as well. And certain indicators suggest that it did. In England, the name grew scarce in political pamphlets, popular literature, and fiction. In France, publishers did not release a single edition of the *Prophecies* between 1740 and 1772. Crises such as the Seven Years' War (1756–1763) generated fewer interpretations of quatrains than earlier ones. It became harder to find popular print that linked these predictions to wondrous happenings. The authorities grew less suspicious of political uses of Nostradamus. Provincial censors occasionally forbade an edition of the *Prophecies,* out of concern with hostile interpretations, but not often. French subjects likewise devised other ways of praising their monarch. In 1716, soon after the five-year-old Louis XV had succeeded Louis XIV, a man named Belier de Saint-Brisson found confirmation of the king's everlasting glory in one of the sixains. The phoenix, it said, would rule for a long time and with as much glory as his predecessors. This was a conventional encomium, but Belier was among the last to make such connections. When he returned to Nostradamus thirty years later, he declared that these predictions were no "erroneous fables." Nostradamus's declining credibility made him defensive. In 1785, a Polish count explained that the quatrains lacked any predictive value whatsoever. They merely portrayed the natural rise and fall of empires. One did not need prophetic inspiration, the count asserted, to claim that such historical events or natural catastrophes would occur.[3]

Still, Nostradamus neither disappeared nor became the preserve of fringe groups. New almanacs continued to provide some of his predictions. Thanks to the growing numbers of peddlers who roamed across the countryside, they also reached broader segments of the population. There are reports that in some parts of France, rural schoolchildren learned to read by reciting quatrains (this remained the case as late as 1881). Within the higher reaches of society, too, people continued to parse his words. Nostradamus was a common presence in the libraries of leading French nobles and ubiquitous in those of rural squires, along with works of piety and heraldry and chivalrous romances. Half of the monastic and abbatial libraries in Champagne and Burgundy owned one of his publications. Unbeknownst to one another, an Avignon lawyer and a Parisian scribe both devoted journal entries to quatrain 1.53 in 1720. Its verses about gold mines and "a great nation in agony" justified their ire against John Law, a fraudulent Scottish financier who had devised a scheme that lured investors with (bogus) promises of profits in Louisiana. His Mississippi Bubble, as it was called, caused a stock market collapse in France.[4]

Seven years later, when an embattled predicator was brought before an ecclesiastical court for his heterodox ideas, he clamored that quatrain 1.7 announced his imminent vindication. A Parisian magistrate noted with astonishment that many people were linking quatrains to this case (this apparently did not include the bishops who deemed the predicator guilty). In 1744, while awaiting news of the French fleet's attack on British warships, a Parisian lawyer found grounds for hope in quatrain 2.68, which mentioned great forces from the north, a door to the Ocean open wide, and London trembling. "If the famed Nostradamus is to be believed," he noted in his journal, "this project must succeed."[5]

All of this suggests that the eighteenth century could open itself to rational as well as magical outlooks, to reasoned interpretation as well as awe, even if the ratio was not always equal. There was no linear progression from an enchanted Middle Ages and early Renaissance to a skeptical modernity. Rather than depicting this period as the heyday of secular reason, some historians have lately spoken of changing inflexions between reason and magic, of cycles of disenchantment and reenchantment during which one resonates more than the other. To distinguish purely rational elites from a naïve populace—as if cultures were fortified castles—likewise misses the exchanges and borrowings, the shared beliefs and commingled horizons that make this period so fascinating. The learned often approached the supernatural with greater distance or diffidence than peasants or artisans, but, even in enlightened Europe, people from all walks of life returned to the notion that spirit could govern matter. They read prophecies, ordered horoscopes, pored over kabbalah, were amazed by the *Tales of 1001 Nights,* practiced alchemy, consulted fortune-tellers, and exchanged mystic secrets during Masonic rituals full of solar mythology. Many did so in private, but the century of Voltaire was also the century of the comte de Saint-Germain, a four-thousand-year-old alchemist who provided the secret of eternal life. It was also the century of Cagliostro, the Sicilian magician-alchemist who claimed to heal ailments through spiritual agencies. And in scattered encounters that can easily go undetected, it was also a century that made room for Nostradamus.[6]

~இ~

It took an unprecedented and unforeseen political crisis, however, for Nostradamus to blast once again into public view and for these guardsmen to single out his tomb. As in the past, the phenomenon came to the fore during a collective effervescence. The French Revolution began swiftly. A fiscal crisis launched a chain of events that toppled the feudal system and turned France into a constitutional monarchy by the end of 1789. The National Assembly enshrined universal rights, abolished ranks, reformed taxes and justice, and held national elections. The scale and speed of change proved dizzying. So much was torn down and so much was erected in a matter of weeks or months. But the new Assembly could not satisfy everyone. Two issues proved especially divisive. The first was the fate of priests, now required to swear an oath of loyalty to the revolution. In Salon, three of them swore the oath in January 1791 and then reneged in May, to widespread consternation. A month later, King Louis XVI and his family tried to flee France and join French aristocrats who had taken refuge in Austrian Belgium. The idea was promising, but the execution lagged behind. The king was recognized near Varennes, a small town abutting the border, and held there with his family above a grocery store until revolutionaries arrived to bring them back to Paris. The botched flight fanned fears of surprise attacks against the nation. It also presented France with a second quandary: what to do with a king who had so clearly repudiated the revolution? The killing of fifty Parisian demonstrators in July deepened antagonisms. Some deemed the Assembly too moderate; others found it too radical. All wondered where the country was heading.[7]

Against this backdrop of uncertainty, violence, dramatic reversals, and soon enough war and beheadings, French men and women projected themselves into the future. They tried to imagine the contours of a world that was confusedly taking shape. Omens and old prophecies grew ever more appealing. So did Nostradamus. Almanacs, newspapers, and pamphlets such as the *Small Nostradamus* commented on recent events while anticipating forthcoming ones. In 1790, the *Journal de Paris* published several quatrains with which "all of Paris is now occupied." Among them was quatrain 2.10, which announced change and then a calmer state of affairs:

Before too long all things shall be ordained :	Avant long temps le tout sera rangé,
We sense a sinister age on its way :	Nous esperons un siecle bien senestre :
The state of marks & seals shall be most changed :	L'estat des marques & des scelz bien changé,

Few to be found content with their stations.	Peu trouveront qu'à son rang vueille estre.

Editions of the *Prophecies* replaced some quatrains with new ones that suited current purposes. One of them announced that nuns and priests would soon perish on the scaffold. A supposed descendant of Nostredame linked the violent tremors of 1789 to a civil war ahead. According to the *Republican Magician,* Nostradamus had announced that this was "the greatest and most wondrous revolution to have ever taken place on the surface of the planet since its creation." In England, too, collections of *Prophetical Extracts* included quatrains. *The World,* a London newspaper, reported in 1790 that Nostradamus had predicted the French Revolution's decree outlawing monasteries.[8]

Most important, Michel de Nostredame had left an explicit prediction about the revolution. It garnered immediate attention and remained in public consciousness for decades. "Beginning with that [unidentified] year the Christian Church shall be persecuted more fiercely than it ever was in Africa," Nostredame wrote in his epistle to Henri II, "and this shall last until the year seventeen ninety-two, which shall be considered the beginning of a new age [*une rénovation de siècle*]." Other medieval and Renaissance astrologers had identified the return of a rare conjunction of planets around 1789 and declared that it would mark stupefying change. But eighteenth-century pamphleteers remarked that none among them had foreseen the revolution as precisely as Nostredame. A leading revolutionary club posted the prediction outside its door for a week, inviting citizens to make up their own minds. Some partisans of the revolution believed that it announced massive political change, including the Civil Constitution of the Clergy (which allowed the state to appoint clerics and required priests to swear this oath of loyalty), the advent of the French republic (which occurred in September 1792), and an era that was free from religious superstition. On the other end of the political spectrum, some readers hoped that Nostradamus promised better times ahead for Catholics, who would no longer be subject to such harassment.[9]

A revolution that sought to establish a utopian world on the remains of an ancient, evil society clearly tapped millenarian aspirations, whether religious or secular. Some contemporaries depicted the revolution as a sign of the

Apocalypse while others announced the imminent arrival of a messianic figure. Nostredame's apocalyptic references and depiction of an epochal break
in time could feed such expectations. Moreover, growing numbers of people
in France assumed that the enemies of the revolution were busy plotting and
conspiring. This was due to a mounting sense of crisis, or even panic, that
was exacerbated by Louis XVI's flight to Varennes. It also owed much to a
collision between the remnants of a secretive courtly society and the revolutionary yearning for open politics. The arcane words of Nostradamus suited
this way of thinking as well. The man who knew everything that had happened since his death would allow "truth to triumph," announced one almanac in 1793. He would shine light on the mysterious forces that were turning
France, and soon enough Europe as well, upside down. Obscure as they
were, quatreins could speak to the revolutionary yearning for transparency.
The point, then, is not that all or most revolutionaries now embraced Nostradamus. It is, rather, that these words could echo and nourish some of the
era's deepest obsessions, even when they contradicted one another.[10]

⁓ᘰᕽ

All of this activity must have come to the attention of our guardsmen. But
something else drew them to Nostradamus and the man's tomb: a mysterious
tale about his death that had nothing to do with the revolution per se. This
story had first surfaced around 1600, when Chavigny claimed that Nostredame had foreseen his own passing. Like a voracious climbing plant, it had
then sprouted off in multiple directions in the seventeenth century. People
heard it from residents of Salon and from the Franciscans who guided visitors through the church. They also read about it in almanacs and prognostications and more respectable publications as well. Oral and written cultures
seem to have borrowed from one another.

According to the first story line, Nostredame had told local peasants that
they would never step on his throat after his death (this claim reflects his
contentious relationship with some Salon residents). This is because he had
ensured that his body be buried standing in a wall of the church. Some versions of the story claimed that this would allow him to remain in contact with
the outside world, others asserted that this burial site captured his uncertain
status between prophecy and sorcery. Regardless, the wall and his body's

location inside and outside the church were fine metaphors for a man who crossed boundaries. Another story line held that Nostredame had built a deep mausoleum in the church and filled it with books, a writing case, candles, ink, and paper. Fleeing worldly corruption and religious strife, he had secretly taken refuge there and bolted the doors shut behind him. The year 1566 marked his death to the world rather than his actual demise.[11]

To deter interlopers, Nostredame cast a fatal curse on whoever dared to enter his vault. This was another story line, and it may have originated in Chavigny's translation of his Latin epitaph. What some rendered as "O Posterity, do not grudge his rest," he translated as "O Posterity, disturb not his ashes and trouble not his sweet rest." Rumor soon had it that Nostredame had inscribed a warning on the vault's stone door: "Woe to the one who opens me." Some almanacs depicted men at arms guarding the entrance in chain mail. In 1714, a French diplomat made a special two-day trip from Marseille to visit the crypt. To his disappointment, he found an ordinary tomb—and no trace of the fearsome inscriptions about which so much had been written.[12]

The diplomat may have read stories about foolhardy visitors who had disregarded these warnings. According to the tale told at London dinner parties in the 1660s, the prophet had made townspeople swear never to open his tomb. Some of them broke this promise sixty years later, and they came upon an engraved brass plate on his breast. It scolded them and provided the exact date of their intrusion. Nostradamus had of course seen it coming. A widely disseminated version of this story held that two death row prisoners, who had been promised a pardon if they lifted the tombstone, died on the spot after doing so. Seated on a bronze chair, the glaring prophet warned future interlopers that they would suffer the same fate. Perhaps Nostredame had never died. Or perhaps the intruders had survived long enough to retrieve new quatrains that he had composed underground. By the late seventeenth century, almanacs provided vivid descriptions of the "opening of Nostradamus's tomb" and then shared newly discovered predictions that readers could not find anywhere else. The legend was also a sales pitch.[13]

These various story lines surfaced in other myths and legends. The seer who had predicted his own death? Simon Forman. The alchemist who had designed his tomb? Nicolas Flamel. The prophet who rose from his grave? Merlin. The astrologer who left new predictions near his tomb? Regiomontanus.

And the prowler who found a mighty book in the soothsayer's vault? This one surrounded the Scottish wizard Michael Scot. Many religious traditions and initiations also featured a magician's temporary death. The Nostradamus phenomenon nonetheless stood out by tapping all of these folkloric or archetypal story lines while leaving a real tomb and an enticing epitaph behind. It was once again about accumulation rather than invention—and about widespread celebrity. The tomb and its "amazing bones" had grown famous in their own right decades before the French Revolution. In 1792, a leading Parisian newspaper ran a letter from a reader who had scoured the crypt and found a prophecy announcing eye-opening happenings for the year to come. Whether one believed such predictions or not, it was now all but impossible to hear the name of Nostradamus, and much less visit his tomb, without entertaining the notion that something mysterious lurked underground.[14]

All of this explains why the guardsmen headed for Nostradamus's tomb that day. But it does not account for their behavior inside the church. Was it necessary to break the crypt open?

Many contemporaries viewed this as a desecration—a charged form of violence that vilifies a person, religious rituals, and the sacredness of eternal rest. French revolutionaries desecrated countless tombs of princes, nobles, and clergymen, all of them symbols of a despicable regime and a corrupt society. This violence grew endemic after the fall of the monarchy in 1792. The royal crypts in the Cathedral of Saint-Denis were defiled, and the bodies of past monarchs thrown into collective graves. Elsewhere, revolutionaries sacked mausoleums and decapitated recumbent effigies. In the town of Corbeil, near Paris, they took bones from church ossuaries, burned them on a public plaza, and then dumped the ashes into the Seine River. Desecration ultimately seeks distance from forces that are deemed reprehensible and threatening. Fashioning a new revolutionary order required the destruction of the old and its deleterious influence. It was a form of purification. Too much may have been at stake in Salon to leave the tomb alone.[15]

In Provence, as politically divided a region as any in France, members of the National Guard took it upon themselves to protect the revolution. Sometimes, this entailed wrecking castles and churches. Marseille's guardsmen were among the most radical. The city's National Guard had come under the helm of the Patriotic Assembly of Friends of the Constitution, a powerful revolutionary club that intervened in neighboring cities—such as Avignon—to keep enemies in check. The guard would soon adopt the bellicose "Marseillaise," France's future national anthem, as its marching song. As they returned from Avignon in the spring of 1791, these revolutionaries may thus have desecrated Nostradamus's tomb and ransacked the church to punish a town that struck them as royalist. Cries against the National Assembly had after all been heard in Salon's marketplace following the king's arrest. These were perilous times, and the guardsmen may have targeted a seer whom they associated with the counterrevolution. By 1791, this made sense.[16]

Nostradamus, as we have seen, had lost political legitimacy since the time of the ghost's visit. And yet the process was not perfectly linear. Isolated pamphlets and ephemeral publications deemed Nostradamus useful at a time in which battles raged and politics seeped into all aspects of life. Everything now became political: the clothes one wore, the name given to one's children, even the sincerity with which one sang during festivals. Popular almanacs taught the revolution's history and values while warring factions used all means at their disposal to express their views and silence their opponents. Polemics could thus trump legitimacy. On the left, it was claimed that Nostredame had predicted the advent of a glorious, harmonious era, free from tyrants and public debt. A pamphleteer named Melchior D'Odoucet declared in 1790 that the soothsayer had foreseen the revolution's outbreak and predicted that it would soon bring glory to France. Quatrain 2.10 announced the end of turbulences: "before too long all things shall be ordained." Some activists were fiercer. According to Nostradamus, they said, France should expect decapitated bodies, war against perverse ministries, and the death of the despot Louis XVI between 1793 and 1800. Whether interpreting quatrains or coining new predictions, these pamphleteers tapped a famous soothsayer who could unite virtuous citizens around a glorious future.[17]

Still, Nostradamus was moving toward the political right, along with prophetic language in general. Disenchanted, anguished, and resentful, royalists found in his quatrains portrayals of an apocalyptic battle and a disastrous finish for the revolution. The populace had usurped an authority to which it had no right. This is why, according to these words attributed to Nostredame, "this unjust, atrocious, vile action, / Will cost it much blood in the end." The royalist *Journal général de la cour et de la ville* declared in 1790 that some of his predictions about the revolution had unfortunately come true: "Let heaven preserve us from the rest." Three months later, it told readers to expect political turmoil and foreign invasions until 1792. That year, another polemicist depicted an imaginary procession that fulfilled one of Nostradamus's supposed prophecies. Having achieved victory, the king and aristocrats paraded across a capital that ex-revolutionaries had swept clean, some of them dressed as monkeys.[18]

Many of Nostradamus's most committed readers were likewise conservative. A member of a prominent aristocratic family copied five quatrains on a sheet of paper then wrote commentaries that betrayed his fears and hopes. The "major massacre" mentioned in quatrain 2.92 pertained to Louis XVI, who was decapitated in January 1793; the great nobleman forced to flee France for Spain in quatrain 3.54 had to be one of the king's brothers. In 1792, a monk roamed Avignon's marketplaces with a quatrain in hand, preaching about the upcoming triumph of monarchy and religion. When the revolution grew more violent a year later, a Scottish countess asked her reverend to explain what Nostradamus had to say. A strict Presbyterian with a doctorate in theology and a command of nine languages, this reverend had recently been appointed president of Dickinson College in Pennsylvania. To quench his curiosity about the future, he interpreted quatrains. He now concluded that a sham trial and an execution awaited Louis XVI following his arrest. One of his friends (a future president of Princeton) wondered how the revolution would end. Nostradamus provided a plain answer, said the reverend: "It will all go to the Devil at last." Perhaps this is what the Scottish countess wanted to hear as well.[19]

～⊙⊙～

It is no wonder, therefore, that radicals equated Nostradamus with counterrevolutionary forces. Some even disqualified rivals by linking them to this figure. Enemies of the journalist Jean-Paul Marat dubbed him a "modern Nostradamus"; opponents of revolutionary leader Maximilien Robespierre likewise accused him of colluding with a prophetess whose annotated copy of the *Prophecies* was full of "imaginings that could be applied to the current revolution." The guardsmen's antipathy for Nostredame was thus part of a broader political climate in which prophecies were deemed anathema to revolutionary virtue and a healthy, well-governed society.[20]

At the same time, these guardsmen took their place in a long line of detractors who had vilified Nostradamus since the sixteenth century. Early critics had questioned the man's poetic and astrological skills, his visions, and the impact of his false predictions and errors. They sought to outline the boundaries of a prophetic universe, establish principles, and distinguish scientific truth from falsehoods or delusions. This continued throughout the seventeenth century. The Puritan preacher John Edwards wrote in 1684 that astrologers such as Nostradamus "step beyond the bounds of their Art, and hold Correspondence with *Lucifer.*" A few years later, a Jesuit heraldist could tolerate the almanac writer but not the false prophet who diluted the sacred mysteries of Scripture. The eighteenth century, however, all but stopped picking on an incoherent sap who, though unable to predict the future, had either believed in his revelations or else penned them to make a living. His behavior was risible, but so what? Why bother debating his prophetic status when the answer was obvious and the stakes insignificant? No institution or body of learning felt threatened to its core by the discredited knowledge for which he stood. The question, then, was no longer who Nostredame *really* was. Instead, it became: How does a rational society respond to such inane predictions?[21]

The heart of the matter was public credulity and what contemporaries called superstition. Clerics had long proscribed improper worship of the rightful God as well as magic and witchcraft. By the late seventeenth century, magistrates, doctors, and men of letters were insisting that feverish imagination combined with superstitious beliefs generated uncontrollable enthusiasm and passions. Mired in ignorance and poor judgment, superstition could lead people astray and undermine the social order. This is why it was so important to free newly-empowered citizens from such beliefs. "What is superstition?" asked an elementary textbook during the revolution. "The fear of invisible forces." How does one protect oneself from it? By dominating one's fears, distrusting imagination, and curbing the desire to know the future. Nostradamus captured all of these dangers: imagination running wild before incomprehensible happenings, credulity before a voice from above, fear before dire pronouncements. The belief that people could predict the future was perilous for it left no room for political will. Stories about Nostradamus's crypt would not circulate as widely if they did not feed on base instincts.[22]

Some eighteenth-century critics now used Nostradamus to deride the Renaissance as a confused, infantile era that believed in judicial astrology, soothsaying, and people burying themselves alive. How could it *not* have welcomed the deluded Nostredame and then made him famous? Catherine de Médicis and the like had believed these predictions and eerie tales and then encouraged others to do the same. This had continued under the Old Regime, but the revolution was mercifully ushering France into a new era. Nostradamus's *Prophecies* "owed their success only to the ignorance and gullibility of his century," remarked the authors of the *French Traveler,* a collective portrait of France, in 1789. Modern citizens, they then added, hardly believed that Nostredame had been buried alive in his tomb. Relegating Nostradamus to a superstitious past made it possible to commend the present era for puncturing such inanities. History was moving forward. We now know that pseudo-prophets cannot see the future or survive underground. What the Renaissance venerated, what the Old Regime manipulated, we judge for what it is worth.[23]

At least, some people do. "Old matrons and ignorant Plebeians" accepted these groundless prophecies, said the English essayist Charles Gildon in 1692. Throughout the eighteenth century, learned writers, gentlemen, and others (including many who adopted Enlightenment ideas) continued to look down upon the weakest, most gullible elements of society: the women and provincials, the peasants and artisans who succumbed all too easily to imagination and novelty. They were the ones who accepted Nostradamus's predictions and gave credence to stories about ghosts or astrologers in crypts. Nostradamus, explained one French legal writer in 1743, is "so disdained by the sane echelons of society, and so respected by the credulous populace." Some elite observers were convinced that the populace was vulnerable to superstitions because of its innate nature. Others blamed the conditions under which these people lived and accused malevolent leaders of dusting Nostradamus off whenever, as one revolutionary put it, they "needed to terrorize the peoples, or release themselves from the torments of their own consciences." It thus fell upon the revolution to turn former subjects into clearheaded citizens who could distinguish truth from falsehood.[24]

These detractors imagined that the Nostradamus phenomenon had not changed since the sixteenth century and that people parsed the predictions in the same way. Superstition was deemed static and unmovable. When they relegated Nostradamus to another era or another social world, they hence depicted a modern, progressive era that was freeing itself from wayward habits. They bolstered their self-worth while drawing boundaries and tracing the contours of modern rationality. Given its fuzziness, magic had long served as a foil in the West. Religious leaders dismissed sects as hollow and immature by accusing them of embracing magical beliefs. The forces of reason could likewise depict their triumphant victory by claiming that they were vanquishing magical tales and predictions. Such beliefs, they said, would soon vanish from the modern world.[25]

This was the expectation, at least. But it is also possible that the guardsmen's sudden, profane violence reflected uncertainty and self-doubt. The boundaries might not have been as resilient as they appeared. If Europe was moving confidently toward an enlightened future, then why worry about Nostradamus and the like? Was it not, rather, because the Old and New regimes had more in common than revolutionaries liked to admit? Was it not because, instead of vanishing, belief in superstitious tales seemed to take new forms? Was it not because Nostradamus expressed all too well the contradictory tendencies of an era that sought to put a certain past behind and yet could not shake off a thirst for intimations of the future? Was it not because elites shared beliefs, rumors, and fascinations that they associated with popular culture? Was it not, finally, because the guardsmen had either felt the force of Nostradamus or else—more frightening yet—doubted their own ability to resist such temptations?[26]

A writer noted in 1792 that even sophisticated minds could end up in Nostradamus's sepulcher. From this vantage point, the guardsmen's actions sought to defuse anxieties about the blurry line between tradition and modernity. Let's not risk it, their behavior in Salon seemed to say. Let's smash the damned thing instead.[27]

⁓෨ᠻ⁓

Violence provides a rich, suggestive way of making sense of the day's events in Salon. But it is not necessarily the only thing that was going on. As they dug out Nostredame's bones, the guardsmen were also interacting with the dead—and this mattered at this time in a way it had not before.

For centuries, death had been part of the natural order in Western Europe. Buried within towns and villages, the dead belonged to the same community as the living. Ghosts, as we have seen, communicated with people and sometimes helped them out. By the eighteenth century, however, this relationship was coming apart. Cemeteries were moved to the outskirts of towns due to new hygienic concerns about foul, infectious odors. As religious practice declined, so did Christian notions of heaven and hell. A growing number of people began to see death as a complete break that left but a void or mystery on the other side. Some were mesmerized by this vertiginous encounter with loss and the passage of time. Many others struggled with this new uncertainty and the prospect of a definitive separation from loved ones. Mourning grew more ostentatious, with grand processions, long eulogies, lachrymose lamentations, and family vaults for those who could afford them. People collected memories that conferred immortality to the deceased. During this time of increasing individualism, they sought out physical traces imbued with the aura of illustrious personages. Soon enough, they would also try to communicate with the departed. Death repulsed, frightened, and intrigued at the same time.[28]

Strange things took place in cemeteries as well. Medical students and anatomists looted graves for bodies that they could dissect. Other robbers, convinced that the shape of craniums corresponded to the sinews of the brain, went after the skulls of great men. To protect their bodies, some people enclosed their tomb behind railings, or bought cast-iron coffins that no crowbar could pry open. The fear of premature burial ran deeper still. Baffled by comas, trances, catalepsy, and other deathlike states, people began to question medical diagnostics of death. Rigor mortis was no longer conclusive. This fear generated other types of coffins, with airholes, shovels, bells, and even ejection devices. Wealthy families hired grave watchers. Newspapers fanned anxieties by publishing stories about people who woke up underground, prey to what Edgar Allan Poe called "the rigid embrace of the narrow house—the blackness of the absolute Night—the silence like a sea that overwhelms."[29]

Our guardsmen were not grave robbers, but they did infringe upon the tomb of someone who had reportedly buried himself alive and then rejoined the living. "I had promised to resuscitate in 1790," Nostredame purportedly declared in one revolutionary pamphlet. "I have kept my word, and here I am, back in the capital of France." Nostradamus hence responded to the era's nervous fascination with death and the afterworld—what some called necrophilia. By penetrating the crypt of a man who may have died or perhaps had not, a man whose indefinite status between the living and the deceased mirrored all too well the era's own doubts, the guardsmen confronted deeper anxieties about the afterworld. They did not necessarily do so in an explicit or conscious fashion. But the tomb and the tales provided a way of dramatizing such questions, grappling with them, and confronting one's own fears and uncertainty. A few decades after the revolution, a leading French magazine recounted—or, rather, invented—Nostredame's last conversation with his son César. The old man told his son that, as death descended upon him in the vault, he would have just enough time to jot down what lay on the other side. "The great secret shall be revealed to the world! I shall write it in a book, and man shall have victory over the universal victor!" The liminal Nostradamus remained meaningful on other planes besides terror. Morbid fascination could accompany desecration.[30]

So could entertainment. If wonder and politics were two angles of the Nostradamus triangle in early modern Europe, then public amusement was the third. Enjoyment and practical guidance had long gone together in almanacs, which often presented their predictions as both useful and pleasant. Satirical farces and songs used Nostradamus to send up all-knowing astrologers or monks. By the eighteenth century, the man also surfaced in theatrical spectacles. In 1756, a French songwriter parodied the opera-ballets of the celebrated Jean-Philippe Rameau in a one-act play about an almanac writer that he titled *Nostradamus.* Twenty years later, Nostradamus gave his name to a play on the bourgeois penchant for astrology. During the revolution, Parisians could watch the drama *Nostradamus, True Friend of the People* and the pantomime *Harlequin and Columbine Protected by Nostradamus.* They could also catch one of the many representations of *The Tomb of Nostradamus,* a comic opera that had first been staged during Parisian fairs in 1714

and then performed repeatedly throughout the century. Its author, the famous playwright Alain-René Le Sage, helped fashion a genre that added
plot, dialogue, and comical or mythological characters to the pantomime's
acrobatics and dances. As they sang the lyrics that actors held up on placards, spectators were equally amused and edified by marvelous spectacles
that were both escapist parodies and acerbic social commentaries.[31]

Set in Salon, *The Tomb of Nostradamus* followed successive visitors into a
book-lined vault that resembled a gentleman's library. Ordinary folk were
too frightened to penetrate the crypt, but these visitors mustered the courage
to enter and consult this strange but wise man about their problems. Harlequin and Octavius went first, and they encountered a fire-spewing monster
(who disappeared once Octavius kissed it) followed by a black magician
whose wand opened the crypt's door. There was the famed Nostradamus,
surrounded by demons and goblins, composing "the resolutions of the fates"
as he had been for two centuries. Octavius asked him to locate his estranged
wife. The prophet obliged, fulfilled the requests of other visitors, provided
sage advice to local residents, and then politely asked to be left alone. "In
peace shall we leave the Great Nostradamus," sang the chorus as the curtain
closed.[32]

Such spectacles brought images of Nostradamus and his tomb into the
era's cultural repertoire. They also show how much the phenomenon owed
to this kind of entertainment. With the proliferation of cheap print, the success of vaudeville shows, and growing doubts about apparitions or miracles,
this was true of all facets of the supernatural. Some historians claim that this
process secularized and domesticated demonic voices and magical forces.
This is true to a point: entertainment tames and makes things less corrosive.
No one would be surprised if the guardsmen had shared a good laugh, albeit
a nervous one, while venturing into the astrologer's tomb. They may well
have been reenacting or playacting a scene that they had first encountered in
an almanac or on a stage. Others had done so in Salon before, though not to
such an extreme. In 1761, two young journeyman glaziers dropped by Saint-
François to see for themselves "all that people say about Nostradamus."
More precisely, they wanted to test the notorious curse. Inside the church,
they slid a knife through the slits of the tomb and waited for something to
happen. Nothing did. The glaziers then resumed their travels. I imagine that

they were thrilled to have shared this moment together, but also relieved after debunking a legend that, as one of them put it, only "commoners believe."[33]

⟐

Like the glaziers, the guardsmen may have playfully tested beliefs that could be true—or not. What happened in that crypt remains shrouded in mystery. This is how it must be, I suppose, when it comes to Nostradamus. But these tales transformed the way people pictured the man. Harlequin, Octavius, the glaziers, and the guardsmen were all looking for a wild magician who had buried himself alive rather than the learned, humane astrologer and prophet whom Chavigny had lionized two centuries earlier. To be sure, many Europeans still entertained images of the Renaissance humanist Nostredame. Biographical sketches could be found in encyclopedias and editions of the *Prophecies*. History did not vanish. But it was dissipating into fictional clouds. Between 1600 and 1800, a biographical Nostredame tinged with legend gave way to a legendary Nostradamus laced with biography.

By the mid-1600s, all kinds of stories circulated about the man's wondrous life and extraordinary powers. In one tale, the astrologer invited the boy Henri IV to undress, scrutinized his body, and then promised that the throne would one day be his. In another story (perhaps the most frequently told), a gentleman asked Nostredame to predict which of his two piglets would be served for dinner that evening. When he picked the black piglet, the gentleman (who wanted to show him up) instructed his cook to covertly prepare the white one. Later that day, a wolf slipped into the kitchen and ate the animal, leaving the cook no choice but to serve the black one. Nostredame had been right, after all. In another popular tale, Nostredame unexpectedly kneeled before a young monk named Félice Peretti. When asked why, he explained that the future Pope Sixtus V deserved such respect. Whether drawn from popular lore, oral traditions, or literary motifs, stories about a wise, prescient seer endowed Nostradamus with new powers and attributes.[34]

Sometimes, these tales erased his life story altogether. Besides a ghost, Nostradamus now came across as an atemporal figure who conversed with mythological heroes, an uncanny sorcerer, and a famed diviner who had left the depths of hell to speak the truth to the imprisoned Louis XVI. Le Sage's play turned the benevolent "papa Nostradamus" into a wizard whose white beard

reached to his belt. He wore a long-eared cap and a violet robe decorated
with talismanic characters. His tomb was both a real place in Salon—the
crypt that the guardsmen sought out—and a fictional one in the mold of Ali
Baba's cave, the setting for another Le Sage production. With their mix of
reality and marvel, the comic opera's dreamscapes helped turn the humanist
into a diviner who embraced all supernatural activities. At once comic and
mesmerizing, the all-knowing Nostradamus joined a universe of magical
forces, potions, fairies, witches, monsters, and the living dead. One of the
ironies of this story is that the learned humanist came to embody forces and
entities that flourished in popular culture. The other irony is that the man
with a real historical pedigree (something that cannot be said of all prophets)
became the most elusive of figures. Unlike Jesus, whose altruism and humanity endured over the centuries he grew estranged from his initial virtues as he
drifted across the hazy landscapes of posterity.[35] Nostredame and Nostradamus went in separate directions.

The closest parallel is the wizard Merlin, another favorite character in
Le Sage's plays. There are differences between Nostredame, who was rooted
in history and whose posterity included multiple threads, and Merlin, who
originated in poetry and fiction and remained wedded to the Arthurian legend. Still, they resembled one another by the eighteenth century, two protean
enchanters who inhabited mysterious tombs and changed shapes to meet the
yearnings of successive generations. While Nostradamus prevailed in France,
Merlin did so in England, where astrological publications carried titles such
as *English Merlin*. French journalists described Merlin as the Nostradamus
of England. Across the Channel, Nostradamus was presented as the Merlin
of France. Prophets and soothsayers would for a time carry passports in the
age of nation-states, but these two legendary figures now marched side by
side in media, entertainment, and the popular imagination.[36]

Nostradamus's legend flourished because the phenomenon's early deficits—
lack of glory and heroism, a structuring myth, and enduring moral content—
deprived it of a sturdy foundation. The man who circulated between realms
could not secure the backing of a collective entity that would enshrine or
protect his life story. Nor could he resemble those compassionate saints who,
in return for solace, ask the devout to keep them in the public eye. Memory
distorts, but it can also preserve when groups feel that they have something

to defend. This was not the case here. As the religious stakes surrounding the *Prophecies* decreased in intensity, as credence in his prophetic status and astrology waned, as cults of saints lost their local grounding, determining Nostredame's status and his relationship to Christian creed grew less urgent. Nostradamian providers could not agree whether he had drawn his powers from poetic furor, astrology, a sixth sense, or an understanding of human psychology. Some stopped worrying about it. Detractors, too, shifted their sights away from Nostredame himself, or else depicted him as a crazed magician in order to better dismiss him. In the "burlesque hell" of one critic, the venomous Nostradamus wore a long robe and muttered devilish formulas.[37]

Nostradamus remained famous—*le fameux Nostradamus*—but the French *fameux* also means memorable or impressive. If impressing readers or spectators required that one take liberties with biography, then so be it. This was especially true in entertainment and popular media, which tend to unmoor traditions from their original settings. Snippets of his life story, anecdotes, titillating tales, and fresh predictions from the grave came together in those marshes where fiction and make-believe seep into truth and history. Unlike cultural traditions that grow meaningless but endure by force of habit, Nostradamus kept on changing. The figure grew yet more fleeting and unstable, yet more illegitimate as a source of information, yet more preposterous and removed from the concerns of many people. At the same time, ignorance about the phenomenon's causes endowed it with an extraordinary, wondrous veneer. Nostradamus also grew more macabre and controversial, more alluring and mesmerizing.

By 1816, an English periodical could thus refer to "the tomb of the prophet, or magician, for he might be called either, or rather both." Whatever. Whether Nostredame had been a soothsayer or a sorcerer was irrelevant as long as he told us our story, a French journalist wrote a few years later. And plenty of people still entertained the notion that, even if they could not place the strange Nostradamus in time, this voice from the past could tell such stories. Most of them did not care that these stories—the ones that endured, at the very least—typically surfaced *after* rather than *before* a given event. [38] After all, one of the most discussed quatrains in the nineteenth century (9.20) was widely seen as a prediction of Louis XVI's flight to Varennes in 1791:

He shall come by night through the woods, of Reines,	De nuict viendra par la forest de Reines,
Two via Pierre Blanche, Herne, & Vaultorte,	Deux pars vaultorte Herne la pierre blanche,
The black monk all in gray within Varennes,	Le moine noir en gris dedans Varennes
Elected cap. causes storm, fire, blood, sword.	Esleu cap. cause tempeste feu, sang tranche.

London's *Gentleman's Magazine* provided a full explanation in 1890. The forest of Reines—or rather Rennes-en-Grenouilles (spelled "Raines" in earlier times)—sat between Paris and the village of Varennes. *Deux pars* designated the royal couple. *Herne* was an anagram for the French *reine* (queen) "by metaplasm of *h* for *i*." Marie-Antoinette wore white clothes—the color of her hair in the wake of her arrest. Louis XVI had chosen an iron-gray coat and a round slouch hat that made him look like a Franciscan monk. *Vaultorte* (an ancient French word for about-face) conveyed his irresolution. Louis could be described as a Capet (cap.), a member of the dynasty that had acceded to the French throne in the tenth century, and as "elected," since the revolution made him a constitutional monarch. "Blood, sword," finally, referred clearly enough to the fate that awaited the king and his wife. Whether in London, Dublin, or New Orleans, there were people who believed, or knew people who believed, that Nostradamus had predicted revolutionary events. "Here again we find a dark record flashing upon us with all the certainty of an eye-witness," said the *Gentleman's Magazine*. Whoever he might be, the famous Nostradamus lived on.[39]

⁂

When the guardsmen left Salon, it fell upon the town leaders to handle the aftermath. The mayor was a moderate revolutionary whose achievements included new markets and new forms of public charity. He was also a local booster who cared about public edifices and monuments, a rarity during these times of widespread destruction. By 1791, revolutionaries had seized, vandalized, and sold off countless ecclesiastical and aristocratic buildings. French churches and convents were now used as prisons, barracks, and warehouses.

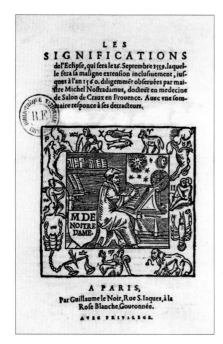

A 1559 chapbook signed Michel Nostradamus, doctor in medicine from Salon de Craux in Provence. Surrounded by stars, books, and an armillary sphere, the astrologer is a picture of penetration and inspiration.

One of the earliest portraits of the man, on a medal dated 1562. The sober robe and hat suited a doctor and astrologer who healed bodies and souls.

Salon-de-Provence, Nostredame's adopted hometown, around 1900. Note the castle to which Catherine de Médicis summoned the astrologer in 1564.

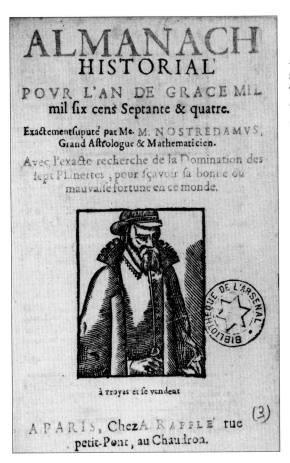

A Parisian almanac for 1674, attributed to Nostradamus. The master had predicted "the good and the bad fortune of this world."

A book-length interpretation of the *Prophecies*, first published in 1693. The author, Balthasar Guynaud, defended the saintly prophet against detractors and provided a key to his predictions.

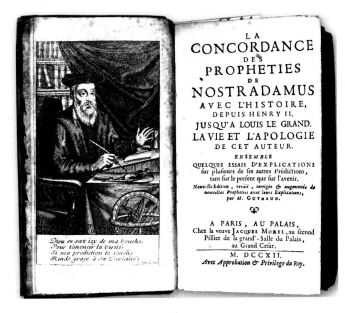

FRANÇOIS MICHEL MARECHAL FERRANT NATIF DE SALON EN PROVINCE

FRANÇOIS MICHEL homme Sage, et de probité
revenant un soir fort tard chez luy, fut arrêté
dans la campagne par un spectre armé d'un flambeau
et en reçut des ordres secrets, qui lont obligé de venir en cour, pour les reveler
au mois d'Avril de cette année 1697.

Prédiction de Nostradamus sur François Michel Centurie 2ᵉ. chiffre 28.

1 Le penultieme du surnom de Prophete,   Loin vaguera par frénétique teste,
Prendra Diane pour son jour et repos: Et delivrera un grand peuple d'impôts.

1. Il y'a un des deux petits prophetes que l'on nomme Michoas, 2. la Mere de François Michel s'ap-
pelloit Diane. 3 frénétique, ne veut pas dire insensé mais inspiré d'un esprit prophetique.

a Paris chez H Bonnart rue St Jacques au Coq

The blacksmith François Michel, who was visited by a ghost and told to deliver a message to Louis XIV in 1698. Quatrain 2.28, which had reportedly predicted all of this, is at the bottom of the engraving.

Une femme consultant Nostradamus sur les evenements il lui presente une Table de Marbre
ou sont ses Predictions et lui dit L'Aigle fera son Nid sur le haut du Chene &c.
Ou le Magicien .....

Nostradamus at the end of the eighteenth century. The soothsayer points toward an oak tree (symbol of virtue and industry) while announcing an invincible empire.

Inklings of the prophet of doom in the late eighteenth century.

Recovering Nostredame's (apocryphal) *Mighty Book of Spells,* with its rules for the interpretations of dreams. Self-help meets Romantic high jinks and the Gothic sublime in this English engraving (1816).

The Wizard Nostradamus laying in his Tomb. with the Mighty Book of Spells at his side.

It was iron Clasped and iron bound
And he thought as he took it the dead man frowned.

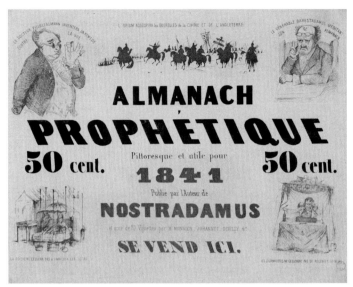

Selling the *Prophetic, Picturesque, and Useful Almanac,* which blended prophecy and irony for a modern readership. Its mastermind, Eugène Bareste, appears in the upper right corner.

Nostradamus combines astronomy, astrology, prophecy, the occult, and wizardry in this French print from the 1860s. The skull is a new touch.

The prophet is flanked by Henri Torné-Chavigny, the French priest who used quatrains to fight secular modernity. In the background of this 1862 print: sixty historical figures whose fates were purportedly inscribed in the *Prophecies*.

A full-page color advertisement for *Le Matin's* latest serial: Michel Zévaco's *Nostradamus* (1907).

The wizard as fixture of mass culture. This poster advertises one of the "fantastic illusions" that Georges Méliès staged in his Parisian theater in the 1890s. Its title: "The Tricks of the Moon and the Misadventures of Nostradamus."

A Nostradamus board game around 1900. Players could find out where to uncover happiness or what their love life had in store.

"Madman gets mad": Hitler learns in the *Prophecies* that his own henchmen are plotting against him. This still comes from MGM's 1944 short *Nostradamus IV*.

The residents of Salon who reenacted Catherine de Médicis' visit to the city in the early 1990s. The Renaissance humanist can only thrive within his local community.

MAYBE IT'S BECAUSE
NOSTRADAMUS DRANK IT.
OR PREDICTED IT.
OR PREDICTED HE'D DRINK IT.

THEN AGAIN. . .

IT COULD JUST BE THE TASTE.™

There is no need to depict the real Michel de Nostredame outside Salon. The name suffices.

A scowling prophet for modern times.

Adjoining cemeteries commonly became vacant lots. Much as he tried, Salon's mayor could not save the Church of Saint-François. The edifice and its convent were parceled into dozens of lots and auctioned off to local residents, who promptly dismantled the buildings and sold the raw materials. All of the bodily remains were moved to a new cemetery—all, that is, except for Nostredame's. The mayor and the city council collected whatever bones they could find—local inhabitants had taken some of them home—and transferred them to the Collegiate Church of Saint-Laurent. Nostredame's new tomb lay across from the entrance, in the chapel of the Virgin Mary, behind protective mesh. There were portraits of Nostredame and César, the family's coat of arms, and a new epitaph honoring a man "whose memory will always be treasured by French patriots given his predictions about the reign of freedom." Salon's mayor reinvented Nostradamus for revolutionary times.[40]

The epitaph said nothing about the guardsmen, but their story endured in popular and commercial culture. A French almanac related in 1794 that the intruders had found a handwritten note predicting the emancipation of France. Later accounts claimed that the men had died in an ambush, or else that Nostredame's body had been reburied in a field. Such tales dovetailed all too well with the era's Gothic literature, which exposed hidden conflicts and secrets from the past by exploring the eerie junction between the natural and the supernatural. Prisons, abbeys, castles, graveyards, and crypts were favorite backdrops. After the revolution, novels and short stories liked to depict Nostredame's funeral and his fate inside the crypt. In some of them, he walked to the vault surrounded by throngs of local residents, pressed a button to lift a huge stone, revealed a quatrain enveloped in flames, and then vanished forever. In others, he went to his tomb carrying royal jewels or his *Mighty Book of Spells,* "iron clasped and iron bound." *Nostradamus,* an 1833 novel of dark predictions, unrequited love, and vengeance, ends with such a tale. The prophet cloisters himself in a vault with a young woman who has spurned his advances. Decades later, interlopers uncover their two skeletons. Nostredame is seated on a chair, quill in hand, while the woman is attached to a gate, the flesh of her wrists eaten off in a desperate attempt to escape. What a haunting "picture of furor and death, terror and rage," gushed one reviewer.[41]

The most memorable picture of terror and rage I uncovered took place in Aix-en-Provence in 1806. A young peasant who fancied himself a prophet decided to emulate Nostradamus and bury himself alive. He began digging a grave on his own and then asked a passerby to complete the job. As word spread, local residents rushed over to pull the peasant out of the ground. By the time they arrived, his skin was black and he could barely breathe. Still, this modern prophet was strong enough to berate his rescuers for thwarting a divine design. The *Journal de Paris* reported the news—a true story that fueled the very legend from which it had sprouted. It was easy and so appealing for educated Parisians to laugh at this superstitious peasant and those strange expanses in which one could not tell what was true and what was not. There is a fine line, however, between laughing and squirming. This morbid incident, like the guardsmen's desecration, captures the uneasy mix of disquiet, gravity, and playfulness that surrounded Nostradamus at the turn of the nineteenth century. Its legitimacy faltered, but the lure and the stakes remained high.[42]

Chapter 8

ᴥᴥ

A World of One's Own

The pseudoprophet from Aix was outlandish and perhaps mentally disturbed. Other Nostradamus aficionados fit this profile between the Renaissance and the nineteenth century, but most of the people whom I have encountered in the course of my research were ordinary folk. A French lawyer wrote commentaries on Nostredame's "magnificent verse" in the late sixteenth century. A self-taught secretary mulled over a prediction about a flood in Grenoble as he traveled across France in the 1730s. And more than a century later, a well-read American grandmother owned a copy of the *Prophecies* with "stained and ragged pages that rustled as one turned them." These people seem perfectly sane.[1]

To figure out why Nostradamus endured across the centuries, we must understand why all kinds of people paid attention to these predictions, whether they trusted the man's predictive abilities or not. We have already encountered some of these readers, but from afar, in the shadows of media and Nostradamian providers. What we have not done is watch and listen in earnest as they grappled with these dark, cryptic words. We have not entered their homes, read over their shoulders, opened their journals, intercepted their letters, eavesdropped on their conversations, or watched them respond to major crises. Doing so is not easy. Exceptional sentiments and occurrences often leave long archival trails whereas indifference goes unrecorded. Illiterate folk are by definition elusive. And the words that historical actors used to describe their emotions do not always express what they truly felt.[2]

Still, it is worth a try. Drawing from history and sociology, we can recover the norms that allowed people to parse the quatrains and the expectations that invited them to do so. When evidence proves frail, we can cautiously extrapolate and pay attention, not just to what people said but also to what they *did* with Nostradamus. We can also derive insights from behavioral psychology, although this requires a soft approach. Successive generations are unlikely to experience similar situations or to register and record their emotions in identical ways. Social forces filter what happens in the body and the psyche. It is nonetheless conceivable that, while emotional frameworks change, some social expectations and behavioral patterns endure or go through gradual evolutions. Even though the field of social neuroscience, which traces the relationship between neural mechanisms and psychological or social processes, is still in its infancy, many scholars agree that brain modules change little over a few hundred years. Without explaining everything (or suggesting that biology determines all), pychology may provide us with something as we seek to understand what Europeans made of these predictions.[3]

What, then, did Nostradamus mean during these centuries? The short answer is that the words that encompassed the world in all of its dimensions, the words that were secular and yet sometimes imbued with religious awe, the words that escaped exclusive ownership by any creed or party also lent themselves to several relationships at once. In fact, the men and women who encountered Nostradamus tend to fall into four families: decoders, awed beholders, persons of leisure, and ambivalent readers. We will meet the first three below and the fourth one in the following chapter.

※

Plenty of readers were distracted in early modern Europe, but some pored over Nostredame's predictions with sharp-eyed focus. They delved into this mystifying text and then furnished the meaning and coherence that were not always apparent. Take the 116-page interpretation of the *Prophecies* held in Lyon's public library. The anonymous, undated manuscript is ungainly, brittle, and partially eaten by rats. But it is important, for it shows that some individuals read Nostradamus with seriousness of purpose. Its author was clearly literate and well educated, most probably a male humanist from Lyon. He began his commentary in the mid-1550s and kept adding to it for years or even decades. He selected dozens of quatrains, copied each one at the top of a page, and then wrote several paragraphs of explanation below. His goal was to extricate the single meaning that, he was convinced, lay hidden within each quatrain. He thus scrutinized lines to explain what each one "meant to say." The task must have taken him considerable time, perhaps whole days or evenings. Each of this humanist's mini-essays received a title and each one pertained to geopolitics, most often the Turkish threat. The "great city" in one quatrain, he wrote, referred to Constantinople. Other quatrains foretold the fall of Tunis in 1638, or the death of a leading sultan in 1640. Again and again, the author concluded that Nostredame had predicted the demise of an Arab or Turkish leader. France may have allied itself with the Turks in the 1520s, but he still concluded that Christendom would vanquish its enemy from the east.[4]

This humanist was an active reader, an interpreter, a translator from an arcane language. One thinks of the counsel that another such reader, the English gentleman William Drake, imparted a century later: "When you read, do it earnestly, gathering together all the power of your mind to the study thereof, neither let your mind wander." Our Lyon humanist never specified what technique he used. This was unnecessary. The quatrains's freedom from institutions and traditions meant that he could interpret them in whatever way he wished. No conditionals or hedging here. Writing in confident, declarative prose, he trusted his ability to unravel a high-stakes mystery. When lines proved opaque, he made the indispensable connections and supplied names and dates. His relationship to Nostradamus rested on a dynamic interplay between words and readers. The former guide and orient; the latter follow these guidelines while imprinting their own direction. Sometimes, this active reading entailed writing. Like modern-day cognitive psychologists, humanists understood that there was no more efficient way of assimilating complex ideas. They accordingly filled the books they read with symbols and abbreviations. Some of them also jotted down thoughts and excerpts from their readings in journals that were called commonplace books. They did so to sharpen their judgment, advance their education, create a bank for future use, and accumulate memories. One Venetian nobleman copied four Nostradamus quatrains in his commonplace book alongside drawings of constellations and considerations on the rise and fall of empires. Readers who annotated, corrected, translated, and rearranged excerpts were free and creative, critical and assertive. They conversed with the words and their author.[5]

Some works lend themselves to active reading better than others. This is true of the Bible, for instance. People could read bits and pieces and make connections between passages and books. Many Bibles handed down to us from the early modern period contain annotations, cross references, and commentaries. Still, the Roman Catholic Church sought to prevent unsupervised access. This was not the case with the inviting Nostradamus. The cornucopia of words, metaphors, and inversions transcends place and time; the discontinuous story lines lack a plot; and the colons separate clauses that relate to one another in all kinds of potential ways. A high-ranking official will be rebuked; temples will be desecrated. Such statements beg for elucidation. Everything is up for grabs in a realm that bridges the true, the plausible, and the conceivable. This universe seems foreign, but the vivid images, the familiar places, the words that most readers had already encountered also provide points of entry. The quatrains are not blank—and hence utterly disorienting, overly demanding of readers who have to do the heavy lifting. Nor are they closed off, constrained by limited horizons, arcane references, and the single connotations of subject-verb-complement sentences. Instead, they provide a vista for reason and imagination.[6]

So does the disjointed nature of Nostradamus's predictions. The presages that he inserted in his almanacs floated on their own. In the *Prophecies*, connections between quatrains were at best loose or veiled. The following musings by the French writer Paul Valéry about Marcel Proust's *In Search of Lost Time* are oddly pertinent: "The interest of his work lies in each fragment. We can open the book wherever we choose; its vitality does not depend on what went before." It was so easy to peruse the quatrains closely though not exhaustively, to consider each one as a stand-alone piece, and then to read it in isolation or else in a sequence of one's own devising.[7]

Nostredame's self-presentation as an inspired human being, rather than the equal of biblical prophets, invited such readings. So did his claims that he lacked the words to express what laid in store, or that he had written but one-hundredth of what he knew: "More things will take place than I have mentioned." He all but dared readers to fill in the blanks. It is not so much that his vague predictions could mean anything. This is true, but then what? It is rather that they became a personal palimpsest, a call to explore, map out, and reconcile one's internal world, the world in which one lived, and the universe that he offered for consumption. To decode the quatrains was to bring together what the historian Anthony Grafton, speaking of astrology, calls the local and the ephemeral: the workings of the universe and those of inner lives.[8]

One of the most forceful arguments for the appeal of divination is that it provides stability and order. This vast cognitive scheme encompasses nature and history, time and destiny, religion and politics. If unexpected events fit within a structured plan, then all is not haphazard. Some scholars hold that people in precarious situations are readier than others to substitute benevolent forces for the vagaries of chance or the deficiencies of reason. Insight into mysterious forces overcomes feelings of aimlessness. Divination thus delivers solace and comfort. True enough, but all kinds of things can bring solace and comfort. We also need to consider the ways divination has helped people make their world meaningful.[9]

Nostradamus provided a coherent framework beneath the surface of the words. Readers had to dig in. The Lyon humanist who parsed quatreins relished this opportunity. Endowed with what psychologists call an internal locus of control, he believed in his own ability to uncover patterns and imprint meaning. Having mastered the text, he could now do the same with the broader world and his own existence. For centuries, people have searched for the hidden and unique signification of Nostradamus's predictions. Those who believe that there is such a thing may derive satisfaction from bringing it to light and hence showing that nothing is utterly incomprehensible. Having fathomed Nostradamus, one can also fathom deeper mysteries. But let us also consider the idea that the reader who felt that she had decoded Nostradamus, or made inroads in that direction, could derive confidence in her broader interpretative abilities. Grappling with the predictions—this open-ended activity—could prove as meaningful as the final result. Nostradamus's semi-opacity may have led our humanist to relive a character-building journey toward contemplation of a broader order, be it cosmic or other. Decoding can be a way of existing in the world.[10]

⁓꙰⁓

Active reading persisted after the Renaissance. French almanacs commonly included blank pages for readers to write comments, relate events that they had witnessed, or even list purchases. Many publishers of the *Prophecies* likewise encouraged readers to determine for themselves what Nostredame had meant to say. "Whoever will apply himself in the reading of this book," one of them explained in 1667, "will be able to discover many more predictions that I have not indicated here." Chavigny ordered and interpreted key predictions but also conceded that he could not explain all of them. Readers with deeper insight should share them frankly, he said. In the late seventeenth century, English pamphleteers invited readers to assess the quality of their interpretations. Sometimes, they even allowed these readers to take over. Quatrain 2.49's references to counselors, conquerors, and the skies of Rhodes proved too perplexing for the translator Garencières in 1672. "I had rather leave it to the liberty of the Reader, than break my Brains about it," he wrote, "considering chiefly that I am going to bed, the precedent Stanza having exhausted all my Spirits."[11]

Numerous readers accepted such invitations. Most of them were educated and wealthy and had sufficient leisure time (although some individuals of lower status also engaged in such reading but without leaving as many traces). The distinguished Godefroy family provides a telling example in seventeenth-century France. The patriarch Théodore, a learned humanist and royal historiographer to Louis XIII, was sober in his religiosity and skeptical regarding astrology and Nostradamus. His two sons, however, were deeply interested in theology and the *Prophecies*. Denys II, who presided over a sovereign court in the city of Lille in northern France, collected transcriptions of sermons, including one that compared Nostradamus's and Joachim of Fiore's predictions regarding the Jesuit destruction of Rome. He also analyzed chosen quatrains line by line. Quatrain 7.43, for instance, depicted a prominent prince's recent flight from the French court in 1662. "The laughing nephew should flee." Denys II's brother Léon, a canon in southwestern France, quoted quatrains in his travel journals and linked them to local floods and other events. Each in his own way, the two brothers fashioned their own meaning out of Nostradamian words.[12]

Several surviving editions of the *Prophecies* from this era likewise contain underlined words, marginal annotations (wobbly lines, parentheses, crosses), boxes around selected quatrains, and impromptu clarifications. Next to the line "The child is born with two teeth in its throat" (quatrain 3.42), one reader penciled "the King" in a 1667 edition. Some contemporaries also kept notebooks with "explanations" of Nostradamian verses regarding the years or decades to come. One of them, by a member of an eminent Avignon family, identified quatrains and sixains about the English Revolution, the Spanish Succession, and the royal house of France. The author then added a section of "strange and extraordinary things that must happen in the century that began in the year 1689." A century later, Bonnie Prince Charlie, the Stuart prince who was exiled to Rome in the 1740s, reportedly combed the *Centuries* for indications that he would accede to the throne of his ancestors. Few readers expected to find explicit references to their personal lot in the *Prophecies,* but most, like the prince, pondered the fate of leaders and nations. The decoder sometimes became a soothsayer.[13]

While active reading was often private, it could also lead to shared and even public experiences. Nothing suggests that the Lyon humanist intended to publish his musings or grant them a public function, say, as a warning. But he may have shown his manuscript to friends, colleagues, or family members and then discussed it with them. Books circulated as gifts, loans, and exchanges among early modern readers. When the lord Picot de Gouberville lent a military officer one of Nostradamus's prognostications in 1562, he asked for a receipt. He wanted it back. There is a good chance that the two men compared impressions. Gentlemen (and some ladies) swapped books and opinions with pleasure during the ensuing centuries. In 1659, an English traveler to France told an eminent friend that the (spurious) line "The heirs of the toads will take Sara" referred to France's recent seizure of Arras. The toad had been part of the French coat of arms, while 'sara' was 'Arras' read backward. During the 1720s and 1730s, two French magistrates discussed chosen quatrains on several occasions, speculating on the identity of the future queen of France and the ruler of the Florentine throne. Neither magistrate was fully convinced by these predictions, but neither one dismissed them either as they debated the meaning and validity of given quatrains. "Is it not clear as day?" one of them once asked the other after linking verses to a legal case. Regardless of the answer, Nostradamus's predictions lent themselves equally well to joint extrapolations and to private meditation.[14]

⁓ᴏ⁓

What some people found bewildering and intriguing, however, others deemed bewildering and alienating. Decoding could constitute an undue burden for individuals who lacked the education, desire, or self-confidence to decipher predictions—and make sense of their world—on their own. This was truer yet for those who believed that a single key unlocked Nostradamus's enigmas but could not easily discern it. One response was to step back and simply behold what Nostradamus had to offer without seeking to disentangle it. The meandering *centuries,* the convoluted lines and prophetic strands, the growing uncertainty around the man, the aura that each crisis magnified— all of this invited readers to enter Nostradamus's universe and accept its covert designs. If anything, Nostradamian providers would crack the code and lead the way. Problem solving is sometimes a lure, but it can also fade behind awe or communion with religious or simply inspiring forces that are greater than oneself.[15]

There are different ways of considering this. Intense stress or even trauma can provoke such levels of anxiety that some people become overwhelmed by stimuli and end up all but paralyzed. Psychiatrists speak of catatonic reactions, which block out affective responses and lead people to abandon initiatve and surrender to existing conditions. From this perspective, Nostradamus's arcane words could contribute to or exacerbate feelings of resignation by displaying all too visibly what lay beyond one's reach. Social critics have likewise accused astrologers of fostering what they call an ideology of dependence and obedience. Accepting external authority—a grandiose framework that escapes understanding—replaces independent, critical thought. This is one perspective on the matter, and it packs a punch. But something else could have been going on. Individuals with an *external* locus believe more readily that outside forces govern their existence. They become less anxious once they relinquish control to a stable entity that seems better equipped to achieve a hoped-for outcome. This handover does not call upon them to abandon self-determination or civic rights (though this can sometimes happen). In emotional terms, some people simply find that the best or sole means of exerting control is to give it up, most often temporarily. Nostradamus thus granted the reader permission to deflect responsibility and stop fighting on her own.[16]

It also provided a framework according to which the world made sense. Nostradamus's impenetrability could itself convey something important. The historian Stuart Clark put his finger on it while discussing the French countryside prior to the French Revolution. "Nature was not mysterious to peasants because it was unintelligible to them," he advanced. "If it was mysterious this was precisely because it was intelligible in terms of a language of mystery." Extended to Nostradamus, the insight draws attention to a language whose very inscrutability, whose lack of discernible meaning could mirror and help people come to terms with broader disruptions. It could fulfill a deeper craving for mysteries. It could also take over when people saw or felt something that was so disconcerting about their own fate or broader events that they could not process it. The same is true of Nostradamus's glum pronouncements. They speak to a pessimistic outlook that faced a disordered world with a triple conviction. Fate lies beyond human sway. Change does not necessarily mean progress. And the best course of action is to reduce expectations and find a way of living with one's troubles.[17]

❦

Collective crises are a case apart. Mysterious forces and glimpses into the future resonate for some people in ways that personal responsibility, reason, and even solidarity may not—or not as strongly. Some crises gestate slowly. Expectations fill the air. Rumors fly. Imagination runs wild. The outbreak then heightens the sense of urgency and disrupts the way people interact with others, perceive state power, or contemplate their future. The locus of control moves easily toward the external pole when events seem to unfold outside one's sway, when outlets for action hover out of reach, when trusted authorities appear impotent and the established order seems hollow or suspect.

This is one reason why, like astrology or fortune-telling or myths about glorious saviors, Nostradamus has loomed largest during such stretches. "It is above all in times of disorder and revolutions that this desire [for Nostradamus] grows," one pamphleteer noted in 1849. "During these moments of instability, the spirit, exhausted by doubt, seeks to fathom the future and find some soothing certainty." That was certainly true of the comte de Moré, a distinguished officer who had served as Lafayette's aide-de-camp throughout his American campaigns and ended up a political exile during the French Revolution. He opened a bank in Italy and eventually recovered his fortune, but decades later he still struggled to make sense of these painful events. Moré came to believe that Nostradamus's *Prophecies* alone contained the history of these years. He strung together a series of quatrains in his memoirs and explained that "the only certain thing about this world is that nothing, nothing at all is haphazard, and that there is no effect without a cause."[18]

There were collective crises besides revolutions. In September 1666, a fire broke out in a London bakery and burned across the city for days. It took few lives but destroyed four hundred acres and hundreds of buildings—the entire medieval quarter. The lord mayor's inability to contain the blaze forced countless Londoners to evacuate in haste and leave their property behind. Among them was Samuel Pepys, the navy secretary, who fled his home in his robe and saw the destruction up close. This was "the saddest sight of desolation," he wrote in his diary. St. Paul's Cathedral, much of Fleet Street, the church in which he had been christened, even his father's house burned down. The fire's rapid, erratic course suggested that it had been started deliberately. Rumors claimed that English Catholics were about to massacre Protestants while the French invaded. Plots seized the imagination of a population that had lived through a plague epidemic a year earlier and found itself at war against the Dutch. Quakers advocated rebellion; Cromwell's veterans were poised to take arms. In earlier years, the astrologer William Lilly had foreseen a burning capital by the river while millenarians cautioned that God would punish England for failing to build a New Jerusalem. Why would warnings about the year 1666, with its "Apocalyptic and mysterious number," not come true?[19]

Pepys had thrived during the plague year, quadrupling his fortune and securing two important appointments. "I have never lived so merrily," he announced at the end of 1665. Few of his diary entries pertained to the disease, as if Pepys were detached from a scourge that was part of the order of things and had somehow spared his family. The Great Fire of London was something else. This "most horrid malicious bloody flame" brought a physical and emotional devastation that seemed to come out of nowhere and last forever. As he walked across the city, Pepys met throngs of distraught Londoners who had suffered great losses. People cried all day, forgot their own names, and sometimes attempted suicide. Pepys's wife began to lose her hair, and he came down with headaches, stomach pains, and bladder problems. He threw himself into work and extramarital affairs, but this was not enough to shake vivid nighmares about the inferno. Five months after the outbreak, smoke still floated above the city and Pepys still woke up in pain. "It is strange to think how, to this very day," he wrote in February 1667, "I cannot sleep at night without great terrors of fire, and this very night could not sleep till almost 2 in the morning through thoughts of fire." He panicked when a neighbor's chimney caught aflame. A contributor to the *British Journal of Psychiatry* diagnosed Pepys in 1983 with post-traumatic stress disorder. There is a risk in transposing twentieth-century concepts to earlier periods, but many of the symptoms are certainly present: health problems, flashbacks and anxiety, difficulties concentrating, and feelings of vulnerability before uncontrollable forces.[20]

That same February, Pepys attended a dinner party at the home of an old friend, the eminent statesman Sir George Carteret. At one point, the conversation veered toward Nostradamus. Carteret recounted the tale of the tomb (it was strange but possibly true, Pepys later noted). Mostly, the guests discussed quatrain 2.51, which was circulating in English almanacs. It seemed to confirm the fire and announce other dire events:

No blood of the just shall be spilled in London :	Le sang du juste à Londres fera faulte,
Six times twenty-three consumed by lightning :	Bruslés par fouldres de vint & trois les six :
The ancient dame shall fall from high station :	La dame antique cherra de place haute,
Many of the same sect shall lose their lives.	De mesme secte plusieurs seront occis.

The first two lines are clear enough. Three times twenty (*vint & trois*) added to six (*les six*) came out to sixty-six. The "ancient dame" in the third line referred to St. Paul's. The last line, however, was more troublesome. Some contemporaries insisted that the members of the same sect were worshippers of the sun and planets while others linked them to warring churches. We do not know what was said about these lines around Carteret's table or how Pepys felt about Nostradamus. After all, he had expressed skepticism about fortune-tellers in earlier years. But innumerable people were now turning to almanacs and the prophecies of Nostradamus and Mother Shipton ("That London in sixty-six should be in ashes"). Dissenters and some Catholics found confirmation that England would finally pay for her sins. While Pepys did not voice such views, this amateur botanist and bibliophile paid attention to a quatrain that he would have dismissed in ordinary times. He contemplated the possibility that it said something meaningful about the events that were making his nights impossible. He remained open to awe, certainty supplanting rumors, and designs underlying catastrophes. Other contemporaries responded similarly. Thomas Tenison, a future archbishop of Canterbury, had derived little edification from Nostradamus in previous years. In the wake of the fire, however, he could not "despise that Stanza of his, which, if it has not satisfied our reason, I'm sure it has astonished the imaginations of many." Whether or not Nostradamus had truly predicted these events mattered little under the circumstances.[21]

Magical thinking—the belief that magical powers animate the world and that human beings can act upon these powers—prospers when social risks are minimal and the rewards most promising. This is especially true during crises, when norms of behavior change and ordinary safeguards are weakened. One of the reasons why Pepys, Tenison, and others now consulted, accepted, or opened themselves to Nostradamus is that conventions made this acceptable—or, at the very least, they reduced social costs such as embarrassment. The phenomenon's recurrence in crisis after crisis provided his predictions with a track record, with bona fides as a suitable recourse during such times. Previous generations had turned to his predictions in similar situations and verified the phenomenon. Respectable individuals and media now gave them credence. Consulting the quatrains seemed normal and certainly less problematic than in ordinary times.[22]

The rewards were numerous. The long-running phenomenon restored the historical span, the mastery over time, even the routine that this sudden crisis had broken asunder. It could both announce the end of times or, in its constant return, intimate that the present ordeal had had historical equivalents. Humanity had survived before and would do so again. It was not only about the long term, however. Enduring crises also alter, dilute, and compress perceptions of time. Two days after the fire began, Pepys felt as if a week had elapsed. "It is a strange thing to see how long this time did look," he jotted down. During the French Revolution, too, time changed countenance. It seemed fleeting, evanescent, and all-powerful. This was partly because the revolutionaries stretched out the present and endowed time with creative powers when they launched what they called a new era and set out to ward off the effects of a detestable past. Freed from divine control and the clasp of tradition, time could shape what people thought and did. The revolution's new calendar would, in the words of the philosopher Condorcet, "put a century of distance between the man of today and that of yesterday." Time also seemed to change because the pace of events grew so frenetic. People hence sought to pin time down by chronicling its course, explaining its jolts, and anticipating its next steps. With its synthesis of past, present, and future, with its multiple temporal frames (cyclical and eternal, ordered and eschatological, and even linear now—a progression from one crisis to another), Nostradamus structured time while opening it up to whatever outcome would best allay anxieties.[23]

Danger lurked everywhere for Pepys, threatening his property, his city, and his country. He felt its physical effects but could not get a handle on it. Anxiety, Freud has taught us, typically operates in this fashion. It is a diffuse state that responds to subjective, often unidentified threats, real or not. Fear, in contrast, revolves around a specific, verified, imminent menace that one can identify. People often find it easier to withstand and sometimes push back against a peril they can name in some way. The Parisian Jewish student Hélène Berr expressed this with startling clarity in 1942: "It's odd: this confirmation of my dread grants it a foundation, reason and force. Rather than intensifying my anguish, it stabilizes it, removes its mysterious and horrible dimensions, and endows it with sad and bitter certainty." Perils suffused Nostradamus's dark universe, but his bank of prophecies could turn anxieties into fears by allowing people to pinpoint their causes, trace their origins, and link them to people and places. In the wake of seemingly unprecedented events, Nostradamus assured contemporaries that they were not prey to mere delusions. Their pain was real and logical given the magnitude of the upheaval, a world historical event that Nostradamus endowed with cold yet glimmering majesty.[24]

Psychologists have paid considerable attention to the kind of confirmation that Berr describes. Few things, they have found, provoke more anxiety than uncertainty. It prevents people from discerning patterns, adjusting their cognitive framework to a new situation, coming to terms with its consequences, and then charting a course of action. "People feel worse when something bad *might* occur than when something bad *will* occur," advances the psychologist Daniel Gilbert. This might be because the human brain needs to control its environment, either by managing a situation as it unfolds or by preventing the return of unpleasant events. One hypothesis holds that the brain experiences electrical stimuli in different ways depending on its internal state. Controlling the circumstances under which the brain receives these stimuli and making sure that they agree with this internal state thus lessens anxiety. This is also true when people simply *believe* that they can control a situation. Neighbors who are invited to complain if a party grows too loud, for instance, tend to mind the noise less whether or not they actually do say something. It would appear that the warning itself and the possibility of acting upon a situation enable the brain to process stimuli. Assuming that one's actions will make a difference may of course be a form of self-deception and yet, this "illusion of control" seems to endow people with self-esteem, enable them to recalibrate their values and priorities, and help them commit to tasks during challenging times.[25]

Individuals who engage in magical thinking thus appear to derive greater confidence in themselves and their ability to make a difference. This is linked to the way they contemplate the future. By Gilbert's estimate, human beings devote 12 percent of their daily thoughts to what looms ahead. The figure is startlingly precise, but he makes the case that projecting oneself into the future enables one to plan, avoid certain events, minimize the impact of others, and change one's behavior if needed. A predictable environment is a controllable one. Because the future we conjure reflects our *current* hopes or worries, it is unlikely to come true as we imagine. Still, delving into the future, even a dark one, can provide a tighter grip on the present, which can seem comparatively more inviting or else find its place within an intelligible pattern. (Apophenia is the name given to our tendency to see patterns even where there are none.) One reason behind Nostradamus's appeal may thus be that the predictions feed misguided expectations about the future (we can anticipate or even shape it) while fulfilling real but misunderstood needs about the present.[26]

Even in times of crisis, moreover, the pain does not have to be unremitting. Patients and accident victims frequently shore up their self-esteem by telling themselves that others have it worse. Feelings of self-worth rest in large part on how one is doing relative to others. This is why personal setbacks often sting deeper than a calamity that affects multitudes of people. The misery of the world can help individuals withstand their own hardships, which seem less terrible in comparison. Readers found it easy to dip into the quatrains and find horrendous tidings about other people, countries, or even eras. In the city of Le Mans on the eve of World War II, to take a more recent example, a boy named Ghislain de Diesbach de Belleroche overheard his father, a bank director, discuss Nostradamus with friends. "Listening to the apocalyptic enumeration of our future misfortunes," he recalled, "I found all the more delightful the comfort of that smoking room where our future and the future of Europe were gloomily discussed. . . . Beyond the green pines darkening in the gray of dusk, war lurked like a ravenous beast in other forests or faraway plains in countries with foreign names." Immediate and yet distant, Nostradamus's vast predictions helped people reframe disquieting circumstances.[27]

The quatrains told people that, rather than simply facing emergencies, they were living through a collective catastrophe. They shared a fate and were now coming together and working toward harmony or redemption. Local or universal communities that coalesce around conceptions of good and evil can face momentous times and enter history as one. Nostradamus's *Prophecies* contained localities, regions, and nations—and humanity as well. Although enduring social movements and rituals did not emerge around Nostradamus, these communities sometimes proved tangible. Pepys and Diesbach de Belleroche were in the company of others when Nostradamus came to their attention. Readers could likewise consult predictions on their own while picturing others doing the same. Whether physical or imagined, these communities could attenuate feelings of isolation. Whereas anxiety tends to draw people apart, fear pulls them together. Nostradamus's evocative words could thus enable people to live with fear—not as mortified stupor but as a controlled, collective feeling that displaces the lonesome terror of the unknown.[28]

⁓ᘗᗢ⁓

Appealing as the quatrains were, certain individuals found it increasingly difficult to espouse Nostradamus publicly by the seventeenth century. Those who rejected the supernatural deemed the phenomenon preposterous. Those whose status rested on good taste and restraint found it unseemly. There was a social price to pay. When a French baron wrote a theologian about Nostredame's insight into some forthcoming marriage in 1659, the prelate exhorted him to trust divine Providence instead. A century later, the friends of an English lord urged him to stop penning reflections on these meaningless quatrains. He was starting to resemble the old fantasist, they warned.[29]

Nostradamus nonetheless endured. This was partly because decoding and awed beholding proved strong enough to withstand such challenges. It was also because a third relationship—private recreation—flourished in aristocratic and bourgeois circles. Sometimes it was about personal enjoyment. Almanacs, for one, were fun to read. In 1551, the pope's vice-legate in Avignon had sent his superior a copy of Nostredame's latest prognostication "to pass the time more than to give it credence." A century later, the future dean of Paris's medical school received Nostradamian verses that, his friends insisted, related to a recent legal case. The doctor deciphered them with amusement. At other times, Nostradamus provided fodder for witty repartee, riddles, and entertaining enigmas. This verbal play thrived in salons, where nothing proved more reprehensible than boredom. With its anagrams and poetic rhythm, its bizarre legends and the wordplay around his name, Nostradamus was tailor-made for this world (prophecy and astrology grew commonplace in early modern parlor games). An eighteenth-century commentator noted that "jokers who have fun with anything" were applying quatrains to current events in order to amuse their friends. The commander of the garrison of Paris was one of them. In the 1760s, he would pull the *Prophecies* from his pocket during social occasions and read out a quatrain that seemed to revolve around a cardinal and the papacy. He laughed every time.[30]

Another favorite activity was to compose quatrains in Nostradamus's style, generally about current affairs. The more they resembled the original, the better. It was all about the artifice, all about flaunting one's talent for poetry and pastiche. In 1694, a renowned Jesuit professor chided the eminent people who wrote quatrains about the Glorious Revolution and then attributed them to Nostradamus. Such rebukes had little impact. In France's Dauphiné region, the lawyer Thomas Delorme entertained himself in the 1710s by composing predictions à la Nostradamus about Louis XIV's campaigns. Farther east, King Frederick the Great of Prussia loved to read such imitations. In 1736, he received a prophecy about the year to come from a member of his court, the count von Manteuffel. Frederick was enchanted. "Nostradamus as you render him has so much wit," he wrote the count. "Only superior geniuses can make the dead speak as they would have during their lifetime." Manteuffel's quatrain was more elegant, intelligible, and "polite" than anything Nostredame could ever have written. The count had bested the coarse prophet at his own game.[31]

Such games subsided when aristocratic entertainment declined along with courtly life, but Nostradamus endured as a learned pursuit or hobby. Clerics, doctors, landowners, and others loved to nose around libraries, dig for archaeological remnants, and collect butterflies. They enjoyed these pursuits for their own sake, took pride in advancing scholarship, and relished the prestige of the local savant. Some of them also grew interested in Nostradamus. In 1722, a Burgundian abbot asked a colleague to send him all references to the astrologer in the *Mercure françois,* a leading journal. Around the same time, a historian of La Rochelle collated the quatrains that mentioned his city. Meanwhile a Belgian canon hired a lackey to travel across France and purchase copies of the *Prophecies.* Using a sixteenth-century edition as his standard, he then corrected the errors that had slipped in. This was "my pastime," he explained.[32]

This cleric cared more about the book's contents than its appearance, but some bibliophiles went after the rare object (the low-end almanacs had less appeal). Aristocrats, wealthy commoners, and clerics owned copies in the seventeenth and eighteenth centuries. One of Louis XIV's sons, the duke du Maine, asked a bookseller to locate a good ancient edition in 1694—not an easy thing, apparently. A century later, a French merchant named Pierre-Antoine Bolongaro-Crevenna purchased four editions of the *Prophecies*

and four book-length interpretations. As bibliophilia grew less exclusive in
the nineteenth century, Nostradamus surfaced in more collections. Alongside
the duke of Roxburghe and the banker James de Rothschild, owners included an English solicitor, a Greek silk merchant, the retired mayor of Marseille, the novelist Walter Scott, and a New York librarian named Wilberforce
Eames. French bibliophiles bought works in their language; the English were
partial to Garencières's translation; and the Americans who later joined them
gravitated toward old French editions.[33]

Other hobbyists chose to clarify the meaning of quatrains or the principles of Nostradamus's universe. These readers were decoding, to be sure,
but they did not feel compelled to believe in Nostradamus's powers, predict
the future, or consider political matters. The implications and the attending
anxieties were both lower. In the mid-eighteenth century, a French gentleman pondered a question posed by a friend: What do you think of Nostradamus? After analyzing dozens of quatrains, he concluded that the *Centuries*
were neither prophecies nor predictions but a veiled depiction of events that
had occurred in Nostredame's lifetime. "They are not announcing the future,
but describing the past," he concluded. The gentleman would not have been
prouder had he proved an intractable mathematical theorem.[34]

Nostradamus continued to generate obsessions in the nineteenth century.
None was more enthused than Jean-Baptiste Boniard, a notary and onetime
mayor of the village of Brèves, in Burgundy. Profession and politics mattered
less to this man than his all-consuming hobbies. He kept a journal, observed
planets, participated in archaeological excavations, and wrote articles for local journals. Nostradamus entered his life in 1837. The circumstances are
unclear, but the sixty-year-old retiree was soon filling his copy of the *Prophecies* with feverish annotations. He refused to let go of a word until he had
figured it out.[35]

Quatrain 9.18 in particular perplexed Boniard. It spoke of "more jail time
for the great Montmorency" and included a mystifying reference to "*a Clere.*"
Boniard suspected that this expression designated the executioner who had
beheaded the rebel duke de Montmorency in Toulouse in 1632 (interpreters
had long linked the quatrain to this event). But he was not sure. There was
only one place to find out: Toulouse itself. Off Boniard went, with a servant
and the local priest in tow. The three men made their away across southern

France. They stopped in a dozen cities, running out of money at one point, but they did reach Toulouse after three months on the road. Boniard discussed the quatrain with the mayor, local historians, and the city's executioner. He pored over registers in the municipal archives and inspected the knife that had severed Montmorency's head. It bore an inscription that was tantalizing but made little sense: "*Celare-Toloze. 1621.*" Unable to figure it out, Boniard and his companions headed home. One morning on that return leg, Boniard had an epiphany: *Celare* was the anagram of *a Clere*. He had proved his hypothesis! For the self-taught, rational notary, Nostradamus provided neither glimpses of the future nor models to live by. It was all about the chase and what his great-grandson (the novelist Romain Rolland) later called exciting charades. Boniard's quest prefigured the Bible codes of modern times but without the apocalyptic overtones.

After solving the riddle to his satisfaction, Boniard moved on to natural history and biblical criticism. He could leave Nostradamus behind since he was neither spiritually nor emotionally attached to the phenomenon. Other amateurs were even more removed. The Dauphiné lawyer Delorme had enjoyed penning quatrains but disparaged the astrologer's "utter foolishness." In 1843, a newspaper editor from northern France purchased the *Concordance of Nostradamus's Prophecies with History* (1712) but pointed out in an inside page that the book was inane. The renowned architect Eugène Viollet-le-Duc acquired two editions of the *Prophecies* for his library that same year, and he, too, questioned the value of these mediocre verses. Why bother, then? Viollet-le-Duc deemed the quatrains curious, especially when they seemed to refer to Napoléon. Other nineteenth-century bibliophiles included the *Prophecies* in their collections of "rare and curious books." One English catalog described Garencières's edition as "an amusing book, full of odd stories." As wonders came to stand for tasteless, plebeian superstition during the late seventeenth century, marvels endured in elite circles as curiosities. One pondered, investigated, or collected peculiar phenomena. The strange words, the underlying design, the rare editions, the meanings attributed to the quatrains, their enduring success across centuries—all this made Nostradamus curious, intriguing, and noteworthy.[36]

These features also infused Nostradamus with something that, given its somber connotations these days, I had not expected to find: pleasure. In the

sixteenth century, words entertained and virtuosity provided a spectacle worth
savoring. Reading could furnish moral and political instruction as well as
delightful dreamscapes and dialogues with ancients. The tale, the lesson, the
well-crafted work were engaging. One is inclined to believe that some early
modern readers enjoyed Nostradamus as well. Why not? It was easy to appreciate vast historical canvases, artful imitations, and ingenious interpretations that required self-direction and yielded mastery. This does not
mean that fun was had by all. Many readers expected clarity and precision
rather than arcane pronouncements. But Chavigny had set the tone by inviting his own readers to enjoy the quatrains in his company. In 1755, a learned
French historian and prelate thanked a friend for lending him a commentary of Nostradamus. He had read it with great pleasure, he said. And while
our Lyon humanist left no record of his sentiments, his manuscript betrays
no irritation before Nostredame's cryptic quatrains. On the contrary, he
tackled them one after the other, moving along methodically and gaining
momentum as he went along. One could swear that, like countless others, he
found this activity enjoyable and perhaps even fulfilling.[37]

✥

Nostradamus once again sated distinct appetites simultaneously. The arcane
yet accessible predictions fulfilled yearnings for self-direction as well as external guidance. In the aftermath of crises, they provided material for narratives that invested events with meaning—narratives that one could either
compose on one's own or accept from others. Nostradamus met the expectations of people who needed to grapple with words and the world and sought
deeper knowledge and direct participation in their own fate. It also spoke
powerfully to those who needed external protection and reprieve from
knowledge. And it drew still others into a realm that seeemed curious, or else
curious and unsettling. In terms of readership or, more broadly, cultural reception, the phenomenon remained open, in flux, and in touch with multiple
expectations.

I have discussed decoders, awed beholders, and people of leisure in turn,
as if they made up separate families, but that is not necessarily the case. The
terms also point toward outlooks that people embraced and then shed, or
embraced partially, or combined with other outlooks. The decoder was not

necessarily a decoder alone, and she certainly did not have to remain one forever. What was intriguing one day could become irksome or merely amusing the next. Many people welcomed Nostradamus during discrete moments in their lives, as their locus of control shifted a few degrees in one direction or another, as their anxieties intensified or waned, as the people around them set different examples. Learned people read Nostradamus "from time to time," one almanac writer noted in 1689. Perhaps they did so the same way on every occasion. Perhaps not. Human beings are multifaceted and rarely free of contradictions.[38]

A final Nostradamian reader, a Londoner whose name and occupation are unknown, illustrates the matter. In 1691, he pored over twelve quatrains and uncovered nuggets about the Fire of London, French defeats, and other timely questions. The decoder in him probed the verses with care, drawing from his knowledge of French, history, and politics to establish his own meaning. The beholder in him allowed that "the hand of some unseen Spirit" could be involved. And the person of leisure collected his thoughts in a long letter to a friend who would certainly find these prophecies and his ruminations equally puzzling and fascinating. Despite his efforts, this Londoner never did pin Nostradamus down. "What to ascribe the Predicting Power to, I leave to yourself," he told his friend. Had someone asked him to explain his interest in the quatrains or define the stakes of the game, he would probably have struggled to answer. But when Nostradamus entered his field of vision, the one thing he could not do was look away.[39]

Chapter 9

✣

We Are Not Nostradamites!

C an a serious person believe in prophecies?"
La Phalange, a French periodical, posed this question to its readers in 1841. It would not have asked if prophecies and supernatural forces did not seem ubiquitous at that time. In the countryside, rural prophets announced the fall of the monarchy or the advent of an Oriental prince. In cities, fortune-tellers, crystal gazers, cartomancers, and palm readers opened shop and answered questions about legal prospects, missing goods, and other pressing matters. Magnetic somnambulists staged public performances in hospitals and universities. This fervor coincided with a religious revival—Catholic in France, Methodist in England—that brought prophecy to the fore in pamphlets and newspapers. It also overlapped with Romantic visions and dreamscapes that connected the soul and the cosmos. "Below what appears to be logical," one French daily observed, lies "a mysterious, horrendous, irrational world."[1]

All of this happened during an era that perceived itself as fundamentally different from the retrograde centuries that had preceded. France had entered an age of constitutional politics, office work, steam engines, and large-scale factories. The nation's heroes were now inventors, writers, doctors, and scientists who could grasp the infinitesimally small and the staggeringly large facets of nature. Paris had likewise begun its transformation into the capital of the nineteenth century, a city of glass-roofed shopping arcades and grandiose salons, where public hygiene mattered as much as banking practices. Soothsayers and believers in supernatural forces did not go unnoticed in this self-consciously modern world. The irrational, declared one newspaper, persisted only because of the enduring frailty of the human mind. Other commentators accepted that the forward march of human civilization was circuitous rather than linear. The flames of imagination still flickered, but not for much longer.[2]

Some people, however, deemed themselves rational and yet could not resist the lure of the supernatural. Among them was a young journalist named Eugène Bareste, the subject of *La Phalange*'s article. Spend enough time in the Nostradamian underworld and you will inevitably run into Bareste. As the author of *Nostradamus,* a heavy tome published in 1840, and the main editorial force behind an annual *Prophetic Almanac* founded that same year, Bareste was the latest in the line of Nostradamian providers who kept the quatrains in the public eye. We could spend time with any number of them, from the mathematics teacher Théodore Bouys, who held that the clairvoyant Nostredame had announced a glorious future for Napoléon's empire, to the Avignon bookseller Pierre Chaillot, who declared that his torch alone would blaze a path across the maze of the *Prophecies.* But none of them did more for the phenomenon in the nineteenth century than Bareste. Innumerable journalists and writers drew from his publications when writing about Nostradamus—in France, elsewhere in Europe, and as far away as Kirksville, Missouri, where a local newspaper translated sections of his almanacs.[3]

From our vantage point, embracing Nostradamus may seem like an odd choice for an enterprising man of letters. What reputable person would give credence to the gibberish of a seer who had resided in a crypt? The writer Auguste Villiers de L'Isle-Adam thus apologized to his friend Gustave Flaubert in 1864 for the plebeian literary tastes of his parents, which barely extended beyond Nostradamus. When a high school teacher from Normandy assigned his students an essay question on Nostradamus a few years later, they staged a mocking show in which the prophet, attired in the requisite robe and pointy hat, sang a ludicrous song about the moon. Such feelings were increasingly widespread.[4]

And yet Bareste was not alone. While many men and women shunned Nostradamus, plenty of respectable individuals and media outlets gravitated toward a phenomenon that they deemed meaningful, intriguing, or full of opportunities—and unseemly as well. If Bareste plays such an important role in this story, it is because he helped anchor Nostradamus in a media culture that remained its strongest base and would now reshape it for public consumption. He also captures the allure of these prophecies and magical thinking in modern times while displaying the ambivalence that accompanied this fascination in middle-class circles. Could moderns believe in prophecies? Could they live with the supernatural vapors, the plebeian passions, and the commercial excess that Nostradamus more than any other soothsayer now embodied? And could they come to terms with their own contradictory urges and feelings? *La Phalange*'s question escaped easy answers, but perhaps there was a way. Bareste certainly thought so.

⁓◌◌⁓

Eugène Bareste was born in Paris in 1814, during the twilight of Napoléon's empire. Despite his modest background (his father was a locksmith), he resolved at a young age to write for a living. Such careers now beckoned in ways that they could not have in earlier centuries, when fewer people were literate, guilds controlled book production, publishers paid little, and intellectual property remained a hazy concept. Without benefactors, writers struggled. The French Revolution upended things by outlawing guilds, ending censorship, and enshrining the rights of authors in law. Publishers took advantage of this new climate and exploited new technologies to quadruple book production and diversify their offerings. The print market exploded, and the daily press took off as well. An American visitor remarked in 1838 that a Parisian breakfast now consisted of coffee, an omelet, and a newspaper. Another American explained that Parisians could no longer be described as a population of talkers. They had become a community of readers. Eager to boost sales and lure advertisers, newspaper editors began publishing commentaries, reviews, and travel accounts along with news reports. This demand for new material created unprecedented opportunities for journalists and writers.[5]

Bareste published his first book (about admirable workers) in 1834. He was twenty years old. During the years that followed, he contributed varied pieces to periodicals and for a while managed a newspaper in the Champagne region. He also headed an arts journal, reviewed art shows, and curated an exhibit at the Louvre. This cultural jack-of-all-trades made up in stamina what he lacked in expertise or superlative talent. In 1840, Bareste turned to Nostradamus. His book provided a comprehensive take on the man and his prophecies, with a biography, an essay on prophecy, and interpretations of selected quatrains that he organized around key historical events. Around the same time, Bareste launched the *Prophetic, Picturesque, and Useful Almanac,* a paperback-size publication with a thin yellow cover. Nostradamus surfaced in many articles as well as the full title: *Published by the Author of "Nostradamus"* or (after 1853) *Published by a Nephew of Nostradamus.* Nostradamus was both a source of material and a name that needed little introduction. The almanac took off at once and came out every year until 1895. "Most of the concierges have heard of Nostradamus," an English magazine reported, "and it fills them with a species of awe to discover that the *Prophetic Almanack* is edited by a nephew of the famous sayer of prophecies."[6]

It was not just concierges. While Nostredame had faded behind the prophets Mother Shipton and Nixon in Great Britain, his prophecies about Varennes and other episodes of the French Revolution retained such a deep hold on French minds that contemporaries equated them with the resurgence of divination. The French no longer believe in ghosts, an abbot declared in 1811, but now they believe in Nostradamus and horoscopes. The *New York Commercial Advertiser* agreed that all kinds of people had been parsing his predictions during the past twenty years. Many inquired about Napoléon Bonaparte, the modest Corsican who had risen through the ranks in the 1790s, achieved resounding victories, become consul, and then ruled France and parts of Europe as emperor until 1815. This saga was the first of several events that drew a new generation toward the quatrains. "Near Italy an Emperor shall be born / Who shall cost the empire a pretty pence": these lines from quatrain 1.60 joined the ranks of his most-quoted predictions. So did another line that seemed to predict Napoléon's ascent: "From simple soldier he shall race to power" (8.57). People turned to Nostradamus for confirmation of the emperor's rise or fall and for insight into what lay ahead for the ruler and his country. In 1813, an imprisoned French soldier reportedly told the crown prince of Sweden that Nostradamus had predicted the emperor's demise, the return of the Bourbons, their own downfall, and then mayhem. In Provence later that decade, a veteran of the Napoleonic Wars grew intrigued by an apocryphal Nostradamian quatrain about a small man and his tomb. Might this relate to the emperor's death? The veteran could not be sure, so he wrote the quatrain on his mantelpiece and then added: "To check." By that time, rumor had it that Napoléon himself had consulted Nostradamus.[7]

The veteran came across this quatrain in his village, when he saw a boy reading a flimsy chapbook filled with such prophecies. It may have been *The French Prophet by Nostradamus, The Great and Double Nostradamus,* or any of the countless low-cost publications that now revolved around the prophet. There were even regional titles such as the *Nostradamus lillois,* named after the city of Lille. The French market for popular print remained ultracompetitive, with innumerable serials, brochures, and engravings sold each year by peddlers, booksellers, and grocers. Publishers targeted a wide readership by reprinting old titles and adapting them to present times. *The New and True Prognostications by Michel Nostradamus for Five Years,* to name but one, provided apocryphal quatrains that, they claimed, came straight from the tomb. The main French purveyor of popular print, publisher Nicolas Pellerin, sold his edition of the *Prophecies of Michel Nostradamus* for a franc and a half, the same price as the *Life of Jesus-Christ* and Aesop's *Fables.* (Workers earned about two francs a day at this time.) In the Vosges, near the Swiss border, the *Prophecies of Nostradamus* had a fifteen-hundred-copy print run for the month of November 1853 alone. This put it among the top five in that region of France.[8]

Bareste was no doubt familiar with such publications, but he lived in a different world: a middlebrow realm that set itself apart from both popular and aristocratic cultures. Here, encyclopedias, newspapers, and magazines embraced reason, progress, and learning, and then packaged them as respectable entertainment for lawyers, doctors, and civil servants—along with shopkeepers, employees, and some nobles. Periodicals such as Charles Dickens's *Household Words* and the *Musée des familles*—the *New Yorkers* and *Newsweeks* of the day—offered historical tales and geography lessons with dollops of current events and sprinklings of fiction. By the 1830s, some of them published articles about prophecy, divination, and Nostradamus.

Middlebrow culture included almanacs as well, though not the low-end ones sold by Pellerin. Publishers modernized an old genre by adding material found in the likes of *Household Words.* "Almanacs have undergone a complete transformation," explained one French official. "They are now real books, full of scientific treatises, considerations on art trades, historical essays—with millions of copies sold." In today's marketing lingo, we might say that publishers were differentiating their product. It was now possible to buy astronomical, agronomical, theatrical, or comical almanacs. Some were aimed at sailors, others at ladies or gardeners. A journalist commented that these publications were entering every recess of society, from the porter's nook and the smoke-filled garret to the mistress's salon and the statesman's office. Bareste's Parisian publishers understood all this. On the Left Bank, Laurent-Antoine Pagnerre sold his almanacs in a small store whose windows were covered with placards. On the Right Bank, the Aubert bookshop stocked them in a brightly lit establishment that overflowed with prints and books of all sizes. To broaden their readership, both of them kept the price of the almanac low (fifty centimes). They also provided more than calendars and feast days, as their publication's full title—*Prophetic, Picturesque and Useful Almanac*—made clear. The *prophetic* encompassed all kinds of articles on the future and the supernatural, from divination to numerological codes. The *picturesque* revolved around odd events, humorous tales, and strange anecdotes. The *useful*, finally, included practical advice and instructive articles on history or political economy. The cover page's motto "Education, improvement, progress" said it all. This was not your grandfather's almanac.[9]

✧

Bareste's book and almanac came out during turbulent times in France. After seizing power, Napoléon had redrawn French legal codes, administrative frameworks, and religious institutions. The man who claimed to have made France a century older (and that much more stable) in four years also embroiled the country in endless wars that led to his downfall. The Bourbon dynasty returned from exile in 1815, governed the country for fifteen years, and then fell victim to a revolution that brought a liberal monarch named Louis-Philippe to power in 1830. The 1830s and 1840s were tense and polarized decades, filled with strikes, riots, plots, and attempts on the king's life. Around 1840, the government responded to political and economic volatility by making a rightward, bellicose turn. Ministers promised to expand

France's natural boundaries to the Rhine and warned Great Britain about its ties to the Ottoman Empire. As new fortifications were built around Paris, war between France and England began to seem inevitable. The *Prophetic Almanac* depicted a French society in agony, dragged down by paralyzed politicians, mediocre thinkers, and bankrupt businessmen. "If Europeans have grown so interested in prophecies these past years," it explained in 1841, "it is because all social classes are suffering while awaiting a better future."[10]

A magistrate from Aix went farther a few years later: "French society is in such turmoil; there is so much uncertainty . . . that our entire curiosity focuses upon the future and more precisely its secrets and mysteries." All kinds of prophecies spoke of disasters, the monarchy's overthrow, and even the end of the world around 1840. In the mid-1810s, the archangel Raphael had appeared before a peasant and announced two decades of calamities—until 1840. In the late 1830s, the so-called Orval prophecy (a forgery) garnered considerable attention in France. It featured an obscure monk who predicted the king's fall and the advent of a Great Monarchy that would unite European powers while returning England to Catholicism. "Several old prophecies, particularly of Nostradamus, refer to the year 1840 as the season of wonderful events," the English banker and dandy Thomas Raikes observed while visiting Paris. Close to twenty publications by or about Nostradamus came out within a few years. Quatrain 9.89 seemed to depict recent and future happenings:

Fortune shall favor Philip seven years,	Sept ans sera Philip. fortune prospere,
He shall put the Arabs back in their place :	Rabaissera des Arabes l'effaict,
Then down south he shall suffer a reverse :	Puis son mydi perplex rebors affaire
A young Ogmion his power shall erase.	Jeusne ognyon abysmera son fort.

This was the quatrain's meaning: after seven years of prosperity, during which the monarchy would put down uprisings in colonial Algeria, the French king would fall to a rival politician, either a royalist or Napoléon's nephew. Bareste contributed to this vatic enthusiasm by publishing articles on prophecy in 1839. He linked the number 40, long deemed momentous, to the year to come, and prefaced a prophetic collection that ranged from the monk of Orval to Philippe Dieudonné Noël Olivarius, an imagined sixteenth-century astrologer who had reportedly foreseen the advent of Napoléon. A year later, he turned to Nostradamus.[11]

Bareste would not have done so with such energy if he did not seek to infuse elemental mysteries and magical thinking into an arid, skeptical, materialistic society. He was not alone. Another man of letters, Victor Fournel, evoked this widespread yearning: "Mystery is always alluring; obscurity with its visions, true or false, both fascinates and frightens us. We like the dizzying depths of the abyss and the revelations of the unknown." The new century, Fournel added, relishes "the shudder of fear." Such sentiments went back to Renaissance pamphlets and horrific plays, but contemporaries now felt chilling yet thrilling tremors while contemplating the immensity of nature, the mysteries of the world, and the fall of civilizations. This was the Romantic sublime: an intimate encounter with terrifyingly beautiful and unmasterable forces. Remote admiration and rational judgment faded behind awe and dread as one became aware of oneself as a tormented, mortal, but acutely sentient being. Prophecies that sprouted from a distant past and pointed toward an infinite future could generate such feelings. So it was with Nostradamus, whose scintillating beauty resided in evocative words, grandiose horizons, and morbid legends. An uncorrupted poetic vein shot up from an underground well deep within the core of civilization. Beyond folklore and the soft glow of nostalgia, Nostradamus's primeval simplicity promised to revivify a sterile industrial age.[12]

Prophecy was not politically innocent, however. Radicals were drawn to a millennial platform that announced a new democratic era of brotherly love. Reactionaries, in contrast, sought to overcome the calamitous effects of the French Revolution by returning to a golden era in which the Church and the Bourbon monarchy governed France. Around 1840, a French prosecutor denounced a *Book of Prophecies* that displayed affection for the fallen Bourbons. Nostradamus could not escape such associations. The counterrevolutionary theorist Joseph de Maistre drew from his predictions to argue that the revolution had launched a sequence of events that would culminate with the restoration of the monarchy. A leading royalist newspaper did the same while condemning a corrupt and doomed liberal era. As Nostradamus continued its move to the political right, people on the left accused his followers of manipulating quatrains to announce catastrophic events. "They take on the mien of prophecy to gain ascendancy over the populace," explained one critic. Some officials shared these concerns and forbade almanacs and pamphlets that bore Nostradamus's name.[13]

Bareste, too, winked in the direction of the right and the Bourbon dynasty. He insisted that Nostradamus had predicted a bloodthirsty revolution followed by a disastrous half century. He also selected several quatrains that, in his view, announced the king's demise. "By avarice, by force & violence / The chief of Orléans will come to vex his supporters" (quatrain 8.42). According to Bareste this chief was King Louis-Philippe, heir of the Orléans family. And yet Bareste's politics fluctuated during these decades. Before pining for a pre-Enlightenment world, he had mourned the Napoleonic empire and embraced freedom of the press. When the Republican left returned to power in 1848, he defended free education and equal pay for women. Perhaps Bareste was politically cautious. Perhaps his convictions evolved over time. Or perhaps his professional disappointment morphed into animosity against the regime in power. However that may be, the *Prophetic Almanac* welcomed contributors from many political schools. It proved as varied in its politics as in its contents and readership.[14]

Beyond prophetic enthusiasm, beyond politics, Bareste expected that a public association with Nostradamus would bring personal rewards. He lived in the age of Chateaubriand and Victor Hugo, beacons who ignited literary ambitions in all corners of France. Thousands of young would-be writers sought glory, influence, and wealth in the capital. Honoré de Balzac devoted one of his best novels, *Lost Illusions,* to the tribulations of a provincial who moved to Paris in order to write and make something of himself. Bareste's literary aspirations were not as defined. He published a novella and essays, but neither plays and poems (the conventional pathways to literary glory) nor novels (the new route). Still, he sought success within a universe in which smarts, ideas, and convictions rarely sufficed on their own. Like so many hopeful writers, Balzac's protagonist failed to conquer Paris. Money and connections proved indispensable, and so did a fine understanding of the literary realm's unwritten rules.[15]

Bareste was a small fish in the Parisian literary pond, a scribbler with sundry publications but scant recognition or success. He joined the new Society of Men of Letters, founded to defend the rights and interests of writers, because he saw himself as one of them. In fact, he signed letters "Eugène

Bareste, man of letters." In 1840, he published an annotated translation of Homer's *Odyssey*, which his publisher advertised as faithful and elegant. He also planned a history of Homeric times that, he said, would appeal to historians, archaeologists, and ordinary readers. In the mid-1840s, he toured German universities on behalf of the French Ministry of Education. Bareste entertained serious ambitions; intellectual recognition mattered. But so did money. It was partly due to financial pressures that he hopped from one literary venture to another. He requested several loans from the Society of Men of Letters, promising to reimburse them as soon as his advances came in. "I absolutely need a reply today or tomorrow at the latest for I am completely penniless," he once wrote the society's secretary.[16]

In order to achieve his twin ambitions, Bareste sought something that could pay dividends while coming across as learned or useful. Like Jean-Aimé de Chavigny and so many others afterward, he settled on Nostradamus. His publisher Laurent-Antoine Pagnerre likewise balanced personal convictions and commercial imperatives. As a political radical, he released popular almanacs that would educate and politicize readers while entertaining them. Around 1850, visitors to his bookstore could find left-wing politicians such as Alphonse de Lamartine and Louis Blanc working on a back table. As a businessman, however, Pagnerre published all sorts of low- and middlebrow almanacs for the French and foreign markets, from the *Picturesque Almanac* to the *Literary and Theatrical Almanac* to the *New Nostradamus*. In the 1860s, he was still printing close to thirty thousand copies of these almanacs each month. The sales potential could not have escaped Bareste, who, like many Nostradamian providers, was trying to make it financially and to improve his position while starting out at the bottom. One finds similar profiles among contemporary mediums, turn-of-the-century occultists, and twentieth-century astrologers and astropsychologists. The self-educated Robert Smith, a product of Bristol's working class and a contemporary of Bareste, made a name for himself as the magus and astrologer Raphael. In France, where it had generated a tradition of providers, the Nostradamus phenomenon promised success, authority, and perhaps a special kind of renown for individuals whose careers had stalled or never taken off.[17]

All of this carried risks within this middlebrow world. Surrounded by ghosts, wizards, and common folk, Nostradamus was both enticing and unbecoming. The Anthropological Society of London reported that fishermen from Dunkirk had found a fish with the semblance of a human head, deemed it a presage, and linked it to Nostradamus. This was not the company Bareste wished to keep. His challenge was to embrace Nostradamus while preserving his social standing, his reputation, and his self-image. It was to reassure readers—troubled by their own curiosity—by convincing them that they had not veered off the deep end. And it was to sell Nostradamus without sacrificing enrichment to mere entertainment. I am not a *"Nostradamite,"* Bareste promised, "and even less *illuminated.*" Saying so was a good start. So was distinguishing his publications from "trash pamphlets that litter the streets." But Bareste knew that this was not enough. He would have to set himself apart from Nostradamites in a more explicit fashion.[18]

Nostradamites made brash predictions about an ominous future. Bareste, in contrast, spoke prudently—as if using such tools to anticipate what lay ahead broke with the measured language of reason and progress. To be sure, his *Nostradamus* and *Prophetic Almanac* mentioned conflagrations, bankruptcies, and other "fatal events" to come. Some contributors uttered traditional warnings about divine ire or else tapped the eschatological fervor of British evangelicals and certain French Catholics. While these movements understood prophecy, the Antichrist, and the imminent return of Jesus Christ in different ways, all sought to process the rise and fall of Napoléon or industrialization through a language of expiation and regeneration that they found in the book of Revelation and prophecies such as Nostradamus's. The *Prophetic Almanac* likewise claimed in 1841 that humanity was nearing a pivotal moment during which it would "shiver, suffer, and tremble." All of this would speak to these people who were now filling notebooks with considerations on the quatrains and France's apocalyptic travails. Still, apocalyptic predictions were rare in these publications. Bareste presented prophecies about the destruction of Paris as thought-provoking rather than conclusive. He also devoted more pages to ancient prophecies and current events than he did to the future. Given the number of almanacs that had drawn mistaken conclusions from Nostradamus, it was best to wait and see which quatrains came true. The *Prophetic Almanac*'s editors singled out prophetic impos-tures and refrained from publishing dire predictions to avoid coming across as irresponsible doomsayers. It was not all about a gloomy future.[19]

Nostradamites furthermore approached the quatrains with credulity and biases. They sensationalized and ridiculed the man by departing from his life story and accomplishments. Bareste, in contrast, gave the phenomenon thoughtful consideration. He situated Nostradamus in a long continuum, clarified his language through close grammatical study, and recovered his biography by delving into ancient sources. "Everyone speaks about Nostradamus, and yet no one knows him," he explained while depicting Nostredame as a devoted doctor and devout prophet whose predictions had sometimes come true. To make him respectable, he coupled divination with scientific veracity and a thirst for curiosities that had become a mainstay of middlebrow media. Just as magazines and newspapers fed their readers a diet of strange but true occurrences, so Bareste presented the quatrains as "curious" entities full of coincidences and puzzling correlations. Antiquaries, librarians, bibliophiles, paleographers, and other learned contemporaries would no doubt enjoy this unusual work. And Bareste himself would become their interlocutor—the first respectable heir of Nostredame in modern times.[20]

Nostradamites, finally, approached the quatrains with mindless enthusiasm. Bareste, in contrast, came across as convinced, inquisitive, didactic, and even amused. He and other contributors to the *Prophetic Almanac* did not commit to a single voice or a single understanding of what Nostredame had said about the human condition. Instead, they tiptoed around the predictions. They considered them through one perspective after another or through several perspectives at once. Readers could not anticipate how each successive article in the *Almanac* would discuss Nostradamus and predictions. Sometimes it was straightforward prophecy. Sometimes it was historical analysis. And sometimes it was something in between. Contributors would sometimes share a prediction and then declare that it might not be true after all. "Before ending our publication, dear reader, we must become less serious (assuming that we had been serious for a moment)," one of them declared. "If future events sadden us, let us laugh while waiting for prophecies to come true." Other articles announced tongue in cheek that judges would no longer sleep in law courts during the year to come and that couples would cease bickering.[21]

This was not the first time that moderns had gently mocked almanacs and prognostications in this fashion. In 1757, *The Modern Nostradamus* had provided a calendar while poking fun at this predictive enterprise: "There is no point in warning readers not to believe the *Oracles of the New Nostradamus*." By the nineteenth century, such publications often embraced irony. Writers and artists were struggling to reconcile dreams of glory with the demands of a new cultural industry that turned them into journalists or illustrators—mere workers for hire. The market had its rewards, but it also flattened aesthetic originality and moral autonomy. Irony seemed to provide a way out, for it enabled writers and artists to participate in this cultural marketplace while telling their audience—and convincing themselves—that they did not really buy into it. Aware of what was going on in this materialistic world, they remained independent, principled, honorable, and perhaps even pure. Irony could similarly defuse unease about one's interest in Nostradamus and the supernatural. Sure, I like Nostradamus, Bareste seemed to tell his readers. Sure, I am awed by magical powers. But rest assured: I am not fooled. I am no Nostradamite and neither are you.[22]

All of these maneuvers—learning, curiosity, irony—were ultimately about the same thing: exploring Nostradamus, mysteries, and dark recesses while maintaining a safe distance. By steering clear of irrational forces, Bareste bolstered his cultural status as a responsible citizen. By resisting popular inclinations, he outlined his social status as a member of an enlightened middle class. And by detaching himself from the market, he shored up his professional and moral status as a writer. It was not just Bareste. *Fraser's Magazine for Town and Country,* a London periodical, reported on Nostradamus's predictions for 1840 with a straight face but soon promised to cease scanning the future. The journalist assured his readers, and no doubt himself as well, that he was no "superstitious dreamer" who believed in a strange seer from ancient times. Moderns, too, could appreciate the quatrains without endorsing divination. They could have a Nostradamus that suited their times.[23]

❧

The first two editions of Bareste's *Nostradamus* sold out within months. Parisian newspapers ran reviews, provincial ones published excerpts, and foreign periodicals reported on this burst of interest in Germany, England, and the United States. *Notes and Queries,* a staid English journal, presented his book as the go-to source on Nostradamus. Bareste's widely advertised *Prophetic Almanac* proved a bigger success yet, with sales of one hundred thousand copies per year. Bareste claimed to have five times as many readers, which is possible. One newspaper reported that no one in France could escape this almanac. Bareste's 1844 stopover in Toulon, for instance, created considerable stir among local residents. Four years later, a French journalist remarked that people now carried three or four prophecies in their pockets and that no writer had derived more notoriety from this trend than Bareste, whom he called Barestadamus. This word had surfaced in the *Almanac*'s publicity posters and then stuck. Bareste had made a name for himself, albeit one that was not entirely his own.[24]

Bareste obtained such success because he met the expectations of many readers. Another relationship to Nostradamus was now coming into its own, and he felt its pulse. While his publications spoke to decoders, awed beholders, and persons of leisure, they were also tailored to those whom we might call ambivalent readers. These men and women delved into the prophetic realm with the same mix of curiosity and self-consciousness as Bareste, the same reservations and shifting convictions, and ultimately the same need for distance. Rather than believing *in* Nostradamus, we might say that they believed *with* him, taking a peek (or more) without fully embracing the phenomenon and its powers.

This stance had slowly built up over the centuries. Soon after Nostredame's death, a French lawyer told a friend that, while he gave little credit to his wild predictions, three lines in quatrain 3.55 had clearly come true while the fourth foretold further commotion. In 1698, a diplomat wrote that he was both curious and dubious about the blacksmith's encounter with the ghost. By this time, some thinkers suggested openly that belief did not have to be an all-or-nothing proposition. People could believe in different entities with variable degrees of intensity. There was a hazy zone between belief and unbelief, filled with individuals who believed in some unseen forces and not others, or in some forces with greater confidence than in others. "One can be skeptical on one side, and credulous on the other," declared the philosopher Gottfried Leibniz. He then provided an example: a prominent theatrical engineer believed in Nostredame's prophecies but not in the Bible's. This stance became more prevalent as the supernatural grew more intriguing and less acceptable in certain circles. By the early nineteenth century, it captured a widespread relationship to Nostradamus.[25]

This relationship was not always public, however. Many people were too embarrassed to consult the quatrains outside their homes. If pressed, they might even deny doing so privately. Such furtive readings rarely enter historical records, but traces surface here and there. Traveling through France in 1785, a Polish count met numerous well-to-do individuals with a public passion for science or literature and a private one for supernatural activities. Following the French Revolution, several commentators noted that even gentlemen and ladies were paying secret visits to the fortune-tellers whom they purportedly scorned. While reflecting on the success of Nostradamus and popular almanacs in the 1850s, the journalist Victor Fournel wrote that "for all the airs of superiority and disdain one might put on," everyone now reads these predictions, "and, for shame, no one dares to admit it." It would appear that such modes of reading have endured or even swelled since that time. We laugh at Nostradamus's prophecies, wrote the *Atlanta Constitution* in 1941, "but secretly practically every one has more or less faith in them."[26]

Ambivalent readers were not necessarily convinced that these prophecies really did predict the future. Many could not tell. Others harbored magical thoughts, or engaged in forms of behavior that they could not understand or that they struggled to reconcile with such core values of the modern West as personal control, autonomy, self-mastery, and disdain for ancient superstition. This is why, like people who touch wood for good luck, they turned to the quatrains without fully committing to their efficacy. They hedged and waffled and belittled their own behavior. The Scottish countess who had asked her reverend what Nostradamus had to say about current events in the late eighteenth century also apologized to him for what she called small talk. Sociologists refer to this attitude—at once serious and skeptical, captivated and doubtful—as half-belief. In some cases, the lure is not so much what predictions say as the ritual activities that surround them: parsing obscure words, consulting interpretations, discussing their meaning. Whether Nostradamus was right or not is beside the point. Despite its uncertain status, the phenomenon could bolster confidence in one's ability to act purposively and intervene in the world.[27]

It also enabled people to play with their own fears by casting sideways glances at ghastly or stupendous events. Some did so to escape a tedious existence or feel the frisson of safe transgression. Some were dazzled by the kind of artful deception that was at play in circuses and other forms of modern entertainment, a deception that generated feelings of curiosity and bewilderment. Some sought to control their mortality. And some inched closer to what proved frightening in the outside world and perhaps within themselves as well, grasping these things tightly to better defuse them. Play has long attenuated anxiety by keeping true horrors at bay and providing a controlled setting in which people can toy with ideas and sensations. This sensibility, too, has grown more prevalent in modern times. In the late 1930s, young Diesbach de Belleroche, the bank director's son, felt "a thrill of fear" while listening to adults discussing Nostradamus's darkest predictions. It took him decades, however, to name his feelings and recognize that a distant, partial, playful relationship with fear could provide relief as well as pleasure.[28]

The Nostradamian universe, this open and over-the-top province in which everything is incredible yet possible, lends itself admirably to ambivalent readings. Individuals can decide on their own what status to give to predictions that might or might not have true historical origins. The contribution of Bareste and other journalists was to draw this ambivalence into middlebrow media and provide it all: history and legend, past and future, reason and mystery, dismay and reassurance, straight interpretations and quizzical riffs. Bareste helped create a safe space in which a self-consciously modern culture could make Nostradamus its own. He told his readers that they could trust his prophecies, but did not have to. They were free to accept what they wanted, wait a while before coming to a decision, or, if they preferred, not decide at all. They could dabble, experiment, and go as far as as they wished while probing their fears and learning to live with them. This was his answer to *La Phalange*'s question. Serious people could indeed believe in prophecies. They could do so when and how they desired. And nobody had to know.

In 1848, France went through another revolution. Bathed in egalitarian and fraternal fervor, this rapid affair brought the Republican left to power for the first time since the French Revolution. Within months, however, half the country was hankering for order and security. This included the new president, Louis-Napoléon, who took France in a conservative direction. When his term neared its end, in 1851, he proclaimed himself emperor and, following in the footsteps of his uncle, took the name of Napoléon III. Prophecies flourished during these chaotic years. "More than ever we pose questions to the future," explained one almanac. "We ask it to illuminate the present, so agitated, so full of thick clouds." Nostradamus garnered new visibility as well.[29]

Bareste planned a ten-thousand-copy run of his book under a new title: *The Political Prophecies of Michel Nostradamus on Red Republicans and Socialists*. The fate of this venture is unclear (I have not located any surviving copies), but Bareste saw other opportunities in this new era. Days after the revolution, he founded a left-wing newspaper that defended political equality, free schooling, and freedom of speech. *La République* endured for three years despite police raids, fines, and even prison time for Bareste, who was accused of defying censorship laws. When the authorities banned the newspaper in 1851, Bareste had had enough. He decided to leave politics, literature, and prophecy behind and devoted the last decade of his life to business ventures. If he now consulted Nostradamus, he did so privately.[30]

Eugène Bareste might not have moved on if his ventures had fulfilled his expectations. Yes, his almanacs sold well, but he did not earn enough to erase his debts. Yes, Bareste acquired a measure of fame, but he did not secure the recognition that he craved so intensely. Some newspapers mocked "Eugène Bareste de Nostradamus." A satirical dictionary mapped with unvarnished cruelty the distance between his ambitions and the place he occupied in the intellectual world. In antiquity, it said, Homer had composed the *Iliad*. In the seventeenth century, playwright Thomas Corneille had penned *The Cid*. As for the nineteenth century, well, it had Bareste and his almanacs. This dictionary grasped the strains of a prophetic venture that, like middlebrow culture in general, carved uneasy paths between reason and magic, between popular and elite cultures, between market forces and respectability. While Bareste's open-ended approach resonated with readers, he also came across as too zealous and too coy, too erudite and too mercenary.[31]

Bareste and his almanac nonetheless achieved something of importance, something that endures to this day. They helped crystallize a way of exploring Nostradamus, a way of living with magical forces that many people could not fully accept, a way of resolving the inherent contradictions of a century that saw itself as modern. Writers shed irony once they accepted the market and viewed journalism as a profession rather than a substitute for literary aspirations. This happened in the second half of the nineteenth century. But things were different when it came to divination and magical thinking. Whether in Paris, London, or New York, all kinds of media outlets continued to tap Bareste's mix of proximity and distance. They provided quatrains and interpretations, praised the prophet's wisdom or style, found confirmation of current events, and warned of dangers ahead. But they also kept their "old friend Nostradamus" at a safe remove. Some did so by recognizing the limitations of such propheteering and adopting a guarded approach. "Let us essay a quatrain or two," the periodical *All the Year Round* cautiously proposed. Others acknowledged that readers would believe only a few prophecies. Still others focused on the talented interpretations rather than the original predictions. All agreed, however, that citizens should arrive at their own opinion about this perplexing matter. "Let our readers judge for themselves," intoned *Household Words*.[32]

These Nostradamian providers did not simply follow seventeenth-century publishers and invite readers to elucidate the meaning of the *Prophecies*. They now allowed their readers to determine on their own what status, what truth-value Nostradamus deserved. They left the matter open (or at least claimed to do so). This ambivalence would endure in a modern media culture that coupled seriousness of tone with laughter or incredulity. Countless newspapers continued to discuss quatrains with ostensible earnestness before conceding that fervent followers alone fully believed such obscure, sinister predictions. One of them, the *Chicago Daily Tribune*, did so in 1941 by framing its interpretation of Nostradamus as hypothetical and then striking a familiar note. Predictions about forty years of blight rattled the mind, said the journalist. "But there is one thing fortunate," he added, as if channeling *La Phalange*'s question and the answer that Bareste had provided. "We don't have to believe it."[33]

Chapter 10

※⁂※

Fin de Siècle Madness

Eugène Bareste outlined one way of living with Nostradamus in the modern world. But when the journalist turned businessman died in 1861, this world was on the cusp of unprecedented changes. People from all walks of life could travel faster and farther than before by hopping on a train. They could acquire and exchange information via telegraphs, the postal service, and cheap newspapers. Strolling down avenues and boulevards, they found themselves surrounded by throngs of people, advertisements, and luminous window displays. There was "noise, commotion, life everywhere," wrote one novelist about the new cosmopolis and the maelstrom of stimuli that now surrounded and unnerved urban dwellers. In the realm of politics, recently empowered voters attended rallies and public funerals, participated in demonstrations, and sometimes went on strike. Amorphous crowds seemed to propel history. Time appeared to move faster than ever before. The West was becoming a mass society.[1]

Was there a place for Nostradamus in this beguiling and unsettling universe? Absolutely. The name was all over the media and jumped to attention every fifteen years or so, in the wake of some crises and in anticipation of others. Around 1900, Europeans and Americans read about Nostradamus in dailies, prophetic pamphlets, and dime novels. They watched him at play in magic shows and short films. They drew from his superlative powers while predicting their own future in dream books. And they purchased clocks, thermometers, calendars, and board games bearing his name or likeness. The legendary seer, the quatrains, and the magical overtones were perfectly suited for a world that was both enthused and dismayed by its own modernity, a world in which persuasion and high emotion seemed to overshadow contained reason, a world that wanted to peer into the future without relinquishing individual volition, a world that sought to contain uncertainty without being convinced that this was possible.

But this did not happen on its own. Nostradamus would not have become an enduring facet of mass society if certain individuals had not grasped these promises. Some of them, like the abbot Henri Torné-Chavigny, came from the religious right and a traditional, provincial milieu. Others, like the pulp author Michel Zévaco, were creatures of the secular left and cosmopolitan Paris. The obscure cleric and the bestselling novelist belonged to different worlds, and yet both publicly linked their name to Nostradamus's. Both tapped mass media and publicity to reach broad audiences. And both transformed Nostradamus in momentous ways. The entity that they and others like them fashioned at this time captured some of the modern West's driving urges and anxieties. Not everyone was enthralled with the modern Nostradamus, but it was perfectly at its place.

⁂

Henri Torné-Chavigny loved to recount how he had discovered Nostradamus. It happened in 1858, when the thirty-two-year-old abbot lived in a small parish in southwestern France. One day, bedridden with the flu, he picked up a book that had been sitting unread on his shelf. It was his mother's worn copy of the *Prophecies*. He turned the pages absentmindedly, paying little attention until he came across a quatrain that seemed to foretell a recent attempt on the life of Napoléon III. Torné-Chavigny sat up. Could Nostredame have been right? He grabbed a pen and decided to draw crosses next to the quatrains that he could link to past events. By the time he was done, 127 of them filled the margins of his book. There was but one explanation: Nostredame had imitated the book of Revelation, he had left prophecies of biblical scope, and he had called upon Torné-Chavigny, the humble dyer's son, to clarify their meaning for his countrymen.[2]

Nostradamus became Torné-Chavigny's lifelong pursuit. He conducted research in libraries across Europe, acquired more than 120 editions of the *Prophecies,* pored over them in his study, and wrote detailed analyses of important quatrains. His method of interpretation, which he called *adaptation,* consisted in tabulating and then correlating all uses of a given word in the book in order to uncover its recurring meaning. *Oemathion* hence designated Louis XIV. In 1860, Torné-Chavigny published the first of many booklets laying out his interpretations. Others came out at a steady clip during the 1860s and 1870s, along with an occasional *Almanac of the Great Prophet.* In 1874, he left his parish for Paris. Only there could he complete his mission.[3]

The abbot's turn toward Nostradamus both drew from and contributed to a spike of interest in the quatrains. In the United States, for instance, a Nostradamus prediction about the Civil War grew ubiquitous between 1861 and 1865. It was a fake (which few people noticed) and announced that "a great quarrel and contest will arise in a country beyond the seas." After four years of war, "prostrate and almost ruined, the people will embrace each other in great joy and love." Launched by the *Courrier des Etats-Unis,* a newspaper founded by French immigrants to New York, the prediction had spread widely by the end of 1861, when a long conflict seemed likely. Other papers reprinted it and added their own interpretations. The *Wisconsin Patriot:* a new Democratic administration would usher in postwar harmony. The *Columbus Crisis:* Northern Democrats would win as long as they waged a war of necessity rather than hatred. The *Daily True Delta* (New Orleans): if Confederates fought with fortitude, their enemies would embrace them at war's end. Not one of these newspapers referred to Providence or American exceptionalism while relaying this prediction. None claimed that old prophecies about an elect nation destined to become the New Rome were coming true. Instead, journalists borrowed from and competed with one another while tapping Nostradamus as a political expedient and an intriguing news item. Without becoming as permanent a fixture as it was in France, the American Nostradamus worked in similar ways in the news media.[4]

Torné-Chavigny, too, was consumed with civil war, but a French one. Like other Catholics, he believed that France was sliding toward oblivion. Instead of obeying the Bourbons, the royal family that had been unjustly deposed in 1830, the French were following a degenerate emperor. Instead of leading moral lives, they worked on Sundays, played the stock market, and attended decadent operas. When war erupted against Prussia in 1870, they did not stand a chance. Otto von Bismarck obliterated the French forces, sent Napoléon III into exile, occupied a third of France, and annexed two of its provinces. Defeat at the hands of Protestants was humiliating for the once-glorious Catholic power. As the Prussians laid siege to Paris, workers and supporters of the far left set up a government of the people—the Commune—that soon battled the French army in the streets of the capital. Thousands died; large parts of the city went up in flames. The moderate left then outmaneuvered royalists to establish a secular regime—the Third Republic—which Bourbon diehards felt they were left to battle alone. This string of calamities made many Catholics despondent.

Prophecies flourished—hundreds of them. Georges Bois, a Parisian student who had sought refuge in the Champagne countryside, saw villagers consult all sorts of predictions about the destiny of France. Nostradamus seemed to surface everywhere, and Bois, too, grew intrigued by the quatrains. A German writer who lived in France in the mid-1870s, Bertha von Suttner, distilled this mood in one of her novels. "The country fell into wild despair," she wrote. "People began to hunt in Nostradamus to find prophecies for the present events, and new seers began to put out fresh predictions." Some people grew so alarmed by quatrain 3.84 that they refused to set foot in Paris. It was dire indeed:

The great city shall be quite desolate :	La grand cité sera bien desolée,
No single inhabitant shall remain :	Des habitans un seul n'y demourra :
Its walls & women, churches & nuns raped,	Mur, sexe, temple, & vierge violée,
All dying by sword, fire, cannon, plague.	Par fer, feu, peste, canon peuple mourra.

One journalist claimed to have encountered many people who believed in Nostradamus with greater confidence than they did in the Gospels. Others read the quatrains and found intimations of a reckoning for the fallen nation. By repenting and expiating their guilt, the elect could obtain salvation and usher in the reign of Christ on earth. A renovated church, a restored monarchy, a new moral order—all of this loomed. Millennialism thrived once again.[5]

Torné-Chavigny's booklets were all the rage, said Georges Bois. The abbot found innumerable signs of the Last Days in the quatrains, from Napoléon's bloody battles to the Italian campaigns that weakened the papacy's temporal power. He then predicted the deaths of Italian king Victor Emmanuel II and Pope Pius IX and the return of the French Bourbons under a legitimate king, the comte de Chambord, who would rule as Henri V. This clear, transcendent framework ordered chaotic events while signaling the end of a century-long civil war. It also fed royalist dreams of victory by reactivating the old messianic notion of the Great Monarch as savior. The abbot was not the only one to reclaim Nostradamus in this fashion: all kinds of people did so in articles, songs, and ten-centime pamphlets. But none turned Nostradamus against the Third Republic with as much vigor as Torné-Chavigny. He captured not only the anguish and desolation but also the fiery self-confidence of Catholics who refused to bow before secular reason. Shining forth from his tomb, Nostradamus's prophetic light would blind materialism and disbelief. Like others, Bois found echoes of his own "hotheaded and unrelenting" royalism in the writings of Torné-Chavigny. Nostradamus's political arrogation by elements of the Catholic right was now complete in France.[6]

The fearless abbot resolved to fight secular heretics and the republic on their own ground. Lobbying conservative deputies and aristocrats would not suffice. In Paris, he went after left-wing intellectuals and freethinkers. One day, it was Ernest Renan, the controversial historian who had depicted Jesus as a charismatic leader rather than the son of God. Another day, it was Victor Hugo, novelist and political radical. Torné-Chavigny followed the same plan each time: "I will find him, my old Nostradamus in hand, and he will be forced to acknowledge prophecy and miracles." The black-frocked abbot dropped by during receiving hours and offered to discuss an author whom he had been studying for years. When his host smiled upon hearing this author's name—this happened every time—Torné-Chavigny was ready with a retort: "With a verse I will shake your skepticism and in five minutes I will make you believe in Nostradamus." He then pulled out his old edition of the *Prophecies* and explained how quatrain 8.46—"Cock vs. eagle, three French brothers wait"—illuminated the fates of France's recent kings. Having sowed doubt (or at least aroused curiosity) in his host's mind, he pounced with one of the famed verses about Napoléon. Torné-Chavigny was just getting started. Jumping from one quatrain to another, he stretched his five minutes into two hours.[7]

The abbot comes across as the kind of lunatic that Nostradamus conjures up so easily nowadays. Was he not deluded in his belief that Hugo and Renan were enthralled by his performance? Renan paid rapt attention, Torné-Chavigny said, and murmured, "How strange! Your explanations are most clever." Perhaps, but he did not greet Torné-Chavigny when their paths crossed on a Paris street shortly thereafter. Hugo's personal secretary recalled years later that the novelist had listened to this cleric only out of amused benevolence. Whether Torné-Chavigny was insane or not (more about his mental state later), he marshaled the quatrains in a public war of attrition.[8]

~⚬~

Michel Zévaco, in contrast, brought the prophet into a nebulous fictional universe. Three decades younger than the abbot, he had grown up in a military family in Corsica, attended a prestigious Parisian high school, and then bounced around for a while. Penniless after failing his university entrance exam, his name besmirched after a scandalous affair, he became a journalist and ghost writer in the 1880s. He also grew politically active. The young Third Republic was busy restoring France's standing in the world. It revamped the educational system, conquered huge expanses in Africa, and staged grand universal exhibitions. Still, the opposition would not relent. On the right, anti-Semitic nationalists joined Catholic royalists such as Torné-Chavigny to denounce a corrupt, emasculated regime. On the left, radicals accused it of abandoning equality and fraternity. Zévaco joined their ranks, veering from socialism and rabid anticlericalism to staunch anticapitalist anarchism. But two prison sentences and infighting among militants led him to shift course. By 1900, the firebrand had become one of the most famous novelists in France, serialized in major dailies.[9]

Zévaco had worked long enough in journalism to understand how the industry operated. Newspaper publishers now owned their own printing machinery, cut distribution deals with railroad companies, advertised massively, and sold millions of issues at low prices every day. To entice and retain readers, they published crime novels, melodramas, and adventures in serial form.

Zévaco set his historical novels in the sixteenth century. He began each one by researching the topic, filling out hundreds of note cards, and outlining 144 installments of equal length. Then he began writing. He was so good that *Le Matin,* one of the leading Parisian dailies, offered him a six-book contract in 1905. The newspaper had initially followed the American example and marketed itself as a source of news. When sales did not follow, its new owner dropped the newsstand price, placed a premium on entertainment and opinion, and published up to three serials at once, all of them by famous writers. Zévaco's first novel for *Le Matin* earned him a 40 percent raise. He immediately began work on another one, advertised as a "novel full of magic, a novel of love, a swashbuckling novel." It had a one-word title: *Nostradamus.*[10]

The novel, which began publication in the summer of 1907, involved imagined characters alongside historical figures such as Catherine de Médicis. This saga was full of romantic subplots, sword fights, ghastly torture scenes, deceitful villains, and court intrigues. The two main protagonists were the magician Nostredame and his (fictional) son, the dashing, valiant Renaud. After avenging the death of his mother, wrongfully burned at the stake as a witch, Renaud defended his paramour from similar accusations. Zévaco followed the formula of swashbuckling novels: star-crossed lovers, a damsel in distress, a hero triumphing over obstacles, vengeance, and a mysterious world that slowly comes to light. In one of the key scenes, Renaud travels to his father's tomb and unearths his will. The parchment enjoins him to enter the bosom of the Great Sphinx and unveil the secret of the Enigma: "During your descent into the belly of the earth, make for yourself a heart of bronze, a mind of fire, a soul of diamond."[11]

This eerie Nostradamus had made his way from theater fairs and pantomimes to historical plays and novels. In an 1829 melodrama, Nostradamus the consigliore tapped magical forces while warning traitorous dukes that God would seek vengeance. A few years later, Balzac included Nostradamus within Catherine de Médicis's college of astrologers and alchemists. By the end of the century, youth magazines and bestselling romances were depicting a wizard who unraveled all things hidden. Nostradamus was at once a deus ex machina and a magical character that moved the plot forward through spells and predictions. He summoned a fiery Renaissance, caught between political passions and mysterious forces. And he blurred the distinction between the natural and the supernatural.[12]

Zévaco now linked Nostradamus to the occult forces that were gaining so many devotees in middle-class circles. Whether in Europe or in the United States, millions of men and women felt that their spiritual needs were unmet. Science explained everything in materialistic terms, while organized religion rested on unproven miracles and antiquated dogma (such as hell and the savior) that contradicted modern values. These people longed for an enchanted yet secular and egalitarian world in which the uninitiated could feel the presence of unseen powers and connect with the afterworld. Some found this in hypnosis. Others, known as spiritualists, communicated with the dead via mediums, levitation, rapping tables, photographs of ghosts, and other observable phenomena. They sometimes believed in reincarnation, which promised eternal life and improvement for the soul. Yet other people were now searching for hidden wisdom in Hebrew, Egyptian, and Far Eastern doctrines—to which they might add alchemy, numerology, and astrology. Members of the theosophical school thus harvested Western and Eastern traditions to uncover a universal, harmonious, inclusive spirit.[13]

A new occultist milieu was taking form, with its meetings and magazines and public lectures. Zévaco himself had explored rapping tables and the esoteric wisdom of the seventeenth-century Rosicrucian brotherhood while in jail. It is not a coincidence, therefore, that one of his novels features the Great Sphinx of Giza. Occultists were fascinated with an Egyptian civilization that, as they saw it, had been saturated with wisdom, justice, and mysteries that opened onto the afterworld. Egyptian motifs and artifacts could now be found in museums, tarot decks, and orders such as the Hermetic Brotherhood of Luxor. The courageous Renaud ventured into the dark passages of a pyramid in which shrill voices wailed from distant recesses. Like a modern-day Indiana Jones, he overcame maggots and skeletons and chambers whose walls closed in on him. Eventually, three magi launched him on a twenty-one-year initiation into the Supreme Rosicrucian Secret. If successful, Renaud would not only save his loved one but also grasp universal wisdom and master the world.[14]

Nostradamus's relationship with this occultist milieu was anything but

simple, however. Madame Blavatsky, the Russian émigré who had cofounded
the Theosophical Society, praised the astrologer for foreseeing the Crimean
War. Some of her followers likewise depicted Nostredame as a clairvoyant
who believed in reincarnation and attained ecstasy through incantation rituals and kabbalistic lore. Like Hindu scripture, his prophecies announced
that humanity would soon pass from one five-thousand-year cycle (or yuga)
to another. But many occultists and spiritualists had a hard time accepting
Nostradamus. Not only was the Egyptian connection a stretch, but they found
neither secret teachings nor natural laws of history nor verifiable messages
from the dead in the Nostradamian universe. More important, these individuals saw themselves as a spiritual vanguard, probing arcane mysteries that lay
beyond the reach of common folk. Nostradamus was simply too popular, too
low-end. Contemporary astrologers who entertained professional ambitions
felt the same way. Dozens of periodicals—with titles like *Modern Astrology,
Modern Spiritualism,* and *The Occult World*—never mentioned his name at the
turn of the century. Some primers on occultism even distinguished authentic
telepathic perceptions from his ludicrous prophecies. In this domain, too,
collective movements and institutions that aspired to respectability tended to
steer clear of the combustible Nostradamus.[15]

Zévaco did not entertain such high-minded qualms. Perhaps it was because
of his politics. Socialists and utopian thinkers had been combining spiritual
language, social reform, and millennialist hopes for decades. Left-wing currents shared with occultism a belief in hidden truths, the prospect of social
harmony, and faith in a glorious age to come. Some of the men and women who
flocked toward spiritualism did so, similarly, because it turned Catholic dogma
upside down and embraced equality and progress. The *Revue spirite,* founded
by the famed spiritualist Allan Kardec, thus ran articles about eradicating pov-
erty alongside pieces on mediums and divining rods. Spiritual forces could
stem the capitalist tide that was draining modern life of its vital energy.[16]

Belle Époque anarchists and radical artists such as Wassily Kandinsky
frequented occultist circles and were enthralled by what they found:
namely, freedom from bourgeois conventions, pure reason, and materialism. Occult forces and art would draw people out of their lethargy and alter
their outlook on the world. Such convictions, coupled with appreciation for
the sheer force of Nostradamus's language, drew members of the avant-garde

toward a Renaissance poet who had anticipated their own efforts to devise new relationships between words and the world. He, too, had shaken the grounds of representation by subverting language from the inside. In the *Prophecies* as in their art, grammatical breaches disturbed literary conventions while random moves disrupted the expectations of readers. The French author Guillaume Apollinaire, who saw magic as a source of new knowledge, praised Nostredame as a great poet in 1915. A year later, members of the Dada movement accidentally discovered Nostradamus in Zurich and felt an immediate sense of kinship. These disconcerting yet brilliant quatrains stretched language to its breaking point. "Nostradamus's mystical poetry resembled the experimentations of our abstract poetry," the Romanian artist Marcel Janco explained. "Our poets found in his writings echoes of, and similarities with our new ideas." Literary and political disorder came together.[17]

Zévaco was no avant-gardist, but his novel did turn Nostradamus into a critic of the king's authoritarian rule. Regardless of his political designs, he also drew Nostradamus and his readers into a magical universe in which Egyptian lore, extrasensory communication, Rosicrucian secrets, and prophetic voices were all but equivalent. All fell under the catchall rubric of magic, which occupied a unique place in nascent mass society. Magic was the counterpoint of modern reason, and yet it captured a fascination with the mysterious, transformative powers of industry, technology, and the market. Nowhere was this fascination more palpable than in show business and popular entertainment. As commercial magic reached its peak, Nostradamus made its way from aristocratic salons and popular almanacs to this corner of mass culture.[18]

Zévaco was not the only one to draw the phenomenon into this realm. The popular magician Harry Kellar toured the United States as the "American Nostradamus" in the late nineteenth century while his Hungarian counterpart Hugo went further and performed dressed as Nostradamus. In Paris, Georges Méliès staged "fantastic illusions"—theatrical shows that mixed magic, illusions, and phantasmagoria. One of his 1891 productions was titled "The Tricks of the Moon, or the Misadventures of Nostradamus." The extravagant, bearded, wizard-like character traveled to the moon and was swallowed up by the celestial body. In 1920s Los Angeles, the Ambassador Hotel held daily performances by "the mystifying, sensational Nostradamus who was buried alive [and] will demonstrate his unsolved, phenomenal, and psychic feats." American and British consumers could also buy booklets that imparted Nostradamus's alleged methods for invoking spirits. One of them, entitled *Art Magic*, told readers to select a pristine crystal, ask to see the name of their guardian spirit, and then request advice. *The Complete Fortune-Teller* had a different approach. Hold the cutout "magic mirror of Nostradamus," it said, and then ask your question while softly uttering the seer's solemn invocation: *Eludor Mirpan Gulith Harcon Dibo.*[19]

The marriage among Nostradamus, the supernatural and the occult (however one defined them), and magic was thus consummated in this commercial realm. There, people from all social backgrounds could obtain secret teachings, guidance, self-help, and distraction. The proportions were left to their own discretion.

Henri Torné-Chavigny devoted all of his energy to a prophetic crusade that would return France to its glory days. Michel Zévaco, in contrast, spent but a year in Nostradamus's company and fashioned a magical universe in which ordinary folk prevailed over princes and prelates. Both men nonetheless understood that what the abbot called the rise of the masses was changing their world in irreversible ways. Both accordingly resolved to reach these masses by coupling Nostradamus with mass media, advertising, and promotion.

This came naturally to the newspaperman Zévaco. *Le Matin* organized massive marketing campaigns on behalf of its star authors. Its budget for *Nostradamus*—roughly two million dollars in today's currency—marked a 50 percent increase over his previous novel. During the weeks that preceded the first installment, daily teasers built up excitement within the pages of the newspaper. No two were alike. The daily also distributed 3.5 million brochures across France and put up more than twenty-five thousand color posters in train stations, outside newspaper stands, and on the advertising columns that dotted the boulevards. Some posters were ten feet high. There was no way to escape Zévaco's Nostradamus.[20]

Torné-Chavigny, too, did everything he could to spread his brand of prophecy. The performances he put on for Renan and Hugo resided somewhere between the magic show and the lecture. In order to reach different readerships, he produced high-priced editions of his works as well as cheap facsimiles, almanacs, posters, and brochures of various sizes. To impress his interlocutors, he made use of popular literary devices (depicting himself, for instance, as David who battled a left-wing Goliath). To promote his publications, he sent advance copies to five hundred eminent clergymen, writers, and newspaper editors. To secure funding, he assured potential advertisers that customers would consult his almanacs throughout the year. To increase sales, he set up a mail-order business that offered bulk prices. And to garner attention, he staged the kind of promotional stunts that were becoming commonplace in the press. Uncover a single lie in my statements about the *Prophecies,* he promised, and receive a thousand francs! Like the French Catholics who financed the Sacré-Cœur Cathedral in Montmartre by selling personalized bricks, like the English Methodists who combined evangelism with leisure, like the American devotional promoters who advertised new cults of saints, Torné-Chavigny blended traditional belief and modern commerce.[21]

He added something else, of course: the unorthodox Nostradamus. Torné-Chavigny and Zévaco both grasped and enhanced its appeal for a mass culture that needed accessible, easy-to-use content for a broad readership and dailies that relied on an uninterrupted flow of material. Whether as serious prediction or playful entertainment, Nostradamus now provided fodder for all sections of the newspaper: news articles about the latest interpretations, editorial columns opining on their validity, dispatches from foreign correspondents, historical features, serialized novels, and wire copy. Most often, readers came across his name in the short items that editors used to fill their columns. These terse entries presented predictions that had come true over the ages, discussed curious interpretations, or related odd stories. In 1860, the *Milwaukee Sentinel* ran an item about a librarian who had seen a deceased patron enter the stacks at night to consult the *Prophecies.* Why not?[22]

This mass culture thus welcomed and magnified the visibility of Nostradamus. In doing so, however, it also transformed the phenomenon in long-lasting ways.

Until this time, most readings of Nostradamus had brought together past, present, and future—while remaining cautious when it came to prediction. The abbot and the novelist, however, looked squarely toward the future. Torné-Chavigny, in particular, provided a precise account of what lay ahead. Newspapers, too, now reported on predictions about the demise of emperors, the death of popes, and political upheavals. All of this happened at a time in which, as Utah's *Deseret News* put it, getting "a peep into the future" became a craze. The colossal scale and pace of change confronted Americans and Europeans with an unstable present and a future that loomed ever closer. Everything about the modern world seemed unpredictable, from the financial markets to geopolitics to the rhythms of everyday life. This is why people now turned to commodity futures, crop estimates, or weather forecasts. It is also why they paid attention to biblical prophecies, trance mediums, and fortune-tellers who charged five cents for their insights. The art of prediction and the science of prospection blended into a business and a national necessity. Both promised to control time and lessen the doubt and uncertainty that weighed on so many people.[23]

It was not always merry tidings, however. Torné-Chavigny announced the destruction of Paris and the end of the world at the close of the twentieth century. Whether this marked the Rapture was not clear to all readers. Zévaco's Nostradamus entered an ominous netherworld where terror penetrated him to the marrow. The popular English novelist Stanley Weyman, otherwise known as the "prince of romance," had Nostredame ride the Great White Horse of Death in one of his books. Newspapers followed suit. In 1904, the *Washington Post* and other American papers ran a short story in which the prophet laughed scornfully while announcing disasters. Such papers also published serious articles about Nostradamus's warnings regarding imminent calamities, such as Paris running red with blood in 1900. Thirty years later, the downmarket *Dimanche illustré* promoted an article on Nostradamus by proclaiming that "the dark kingdom of the afterworld is here." Tabloids and respectable newspapers may have used different languages, but they pulled their readers into the same gloomy universe.[24]

While darkness had surrounded the *Prophecies* from the start, earlier interpreters and ordinary folk had also emphasized reassuring or self-affirming facets. "The more I probe the chaos of the future," explained one 1792 interpreter, "the more I see marvels and tyrants perish." In the late nineteenth century, however, the balance shifted toward doom. The *Prophecies* are like a fireworks show in the darkest of skies, explained one commentator in 1867. This evolution owed as much to religious revivalism as it did to turn-of-the-century anxieties and media operations. Some people were deeply shaken by the vast transformations under way in the West. In France alone, peasants moved to cities and industrial centers; universal suffrage transformed the political game; religious observance declined; Jewish immigrants seemed to imperil national identity; women made bids for independence. No one was grounded anymore. Distant economic forces could alter everything from afar. Civilization, one writer lamented, "no longer knows where it is going, toward what nights, into what abysses it is drawn."[25]

Fears about forthcoming cataclysms, apocalyptic or not, grew intense. With 1900 on the horizon, some Christians believed that massacres in Armenia or insurrections in Cuba announced the end of the world. Theosophists held that the passage from one yuga to another would involve unimaginable horrors in 1897. A series of natural disasters—the Krakatoa volcanic eruption of 1893, the San Francisco earthquake of 1906, the Paris flood of 1910—led scientists and journalists to suggest that Earth's crust was not quite done and that human civilization had come too soon. Even Emile Zola, the level-minded French novelist, confessed to sensing "the end of everything," an end that he linked premonitorily to a vast pan-European conflict. The untold pages that newspapers devoted to such cataclysms—not to mention accidental deaths in the modern city—tapped the full range of human emotions, including trepidation. Whether thrilling or alarming, the hues of wonder grew ever more somber.[26]

The West seemed to want or need a prophet of doom to play with its fears, conjure them, and anchor them in a meaningful collective framework. Nostradamus was perfect for the part. There was no mythic story or discernible moral content to redeem the man. There were no institutions to object to this dark incarnation. And it was easy to dive into this ocean of words and emerge with apocalyptic strands, searing scenes of horror, and a long line of catastrophic events that now reached their pinnacle. Journalists did so with relish. Sometimes, they claimed that Nostradamus announced a major cataclysm— or worse. At other times, they found confirmation of a crisis or its outcome. Witness the U.S. Civil War, when Nostradamus was filtered into America not only through new media, but also via an apocalyptic language that led Northerners and Southerners alike to depict themselves as the righteous side in a holy war pitting good and evil. In the early 1880s, the following prophecy attracted widespread attention:

When on St. George's Day the Crucifixion,

And Jesus Rising on St. Mark's Day fall;

And John the Baptist bear him, great affliction

Upon the world shall come, the end of all.

Commentators agreed on its meaning: the world would end the next time that, in a given year, Good Friday fell on St. George's Day, Easter on St. Mark's Day, and Corpus Christi on St. John's Day. This rare trifecta loomed in 1886. Whether they endorsed this prediction or not, most newspapers claimed that Nostradamus had written it (false!) and that it had first appeared on a marble tablet in Germany. By the early 1880s, the quatrain was discussed in Munich, Trieste, New York, and countless other cities. King Ludwig II of Bavaria found it haunting. Theological publications suggested it as a seed thought for sermons. Some occultists paid close attention, but mostly the prophecy circulated in the mass press, which told readers that the fatal year would witness the downfall of European monarchies, the advent of communism, or "the End of the World at Hand."[27]

This prediction surfaced in several locations at once—Europe, the United States, and the British Commonwealth—and promised to affect all of humankind. The famous all-encompassing Nostradamus suited an age of transatlantic cables and wire services, when newspapers borrowed from others across the oceans and reported increasingly on distant events. Yes, the phenomenon had resonated in multiple countries during earlier centuries. Yes, Nostradamus retained pride of place in France. Foreign correspondents continued to report on his predictions about the French. And yes, some crises resonated in only a single country. The European press all but ignored the Nostradamus prediction that had surfaced in American newspapers during the U.S. Civil War, for instance. But the 1886 Nostradamian effervescence was an instantaneous worldwide event, capable of feeding Christian apocalypticism as well as secular notions of world's end.[28]

⁓౧⊱

The mysterious name of Nostradamus endowed this prediction of uncertain provenance with a lineage from the fogs of time and what one journalist called "another authority for the date of the world's doom." This was enough: there was little need to identify the author or justify the prophecy's authenticity. Once Torné-Chavigny had rehabilitated the great prophet Nostradamus, he focused on stand-alone verses rather than his life story or legendary adventures. As for Zévaco, he turned Nostradamus into a minor character in the story of a young hero. The posters that advertised his novel depicted Renaud in the midst of a skirmish while screaming in bold, oversize, bright-red letters: *NOSTRADAMUS*. With the man out of the picture, the name shined brightest. This was the final transformation of Nostradamus in mass society.[29]

Some people had gravitated toward the name before. In the seventeenth century, polemicists signed articles as Nostradamus the Hobbler while playwrights depicted characters as "old Nostradamus." A century later, the writer Horace Walpole described a mystical acquaintance as a cousin of Nostradamus. The name served as invective, too. Here is the poet John Dryden, in a stanza on prophets: "Each *Nostradamus* can foretell with ease . . . / One casual truth supports a thousand lying rhymes." By the mid-1800s, contemporaries claimed that it did not matter whether Nostradamus had written his prophecies in 1555 or not. It sufficed that some person—anyone, really—had composed predictions before the fact and attributed them to Nostradamus, and that these predictions seemed to have been on target. Around 1900, contemporaries agreed that "little is generally known of Nostradamus but his name." Given the growing distance between cultural producers and consumers in mass culture, this is all that was required.[30]

Nostredame's biography had faded because it lacked committed advocates. (The four hundredth anniversary of his birth went unnoticed in 1903.) The legend that had then taken center stage faced the opposite problem: a lack of natural limitations. Without a mythic narrative or institutions to keep it together, Nostradamus sprouted in innumerable directions. The prophet and the magician, the ghost and the alchemist existed separately, but they also melded into an all-purpose wizard. There was a whiff of medieval and Renaissance forces in this evolution from a living prophet to an imaginary character. But Nostradamus also became something else: one of these instantly recognizable stock figures, or stereotypes, that writers and journalists began to use to communicate quickly and distill complex notions for a diverse readership. The era needed a way of talking about this otherworldly realm and its secret forces, arcane teachings, and sundry forecasts. It needed an emblematic figure whom it could praise, sell, or invoke to generate magic, mystery, and meaning. Nostradamus fit the bill. In the process, he became a necromancer, a crystal seer, and a medium as well. Some of Zévaco's advertisements depicted him in a magician's workshop, complete with a workbench, skulls, a stuffed owl, and hieroglyph-like signs. "Magic! Conjuring the dead! Telepathy! Divination! Knowledge of the Future!" they exclaimed. "What is this strange science that suddenly, in our own time, seems to be rising from its ashes?" Whatever it might be, Nostradamus encompassed it all.[31]

This stock figure grew so ubiquitous that the image of the wizard became superfluous. The name alone remained in the forefront, louder and freer and more enticing than ever. This name was not only a verbal shortcut and an authority but also a brand. Almanacs had long lured buyers by claiming Nostradamus as their author. As time went on, some publishers stopped including quatrains or sketches of the prophet. They simply attached the name. In Edwardian London, a certain Gabriel Nostradamus published a primer on the unseen world while a Professor L. Nostradamus sold horoscopes by mail order. Untethered from the man, floating above distant legends, the brand revolved around wonder, mesmerizing gloom, and paranormal powers of unknown origin. The fleeting name enhanced the lure of a mechanism whose own workings seemed as puzzling as those of mass society. One thing was clear: the Nostradamus phenomenon found within itself and within history new sources of energy. After that, people could use it however they so desired.[32]

⁓᷎᷎⁓

Neither Torné-Chavigny nor Zévaco allowed Nostradamus to stand alone, however. Instead, both mingled their own names with his and then placed theirs on top. *Le Matin*'s promotional campaigns ultimately revolved around Zévaco, the "great popular storyteller" whose dramatic intuition would resurrect vanished eras. Torné-Chavigny presented himself as Nostredame's chosen heir, a national prophet whom the quatrains had depicted as *"luisant torné"* (this could be translated as ornate and shining, but it was the reference to his name and the resemblance to Jean-Aimé de Chavigny's that mattered). While Chavigny had published his own compendium of prophecies, he had not talked about himself ad nauseam or depicted himself as Nostredame's quasi-divine translator. Nor had Eugène Bareste, whose main contribution was a complete edition of the *Prophecies*. By the late nineteenth century, interpretations, tales, and Nostradamian providers came to the forefront. The reasons for this include doubts about the masses' ability to judge the quatrains on their own and the growth of the entertainment and forecasting industries. The pressures of self-promotion also came into play. The abbot and the novelist had both entered fiercely competitive domains, filled with clerics who deemed themselves prophets and novelists who claimed to speak to the people. It was impossible to succeed without putting one's name forward.[33]

Torné-Chavigny and Zévaco both became media celebrities. In Paris, Catholic bookstores near the Saint-Sulpice Church placed the abbot's brochures in their windows. Leading politicians and the pope's secretary of state read his interpretations. Royalist pamphleteers used them as ammunition. Many readers thanked him personally for providing relief and the hope of forthcoming deliverance. Translations and commentaries came out in Spain and Denmark. Zévaco's star kept on rising as well. In 1909, the Fayard publishing house released his *Nostradamus* in its new highly profitable collection of dime novels. Like so many others, the young Jean-Paul Sartre read with delight "that author of genius [who] had invented, under the influence of Hugo, the republican cloak-and-dagger novel." Zévaco, the onetime anarchist, moved his family to a posh Parisian suburb and vacationed in Monte Carlo.[34]

The operations of the press, the strategies of cultural producers, the expectations of readers, and the demands of modern life all came into play to reconfigure Nostradamus. They divorced the man from biography, projected his words into the future, and drew it all into dark recesses. With its mix of reliable reports and fears, mysteries, and thrills that seemed to escape rationality, Nostradamus was perfectly at home in a media culture that struggled to separate fact and fiction. The phenomenon's evolution thus responded to publicity, titillation, and sensationalism. But there was more. By tapping a vast range of emotions, Nostradamus could help people manage the sensory overload of modern life. By depicting somber realms and tomorrows, it could bolster their immunity before the unpredictability of this life. And by delving into past, present, and future, it lessened feelings of uncertainty while, like the new media, allowing contemporaries to encounter and perhaps tame a history that was now unfurling so quickly, a history that seemed ever more remote and yet ever so present in their daily lives now that distant events seemed simultaneous and far-flung countries seemed connected. The parallels with the Renaissance Nostradamus are as glaring as the disparities.[35]

✾

This kind of success drew scrutiny and hostility. In his own time, Bareste had been mocked as the *Stradumuste,* a wordplay on Nostradamus's name and Bareste's pseudo expertise. Torné-Chavigny became the "sorcerer abbot" or *torz né,* a wordplay around his name that meant *twisted nose* (and perhaps lying scoundrel). Salon's town historian scolded him for feeding an impatient readership unverifiable predictions about a distant future. In England, a journalist used more graphic language to deride the "crotchety fellow who has racked up a prophecy of Nostradamus out of the dusty limbo of the past and is shaking it before the eyes of the world as a terrier shakes a rat."[36]

As in earlier centuries, people went out of their way to vilify Nostradamus. But the main concern changed once again. "Even in this present century the name of Nostradamus has weight," regretted Boston's *Every Saturday* in 1874. "Astrology is dead—true; but the spirit which led to a belief in astrology is not. . . . What else mean the Spiritualist journals, the séances, the mediums?" How, in other words, could the patently false spirit of Nostradamus take on new spiritual and commercial forms in this modern era? It was pointless to blame the hapless soothsayer or the hordes that yearned to know the future. They did not know any better. No, the true culprits were the peddlers of miracles, the fanatics who made Nostradamus a prophet in spite of himself, the callous commentators who did not always believe their own interpretations. Such complaints had been voiced before, but the nineteenth century granted them new inflexions and a new urgency.[37]

The forces of religion and reason both found cause for concern. The eminent bishop of Orléans accused Torné-Chavigny of drawing disoriented readers toward chimeras and absolving them of responsibility for their mistakes. He also felt that Torné-Chavigny's millennialism and unyielding opposition to the republicans in power would harm the Catholic cause. But Torné-Chavigny did not secure a consensus even in millennialist circles. Some ultra-Catholic apocalyptic authors asked how this provincial cleric could present himself as the leading prophet of modern times while trusting a crazed old magician. Devout Catholics would lose their faith and their minds in this magical morass. On the other end of the spectrum, rationalists put Torné-Chavigny's prophecies on a par with belief in werewolves. America's leading nature writer, John Burroughs, debunked the notion that Nostradamus had predicted the end of the world for 1886. Nothing displayed more clearly the chasm between scientific facts and those "personal wants, fears, hopes, [and] weaknesses" that prophecy and theology exploited. While science was coming into its own in universities, laboratories, and popular journals, there was no agreement regarding its methods and designs. Nor were its dikes necessarily strong enough to withstand the attacks of ignorant amateurs, religious devotees, and resurgent astrologers. The magical spirit endured—and, like science, it sought to unravel the hidden principles of nature. Budding, shaken, or insecure institutions once again went after Nostradamus to shore up their legitimacy.[38]

It was their powers of persuasion that made Nostradamian providers so threatening. Religion and science denounced a moral danger, a modern-age con, and "prophets of evil" who played the fear card. The bishop of Orléans and Pierre Larousse, the editor of the left-wing dictionary that bears his name, were political enemies, but they agreed that Torné-Chavigny made an entire generation tremble before apocalyptic calamities. Reports about the "mysterious and blood-curling prediction of evil" for 1886 had the same effect. This was one reason to denounce the modern Nostradamuses. The other one was their craving for personal gain. In his time, Nostredame had cornered the Renaissance almanac market. In theirs—a time of unprecedented commercialism—individuals sold Nostradamus in all venues at the expense of truth. Starting in the late eighteenth century, detractors had used Nostradamus to condemn a marketplace that promoted shams, greed, and deception. The main character of the 1779 play *Nostradamus, or the Pleading Physician* was a doctor and lawyer who misled public opinion by hectoring and penning misleading pamphlets. Later, Bareste was accused of hawking his almanacs wherever he could. Money trumped principles. The speculator Torné-Chavigny likewise sold empty oracles to gullible consumers.[39]

Intent on becoming as famous as the Renaissance astrologer, these Nostradamian providers captured broader anxieties about deception, commercial fraud, and speculators who created something out of nothing in order to better themselves. This, too, reflected a deeper trend. The eighteenth and (especially) nineteenth centuries made it easier for people from humble backgrounds to rise up in society, obtain public recognition, and even become celebrities. Thanks to the mass press, ordinary citizens now felt as if they could gain intimate proximity to writers, artists, or virtuosos whom they had never met. "The best path to success these days is to get oneself noticed," declared the writer Chateaubriand. In literature and politics and countless other professions, self-promotion seemed to veer out of control. People appeared to care more about personal distinction than they did about their fellow citizens or higher ideals. They said or did whatever it took to earn attention and, alas, they succeeded all too often. Loud celebrity was drowning out self-sacrificing glory.[40]

The Nostradamus phenomenon expressed this feature of the modern world as well. Detractors lambasted "the much too famous Nostradamus," the man who had spurned medical glory for astrological fame, the alleged genius who had obtained more attention than industrious yet modest citizens. He had "taken advantage of his era's dominant ideas to obtain recognition and wealth," explained Salon's town historian in 1883. "Were he alive today, he would meet our century's standards and hold his own among our modern celebrities." But if Nostradamus had become the world's leading astrological celebrity, if his posthumous fame surpassed that of Shakespeare (as some asserted), it was again because these new Nostradamian providers were manufacturing their own celebrity by amplifying his. Detractors now linked Bareste to the deification of fame and berated Torné-Chavigny for turning the press into a self-serving pulpit. All of these providers were offspring of a society that allowed ambition and magic tricks to eclipse virtue and honest exchanges.[41]

The nineteenth century called upon many stereotypes and fictional characters to make sense of rapid transformations. Frankenstein famously served as an admonition against misguided hubris. Nostradamus was not alone. Still, the phenomenon was distinctive. It embodied the persistence of archaic beliefs, but it also came across as modern in its reliance on media, its connection to spiritualism, its freedom from old institutions, and its appeal to striving, fame-hungry providers. Like the fortune-tellers who seemed to be sprouting on every street corner, these swindlers preyed on unsuspecting men and women and threatened the nation's work ethic and social stability. When people needed reassurance against these changes—changes that recast their world and their place within it and perhaps the way they viewed themselves—they could push back against Nostradamus and his modern epigones. The name, too, was good to think against in late modern times.[42]

～⊗◦～

In 1880 an old man approached a newspaperman at a royalist meeting in Paris. He introduced himself—Henri Torné-Chavigny—and began speaking passionately about Nostradamus's predictions for the years to come. After listening to him for a few minutes, the newspaperman interjected that some of his interpretations had failed to come true in recent years. Such objections merely fueled the abbot's ardor. The man still enjoyed a good fight. Following the death of Pius IX in 1878 and the consolidation of France's Third Republic, a regime that many Catholics eventually came to accept, eschatological fires lost some of their incandescence. Torné-Chavigny was now scrimping by. He relied on the hospitality of a Catholic printer near Saint-Sulpice. A doctor who ran into him a few months after the political meeting was struck by his manic agitation. Perhaps the abbot was insane after all.[43]

Many people thought so. Pierre Larousse deemed him fit for the asylum. A rival interpreter dismissed his approach as "utterly eccentric." Mainstream Catholics depicted the abbot and others like him as unhinged minds whose enthusiasm for the *Prophecies* was as crazed as spiritualism. Nostredame had been dismissed as a lunatic before (even in his own time), but the entire phenomenon now generated medical diagnoses. When a Cambridge undergraduate began reciting quatrains, his classmates depicted him as prey to nervous obsessions. Journalists likewise consigned Torné-Chavigny, mediums, and séances to "that long chapter of human folly which treats of men's distrust of themselves." As psychiatry came into its own as both a profession and a discipline, references to insanity began to surface in all kinds of places. Journalists, writers, lawyers, and others used this language with equal abandon. One had to be crazy, they said, to associate oneself with Nostradamus in the present age.[44]

The abbot's true mental state matters less than the way people perceived him. But Torné-Chavigny certainly was mad if we eschew medical definitions and instead view madness as an unwavering commitment to one's worldview, regardless of the consequences. Whereas melancholy people resign themselves to the order of things, madmen fashion their own reality. Torné-Chavigny was prepared to rewrite the rules in order to carry out his vision for France. He never changed course or questioned himself. This is why he earned a place within the studies of literary madmen that began appearing in France in the early 1880s. These were defined as idiosyncratic authors who devoted all of their energy to disseminating their extravagant views. Afflicted by delusions of grandeur and a persecution complex, these philosophers, mystics, and alchemists toiled tirelessly for a vindication that would never come.[45]

The label of madman relegated to the margins individuals who were deemed abnormal. This is where Torné-Chavigny and Nostradamus ended up. The abbot brought the quatrains into an arcane subculture of Catholic dissidents, nostalgic reactionaries, esoteric devotees, and occultist journalists that married conservative tirades with apparitions, hypnosis, and apocalyptic prophecy. Following Torné-Chavigny's death in 1880, a rural priest from northern France retired to a reliquary-filled presbytery and spent sixty-three years completing his grand work. In the early 1900s, occultist periodicals received letters from subscribers regarding Torné-Chavigny and Nostradamus's predictions about the demise of Paris or the return of the Great Monarch. Meanwhile, Zévaco and the like drew the phenomenon into a sensationalist maelstrom of media and entertainment that appealed to the lowest common denominator. Other books were similarly caught up in the century's commercial culture, including the Bible. Publishers now put out family Bibles, customized King James Bibles, and illuminated Bibles with embossed leather covers. The holy book was a mass product, with more than a million copies published each year in the United States. But biblical entrepreneurs knew that their reinventions could go only so far. And the Bible retained its respectability. It was a decorative object in Victorian parlors and a key component of American presidential inaugurations. The Bible "carries a dignity with it that is found in very few other lines of business," declared one catalog. Nostradamus, in contrast, grew ever more dubious and illegitimate.[46]

And yet the phenomenon was not confined to barren cultural borderlands. Refashioned for mass consumption, the glowering predictions and floating name infused the respectable center on both sides of the Atlantic. The *New York Times* published considered reports on Torné-Chavigny's interpretations in the late 1870s. In 1913, a respected speaker presented Nostradamus's views before an audience of high-society Parisian ladies. And three decades later, the *Los Angeles Times* discussed the predictions of an old French prophet who had reportedly studied Egyptian lore. With his single-minded focus and his grip on new media, his sense of self-importance and limitless possibilities, his ability to mix emotional appeal and deduction, his hopes and fears and (perhaps) psychoses, the madman found his place within a mass society that requested surefire forecasts while accepting the unpredictability of modern life. He captured the era's awkward dances between magical thinking and rational assumptions about causality and progress. In so doing, he tapped the era's thirst for meaning and relief, destiny and delight, play and certainty—all of them at once. The modern Nostradamus, too, crossed boundaries.[47]

Chapter 11

❧

Nostradamus Is Adolf Hitler

A couple of years ago, an elderly gentleman came up to me during a cocktail party in Boston. I had just given a talk on the nineteenth-century Nostradamus, but this retired doctor wanted to discuss World War II. More precisely, he wanted to share memories of his first encounter with Nostradamus, which had taken place in a Brooklyn movie theater in 1944. A teenager at the time, he had never heard of the quatrains until he saw a film about the astrologer and his predictions. It was an MGM short titled *Nostradamus IV*, the kind of fare that used to accompany feature presentations. It impressed the young man so much that sixty-five years later he could still recall its images of modern weapons and impending calamities for the Axis. Within days, he had gone to the Borough Park public library and borrowed its copy of the *Prophecies*. He had to find out for himself what Nostradamus had to say.

Other people have asked me about the wartime Nostradamus over the years. Did he not make an important prediction about Adolf Hitler? World War II has joined the Fire of London and the French Revolution as touchstone moments that settle in the collective imagination and endow the phenomenon with another layer of mystery or credibility. During one of the deadliest conflicts the world has ever known, during a time of displacement and hunger and persecution, the quatrains resonated with greater reach and intensity than at perhaps any other historical juncture. This does not mean that other modern wars had not been good to Nostradamus. The U.S. Civil War and the Franco-Prussian War played their parts, as we have seen, and so did World War I. The quatrains circulated in the trenches and on the home front, within the press and among literati. Germans, Britons, and others uncovered references to the invasion of Belgium, the invention of submarines, and the kaiser's defeat. The artist Amedeo Modigliani was convinced in 1915 that Nostradamus had foreseen the advent of a cruel ruler and a mass exile to distant islands.[1]

Still, World War II stands out. In one respect, this is a story about ordinary citizens who, from the late 1930s on, turned en masse to the quatrains in order to peer into their personal and collective future, make sense of seemingly unprecedented events, stare into the abyss, and connect with a world historical event that was equally catastrophic and momentous. One American wartime edition proclaimed that Nostradamus "makes for fascinating reading when related to the catastrophes announced daily while the world is in crisis."[2]

But there is another story to be told. This one revolves around new uses of Nostradamus and especially propaganda, which is partly what MGM provided on the home front. World War II propaganda conjures up images of Leni Riefenstahl documentaries, Rosie the Riveter flexing her biceps, and Robert Taylor fighting the Japanese in the jungles of Bataan. Add Nostradamus to the mix. In earlier centuries, the phenomenon's political life had rested upon individual efforts. After Catherine de Médicis, no regime or ruler made a concerted use of the quatrains or directed them toward the masses. But during this conflict, rival propaganda outfits turned to Nostradamus to impress public opinion at home and abroad. In a context of total war, the Axis and the Allies tried anything to gain an advantage. Strangely or not, four-hundred-year-old predictions made for an alluring instrument of mass persuasion.

⁘

It began once again in France. The Depression had come late to the country, but it lasted longer than elsewhere. As industrial and agricultural production collapsed during the 1930s, public deficits and unemployment ballooned. Frustrated by the apparent paralysis of the state and traditional parties, growing numbers of people gravitated toward communism and the xenophobic right. An antifascist, leftist coalition won the 1936 elections and passed several progressive laws, but this Popular Front could not stem a conservative tide two years later. France seemed punch-drunk, oscillating between left and right, with no clear sense of direction. By 1938, furthermore, war against Germany seemed imminent—a frightening proposition for a country that had lost one citizen out of eighteen and seen a thousand towns vanish between 1914 and 1918. The Munich Agreement, which placated Germany by allowing it to occupy the Sudeten territory in Czechoslovakia, was greeted with relief, but it hardly provided long-term security or a grip on current and future events.

The future had already beckoned following World War I. People used rational methods of analysis and deduction (anticipating our own economic and political models) to forecast the nature of the next war, the growth of urban centers, and technological advances. This form of planning would help manage and regulate a world that, as one journalist put it in 1932, seemed to advance at three hundred miles an hour. Divination, that older window into the future, continued to flourish as well. Almanacs had declined, but thousands of fortune-tellers plied their trade in Paris. Newspapers, mail-order services, and publishers peddled a secular, accessible, and supposedly scientific astrology that revolved around zodiac signs. A deluge of predictions flooded the country. Not all astrologers embraced Nostradamus, but the quatrains seemed to provide answers or at least a way of posing questions. In the early 1930s, a Parisian could begin his day with an astrological consultation at the Nostradamus Institute, located on the rue du Faubourg Saint-Honoré. After lunch, he could attend a public talk on these predictions. And before returning home, he could purchase a new interpretation of the *Prophecies* or *L'astrosophie,* a magazine that paid close attention to the tantalizing quatrains.[3]

The output kept mushrooming as one ominous event followed another: Italian incursions in eastern Africa, the rise of Hitler, the Spanish Civil War. An astrologer from Marseille rendered the mood in 1937: "All we hear about are revolutionary uprisings, political wars, economic wars, civil wars. Everyone is worried and seeks to know the future." As in earlier centuries, uncertainty drew attention to Nostradamus. Mainstream and fly-by-night publishers alike released more than twenty Nostradamus books between 1937 and 1939 alone. *The Collapse of Europe According to Nostradamus's Prophecies* was typical. Complete editions of the *Prophecies* sold for thirty francs while condensed ones could be had for two francs. Louis-Ferdinand Céline, the novelist and notorious anti-Semite, commented that turmoil always brought forth Jewish prophets and oracles such as Nostradamus and Karl Marx. Detestable as they were, they could feel presentiments of what he called "great Jewish upheavals."[4]

Germany's invasion of Poland in September 1939 triggered the long-awaited war. The French high command sent conscripts to the Maginot Line, the massive fortification line that stretched between Luxembourg and Switzerland, but instructed them to wait. They bided their time, wrongly convinced that the French army needed two more years to catch up with Germany's. As they waited for an attack that did not come, soldiers and civilians grew increasingly fretful and wary of their tentative leaders. The *New York Times* reported that men and women of all social stations, including officers at the front, were combing the *Prophecies* for insight into current and future events. In the town of Versailles, a taxation official welcomed a new underling by pulling out his copy and reciting a quatrain that announced terrible dangers in various regions. On the quays of the Seine, strollers asked booksellers for books on magic or spiritualism and above all the *Prophecies*. One Parisian bookstore sold three thousand copies in a single month that fall. The American journalist A. J. Liebling bought a book of interpretations soon after landing in France. It predicted the destruction of Paris by birds from the east and the advent of a French king (often depicted as a white knight) who would defeat the Germans in the Loire Valley a year later and then rule from Avignon. If all of this came true, Liebling reflected, Nostradamus would become as revered as experts on European affairs.[5]

Commentators drew attention to quatrain 2.24, which had barely registered beforehand but would circulate widely during the war:

Beasts wild with hunger shall swim the rivers :	Bestes farouches de faim fleuves tranner,
Most of the host shall move against Ister :	Plus part du camp encontre Hister sera :
He'll have the great one dragged in iron cage,	En caige fer le grand fera treisner,
When the child the German Rhine surveys.	Quand Rin enfant Germain observera.

Ister (spelled Hister in the Old French) most probably referred to the Danube River. Nineteenth-century commentators had presented it as an anagram of Thiers, the name of an important minister. Now they equated it with Hitler, about to cross the Rhine and launch new conquests. Some added that his early victories would soon give way to defeat. In the town of Le Mans, a bank director and his friends could not stomach another protracted war. They accordingly parsed the quatrains and prophecies attributed to the Irish Saint Malachy to uncover cheerier prospects. Meanwhile, a *Figaro* journalist recounted the visit he had paid to fashion designer Paul Poiret in Saint-Tropez. Within minutes, Poiret had whipped out chosen quatrains and told his guest to expect a German invasion during the coming year followed by the devastation of Paris and the reunification of France in 1944. Poiret and the *Figaro* captured the modern machine in full drive. Providers made Nostradamus available by pointing to quatrains that had come true and then peering at the future. Growing numbers of people, facing uncontrollable forces, dipped into this universe and spread what they found by word of mouth. Changing norms made it acceptable to engage in such behavior without losing face. The media, finally, fed and amplified a process that was repeating itself on a broad scale.[6]

⁓᳓⳾⟋

When fighting broke out on the Western Front in the spring of 1940, it was swift and brutal. The German army powered through Holland and Belgium and overwhelmed French and British forces. Within weeks, they had inflicted three hundred thousand French casualties and taken two million prisoners. Not even Hitler's generals had expected a victory of such magnitude. Roosevelt reckoned that France had lost its place in the world for decades to come. Terrified of German exactions, civilians packed up their belongings and headed south—by car, train, buggy, bicycle, or foot. The Dutch came first, followed by Belgians, residents of northern France, and finally Parisians. Some French towns lost more than 90 percent of their residents. Altogether, eight million people clogged the roads, civilians alongside soldiers, mayors, prefects, policemen, and firemen, all of them in full retreat during the greatest exodus in French history. The government took off as well, first to Bordeaux and then to the spa town of Vichy. On July 10, the French parliament called for a new constitution and granted full powers to Marshal Philippe Pétain, an old ultratraditionalist war hero whose authoritarian regime would restore the country's ancient values while accepting German conditions, including a partial occupation of France.[7]

In a matter of weeks, France had lost a war, two-thirds of its territory, its republic, and its independence. This massive crisis raised unsettling questions about the country's military, its political leadership, and French society itself. What had happened to the army and its war plans? Where did political legitimacy reside? Did latent ills and social disfunction cause this debacle? The shock and the divisions that ensued were so deep that eminent scholars have spoken of a national trauma—a collective denial of painful memories or a compulsive, haunting reliving of the event. *Trauma* is a catchall term, too broad to do justice to the unique experiences of individual men and women. Still, studies have shown that civilians who saw their country fall apart, lived through German airborne attacks on the roads of France, or survived bombardments suffered severe psychological effects. It may not have been traumatic for all, but the wounds and the anguish ran deep. By the summer of 1940, citizens of France (and countless foreigners as well) had to accept almost overnight the bankruptcy of what they had taken for granted. "France no longer exists; in a few weeks, a thousand years of culture have vanished," the young writer Julien Green noted in his journal. "We believed that the foundations were strong; they were collapsing." The same was true of people's cognitive foundations. Many in France struggled to ascertain what they could know about their world and its future and their place within it. The prevailing emotion, according to Green, was stupefaction.[8]

Interest in Nostradamus's predictions intensified that year. Never had the quatrains been read with greater eagerness, declared one journalist. After watching people consult these prophecies, Green noted that "a kind of popular naïveté was emerging and grasping at hope wherever it could find it." In truth, people from all walks of life were once again intrigued. An officer who had fought the Germans that June later recalled the comfort that members of his unit drew from Nostradamus while trying to process what he called "our disaster." In the midst of the exodus, the high school teacher Germaine

Dauchat spent a night in a village surrounded by women who listened raptly to a clairvoyant who, quoting Nostradamus, spoke of a German retreat. Elsewhere, a Communist schoolteacher drew from geopolitics and Nostradamus to predict the outcome of the Battle of Britain. And somewhere on the Atlantic, aboard the ship that ferried them from France to Casablanca, a group of naval officers discussed the meaning of selected quatrains. News of this French obsession even reached Warsaw, where a school principal concluded that the country's tragic defeat had spawned "a spirit of mysticism in her oppressed people."[9]

French intellectuals could not agree on what this meant. The surrealist André Breton told an interviewer in 1941 that the Nostradamus vogue represented one of the most troubling psychological facets of the war. The Communist poet Louis Aragon likewise declared that stunned folk were making Nostradamus "their shadowy, stupefying refuge." Léon Werth, a critic who lived through the exodus, was more indulgent. The people whom he saw invoking protective divinities and apocalyptic beasts on the roads of France were less crazed than one might think. "Nothing, since we have left Paris, can be explained by the laws of reason," he wrote in an account of those events. Indeed, some people found confirmation of their fears while others rebuilt an interpretative framework. A journalist linked quatrain 2.68, with its great northern forces and London trembling, to the German offensive and the Battle of Britain. Elsewhere, rumors asserted that Nostradamus had warned the French republic that its errant ways would lead to cataclysm in 1940. For the most part, people sought news of a favorable resolution to these chaotic, paralyzing times.[10]

The prevailing interpretation held that Hitler would be stopped in Poitiers and that a great white prince would save France. But who might it be? On the Casablanca-bound ship, the officers settled first on Pétain, great in repute rather than height, and then considered the little-known general who was telling the French on the BBC that the war was not over. Charles de Gaulle was six foot five. The officers could not settle the matter, but on the mainland two young social workers accepted that de Gaulle was the savior whom Nostradamus had announced. "We put all of our trust in this de Gaulle," they wrote in the chronicle they kept that summer. "Nostradamus is quite something!" It is difficult to gauge how widespread such feelings were, but we should consider the possibility that sixteenth-century quatrains helped shore up the standing of France's future war hero. After all, one of the speakers at a Washington, D.C., benefit for the Free French claimed in 1941 that Nostradamus had predicted de Gaulle's triumph. There was nothing shadowy or stupefying about this.[11]

The more the French lost confidence in their military forces, Julien Green concluded, the more they trusted the *Prophecies*. Beyond the army's failures, history appeared capricious and every social institution was disintegrating. No traditional figures of authority—political leaders, clergymen, policemen, teachers, unbiased journalists—seemed to remain. Nostradamus was not the only source of protection and certainty during this time of confusion. People turned to the Bible, astrological forecasts, and the prophecies of Sainte Odile (which were said to predict Germany's downfall in 1941). They also listened to reports that a saint had appeared before a nun to predict Hitler's defeat. All of them were carried by the rumors that flourished during the war. But Nostradamus did stand out. The phenomenon carried the aura of past conflicts, from the Franco-Prussian War to the Great War. It exuded a mix of mysterious power and tangible evidence lodged in actual quatrains. It continued, finally, to marry prophetic and astrological traditions, secular and religious strands in an ecumenical synthesis that spoke to people from different sexes, classes, political leanings, generations, and faiths.

This remained the case throughout the war, during these years of deprivation and terror in France. Four citizens out of five were undernourished; deportations of Jews, Communists, and other such public enemies became commonplace; bombardments killed tens of thousands. The authorities intervened in all realms of everyday life, and yet they could not provide security or a clear sense of where the world was headed. Ordinary folk gravitated effortlessly toward Nostradamus when, as in previous crises, political leaders and social institutions seemed deaf, remote, or powerless. Once Germany began suffering military setbacks, they anticipated the end of the war. A Marseille daily reported that people were parsing the quatrains for signs of "the end of their misery, which is also ours." Among them was the Jewish novelist Irène Némirovsky. While hiding in a French village until

her deportation in 1942, she trusted Nostradamus's prediction about a favorable outcome two years hence. Her daughter was so mortified decades
later that she dismissed this fancy as a brief childish moment.[12]

⁓⊙⊙⁓

However we consider this collective fascination, it was not limited to France.
In London, a Belgian refugee—a secretary to exiled political leaders—wrote
in her diary that Nostradamus had predicted an assault against an Italian
dignitary before the end of 1940: "We firmly hope that it will be Mussolini."
In the Soviet Union, admirers of Marshal Timoshenko, the defender of Sta-
lingrad, claimed in 1943 that Nostradamus had forecast further triumphs for
the "bald eagle of the Ukraine." Further research is needed to fill in this international tableau, but European propaganda shops took notice. Nostradamus's omnipresence suggested that his predictions could gain a grip on
psyches—and this had been the order of the day throughout the 1930s. This
was a decade of Nazi rallies, Stalinist posters, and antifascist movies by the
likes of Jean Renoir. On the eve of the war, every major country except the
United States had set up a propaganda agency to mobilize its citizenry around
shared goals and soften its enemies. The need for propaganda was one of the
lessons learned during World War I but the focus was shifting from political
allies, enemies, and neutral powers toward civilian populations and public
opinion.[13]

The French entered this Nostradamian field first. With war looming in
1939, ministerial officials asked a Parisian astrologer named Maurice Privat
for favorable interpretations of Nostradamus. This onetime journalist had
made a name for himself between the wars as an astrologer. He wrote several
mass-market books, sold mail-order horoscopes, and in 1933 launched a magazine on "conjectural studies" titled *Nostradamus*. Two months after France's
declaration of war, he published a book titled *1940, Year of French Grandeur*. Drawing from the quatrains, Privat predicted misfortunes for Franco,
Stalin, and the Nazi propaganda minister Joseph Goebbels. As for France,
the title said it all. Its strong government would stand up to Hitler, weaken
the Axis, and avert war. "The West will not kneel down," Privat promised.
"France and Great Britain have no reason to worry."[14]

Once it became clear that events would follow a different course, Privat became quiet and Nostradamus faded from French propaganda. The collaborationist regime of Vichy sought to unite the population around Catholic patriotism, military honor, rural purity, and familial harmony. If any historical figure could embody such values, it was the saintly peasant girl Joan of Arc, who had sacrificed herself while serving her king (and her fatherland, it was now claimed) against England. Nothing of the sort could be said about the unattached and unreliable Nostradamus. The French authorities were also concerned about interpretations that might offend their new German partners. In the fall of 1940, they went after two other books that drew from the quatrains: Emile Ruir's *The Great Carnage* and Max de Fontbrune's *Prophecies of Master Michel Nostradamus*. The first announced a Nazi assault on Christianity and a French resurgence thanks to British aid in 1944. The second predicted tribulations for France under the rule of an old man and depicted Germany as a brutal enemy. Quatrain 2.9, which we encountered in a different context during the Renaissance, was now linked to the doomed chancellor:

The thin one shall rule for nine years in peace,	Neuf ans le regne le maigre en paix tiendra,
Then fall into an immense thirst for blood :	Puis il cherra en soif si sanguinaire :
For this lawless one a great people dies,	Pour luy grand peuple sans foy & loy mourra,
To be slain by a rival far more good.	Tué par un beaucoup plus debonnaire.

Meanwhile, the German embassy's lists of forbidden publications included a selection of quatrains predicting France's victory over barbarians. Michel de Nostredame joined Freud and Einstein among the ranks of "undesirables."[15]

※

Or did he? In Berlin, Nazi officials looked at Nostradamus with greater benevolence. The young Hitler himself had bought books on spiritualism and the occult while living in Munich in the 1920s. Among them was an interpretation of the *Prophecies* by Carl Loog, a postal official who claimed to have discovered the book's numerological key in 1921. According to Loog, Nostradamus had predicted that a "prophet with a raging head" would liberate the German people and then transform the world. France would decline, he said, and war would begin in 1939, a year of crisis for Poland and England. By 1940, this book was in its fifth edition.[16]

Hitler's moldering copy—one of eighty books found in his bunker after his death—contains no marginal notes, and some of its pages remain uncut. We cannot be certain that he consulted these predictions before or during the war. Indeed, there is no conclusive evidence that astrology shaped his decisions or those of other Nazi leaders. Hitler reportedly met the mentalist Erik Jan Hanussen—known as "Europe's Greatest Oracle Since Nostradamus"—on several occasions in the early 1930s. He expressed interest in his clairvoyance and listened to Hanussen explain that the stars and planets were aligned in favor of the man who embodied German destiny. Whether Hitler believed such predictions or merely sought out a seer whose tabloid reached millions of Germans is unclear. In his entourage, Deputy Führer Rudolf Hess gazed at the stars and reportedly recited passages by Nostradamus. SS commander Heinrich Himmler was engrossed by Nordic myths and may have inquired about Hitler's astrological prospects late in the war.

Still, distrust prevailed. Himmler outlawed public uses of astrology, which hinged on a universal soul untouched by racial differences. In 1941, the Gestapo blamed Hess's ill-fated flight to Scotland (an apparent attempt to broker a peace) on pernicious astrologers and then purged their ranks. The horoscope's focus on individual self-development did not sit well with Nazi ideology. Likewise, its neopagan, anti-Christian beliefs could antagonize the Church. More to the point, predictions defied central control. After 1934, horoscopes about Nazi dignitaries and speculation about the Third Reich suddenly came to a halt, probably due to an official order. Occult activities were outlawed a few years later, and Germany's rich astrological life went underground. "In the National Socialist state, astrology must remain a *privilegium singulorum*," Himmler declared. "It is not for the masses."[17]

More precisely, it was not for the German masses. Enemy populations were another story. The goal of psychological warfare was not only to tame ordinary Germans but also to create a more favorable terrain for military operations. Although Goebbels dismissed astrology as a medieval throwback, he paid attention to Nostradamus's predictions that fall. One version of the story holds that his wife woke him one night after reading a startling book on Nostradamus

(Loog's perhaps). Goebbels's first instinct had been to avert unfavorable predictions by banning fortune-tellers and almanacs. But he now saw potential benefits for the Third Reich. He simply needed someone to pen suitable interpretations. Goebbels asked Loog to do it, but he bowed out, so he turned to Karl Ernst Krafft, a Swiss-born "psychological adviser" who had recently published a treatise on astrobiology. A second version of this story holds that Krafft himself had warned Hitler in 1939 that the stars announced an upcoming plot against him. The Gestapo brought him in at once. In the course of his interrogation, he talked about Nostradamus and disclosed that quatrain 5.94 mentioned a great leader who would "shift toward greater Germania / Brabant & Flanders, Ghent, Bruges, Boulogne." This is exactly what Goebbels was looking for.[18]

By November 1939, Goebbels was telling underlings that Nostradamus would yield dividends for a long time to come. He commissioned forecasts and ordered agents to spread the rumor that quatrain 5.94 predicted the temporary occupation of France and a thousand-year empire. Given the French population's misgivings about a new war, it should prove easy to weaken their resolve. In March 1940, Goebbels approved a Nostradamus pamphlet announcing the demise of France and Great Britain. Eighty-three thousand copies were printed, one-quarter for France, and the rest for Italy, Serbia, Croatia, Romania, Sweden, and the Netherlands. Secret radio transmitters broadcast quatrains about the French government's flight and German plans to confiscate bank deposits. They also announced that a white man from the Danube would defeat France and establish the most powerful kingdom in history. Meanwhile, secret agents and warplanes distributed pamphlets in which Nostradamus predicted that German "flying-fire machines" would target northern France while sparing the southeast. The goal was to sow panic, create a glut of southbound refugees, make roads impracticable for the French army, and turn German victory into a fait accompli.[19]

Nostradamus seemed so effective that the Nazis enlisted the quatrains in other campaigns. A British speaker on German radio quoted the *Prophecies* to announce the destruction of London and demoralize the English during the Battle of Britain. In 1941, Krafft's *How Nostradamus Perceived the Future of Europe* predicted a collective nervous breakdown in London, world domination for totalitarian states, and the reign of Great Germania. That same year, the propaganda bureau of the German Ministry of Foreign Affairs released a brochure titled *The Prophecies of Nostradamus.* The leader who hailed from the Mountains of Noricum would fell the British Empire and regenerate Europe. At the ministry of propaganda, Goebbels continued to deem the quatrains effective. They "must once again submit to being quoted," he declared in 1942. And so they were, in countless languages.[20]

By this time, the Nostradamus phenomenon no longer played the same political role as in earlier centuries. It no longer fed political theories, promised divine protection, or influenced negotiations. And yet it could still tar enemies and order chaotic events by providing a distant stamp of authority in uncertain times. These secular predictions, written by a French prophet rather than a threatening German, lent themselves to repeated use across the continent. They corresponded so well to propaganda as Goebbels understood it: penetrate the psyches of ordinary people by appealing to their emotions; repeat simple, unequivocal notions with unwavering certainty; spread truths but do not hesitate to impart lies as long as no one can disprove them. In Germany, Nostradamus's forecasts might demoralize the population by raising false hopes and sowing anxiety. Abroad, however, his resurgent appeal and global fame made it possible to repackage rumors in campaigns that frightened enemy populations while promising a reprieve if they accepted Nazi supremacy. Nostradamus's apocalyptic images would tap fears, intensify feelings of panic, and prevent people from acting decisively. "The Americans and English fall easily for that type of thing," Goebbels assured his staff.[21]

❧

Goebbels may have read English surveys in which nearly half of the respondents claimed to believe in astrology. Regardless, Great Britain marshaled Nostradamus in its own propaganda ventures. In 1943, agents smuggled into Germany fake issues of the astrological magazine *Der Zenit* and a pamphlet titled *Nostradamus Predicts the Course of the War.* The operation was the brainchild of Louis de Wohl, a colorful Hungarian journalist who had moved from Berlin to London in 1935 and become a professional astrologer. By 1941, he was also attached to British counter-intelligence and propaganda services. The eccentric de Wohl, who stayed at the ritzy Grosvenor House and liked to parade down Piccadilly in his captain's uniform, was convinced that Hitler consulted Krafft before making strategic decisions. He thus challenged the astrologer to a long-distance duel. "I realized the danger: Hitler now had first rate astrological advice," he explained in 1945. "This man Krafft had to be fought." De Wohl devised a war on several fronts. His calculations would divulge Krafft's advice to Hitler and help the allies time their actions. His horoscopes of leading German generals would grasp their temperament and anticipate their decisions. And his interpretations of fifty quatrains would demoralize the German population. Having accurately predicted Hitler's rise to power, Nostradamus now announced his demise in Italy as well as devastating Allied air raids. While some English officers looked askance at this unpredictable astrologer, others lauded his "great gifts as a psychologist and excellent insights into the Continental mind." [22]

Prior to writing this pamphlet, de Wohl has been sent on a propaganda mission to the United States in the summer of 1941—part of the effort to draw Roosevelt into the war. In lectures and radio talks, this "modern Nostradamus" warned about a Nazi invasion of the U.S. through Brazil once Saturn and Uranus entered Gemini, America's ruling sign. As he addressed the American Federation of Scientific Astrologers in Cleveland, de Wohl may well have marveled at the country's craze for divination. Fortune-telling had become a multimillion-dollar business. Soothsayers received top billing on the lecture circuit. Prophecies attributed to Mother Shipton and others circulated widely. As for Nostradamus, Americans had begun turning to the quatrains in the late 1930s for a handle on the global crisis. This interest intensified after Rudolf Hess's flight to Scotland and Hitler's invasion of the Soviet Union in 1941. Wire services reported that spring that an Indianapolis librarian had linked quatrain 9.90 to Hess: "A captain of Great Germania shall come to yield himself." After Pearl Harbor and Germany's declaration of war on the United States, Americans applied the quatrains to their own situation, just as they had during the Civil War, but on a much grander scale. [23]

Within a couple of years, American astrologers, journalists, translators, and librarians had published a dozen books relating the quatrains to world events. They linked Nostradamus to esoteric traditions and Egyptian cosmogony or else maintained that the telepathic prophet had tapped what psychiatrist Carl Gustav Jung called the collective unconscious, a world soul that apprehended past and future within an eternal present. Nostredame's main interest, they insisted, had always been the current conflict. Since so many of his earlier predictions had come true, why not listen to what he said about future battles and the war's outcome? The esteemed Modern Library reprinted a fifty-year-old interpretation of the *Prophecies,* added an afterword, and sold it for ninety-five cents. Librarians recommended such books as "background on the news" while newspapers published hundreds of articles on Nostradamus. The syndicated columnist Elsie Robinson claimed that the astrologer had urged Americans to shape their destiny by combining high hopes with hard work. "We could all be Nostradamus," she wrote. Books about the predictions climbed the best-seller lists. The *Prophecies,* declared the *Washington Post,* have "replaced *Mein Kampf* as the infallible authority on what is going to happen next."[24]

But the nation of readers was increasingly becoming one of moviegoers. Three-quarters of Americans now went to the movies every week. This was Hollywood's heyday, and the studios knew how to spot an up-and-coming trend. On the West Coast, Nostradamus became a "U.S. cinema star," per *Time* magazine, and an American tool of propaganda.[25]

Nostradamus was in some respects a natural for the screen. As the poet Harold Norse (a Nostradamus aficionado during those years) put it, "The great psychic physician saw the future like a Fox Movietone newsreel." Catastrophic panoramas and legendary tales provided rich visual material. Building on his theatrical productions, Georges Méliès had included Nostradamus in *A Trip to the Moon,* his 1902 short film about six zany astronomer-magicians who encounter man-eating aliens on the moon. Five of the characters were fictional (with names like Barbenfouille and Alcofribas), and Nostradamus came across as such as well. Soon afterward, the Gaumont movie studio commissioned a historical fiction about the astrologer, his imaginary daughter, and King Henri IV. There was even a Mexican adaptation of Michel Zévaco's novel in 1937. But the phenomenon's punch had always rested on its proximity to reality, on the possibility that, even if the man eluded our grasp, the predictions might be true. As biography and legends faded from view, it became more difficult to make movies around Nostradamus. Features that borrowed from the documentary were better fits.[26]

The documentary had come into its own between the wars as a genre that aimed to record reality instead of fictionalizing it. There were social advocacy films and political manifestos, avant-garde adventures and ethnographic depictions of distant peoples. In the 1930s, Hollywood shorts began blending the documentary's informative stance with the feature's entertainment value. These shorts were highly profitable, and MGM's unit was considered the best at turning cultural trends into tight cinematographic concentrates. In the late 1930s, it launched a series that, in the words of one reviewer, would "educate the public in regard to the facts of psychical research." Each episode investigated a strange occurrence that could be explained as a coincidence or the result of supernatural forces. Early topics included telepathy, ghosts, and encounters with the dead. The host was Carey Wilson, a dapper producer whose life followed the arc of a rags-to-riches story. By age twenty, this upstate New York native had dabbled as a projectionist, a production hand, a traveling film salesman, a foreign rights agent, and a scriptwriter. But he still scrambled to make a living and spent many nights in Manhattan subway stations. Then came his break: a fortuitous encounter with studio head Samuel Goldwyn on a midtown sidewalk in 1921. Goldwyn requested a script; Wilson wrote it overnight; a Hollywood contract ensued. Out west, Wilson quickly made his mark as an indefatigable scriptwriter and rewrite man who understood the business. His motto was to give the public what it wanted, whether it was a star or a story. This served him well as he climbed the rungs at MGM and soon hobnobbed with the likes of Greta Garbo.[27]

In 1937, Wilson came across a magazine article on Nostradamus—an ideal subject for this new series. The short that ensued, *Nostradamus: A Historical Mystery*, was a fast-paced eleven-minute movie full of flashbacks, lantern slides with off-camera commentaries, and interpretations that traveled across time. The producers included a reference to the German annexation of Austria (across the Hister) and ended with the annihilation of Paris in the year 3420. Their Nostradamus was both a star and a story. But the film said nothing about politics. Unlike the French, Americans did not feel an existential threat at home. Instead, MGM played on wonder and curiosity. At once thrilling and accurate, its "riddling of the future" joined the spirit of seventeenth-century broadsheets (without the gore) with the inquisitiveness of Eugène Bareste (without the erudition). Nostradamus was present at the birth of a new genre— the probing, entertaining journey into the strange and the mysterious, the incredible but true—and then accompanied its formidable growth throughout the twentieth century, when it sometimes morphed into docudrama. The radio show *Strange as It Seems* devoted a segment to Nostradamus in 1939, and others followed. With its didactic yet spirited tone, its authoritative commentator who distilled the results of research, its music and special effects, and its claim to serve the public interest, MGM's Nostradamus dwelled somewhere between middlebrow and lowbrow cultures.[28]

This short was so well received that the studio produced three others of the kind between 1941 and 1944. Following their usual assembly line approach, the producers recycled material from one to the next. But each film provided "new and even more amazing predictions." To cull this material and make these shorts credible, Wilson enlisted three Los Angeles–based experts. Franco Bruno-Averardi, an Italian literary scholar who had cofounded UCLA's Italian department, translated quatrains. Nina Howard, an astrologer who had published *Follow Your Lucky Stars* ("a stellar road map" to life), identified quatrains that could be linked to the Nazis. And Manly P. Hall, a creature of California's occultist milieu, wrote commentaries that, he insisted, pertained to the war. A magnetic presence, Hall had turned his mystic retreat in Los Angeles's Griffith Park neighborhood into the headquarters of a venture that sold magazines, correspondence courses, and self-improvement plans. Building upon theosophical teachings, he linked the psychic instability of humanity to current crime waves, pollution, and the World War. To recover lost feelings of community and sacrifice, modern civilization had to delve into a trove of esoteric wisdom that ranged from Indian rituals and Greek allegories to the predictions of Nostradamus.[29]

MGM had brought together academia, popular astrology, and occultism around Nostradamus. It was an odd partnership, but all three of these purported experts belonged to the entertainment-publicity nexus. Even Hall believed that cinema would impart metaphysical themes in ways that no book or lecture ever could. Like other media figures before them, the studios recognized a commercial opportunity, tapped a preexisting interest, and sought to create broader demand. MGM's publicity department thus instructed theater managers to capitalize on the appeal of astrology in order to launch these shorts. Bundle advertisements with predictions about local and national events, they said. Invite local astrologers, psychics, and clairvoyants to advance screenings. Organize Q&A's between these seers and the audience. And play the press, of course. Wilson told journalists in 1943 that his team had studied only seventy quatrains so far. They were far from done. "Now, we're digging for something on the Roosevelt-Churchill conference at Casablanca."[30]

⁓ꙮ⁓

By then, such digging contributed to wartime propaganda. Like de Wohl, many Americans seemed to believe that the Führer gave credence to Nostradamus and kept several astrologers on hand. "Read the fateful happenings predicted tomorrow for Europe and America by the sixteenth century soothsayer whom Hitler relies upon today," beckoned the Modern Library. Newspapers reported that Hitler was terrorized by quatrain 2.24 and the prospect of ending up in an iron cage. One Long Island resident wrote to *Life* magazine suggesting that a giant cage should be built, with a placard announcing that it awaited the superstitious dictator. This never happened, but Nostradamus seemed to offer a good way of beating Hitler at his own game.[31]

Most studio heads were Jewish immigrants with little sympathy for fascism or isolationism. Still, they remained politically cautious during the war's early years in order to retain access to foreign markets. Once Hitler forbade the distribution of American movies in Germany, they contributed generously to the war effort. In Washington, Roosevelt was convinced that the heavy-handed European approach to propaganda would backfire in the United States. Public entertainment was more promising. Films, in particular, could influence viewers without their being aware of it. They could sell the war, energize the home front, and entertain soldiers. The Office of War Information and other agencies thus commissioned movies and encouraged studios to produce battle dramas, training films, newsreels, documentaries, and shorts. The agency provided what Richard Goldstone, production supervisor in MGM's shorts unit, called "a certain doctrinaire policy line to follow." The studios followed this line, but without heeding every recommendation. Who, after all, knew the American public better than they did?[32]

MGM's Louis B. Mayer put his shorts department to work. Its output ranged from paeans to Max the Mechanic to cartoons about Adolf the wolf to Nostradamus. Seeing no contradiction between universal wisdom and patriotism, Manly Hall had provided quatrains that denounced what he called the idiocies of isolationism and fascism, announced an allied invasion of France, and prefigured the demise of Hitler and Mussolini. This was standard fare in these shorts.

MGM's Nostradamus told different things to different peoples. The French should not surrender their fleet. The British would regain strength and contribute to a united democratic front. The Italians were done for. Hitler could not trust his own henchmen. Latin American countries should beware Nazi invasion plans. Americans, finally, should expect tribulations but remember that commitment to the war effort would usher in a reign of peace and justice. "The United States will be prominent in reestablishing unity," Wilson said, claiming to channel Nostradamus, "and war will be outlawed for centuries to come."[33]

The facets that made Nostradamus so appealing to Goebbels applied here as well, but with notable differences. MGM began with entertainment and ended up at the junction of show business and propaganda. The studio moreover targeted its own population without worrying about subversive readings of the quatrains. Finally, Wilson and his colleagues moved organically toward Nostradamus, without heavy governmental oversight. This is why the shorts combined the media figure's multiple dimensions: learned yet distant earnestness, flights of fancy, and urgent projections into the future. The multifaceted Nostradamus proved ideal for films that sought not to pummel or frighten enemies but to astound, entertain, reassure, and energize during uncertain times. It was a playful affair, and yet deadly serious.

It also had to seem true. One of the challenges facing democratic propagandists was to reconcile political designs with an attachment to truth. They could not come across as liars. The Office of War Information warned filmmakers not to give audiences reason to believe that they were being misled. Here too, Nostradamus was well suited to modern persuasion since producers could combine history and outright invention while remaining loyal to their principles. In their postwar oral histories, Wilson and other producers explained that they had tried to get Nostredame's life story right and devoted several months to each short for the sake of accuracy. At the same time, they felt free to draw from what they called the Gothic legend. One short opened with eighteenth-century intruders violating the prophet's tomb in the middle of the night. This ghoulish scene was straight out of the old almanacs. Interpretations of quatrains followed. MGM granted itself the latitude to select and then elucidate verses that Richard Goldstone later deemed easy to manipulate. The task, he explained, was to "make a given verse say what you wanted it to say, in terms of the times and in terms of the interest and in terms of the dramatic value of your interpretation." It was not difficult to come up with explanations that seemed to pertain to specific events.[34]

MGM spoke in one respect to the awed beholder in each spectator. "The psychology of these Nostradamus features is irresistible," marveled one American columnist in 1942. "You sit back and watch Carey Wilson conclusively prove that this monk of medieval times forecast the present war," and you exhale after hearing about Hitler's inglorious end. The English critic J. A. Hammerton was less charitable in 1943, when he wrote that these movies added to the mental confusion of a thoughtless public. Perhaps, but American propagandists were sensitive to their audience members' sense of themselves as citizens and consumers in ways that Goebbels was not. They hence appealed to the decoders and ambivalent spectators as well. Each short ended with a question followed by the same tagline. Could Nostredame peer into the unknown? *What do you think?* Would Hermann Göring or Himmler slit Hitler's throat? *What do you think?* "We toss you a little problem to work out for yourselves," Wilson said on camera in *Nostradamus IV*. It was up to the spectators to answer the question, examine the prophecies, and either make up their own minds or carry the uncertainty home. Wilson does not provide answers, explained *Coronet* magazine. "You have to seek out Nostradamus yourself and become your own interpreter."[35]

This was not accidental. The producers wanted spectators to wonder whether all of this could possibly be true. For dramatic and perhaps political reasons, they deemed question marks more effective than definitive statements. Like others before them, these Nostradamian providers exploited the phenomenon's remote authority and open-ended mystery. As they guided Americans, they supplied the illusion of control, coupled with distance for those who needed it, and an invitation to dig deeper on one's own. The Brooklyn teenager who rushed from the movie theater to the library in 1944 played his part perfectly.

⁓◌⊙◌⁓

One of the lessons of World War II is that the quatrains could maintain and perhaps magnify their wondrous appeal in the mid-twentieth century. In the United States, they could espouse the contours of a noble American destiny, written in the stars and in the past, but doomed to failure unless the country's citizens worked, fought, and made sacrifices. The quatrains reached more people and at a faster speed than ever before, even though some people remarked that, like a pendulum, Nostradamus resurfaced during each major crisis. *Time* explained in 1941 that "new generations have constantly dusted off its well-worn prophecies to fit newborn events." Two lasting notions rooted themselves in the media at this time. The first held that the present frenzy for Nostradamus was unprecedented: a small cult was morphing into a mass phenomenon. The second, in contrast, depicted this frenzy as a cyclical delusion. The latter drove some people away, but not all. In 1944, two Texas pilots looked to Nostradamus for the date of D-day. How they came upon him is unclear, but the very media that fostered critical awareness continued to feed curiosity as well.[36]

Propaganda also played a part. The Nazi counterintelligence officer Walter Schellenberg reflected after the war that, due to Nostradamus, French efforts to "divert the great streams of refugees from attempting to reach southeastern France proved useless." I have been unable to confirm this assertion—foolproof sources just are not there. It is equally possible that Nazi Germany drew people involuntarily toward the great white man in London. Still, propaganda heightened Nostradamus's visibility in Europe. The Modern Library and MGM did the same in the United States. The shorts played in hundreds of theaters and earned an Academy Award nomination. Educational catalogs recommended them for high school and college courses in history, English, and psychology. Wilson obtained recognition as the "energetic movie scholar who discovered Nostradamus for the screen." Thanks to him, said *Coronet* magazine, "a whole army of Nostradamus addicts has sprung up all over the country." More mail reportedly poured in for Nostradamus at MGM than for the studio's own Mickey Rooney. Wilson claimed to have answered five thousand letters, from Catholic priests in Texas, lumbermen in Wisconsin, and book collectors in Atlanta. Some treated Nostradamus as their personal astrologer, though most wanted to know when the U.S. air force would next bomb Tokyo or when the German people would revolt.[37]

The shorts' prophetic strand and hopeful endings played upon deep-rooted notions of national destiny while promising an American victory. Spectators could nonetheless take Nostradamus in whatever direction they wished. What Goebbels called "occultist propaganda" could both deny human powers of decision making and at the same time spur people to action. It could provide authority and at the same time discredit. But perhaps it had become too obvious for an increasingly savvy era. *Time* denounced this avalanche of Nostradamus books, and a Manhattan rabbi compared the true prophet Isaiah to this false one in one of his wartime sermons. These objections were not new, but something else was: criticism of such interpretations as modern propaganda and mass persuasion. In 1940, leading newspapers in England, Sweden, and Spain responded to Krafft's pamphlet by printing the headline "Who Is Nostradamus?" The answer came days later: "Nostradamus Is Adolf Hitler." Shortly thereafter, André Breton scolded the European masses for attributing extrahuman powers to Hitler and assuming that he consulted astrologers before making decisions. These kinds of assumptions fed Nazi designs as well as collective psychosis. By 1942, some American journalists were mocking MGM and others for claiming that the Allies would lick Hitler in no time. How could we conclude otherwise, asked the *New York Times,* when we make Nostradamus "an ally on the propaganda front"? Should the United States ever create a Ministry of Fun, added one syndicated columnist, its *"Mein Kampf* for propagandizing" should go to Nostradamus.[38]

Perceptions of propaganda had changed since World War I. In some quarters, a term that had once described public-health campaigns now denoted deceit and indoctrination in the service of the state or capitalism. The massive Fascist campaigns did not help matters. During the war, Americans debated whether *propaganda* was a curse word or not, and whether it lurked behind every billboard or screen. Some diplomats and members of Congress were alarmed. From a practical perspective, moreover, propaganda is most effective when it remains subtle and seems plausible or at least sincere. These uses of Nostradamus did not fit the bill. What made the phenomenon so appealing as a political device also made it appear coarse, if not blatantly cynical. Could Nostredame have been as sanguine about our side or as glum about our enemies? Should we really give credence to these arcane prophecies? And did the Nazis and MGM producers even believe their own interpretations? Goebbels referred privately to the quatrains as "silly rubbish" that was good enough for the French. In Los Angeles, Wilson was intrigued by the occult while Hall included the quatrains within his philosophical framework, but other producers claimed privately that no member of the shorts unit wanted to be identified with "this superstitious philosophy." Political opportunism seemed more naked than at any other time in Nostradamus's history.[39]

This transpired in the final product. By 1944, some Nazi counterintelligence officers felt that Goebbels's uses of Nostradamus had proved clumsy. That same year, German forces in France contemplated a different approach. This time, they would use the name to *taint* the Resistance. They prepared a clandestine edition of the *Prophecies* that bore the imprint of the leading underground publisher, the Editions de Minuit, and printed eighty thousand copies. When one of Minuit's cofounders, the writer Vercors, saw a copy, he found it laughable. "It was an anti-English ersatz of Nostradamus's prophecies, so foolish that one almost wishes that it had circulated," he wrote in his memoirs. This edition was never released, perhaps because such operations seemed futile at this time or because priorities shifted as the Allies gained ground. Nostradamus now came across as an instrumental device, both in Nazi Berlin and Hollywood. The propagandists had gone too far. They had stained the phenomenon with pejorative connotations and sucked out what remained of its political respectability. World War II was thus the zenith of Nostradamus propaganda and also its nadir—the coda to a political history that had begun four centuries earlier. Since then, no state has marshaled Nostradamus in this fashion. Saddam Hussein commissioned a translation of quatrains because he was convinced that they mentioned him, but even the Iraqi dictator kept this to himself.[40]

In 1945, three convictions thus surfaced in the American media. The first held that Nostradamus had been proved wrong. Most of these wartime prophecies had failed to come true, including those about VE Day. "Possibly as the seer looked farther into the future, his vision became clouded," wrote the science-fiction writer De Witt Miller. Second, the West had reached its limit. "Enough of Nostradamus!" exclaimed the *Atlanta Constitution*. Third, there would be no place for the ex-king of prophets in the postwar order. "Amidst the jubilation of the Allied world, poor old Nostradamus was forgotten," declared the *Fairmont Herald-Mail*. It was not just the demise of Nostradamian propaganda. Military victory and the prospect of a lasting era of peace also erased the chaos and uncertainty under which the quatrains had thrived. But this prophetic fatigue, too, was but a fleeting moment. The idea that Nostradamus was finished, that the modern world had vanquished its demons and moved past an era in which such predictions were both needed and pertinent— this illusion and this mantra, too, became part of the modern phenomenon.

Chapter 12

☙☙

Apocalypse Now?

If Nostradamus was forgotten, it was neither completely nor for long. When I first encountered his predictions in the early 1980s, French journalists spoke of *Nostradamus superstar.* "This fall, what are people talking about in offices and workshops? What are they reading in subways and buses? What fills the window displays of our bookstores?" one of them asked in 1981. "Nostradamus."[1]

I remember watching a well-groomed fellow named Jean-Charles de Fontbrune speak somberly about the prophecies on television. Fontbrune was the latest Nostradamian provider to surface and perhaps the most successful one since the Renaissance. Most of the articles I was reading in *Paris-Match* and elsewhere revolved around him. Fontbrune had the advantage of entering a family business. His father, a doctor named Max, had written the interpretations that the French authorities banned in 1940, taken a hiatus during the war, and then continuously published books and newspaper articles about the quatrains until his death in 1958. At that time, Jean-Charles was studying business and beginning a career as a pharmaceutical executive. In his spare time, he immersed himself in the *Prophecies,* combining his father's Catholicism and philological inclinations with computer programs that, he said, could uncover undetected word patterns.[2]

In 1980, a small French publisher released Fontbrune's *Nostradamus:*

Historian and Prophet, which laid out predictions for several decades to come. The initial print run and marketing budget were modest, but a year later readers noticed that Fontbrune had predicted the election of the Socialist president François Mitterrand as well as an assassination attempt against Pope John Paul II. It was quatrain 2.97:

Pontiff of Rome, beware of approaching	Romain Pontife garde de t'approcher,
The city where the two rivers pool :	De la cité que deux fleuves arrose,
You shall come to spit up your blood here,	Ton sang viendras au près de là cracher,
You & yours, when the rose is in bloom.	Toy & les tiens quand fleurira la rose.

The rose, symbol of the French Socialist party, provided the connection with the presidential election, which took place in May 1981. Fontbrune's book now became a colossal hit, selling 500,000 copies by the end of the year and 1.3 million within three years. A poll showed that three-quarters of the French population knew about it. Nostradamus was in the air—so much so that the eminent philologist Georges Dumézil claimed to be fascinated by these verses and penned a book-length essay on the quatrain about Louis XVI and Varennes.

The fervor spread beyond France. Fontbrune's book was translated into twelve languages. Spaniards focused on an Arab invasion of the country and the army's tolerance for civilian control. German weeklies devoted cover stories to the brouhaha; the *Chicago Tribune* and other American newspapers summarized these forecasts. Meanwhile, the publishing house Farrar, Straus and Giroux hastily repackaged an old volume of Nostradamian interpretations that had lain dormant in a subsidiary's backlist. On the West Coast, the producer of the *Roots* miniseries featured Nostradamus in a docudrama titled *The Man Who Saw Tomorrow.* Like an extended MGM short but without the propaganda, the film cast the aging Orson Welles as its host. With his floppy cravat, his cane, and his cigar, Welles bore a resemblance to the prophets and magicians whom he had played in his younger years, but his predictions of natural disasters and world wars were all too serious. As in his 1938 radio broadcast about a Martian invasion, a distant voice depicted a catastrophic attack on American cities.[3]

This resurgence lasted throughout the decade, but it was not the first of its kind since World War II. Older generations could remember Nostradamus's presence during what contemporaries called the Age of Anxiety. The bombs on Hiroshima and Nagasaki, the Holocaust, the testing of thermonuclear weapons, and the Korean War cast a shadow on the late 1940s and 1950s. Atomic fission provided a new source of energy, but it could also disrupt nature and flatten entire nations. The historian Arthur M. Schlesinger, Jr., famously declared in 1948 that inhabitants of the West were tense and adrift, bereft of the ideas and institutions that had provided certainty in the past. They contemplated another world war and faced hard questions about the uses of science, the purview of reason, the very idea of progress, and the right choices to make in this new world. "It is difficult," the scholar Henri Peyre wrote in 1950, "not to keep one's eyes riveted on the present and on a future which appears to many to be wrapped in clouds of threatening gloom."[4]

Nostradamus's predictions flourished just as they had during previous crises. Holly Beye, a struggling beat writer living in Greenwich Village, devoted a journal entry to Nostradamus in September 1950. Five months from now, she wrote, "a war will end in seven days from which it will require seven months to bury the dead." This nervous fascination percolated into dailies, women's and science fiction magazines, and digests. *Fantastic Adventures* asked its readers in 1947 whether they would "like to know if the atomic bomb will ever be used in warfare, if the world government envisioned by the United Nations will succeed, or what nation will be most powerful fifty years hence." Nostradamus might just have the answer, suggested the magazine.[5]

One of the publication's contributors, Henry C. Roberts, published the *Complete Prophecies of Nostradamus* that same year. The owner of a knick-knack shop in lower Manhattan, Roberts interpreted Nostradamus with regard to Arab nationalism, Korea, the Middle East, and other hot spots. Quatrain 9.44, he explained, referred to atomic power:

Flee, flee, O Geneva, every last one,	Migres, migre de Genesve trestous
Saturn's gold for iron shall be exchanged :	Saturne d'or en fer se changera,
RAYPOZ shall wipe out all opposition,	Le contre RAYPOZ exterminera tous,
Before his advent, the sky's signs shall change.	Avant l'a ruent le ciel signes fera.

Without explaining the meaning of RAYPOZ, Roberts declared that Nostradamus warned "with terrifying finality . . . of the eventual destruction of our civilization by means of the release of atomic energy." The quatrain's last line, however, provided one last hope for humankind, one last possibility for collective salvation even in these ominous times. Like other Nostradamian providers before him, Roberts drew out the quatrains' twin dimensions. He also promised to enhance the psychic abilities of his readers. The *New Yorker* was not impressed by this "short, gnarled, nervous man" who became "a one-man corporation devoted to disseminating the message that Nostradamus and other great adepts have for a groping humanity." Regardless, Roberts earned a wide audience in the United States and Europe, where middlebrow magazines relayed his interpretations. Whereas Nostradamus had hitherto traveled to American shores from Europe, American Nostradamica was now exported to the rest of the world.[6]

It is possible to find interpretations of Nostradamus during the 1960s and early 1970s. A *Chicago Tribune* writer suggested in 1963 that quatrain 8.97, which referred to "three fine children," predicted that three brothers would govern the United States. It was of course the Kennedys. (In later years, commentators would link quatrain 1.26 to the assassinations of John and Robert Kennedy. "During daytime a great clap of lightning": the president was shot down by a sudden thunderbolt in broad daylight, while his brother died in the early morning. "Ill omen from the bearer of tidings": both brothers had received countless threats. "Conflict in Reims, London: Tuscan blight": the international repercussions of their deaths.) Still, Nostradamus grew more discreet during a time of affluence and stability in the West. People who looked to the future—demographers, policy planners, academics, the RAND Corporation—were more likely to imagine technological advances, track trends about wealth distribution, and plan a better society.[7]

While this new futurology was bathed in optimism, futurist Alvin Toffler's mega best seller *Future Shock* did warn in 1970 of the psychological cost of incessant, overwhelming change and information overload. Military worries did not vanish either (the Cuban missile crisis provided an all-too-vivid reminder). These concerns deepened in the late 1970s and 1980s, with the Soviet invasion of Afghanistan and the reigniting of the cold war. Europeans feared a nuclear winter on the continent while Americans began to imagine a conflict waged on their own soil. Washington, D.C., hosted a conference on the post–nuclear war world in 1983. That same year, half the adult population watched ABC's *The Day After,* a graphic depiction of a nuclear attack on Middle America.[8]

All indicators pointed downward. The Vietnam War, the Iranian hostage crisis, and terrorist strikes across Europe shook the West's confidence. Colonial empires were a thing of the past, and so was the postwar economic boom. Against a backdrop of monetary inflation and oil shocks, industrial output declined and unemployment soared. In the United States, Bruce Springsteen belted out, "Lights out tonight, trouble in the heartland." The crisis was felt acutely in France, where it followed a massive thirty-year program of urban and industrial development. Europeans began feeling that society was ungovernable. Moreover, the planet was looking at overpopulation, severe depletion of resources, famines, and an energy crisis. Around 1980, accidents in French and American nuclear plants illustrated the environmental and medical perils of technology. A few years later, the American surgeon general described the AIDS epidemic as the biggest health threat the country had ever faced. Publishers released books with titles like *The Population Bomb, Facing the Bomb,* and *The Beginning of the End* (a collection of Bible prophecies). In England, a politician complained in his diary in 1979 that "the press is just full of crises, anarchy, chaos, disruption. I have never seen anything like it in my life." He was not alone.[9]

All forms of authority now came under attack in Western Europe and the U.S. The counterculture had done its part by questioning the power wielded by the patriarchy, parents, schools, and other institutions. Science was accused of polluting the atmosphere, enriching unscrupulous corporations, and contributing to genocides. Predictive models rooted in macroeconomics and the social sciences were seriously compromised after the oil crisis. Watergate and later the Iran-contra affair sowed doubts about the probity of governments and politicians. Individual choice and autonomy grew ever more appealing, making it difficult for leaders to secure a consensus around universal values or stable ideologies. Political parties found it increasingly difficult to enforce discipline and inspire voters to turn out at the polls. One of the ironies of the era is that institutional religion suffered as much as reason and science. Mainstream churches now came across as tools of the establishment rather than benevolent caretakers. Fewer parishioners were ready to commit to a single denomination and embrace its absolute truths. The decline in trust and devotion was steepest in Europe, but in the United States, too, changes were afoot. Growing numbers of Americans began searching for spiritual fulfillment, mystery, personal growth, and healing outside traditional institutions and the Judeo-Christian tradition. In 1972, *Time* subtitled its cover story on the occult, witchcraft, and Nostradamus, "A Substitute Faith." Since that decade, the number of palm readers, New Age bookshops, and fortune-telling conventions has exploded, along with belief in reincarnation, ghosts, and spiritual energies.[10]

Nostradamus has always thrived when defeats or catastrophes degraded the legitimacy of government and other institutions. This situation was different—a diffuse crisis of authority that was not connected to a cataclysm—but it lasted longer. Nostradamus was ideally suited to these circumstances as well. The phenomenon has after all endured without the permanent or exclusive seal of any institution or seat of power. This has deprived Nostradamus of recognition but also of any definitive association with the churches, political institutions, and learned bodies that were now contested. Free from norms and oversight and yet respectful of the West's moral and political foundations, Nostradamus could travel from one realm to another and draw from all of them. As a perpetual work in progress, it is tailor-made for the unstable landscape and composite cultural life that have been gaining ground since the 1970s.

The one institution that increased its reach during these decades was the news media. The printed press, radio, and television did not escape ambient distrust, but they broadened their presence as cultural providers. Some of them took advantage of the discredit of other institutions to magnify their role; others simply enlarged their fare, which came to encompass religion and the supernatural. Many people have grown more comfortable espousing beliefs that they uncover in the media. Since World War II, astrology has likewise become more present in newspaper columns, radio shows, paperback series, and book clubs. Nostradamus has followed suit. The phenomenon's political illegitimacy at war's end did not make it any less appealing for mass outlets. Henry C. Roberts promoted his interpretations on radio and television. Max de Fontbrune was a regular contributor to *Ici-Paris,* the large-circulation newspaper that told readers in 1948 that Nostradamus had predicted a half century of wars and revolutions (afterward, all would be well). Three years later, the paper awarded a *Grand Prix Nostradamus* of one hundred thousand francs to the reader whose predictions came closest to the truth. As for Jean-Charles de Fontbrune, a fixture on TV and in magazines, television producers brought him to Salon in 1981 for a week of shooting in the castle that had once welcomed Catherine de Médicis. The show's title, *Time X,* captures the enduring interface between Nostradamus and a media culture that tries to to pin time down while allowing it to escape its grasp. Both relay stories that revolve around defined locales and distant, abstract spaces. Both buttress national sentiments (by identifying looming threats, for one) while diluting them in a global sphere. And both continue to inhabit a foggy realm in which popular science and curiosity encounter mystery and high emotions.[11]

❧

During the 1990s, the quatrains surfaced in supermarket tabloids and on cable television. They were also linked to AIDS, the first Gulf War, and earthquakes in Umbria. Then came the effervescence around the new millennium, 9/11, and 2012. While the Middle East, Asia, and Africa were all but absent from the *Prophecies,* Nostradamus now made inroads outside the West. An Iraqi sheikh studies Shiite theology, Catholic doctrine, Greek philosophy, and Nostradamian quatrains during his youth. A Senegalese bishop brings up the quatrains during a papal audience in Rome. Nostradamus develops a new presence in China during the late 1990s. These are merely anecdotes, but they point toward a globalization of Nostradamus. Earlier evolutions grew more pronounced: the floating name, the spotlight on the future and predictions, and the apocalyptic horizon.[12]

In 1981, a French journalist described Nostradamus as "a kind of Ayatollah Khomeini with flashes of lightning darting from his eyes." By 1999, the *Sunday Times* could dub him "the star of Apocalypse Now." The year 1999 loomed large in the Nostradamian firmament, an appointment with destiny that had been set centuries earlier, in quatrain 10.72:

The year nineteen ninety nine, seventh month,	L'an mil neuf cens nonante neuf sept mois
The sky shall send a great King to defray	Du ciel viendra un grand Roy deffraieur
And restore the great King from Angoumois :	Resusciter le grand Roy d'Angolmois.
Before, after March, blessed be his reign.	Avant apres Mars regner par bon heur.

The first line referred to a momentous event that summer, perhaps the lunar eclipse scheduled for July 28 or the total solar eclipse that would take place in August. The second line suggested what this event might be, although the words had changed over time. The original had mentioned a great king *deffraieur:* one who defrays. Within decades, however, editions of the *Prophecies* inserted an apostrophe and made this king a *d'effrayeur:* one who startles and frightens. From then on, the quatrain was linked to a great king of terror. "From Heaven a great terrible King," announced Theophilus de Garencières in 1672. The last two lines remained open to multiple readings regarding airborne attacks, a Soviet space probe crashing on Paris, or a savior figure.[13]

As the millennium approached, the quatrain shot up within collective consciousness. In the late nineteenth century, Catholics like the abbot Torné-Chavigny had already spoken of a "day of judgment" in 1999 while secular journalists anticipated the destruction of London and Paris. By the middle of the twentieth century, American dailies declared that 1999 would witness a "cataclysm which will leave few of the human race to bother about anything." Cold war interpreters tended to evoke an invasion of Europe by a Tatar or Islamic king whose hordes would usher in Armageddon and World War III. For the novelist Aldous Huxley, this was the price that the West had to pay for four centuries of imperialism. "Nostradamus prophesied that in the year two thousand or thereabout, yellow men would be flying over Paris," he wrote his brother in 1957. "It may easily turn out that he was right."[14]

From the 1970s on, it was all about Arabs and Muslims (not exactly Nostradamus's Turks but close enough) and eventually the Islamic Jihad. These decades began, after all, with Palestinian hijackings, continued with Algerian terrorism in France, and ended with Al Qaeda. Orson Welles declared that the king of terror would rise to power in Greater Arabia and spread Islamic fundamentalism around the globe. Fontbrune predicted a furious Muslim attack and a twenty-seven-year war between the West and a coalition of Russian and Islamic forces. In 1995, two years after the political scientist Samuel Huntington had advanced his famous theory about the break-up of the world into incompatible and antagonistic civilizations after the fall of Communism, Fontbrune warned that "the confrontation between the West and Muslim countries would prove catastrophic." In Japan, meanwhile, a science-fiction writer named Ben Goto published several books on the *Prophecies* and the impending nuclear war of 1999. They touched a nerve during the 1990s, known as Japan's Lost Decade. Following the collapse of the asset bubble, the country fell into a deep recession, with untold bankruptcies, high unemployment, and a rising suicide rate. Japanese society's ingrained sense of interdependency and cohesion came under stress. Corruption scandals and the government's inadequate response to the Kobe earthquake in 1995 exacerbated feelings of vulnerability and distrust toward political leaders. Hidetoshi Tahahashi, a graduate student who read Nostradamus with care during those years, later recalled that "all Japanese at that time had the idea drilled into them of 1999 being the end of the world." That was just his impression, but Japanese journalists flocked to Salon throughout the decade.[15]

In the spring of 1999, the number of television crews in the town topped twenty-five on some weeks. Britain's Channel 4 programmed a "Nostradamus Night" while the *Daily Mail* asked whether there might be "more to this enduring figure than meets the sceptical eye." Regardless of the answer, it named him its man of the year. Other newspapers wondered what the sky might send down, from meteorites to a crashing space station. Astrologers and other interpreters declared that the quatrain announced a mass catastrophe or even a nuclear war. Polls indicated that a fifth of the Japanese population felt that this doomsday prediction contained some truth. Callers from distant continents dialed up Salon's newspaper and tourism bureau to find out what loomed ahead.[16]

Once the eclipses had come and gone without disastrous consequences that summer, the interpreters apologized or recalibrated. Fontbrune admitted to an error rate of 20 percent, an improvement over his father's, which he put at 80 percent. As in the past, failures of this kind were either forgotten or else papered over by people who could not bear to part with their belief system. With the year 2000 on the horizon—a year that had long been linked to a

Great Monarch and apocalyptic battles—and then the controversial American presidential election that year, Nostradamus did not have time to vanish. When he returned in full blast after 9/11, one of the predictions that went around the Internet was all too familiar: "From the sky will come a great king of terror." These ominous verses remained fresh in collective memory two years after 1999. By that time, commentators were beginning to warn about the Mayan calendar's cycles and the critical juncture looming in 2012. A book titled *The Mayan Factor* explained that reliance on fossil fuels and metals was depleting Earth's energy reserves. Governments, media, and other institutions, the book added, were concealing the gravity of the situation. "If we don't wake up, the planet will naturally self-destruct because it is already so far out of balance." The 2012 predictive juggernaut brought together New Age belief in a shift of consciousness with Christian apocalyptic currents and claims that a Bible code announced cataclysmic divine ire. Commentators and media outlets such as the History Channel then added Nostradamus to the mix. The process is by now familiar.[17]

The somber Nostradamus channeled apocalyptic fears that had taken hold during the cold war and then tightened their grip. A Christian strand revolved around fatalism, moral order, and a millennial realm of peace and justice. From the persecution of Catholics in Eastern Europe to the rise of the counterculture, innumerable signs seemed to suggest that the end of times had begun. In 1999, 40 percent of Americans and 78 percent of U. S. Evangelical Protestants believed that the world would end in a battle between Jesus and the Antichrist (the numbers climbed higher after 9/11). A second apocalyptic strand—secular and more pessimistic—anticipated atomic annihilation without any hope of salvation. Fifty-four percent of respondents in a 1979 French poll expressed dread about the year 2000. By the end of the century, a third, more eclectic strand combined Christian collective redemption with final obliteration and elements that various individuals drew from their respective belief systems. While the Apocalypse continued to seduce fringe groups, it also migrated beyond such confines. Without believing in the imminent end of the world, ever more people have come to understand their lives and broader events through a framework of crisis, all-or-nothing struggle, and sometimes survival and regeneration. "Modernity," contends one sociologist with only a dash of hyperbole, "has become apocalyptic."[18]

Nostradamus contained it all once again. For the Christian strand, listen to Max de Fontbrune speak about decadence, millennial conflagrations that would dwarf atomic explosions, and then salvation and redemption. Nostredame, he said, was no "sadistic prophet of gloom." The American writer Kym Ragusa recalls in a memoir of her childhood that whenever her three aunts—middle-aged African American women from Detroit—visited her family in Harlem in the 1970s, they sat around the kitchen table and quoted Nostradamus and Revelation while drinking coffee. The Last Days are upon us, they said, and Jesus will judge our souls. For the secular apocalyptic strand, read Roberts's predictions about the demise of New York City and global destruction. Nostradamus's dark language and reputation infused and at the same time drew from what the host of *Time X* termed "acute catastrophitis." For the syncretic strand, finally, consider Jean-Charles de Fontbrune's claim that 1999 would mark the end of *a* world, not the end of *the* world. Then ponder his book's American subtitle (*Countdown to Apocalypse*) and the titles he gave to quatrains ("The Burning of Paris"). Consolation could be found, but it remained faint in publications that deepened the association between Nostradamus and what the gonzo journalist Hunter S. Thompson memorably called the Final Shit Rain.[19]

⁕

Five centuries into this journey, Nostradamus's enduring hold no longer surprises. But it remains startling—and revelatory. This phenomenon says something about the world that continues to house and refashion it. The question, of course, is what?

It is easy enough to frame it as a story of loss and impoverishment. One of the facets of this book has been continuity across the centuries, with repeated surges during crises, recurring distance from established authorities, convergence with successive media, stable profiles among Nostradamian providers, and even similar yearnings on the part of readers. This said, many facets of the phenomenon have wilted or vanished over time. The deep connections with wondrous words and moral blueprints have grown elusive. The *Prophecies* have long ceased mirroring their times and helping people visualize or navigate a just world. Nostradamus does not assuage anxieties about being buried alive since this is no longer a widespread concern and the Nostradamian legends are now forgotten. Without a strong story or message, the figure has even become scarce in the world of entertainment. The same holds true in politics. Nostradamus is just too discredited nowadays, even in right-wing or Catholic circles. One can find exceptions, such as Fontbrune father and son, but they hardly count as public ideologues. Some would argue that something similar has happened to the Bible. People in the West are less attuned to its complexity and its multitude of voices.[20]

This rings true, but the holy book has also taken on new forms and functions in the last century, from family record keeping (including photographs) to feminist editions. This is not the case with the *Prophecies*. What remains, then, when it comes to Nostradamus? For one, the commercial opportunities that even highbrow publishers cannot resist when the conditions are right. In 1982, the American publisher Roger Straus wrote to a British colleague that he was putting out an edition of Nostradamus in order "to cash in on this nonsense." Run-of-the-mill stuff, perhaps, but commercialism can easily lead to sensationalism and paralyzed trepidation. When I reread the *Paris-Match* articles that had seared my mind in the 1980s, I could not help but admire the skill with which these journalists juggled Eugène Bareste's distanced register with in-your-face relish before horrors to come. We are merely trying to get to the bottom of this thing, they said. We will debunk false alarms and ask clerics and psychotherapists what they make of these eerie predictions in order to provide a complete view. Fine, but these same journalists published predictions of world's end under blaring headlines ("The War of Nostradamus"), chose lugubrious illustrations, and fabricated controversy by commissioning pro and con opinions. In his interviews with *Paris-Match,* Fontbrune announced the fall of a calamitous meteorite and told readers which European cities would survive and which ones would not. So many readers reportedly asked the magazine where to take refuge that he grew defensive. "Morbid speculation on uninterrupted catastrophes" was the farthest thing from his mind, he insisted.[21]

Events took a similar turn in California where, according to Orson Welles, Nostradamus had predicted an earthquake for 1988. That year, travel agencies, moving companies, and real estate agents told the *Los Angeles Times* about Southern Californians fleeing the area before the Big One hit. The Griffith Observatory deemed it necessary to proclaim that the gravitational force of planets could not cause earthquakes. At the time of this writing, the Amazon page for Welles's *The Man Who Saw Tomorrow* contains revealing viewer comments. "You will live in fear after seeing this tape," one of them warns. It will make you lose sleep, adds another. "If you are easily persuaded, please watch this with someone else so they can maybe calm you down," advises a third. In Japan, the graduate student Tahahashi recalled that in the late 1990s "the sense that 'The End Is Nigh' wedged itself deep into my consciousness through mass media." And in 2009, four million viewers made *Nostradamus 2012,* the History Channel's gloom-and-doom special, the most-watched cable show of its night. Viewers learned, among other things, that quatrain 2.3 foretold global warming and massive ecological crisis ("The fish half cooked by the heat of the sun") and that quatrain 5.98 announced a depletion of grain reserves ("At forty-eight degrees of latitude, / At the end of Cancer a drought so dry"). It was a cataclysmic convergence of natural disasters.[22]

Years ago, the philosopher Theodor Adorno penned a vitriolic takedown of the *Los Angeles Times*'s horoscope columns. These vague and unfathomable pronouncements, he argued, invite readers to accept irrational forces and comply with norms instead of pondering the inequities of the world. Fear and consolation, resignation and solace go hand in hand. Today's frightening Nostradamus may be seen as both the equivalent of a horror movie—providing a playful but controlled experience of terror—and an illustration of Adorno's critique. Its abstract authority is accepted simply because it has been around forever, simply because others give it credence. It fosters compliance rather than engagement. Like the alarming stories about impending crises in our newspapers and cable docudramas, it makes it difficult for distressed consumers to see beyond imminent troubles and truly contemplate the future. The Nostradamus phenomenon's "rising spiral of bloodshed and uncertainty," to quote one tabloid, amplifies threats, generates moral panic, and then invites readers to accept external guidance and a return to order.[23]

This has happened before our era, but not with such unremitting single-mindedness. The demise of propaganda, which can frighten but also promises good things ahead, allowed Nostradamus to become darker yet. The phenomenon also fed a media machine whose dramatic stories fuel public worries that in turn generate more coverage. The cycle then repeats itself. This harks back to Renaissance chapbooks and nineteenth-century almanacs. For Adorno, though, the marriage between dailies and horoscopes expresses something specific about our mass culture and a cultural industry that takes advantage of new technologies to sell standardized, stereotypical images that consumers passively imbibe. No need for a direct grounding in current events for the phenomenon to have an impact. The elusive words accrue more power in a world that pledges allegiance to verifiable facts and yet lacks the time or desire to confirm them.

Media do not, of course, manufacture fear out of thin air. To have any staying power, they must feed off broader sentiments. The dark Nostradamus thus provides fodder for those who bemoan the West's drift toward what they call an age of fear. It takes but a few minutes of online searching to come across droves of Web sites linking Nostradamus to meteor showers, continental shift, and a world war between Christianity and Islam. An essayist recently remarked that Americans live under "something approaching a collective siege mentality," afraid of diseases and immigrants, terrorists and global warming. While we are not more fearful than our ancestors (and do not necessarily have reason to be), the nature and scope of our fears may well have broadened. It is increasingly through this lens that many media and others view human experiences: change, fueled once again by technological innovation, keeps coming faster and faster. Without trustworthy institutions to comfort or protect us, we are left to our own devices to calculate risks and chart a course in a world that keeps on generating alert codes, advisory systems, and public-health campaigns. Nostradamus draws from and contributes to this as well.[24]

The heat wave that I experienced in Salon in 2003—when thousands of elderly people were left alone in their unventilated homes—had deepened feelings of vulnerability before social or natural forces that governments could neither avert nor regulate. The recent Slate Magazine article "The Century of Disasters" devotes twice as much space in its concluding recommendations to community resilience and personal emergency plans as it does to regulation, as if there was little to expect on that front. The crisis of authority has placed individuals at the center of social life but also has left them lonelier and more exposed. Faced with nothingness or else a bevy of conflicting choices, none of them more compelling than the others, they cannot be blamed for giving up critical judgment while submitting to higher forces, even if these forces point to a petrifying Apocalypse.[25]

This goes beyond the media. When the graduate student Tahahashi consulted Nostradamus, he was a member of Aum Shinrikyo (Supreme Truth), a Japanese authoritarian cult that sought liberation through a program of austerity that included yoga, drugs, beatings, and sleep deprivation. By 1995, nine years after its creation, Aum had a hundred million dollars in cash, branches in most Japanese cities, and thousands of followers who embraced a theology that fused different strands of Buddhism, Hindu deities, and Nostradamus. Its leader, Shoko Asahara, sent disciples to France to consult original editions of the *Prophecies*. Japanese religious traditions had long mixed currents and beliefs—including Shinto and Buddhist rituals—but several of them now drew from Western sources as well. Aum went farther than others by sketching a theology of destruction aimed at the materialistic West and the Jews, which it accused of plotting against Japan. The final outcome was a nuclear war from which Aum's superhuman race would emerge victorious in 1999. To accelerate this apocalyptic process, the cult released sarin gas in the Tokyo subway in 1995, killing thirteen and poisoning thousands.[26]

Beyond the doomsday cult, it is the conspiracy thinking that grabs our attention. The age of fear is also one of suspicion and distrust. The crisis of authority and the shocks of globalization have opened a space for theories that, since the days of McCarthyism, have seduced people from all classes, races, and political backgrounds. The formula remains the same. In order to end the struggle between good and evil, we must defeat the powers that are acting covertly to achieve malevolent aims. Such simple yet all-encompassing explanations infuse a complex world with mystery and meaning. Their appeal extends beyond conspiratorial undergrounds. In 2007, for instance, 42 percent of Democratic respondents told pollsters that American government elements had either allowed the 9/11 attacks to happen or actively contributed to the plot. Nostradamus has been linked to plots since the days of the blacksmith François Michel and the French Revolution, but this has intensified in recent years. The phenomenon now feeds conspiracies about 9/11, a new world order, or Russian designs on Libya. Today's Nostradamus, the conspiratorial revival, and the paranoid style of politics all play between fact and invention, make leaps of imagination, and share a predilection for naming and emotion. All are partial to a coded language that requires decryption and hidden, seemingly unfathomable schemes. All also agree that we are living through a historical turning point, that nothing is what it seems (and hence that no one should be trusted) but that everything is connected. "Shocking Nostradamus Cover-Up!" the American tabloid *Sun* blasted in 2004 while revealing that world leaders were hiding seven quatrains from the rest of us.[27]

In some situations and for some people, Nostradamus thus reflects and feeds feelings of alienation and retreat from political life. Even when the predictions do not cause full-blown panics, a case can be made that they prey on people's vulnerabilities during an era that struggles to believe in peace, progress, and our collective ability to master massive change and chart a common course. Nostradamus may well encourage submission and passivity. It may well hold a special appeal for the powerless and the disenfranchised—poor or unemployed, divorced or lonely, ill or elderly—in ways that it had not (or not as massively) in earlier centuries, when apocalypticism was not its dominant hue. According to some sociologists, it is largely among such people and disaffected Christians that astrology has lately found most of its adherents in the United States and France. Many Aum members were likewise young and down-and-out—dropouts, educated but unemployed, or frustrated at work. Whether they read Nostradamus before joining the cult or encountered the prophecies during their indoctrination, they looked forward to the demise of an unjust world.[28]

Aum is of course extreme, and so are the scares around specific dates such as 2012. These come and go. The capacious Nostradamus phenomenon continues to fuse prophecy with astrology and paranormal forces whose appeal is more evenly distributed among social classes. Still, the larger point is that today's Nostradamus does not endow our public arena with civic or ethical foundations. It does not outline a more equitable society or generate meaningful political exchanges. It does not point toward ideals of justice, democracy, or love that might spur people to act on behalf of something larger than themselves. Nor do its intimations of hidden designs help men and women sketch their own future as citizens. Nostradamus is not a myth but it now functions like one, with a predetermined framework of time that is governed by gods, stars, or scientific precepts, and hence leaves little space for change or individual control. Whereas history rests on human intervention and grants citizens responsibility over their own destiny, myths turn the world into an inescapable fate. As they face ecological disorders and economic imbalance and find it difficult to imagine a shared future—or even trust that giving form to such a future remains possible—some people find this kind of framework enticing. While Nostradamus does not on its own threaten our democratic institutions, what its enduring presence says about collective horizons and civic participation in our era is not always heartening.[29]

~ফ্টে~

It comes as no surprise, therefore, that Nostradamus has once again come under attack. Journalists, scholars, and clerics have weighed in during these past decades, along with Fontbrune's brother, who sued him for creating a frenzy that sullied their father's legacy. In the late 1980s, there was talk of a Nostradamus syndrome. A decade later, the *Figaro Magazine* ran a cover story on the Nostradamus Craze. Weeks after 9/11, Edinburgh's *Scotsman* titled a piece "Don't Ring Nostradamus, He's Panicking, Too." And by the middle of 2012, an online article titled "The 6 Best 2012 Apocalypse Theories (Are All Bullshit)" had generated more than 1,800,000 views (Nostradamus was the leading such theory). Fear and panic are the features of late modernity that now prove most unsettling. Like Thomas Hobbes three centuries ago, some detractors lambaste fearmongers who use Nostradamus to unnerve the masses. But it goes deeper than that. It is about the sense that fear has become the prevailing mood of the modern West. As one historian put it in 1989 regarding Nostradamus: "This is about the crisis of modern society, a crisis that is deeply moral rather than material."[30]

Hobbes had denounced fear as a passion that afflicted the common folk and threatened the social order. Postwar detractors, in contrast, see it as the symptom of a disease that has been gnawing away at an entire civilization ever since the rise of totalitarian states, the atomic age, and the decline of family, religion, and moral frameworks. The belief that technology dehumanized the West goes back to the nineteenth century and then reached a fever pitch around 1900. The carnage of World War I, made possible by science and rationality, showed that the Western world was self-destructive and mortal.

Technology and material progress could themselves generate cataclysms. Sigmund Freud framed it a bit differently in 1915 when he wrote that European civilization was but an illusion, a repressive veneer that could not hide savage instincts. But skepticism about this civilization was growing, and it was soon fueled by the Holocaust and Hiroshima. Bureaucratic systems and weapons that can kill millions and possibly extinguish humanity also destroy ethics and the value of human life. Dread of nuclear carnage plunged humanity into what critics called fear psychosis and universal terror after World War II.[31]

Similar concerns about all-pervading fear could be heard in the 1970s and 1980s, when people seemed increasingly distraught and isolated, and again between 1999 and 2001. Fear, said the London *Times* in 2001, "shreds away at our humanity until we are hollowed out by it, whittled away to the sum of our neuroses." Wills grow limp; trust evaporates; moral obligations become perfunctory. Terrified men and women simply cannot resist conspiracy theories, charismatic gurus, apocalyptic nightmares, and predictions of the world's end. Here is one take on end-of-the-world fears: "In response to an anguish that is rooted deep within itself, the European world, the western world invents a thousand Apocalypses." This includes cults. Religious circles began denouncing them in the 1950s and secular critics followed suit in the 1980s, especially in France and Germany. New antisect associations and books with titles like *Dangerous Persuaders* have responded to something real, but they also betray a deep disquiet about an infection that seems to poison the social body from the inside.[32]

As both an agent of fear and proof of its advances, the Nostradamus phenomenon has captured all of this. In 1987, an anti-Nostradamus pamphlet decried an ailing civilization in which archaic fears were degenerating into collective obsessions. "When faith goes astray," echoed the *Guardian* in 1999, "Nostradamus has laid down many strange channels into which it can flow." As in earlier centuries, the anxiety that we project onto the phenomenon revolves around change and the transition toward modernity, or the transformation of modernity and its relationship to the future. But Nostradamus has also moved to another location. The external menace has become an internal one: a destructive, fear-stricken pessimism that corrodes our psyches. Governments cannot stop this and neither can religious institutions or universities. Self-control alone is able to stem this civilizational crisis. To stop trembling and recover our humanity, we must look within, identify our fears, and reject seductive yet damaging fixes. As the *Daily Telegraph* put it a month after 9/11, we must silence the "nattering Nostradamus" that lurks inside.[33]

To think against Nostradamus in our age is therefore to think against ourselves. Or rather, it is to find within ourselves the resources to rebuild a new civilization. When political action seems out of reach and authorities appear powerless and society comes undone, individual liberation is the sole remaining option. As in past centuries, denouncing Nostradamus restores order and outlines a way forward. It also tells us who we are.

⁊ᴏᴇ⁊

But these detractors should also give us pause. If the knee-jerk debunking of past centuries has taught us anything, it is that Nostradamus is first and foremost a Rorschach test for each era's anxieties. Things are not different now. There is no reason to conclude, therefore, that Nostradamus's lasting presence betrays nothing but a crisis of civilization. There may be other stories to be told about Nostradamus in our own times besides cautionary tales.

After all, the frightening Nostradamus has never seized complete control of the collective psyche. In 1999, a poll showed that 18 percent of the French population feared these apocalyptic predictions (or, at least, admitted to it). This number is both high and relatively moderate. While some conspiracy theorists have taken up Nostradamus, countless have not, either because the *Prophecies* do not channel their anger against governmental abuses or they fail to provide the coherence and certainty that those people seek. Nor do the quatrains necessarily foster feelings of persecution and crusades against other nations or cultures—other aspects of the paranoid style. We can certainly find cults and occult organizations that, like Aum, have tapped Nostradamus. In 1953, the Brotherhood of the White Temple built an atom-proof refuge in the Rockies to survive the Soviet attack that, according to their reading of Nostradamus and other sources, would destroy most of the world's population. But this is not a pattern. Among the doomsday cults that the French government identified in 1998, Aum alone took up Nostradamus. The phenomenon has no exclusive connection with cohesive, elect communities that obey charismatic leaders, enforce a single ideology in the name of the true God, claim to battle Satan in an apocalyptic struggle, and reject the modern world instead of searching for compromise.[34]

We cannot assume either, as detractors often do, that all of the people who consult Nostradamus today do so in the same way, or that they are as easily manipulated as Adorno suggested. All are not necessarily—or exclusively—conspiracy buffs, prey to modern delusions or the mass media. Even if few people today parse the quatrains with the dedication of the sixteenth-century Lyon humanist, there are men and women who continue to decode, debate the matter, and decide for themselves. Some of Fontbrune's readers wrote him in the 1980s to obtain more information, discuss his interpretations, and compare them with others, including their own. Other men and women continue to behold the Nostradamian universe and their world with awe. When the television producer Fern Field Brooks came across the Orson Welles docudrama after the fall of the Berlin Wall, she felt wonderment and fascination rather than fear before these uncanny predictions. A sociologist has suggested that readers of the *New York Times* like to forward articles to friends, not merely to impress or provide information but above all to commune with them through shared wonder. The same still holds true when it comes to Nostradamus's predictions about a bewildering world.[35]

This is one of the dimensions of the phenomenon that has not vanished. Its mesmerizing density still allows us to peer into the immensity of time, untangle its thicket, and gain a sense of history in the making—especially when the pace of change unsettles our senses of time and self. Nostradamus still tells us that we are fragile, solitary beings while drawing us into a wondrous universe in which we can connect with transcendent forces. We are not alone; all of us are equally limited: such thoughts may resonate more than ever in our fragmented era. The words continue to float above the surface of things while plunging us into the magma of human life and opening our lives to mystery and forces operating below the surface. They can dramatize the unjust and sometimes catastrophic violence of our world and the sorrow that punctuates the human condition. Haphazard and ineluctable though they may be, this violence and this sorrow can find their place in a story that we help to write.

That is not all. The words of Nostradamus can still put us in touch with yearnings and emotions that, from rancor and despair to empathy and community, we cannot always pinpoint. They also allow us to express vulnerabilities that we often conceal, from ourselves and from others. And death, too—which remains so elusive in the West's public space. In quiet moments, we can contemplate Nostredame's simulacrum of collective death and imagine what lies beyond. In times of crisis, when death is all too present, we can feel the tremors while remaining at a remove. The apocalyptic strand opens up similar vistas. For some, it is the deeper reaches of time and space. For others, it is a collective doom that proves more soothing than lonely death and more certain than possible war. And for still others, it is the invigorating sentiment of living through exceptional times. Nostradamus continues to deliver ways of knowing and being and circulating within the world.[36]

This was certainly the case for the novelist Henry Miller, who read quatrains and their interpretations throughout his adult life and claimed to feel at home while doing so. "A name like that of Nostradamus always strikes a responsive chord in me," he said. The author of *Tropic of Capricorn* and other licentious works, the writer who sought to mold his own singular self, the man who berated foreigners as well as Americans hardly embodies the mainstream. But he is emblematic of a distinct presence of Nostradamus in the West's late modernity.[37]

Between the late 1930s and mid-1940s, Miller read Nostradamus to confirm his premonitions regarding German advances and atomic bombs. He also grew convinced that capitalism and democracy were inhibiting true creative forces and propelling the West into a downward spiral. After World War II, he, too, lamented the corrosive impact of fear, which led the masses to retreat into themselves. The belief that he was witnessing the death throes of Western civilization never left him. This was what the popular philosopher Oswald Spengler, whose *Decline of the West* Miller read with care, termed the civilizational phase. Religion faded, cold intelligence ruled, and organic unity fell apart. Nostradamus seemed to echo such sentiments while capturing the notion that moderns were creating the condition of their own collective death. In words whose rhythm mirrored Nostredame's own gloomy enumerations, Miller wrote in the 1970s that all was now "strife, confusion, mendacity, and buggery."[38]

Pessimism colors Miller's outlook, but he was not frightened while reading Nostradamus. Like Max de Fontbrune, whom he met in the 1950s and visited once in southwestern France, he entertained the idea that a great king would emerge from the upcoming "smash-up" and restore a harmonious order. Miller also joined the string of avant-garde writers and modernist artists who, in the wake of Guillaume Apollinaire and Dada, reclaimed the free poet Nostredame as one of their own. In 1929, the Surrealist Max Ernst included a nineteenth-century depiction of Nostradamus (along with images of a baby and Blanche of Castille) in one of his collages—an artwork that, like the *Prophecies,* mixed incongruous elements to disrupt logic and the fetter of reason. The poet and mystic Catholic Max Jacob likewise consulted quatrains that contained the universe. Miller did the same. Sometimes, he tried to interpret the quatrains on his own to gain glimpses of the future. Sometimes, he trusted Max de Fontbrune's readings. And sometimes he simply surrendered to the mysteries of an inexhaustible universe that resisted rational explanation but said as much about the outside world as it did about him. Nostradamus provided Miller with a window into the "vast multitude of worlds" that surrounded him. This encompassed the worlds that he could see, from China to South America, and those that he could not.[39]

Invisible worlds led to uncharted spiritual expanses. Miller saw himself as "fundamentally a religious man without a religion." Churches and sects had no monopoly on truth. Instead, one had to look inside oneself to uncover what a minister whom Miller esteemed called the divinity within. Miller began seeking this truth as a young man while living in Greenwich Village during the 1920s. Séances and telepathy were as common in downtown circles as Rosicrucians and other forms of occult belief. Miller attended lectures at the Theosophical Society, read Madame Blavatsky, and later immersed himself in astrology, Buddhism, and Taoism. Nostradamus was thus one component of a personal theology that he created out of diverse traditions. Whether or not Max de Fontbrune's interpretations corresponded to any reality hardly mattered. Nostradamus granted Miller an acute awareness of himself, internal peace, and deeper relationships to other people and history. The quatrains helped him chart a meaningful conception of himself in relation to a broader cosmological and social universe.[40]

Miller was not the only person to fashion his spirituality outside the confines of institutional religion. Indeed, he heralded the New Age constellation, which came into its own in the 1970s. This eclectic movement juxtaposed esoteric traditions with the millennial conviction that human consciousness would rise out of its material morass and evolve to a higher stage. Now that spiritual illumination was freed from allegiance to a single religion, theosophy and the Second Coming could meet up with Aztec prophecies and Nostradamus. By the 1990s, such fusions had even made their way to South Korea, where the Chungsan-do movement married New Age tenets with Confucianism and Nostradamus. But Miller also announced a broader transformation in industrial countries. Since the 1970s, growing numbers of men and women have been moving away from an understanding of religion as a doctrine that is handed down from above and requires formal participation in churches. Instead, their religion has become a free-floating cultural resource, a set of symbols, meanings, and values that they cobble together on their own, like a collage or a patchwork. People may pick and choose and retain whatever suits their spiritual, emotional, or ethical needs at a given moment. There are no rules to follow, no obligation to commit in full, and no expectation that this process will ever end. Meaningful experiences and verities may be found in all kinds of places, and these places can change.[41]

The Nostradamus phenomenon has never resembled traditional religions. It bears repeating that there are no emotionally intense rituals here, no institutional framework or clergy, no physical community that could serve as a surrogate family, no formal process of socialization, and no notions of salvation or the afterlife. Nothing indicates that belief in Nostradamus has ever supplanted religious observance in any significant manner. On the contrary, the phenomenon has functioned as a complement to religious beliefs and practices or else as an activity that served different purposes altogether. To depict Nostradamus as a replacement faith, as if disaffected people now sought outside organized religion what it used to provide, is hence to misunderstand the phenomenon. But Nostradamus is also perfectly suited to a religious landscape in which growing numbers of people seek out direct and authentic connections to supernatural or transcendent forces. What they call the sacred or the spiritual may still be found in churches, but not only: it has seeped into everyday life. The unclassifiable Nostradamus espouses the fluidity of a landscape that encourages borrowings, experimentation, and idiosyncratic (re)enchantments of the universe. Accumulation—the phenomenon's modus operandi—prevails in a world that is being shaped by new spiritual yearnings and changing understandings of self and collective norms. Instead of promising universal truths and requiring that one commit to a fixed creed, the quatrains remain caught in a perpetual state of becoming. They invite personal and intermittent readings rather than collective and binding ones. People from all creeds and walks of life are thus free to share and adapt them as they see fit. They are also free to combine them with other religious or spiritual traditions while fashioning their own private cosmological frameworks.[42]

The story that Nostradamus has told since the Renaissance has not revolved around collective rites or institutions. Instead, it is about the endurance of an autonomous phenomenon that speaks to men and women as individuals and provides multiple points of entry, multiple ways of proceeding rather than a single path. Nostradamus displays the vigor of an individualistic strand in the modern West, a strand that pervades the religious landscape in which Henry Miller and others have found themselves at home but that we can find elsewhere as well. In recent years, this has included the Internet, the latest mass medium to embrace Nostradamus. This flow of unmediated information exacerbates the crisis of authority by making leading institutions, from political parties and schools to corporations and churches, seem ossified and untrustworthy. The medium also brims with hoaxes and conspiracy theories. One understands why the London *Times* would claim that it breeds "scaremongering misinformation of the sort that would put the fear of God into the least credulous individuals." But the Internet also shifts the balance from producers to creative consumers who can make their way within an endless trove of cultural material that remains open to all. Nostradamus is tailor-made for a technology and a culture that embrace fragments and discontinuous readings. While our era may generate conspiracies and terrified readers, it also provides ways of making the quatrains and possibly the world in which we live our own.[43]

⌘

So what is it? A fear-laden society? An age of conspiracies? An era of experimentation and do-it-yourself spirituality that some will praise for its freedom of choice and others will accuse of shrinking from collective life? Readers will make up their own minds, but we do not necessarily have to choose. Perhaps what Nostradamus says escapes sweeping labels and revolves instead around deep but oft-hidden contradictions. If the phenomenon has continued to speak powerfully from one generation to the next, and then rebounded following the disaffection of 1945, it is not only because these opaque words could mean anything. The lasting idea to take away is that the Nostradamus phenomenon has captured conflicted yearnings in the modern West for five centuries and that it continues to crystallize them today.[44]

Nostradamus has from the start circulated between realms and registers. The phenomenon has consistently inhabited an indeterminate space, where emotion bleeds into reason, tradition overlaps with innovation, imagination accompanies information, darkness surrounds hope, and the margins nourish the center. It now brings together the dark tone and providential forces of *Revelation,* the media's spectacles near and far, and the mix of serious forebodings and games at play in modern astrology. This peculiar location has made the phenomenon ubiquitous and familiar but also fleeting and foreign. Nostradamus remains a Renaissance monster who surfaces at key historical junctures without limiting itself to any one of them. Its presence is indelible and yet impermanent. Anthropologists might speak of a floating signifier—a word or concept that instead of designating a single and fixed object encompasses contradictory meanings. This "symbol in its pure state" is wedded to each of these meanings but not exclusively. It always points beyond itself; it is always directed toward something else. This is why Nostradamus has retained its roots in the Renaissance while looking to other historical eras, why the phenomenon is both ancient and topical. This is why, despite lacking legitimacy and institutional anchors, it has attached itself again and again to new realms, from Christian dogma to Mayan prophecies. This is why, finally, Nostradamus has elicited such conflicting reactions.[45]

In his essay on media and astrology, Theodor Adorno proposed that the modern West has come to accept horoscopes simply because they appear in the morning paper. Results alone matter nowadays, not their origin. People "don't even see the sorcerers at work anymore. They simply 'get the dope.'" Adorno was on to something. Nostradamus has sometimes worked alongside established religious and political authorities, especially in the sixteenth and seventeenth centuries. But we have seen that the quatrains have flourished during crises of authority, when recognized institutions appear ineffectual or bankrupt, or at the very least display their limitations and open a space for impersonal, unattached, and impenetrable forces. This has grown increasingly noticeable in recent decades. At the same time, our era remains partial to the idea of all-powerful secular geniuses who, like Steve Jobs, promise to save us or at least solve our problems and blaze a path from their superior perch. Over time, Nostradamus has become a suspended name, at once empty and overfilled, at once transparent and opaque. This transformation has never turned it into pure abstraction, however. The name remains laden with the dust of distant origins, the scent of mystery, the glow of celebrity, and the shadow of a human being who must have existed. When a phenomenon combines the lure of impersonal forces with the aura of transcendent geniuses, anything is possible.[46]

And so Nostradamus continues to speak to contradictory yearnings. The quatrains still fulfill our desire for deeper knowledge about an ever-bewildering planet while providing relief from too much information. They assuage our fear of not knowing and our fear of knowing too much. Its floating horizon allows us to avoid too much contact with reality while recasting our everyday lives. The distant authority guards us against imponderable threats while enabling us to participate in our own fate. We can find protection and we can find autonomy. The open-ended lines satisfy our need for individual projection while drawing us into a vast community. The endless flow of words tells us that everything is ephemeral while grounding us in times past and narratives that imbue the chaos of life with meaning. The interpretations, finally, allow us to confront global perils with sober urgency while feeding our disillusioned outlook on a world that is so saturated in commentary that everything has been said and nothing truly holds.[47]

When Henry Miller wanted to grasp the "uncertain reality of life," he turned to the quatrains with seriousness and playfulness. Of course he did. Where else would he uncover as complete, as conflicted an image of himself and his worlds?[48]

Epilogue

✦

Times for Nostradamus

It all began in Salon-de-Provence. I made my way there early and returned often, convinced that it was impossible to understand Nostredame and his cultural posterity without spending time in the man's adopted hometown. But there was something else. It is easy for Springfield, Illinois, to take pride in its Lincoln Presidential Library and Museum or for Menlo Park, New Jersey, to devote an educational center to Thomas Edison, the inventor who made the town famous. Things might be more complicated when the local son in question is a notorious figure whom the outside world shapes as it sees fit. If I was drawn to Salon, it was because this middling town could not elude national or international forces that tend to flatten everything out. I wanted to find out how things played out in the city to which Nostredame had linked his name in such a public fashion, without asking permission.

All kinds of people agreed to answer my questions: local activists and artists, office workers and policemen, journalists and deputy mayors. None, however, conveyed the town's singular position with greater verve than Françoise Wyss-Mercier, an energetic fifty-something woman who helped put Nostradamus—or rather a particular vision of Nostradamus—on the local map in the 1980s and then again in 1999. Wyss-Mercier began doing so as a young freelance journalist and a member of Salon's cultural commission, a semi-public agency that had been set up to energize the local cultural scene. With

Nostradamus all over the news, Jean-Charles de Fontbrune now made frequent stops in Salon to promote his book. He even invited the town to become the world's leading research center on the *Prophecies*. Wyss-Mercier was not against the idea, but she could not bank on much local support. Growing up in Salon, she had heard repeatedly that townspeople paid little attention to the man. She also knew that the local authorities had failed to preserve Nostradamus's memory since the French Revolution.[1]

The town's archives enabled me to fill in the story. During the nineteenth century, Salon did little besides naming a street after Nostradamus in 1808. The city did not concern itself with to his tomb and his original home—"nothing interesting," said the mayor in 1818. The three hundredth anniversary of his death passed unnoticed in 1866. Nostredame did secure a statue that year, but it was only because a local artist donated it to the city. While some residents may well have venerated the tomb (as some visitors claimed), I have uncovered no traces of such rituals or oral traditions. The nonheroic astrologer who had entertained a difficult relationship with some locals had failed to anchor himself in Salon's memory. Other factors came into play as well, including the meager cultural resources of small provincial towns. Provence's regionalist writers, the *Félibres*, also dismissed a man who had said little about the region's spiritual poetry and had written in French rather than the Occitan dialects spoken in southern France. By the end of the century, Salon was furthermore defining itself as modern and forward-looking. The arrival of the railroad had enabled the town to become a leading exporter of olive oil, soap, and roasted coffee. New factories produced metal drums, barrels, and soap boxes. Banks opened agencies; workers flocked from Italy and Spain. The heart of the town moved from the old quarter surrounding the castle, the neighborhood in which Nostredame had made his home, toward the train stations and the surrounding boulevards, where Salon's new business leaders now built gaudy villas. These entrepreneurs attributed the town's prosperity to its dogged, industrious character.[2]

If a local personage could embody these qualities, it was the engineer Adam de Craponne, whose canal had irrigated the city and its surrounding plain during the Renaissance. The enterprising and optimistic engineer was an ideal local hero for modern times. In the late nineteenth century, Salon erected his statue and gave his name to a boulevard, a musical society, and an agricultural syndicate. When a local newspaper asked its readers to elect the city's greatest historical figure in 1949, Craponne beat Nostredame by more than a thousand votes. Salon, the newspaper concluded, preferred "engineers to shifty types" (*les ingénieurs aux ingénieux*). Nostredame was the anti-Craponne personified: notorious rather than glorious, enthused with astrology rather than science, concerned with personal success rather than the public good, gloomy rather than optimistic. Local politicians, industrialists, clergymen, and intellectuals refused to turn the wizard into a symbol of their town. They preferred a great man who had a local resonance but no purchase whatsoever outside Salon. Not even the prophetic revival that took place during World War II could spark local interest in Nostradamus.[3]

This line prevailed during much of the twentieth century. Salon went through rough times between the 1920s and the 1940s, when the market for olive oil dried up and the nearby port of Marseille siphoned off business. Following World War II, however, the city took advantage of large-scale industrial ventures in Provence to reinvent itself. The mayor who ran Salon from the 1950s to the 1980s, Jean Francou, was convinced that the region's new dam and petrochemical plants would attract investments and white-collar residents. Salon could become a commercial center and a middle-class bedroom community, prized for its quality of life. As the population doubled, the municipality built waterworks, hospitals, schools, and stadiums. Like other Christian Democrats, Mayor Francou believed in social services as a means of outreach and political patronage. He also took aim at Salon's squalid medieval quarter, now inhabited by poor families and North African immigrants, most of whom lacked running water and electricity. A modern city could not let this stand. The authorities launched an urban renewal plan that would destroy much of the neighborhood, erect cubelike buildings, and transfer residents to housing projects on the town's outskirts. Only at the behest of the national heritage agency did Francou agree to protect a dozen medieval houses and highlight Nostredame's home.[4]

By then, the building was in shambles. Henry Miller was horrified when he came through Salon in 1964. "What's the reason behind that neglect?" he wrote the photographer Brassaï, a friend of his. "The most illustrious person in all of France!" The house told visitors all that they had to know about

Nostradamus's place in Salon. Between the wars, local historians and tourism officials had occasionally made room for him. When the town struggled to project itself economically into the future, the past beckoned as a bewitching dreamscape, a picturesque Old France that might seduce visitors. This was still true in the 1950s. "Salon the tourist center can be represented by Nostradamus," a local hotel owner declared in 1954. The prophet's name now appeared on road signs and a marketing slogan, *Salon, City of Nostradamus*. But these steps remained timid. The *Salonais* derived few local benefits from linking their name to someone who was both familiar and estranged from regional traditions. It was difficult to perpetuate a mystery around Nostradamus—or to convince compatriots to suspend disbelief. More to the point, the forward-looking mayor and most residents had little interest in culture, tourism, astrology, and dusty Provençal folklore. In our "century of speed and comfort," explained a local journalist in 1960, "things of the mind are secondary." The prophet had little traction, except perhaps as a counterpart to modernity. When it came time to name the middle school that had been built on the ruins of the medieval quarter in the 1960s, Craponne was the obvious choice.[5]

And then everything changed. The oil crisis hit Provence hard in the mid-1970s and dimmed Salon's prospects. The town's dependence on services meant that fiscal returns could no longer fund its generous social programs. As elsewhere, unemployment exacerbated xenophobic and anti-immigrant sentiments. Journalists and politicians worried that Salon's North African population refused to embrace French culture. Some residents complained that immigrants had turned the old quarter (whose renovation had run out of funding) into what they called a "kasbah." These immigrants' delinquent children, they said, now descended from their housing projects to "impose their rule on the city of Nostradamus." A public-health issue in years past, the decay of the city center had come to symbolize social decomposition, crime, and loss of identity. Salon "is no longer what it once was," regretted one local editorial. By 1984, France's extreme-right party, the National Front, was winning more than 20 percent of the votes in local elections. During a national referendum held a few years later, just over half Salon's population voted against the treaty on European unification. Such results reflect vulnerability, a yearning for protection, and unease regarding a future that, in this town, seemed once again to be local rather than regional.[6]

City Hall accordingly charted a new course. Urban renewal and heritage would now supplant growth. The goal was to improve the city's image, draw tourists, and unite residents around a shared past and moral values. The better local residents knew their traditions, the more they would love the town and respect one another. So began the "reconquest" of the old quarter, with faux-Mediterranean buildings and pedestrian streets, food markets and folklore festivals. The decision to turn Salon's past and city center into historical make-believe exemplifies the way European cities were transforming the past into a resource that would advance modernist agendas. It also tapped the population's desire to shelter the environment and local culture from pollution, developers, and a mass-market culture that the French often associate with the United States. Wyss-Mercier called upon Salon to protect authentic local traditions against the American cultural tsunami. European public festivities, she wrote in the local newspaper in 1985, are increasingly modeled after American entertainment, with its twirlers, boxing matches, and hot dogs. When I met her years later, she still professed her love for the endangered *terroir*—a word that could be translated as soil but really denotes a sense of place.[7]

What about Nostradamus, now back in the global spotlight? Could Salon succeed without the help of the prophet who was garnering attention across the planet? This was the question in the 1980s, and in 1999 as well. Mayor Francou was skeptical, but one of his deputies convinced him that this extraordinary figure could hasten the town's renewal. First came Nostredame's home, still in shoddy condition and open to visitors only at select times. At the deputy's instigation, City Hall acquired the entire building, began renovations, and turned it into a four-room museum. Budgetary constraints kept it modest but a new mayor entertained loftier aspirations in the early 1990s. He entered into a partnership with the Maison Grévin, whose famous wax museum has delighted visitors in Paris since the nineteenth century. The Maison Nostradamus, as it was called, tells the astrologer's life story in ten tableaus. Nostredame invites visitors into his home, where each room is filled with wax figures, sound effects, and light shows. "Everything has been planned to allow spectators to live and feel history," explained the new team.[8]

In the early 1980s, Wyss-Mercier felt likewise that Nostradamus's time had come in Salon. Things were so bleak, she wrote Francou in a memo, that people were looking for some kind of utopian ideal. After pondering the matter, she concluded that Nostradamus could fulfill social needs and provide an economic bonanza in ways that Craponne could not. The phenomenon would allow Salon to attract huge crowds. It was a sure thing. Soon enough, a local alliance took form around this project. Some of the people involved—journalists, tourism officials, and local erudites—had been around for a long time. Others belonged to new business, neighborhood, and cultural organizations and shared Wyss-Mercier's enthusiasm for cultural marketing. Thanks to these local providers, Nostradamus appeared in exhibitions, comic books, outdoor frescoes, and guided walks for tourists. From 1986 on, the town's summer pageants also revolved around him.[9]

But what Nostradamus would it be? The astrologer or the seer? The humanist poet or the consigliore? Unless, of course, the prophet of doom imposed his will. Salon initially tapped Fontbrune and his unmatched media connections, but few townspeople were ready to live in what *Paris-Match* called the "Mecca of the occult." Wyss-Mercier and her partners asked Fontbrune to focus on Nostredame's life and his encounter with Catherine de Médicis during her visit to Salon. He agreed, but this partnership lasted less than two years. Salon then resolved to recover Nostredame the "super-genius": a devout yet free-thinking Renaissance man who had combined prescience and science, scanned his times and the souls of his compatriots with piercing clarity, spoken the major ancient and modern languages, and recognized the genius of Craponne. His resourcefulness and openness to others, his affinity for tradition and new ventures, and his "cultural versatility" (as the press kit put it) were exactly what Salon needed to overcome the present crisis. Nostradamus had put Salon on the map. If the *Salonais* pitched in and worked together, they could do the same. A new Renaissance awaited.[10]

The organizers of the historical pageant put this into action. Each year since the mid-1980s, hundreds of volunteers from all social classes have contributed to a reenactment of Catherine de Médicis's visit (or sometimes another historical scene). They have sewn costumes, built sets, and played peasants or innkeepers in the Renaissance village that has been set up in the old city center. Prophecy and predictions have remained in the background, even in 1999, which the organizers deemed the "Nostradamian year par excellence," when they faded behind the history of a Renaissance man and a town that had welcomed Catherine. The festival blended a do-it-yourself Renaissance fair, cultural marketing, and grassroots neighborhood activism. Many participants appreciated this opportunity to fashion a new social identity, feel deep ties of camaraderie, and recast their relationship with the town. This, at any rate, is how they described it to journalists and to me as well when I interviewed them. "We were in the city, we owned the city, the public space," a pharmacist from the housing project explained. "We set up our shacks, our taverns. All of this was ours. In some ways, afterward, you don't see your city the same way." Nostradamus, too, contributed to the reconquest of Salon.[11]

As I listened to Wyss-Mercier talk about these festivals, I could not help but draw a parallel with the resurgence of astrology and the occult that was taking place at the same time. The two are not identical: whereas astrologers promise to disclose underlying patterns on their own, the town's cultural endeavors rested on a mix of private initiative, public planning, and shared undertaking. But the astrologer and the Renaissance man emerged around the same time to provide fodder for dreams—"dreams of a future drawn in the stars," the pageant organizers said—and deepen the connection with the everyday world. Both feed yearnings for a deeper sense of self, for intuition of larger forces, and perhaps for what a local volunteer called a soul. Besides the city, it is also oneself and one's place in the world that one sees differently afterward. This overlap goes a long way toward explaining why at this precise moment Nostradamus reentered Salon's public space and collective life for the first time since the early modern age.[12]

This happened during an era that was losing confidence in grand historical narratives and vast theories about the state, society, or the human condition. This confidence, too, may be seen as a casualty of the West's crisis of authority. The same holds for the future, which is difficult to imagine as a collective horizon—of progress, revolution, or restoration of the past—when change is spiraling out of control and one worries about the next unemployment check. The future has come to loom as alarmingly impenetrable, severed from a history that can no longer provide guarantees or shared models of behavior. We are thus left with local stories and an ephemeral present that stockpiles memories of a mysterious and indeterminate past.[13]

It is clearly not because residents believed that predictions would now come true that Nostradamus acquired a new presence in Salon. Rather, this inherently local venture promised to slow time down and to stretch it out. When Wyss-Mercier said that Provence could save itself only by recovering its traditions, she did not simply embrace a nostalgia-tinged, immobile past. Instead, she and others responded to contemporary anxieties by trying to reconnect past and future. "Nostradamus jostles temporality and draws Salon and its residents into a great transmutation," explained one festival program. I cannot vouch that the organizers deliberately sought to recover Nostredame's own plays among past, present, and future, but they did speak of time reversing itself, of time growing active and transcendent. In 1999, they promised to link the sixteenth century with the third millennium. In that year's festival, the character of Nostredame describes himself as a tree, with roots that sink deep within the *terroir* and branches that reach into the skies. He points toward a collective transformation of time and a future that is rooted, regulated, orderly, and also full of possibilities.[14]

These local aspirations could speak to people within and outside Salon. It is partly for this reason that the pageants energized local residents and drew up to eighty thousand spectators. But ultimately they did not speak loud enough. Part of the problem is that Nostredame has not left a cultural legacy, a moral foundation, or an image of the community around which Salon's residents could fashion a proud collective project. The other problem is that the web of meaning surrounding Nostradamus has grown too dense. Many of the townspeople to whom I spoke explained that they knew little about the man and did not care to learn more. A seventy-something woman captured the prevailing indifference at an open-air market. It might serve Salon to recover its Renaissance prophet in order to draw visitors, she said, but "we don't know who Nostradamus is. We know where he lived, we know what he did, that's it. We don't believe in it." Others were more vocal. Enough already of Nostradamus! said the young woman who cut my hair one afternoon in a small salon on the city's main street. During the festivals, many participants gravitated not to the man but to "the times of Nostradamus," a place and a moment out of time in which they could reinvent themselves and escape the constraints of their daily lives. One volunteer, an ex-policeman, explained that he had relished the direct connection with history and the feeling of freedom. But he eventually grew tired of hearing about Nostradamus: "People were saying so many things about him."[15]

In the right circumstances, small towns or local movements can provide the broader world with objects of devotion or collective memory. For this to happen, they must embrace modern commerce, rise above parochialism, and speak to widely shared aspirations. This is what Chicago's Claretians did in the 1930s when they launched a national cult around the all-but-unknown St. Jude. Their medallions and rosary rings spread the image of a placeless saint that was available to all. Salon, however, has played it safe commercially to avoid becoming what one official called the Lourdes of fortune-telling. Its leaders and its residents were equally concerned about what the prophet's presence in Salon said about them. Unlike broader media forces, unlike those Nostradamian providers who reshaped the phenomenon in ways that they deemed meaningful or profitable, Salon has anchored Nostradamus in the local past to protect its own reputation. As the deputy mayor put it, the city sought to "flesh him out so that people could see past the antediluvian wizard." Only by explaining precisely who Michel de Nostredame was and who he was not could Wyss-Mercier and others make him palatable.[16]

These local actors are no match, however, for this antediluvian wizard, bathed as he now is in global anxieties and commercial ambitions. In the late 1990s, festival organizers denounced both the Aum sect and what they called "the business of fear." The director of the Maison Nostradamus likewise told a newspaper that predictions about the end of the world in 2000 were unconscionable: "Less than scrupulous interpreters are enabling potential lunatics to cultivate their madness." Outside the town, the quatrains continue to float in the ether while ominous interpretations hog the attention. Few people can picture the Renaissance man. As a result, this wizard has become the absent center in Salon. Outsiders search for him in vain while local residents cannot escape him. The Japanese television crews that descended upon Salon in the 1990s asked the man who played Nostredame to predict the end of the world for their cameras. Whether he accepted or not to do so, the request displays the chasm that separates Salon from the rest of the world.[17]

A century earlier, Salon's local historian had declared that Nostradamus was "as linked to the city as Muhammad is to Mecca." Unlike its Muslim counterpart, Salon's prophet has never been just a prophet; he could neither secure local consensus nor draw pilgrims. And yet he has never gone away. This is why the local sphere has proved a shaky foundation for his modern posterity. This is why in Provence as elsewhere, Nostradamus continues to eschew collective moorings. And this is why Salon has joined the long list of institutions and social groups that have kept Nostradamus at bay over the centuries. Not even Nostredame's hometown is powerful enough to halt the tides of history.[18]

⌖

As this book neared completion, it dawned on me that something else had drawn me to Salon. Here was a place, the only one perhaps, in which the rational historian in me (or at least the person who saw himself as such) could approach Nostradamus and ponder the phenomenon's lasting presence without coming too close to the magical thinking, the apocalyptic doom, and the collective fears that had entered my life in the 1980s and proved so disturbing. Salon was safe. Wyss-Mercier herself had said so to the London *Times* in 1999: "We don't get too worked up about anything in these parts." Though I did not frame it this way at the time, I, too, wanted to delve into the Nostradamian world without getting worked up—about the fate of the world or passions that might lurk within me. Like residents of Salon and so many others before them, I wanted to peek in while keeping a distance.[19]

This proved more difficult than I had expected. At one point, I asked a leading French commentator of Nostradamus for permission to read his fan mail (for reasons of confidentiality, I will not reveal his name). This seemed like an ideal way of understanding what a cross-section of the population makes of these predictions in our times. Following an initial e-mail exchange, he invited me to his home in central France. I made plans to visit the following week, after giving a talk in Paris. Everything was set, but a day later, his tone suddenly cooled. He now complained that people had repeatedly taken advantage of his scholarship. I tried to reassure him, but on the third day he informed me that his private papers were his alone. He then rescinded his invitation: "Sorry to disappoint you, but I will retain for myself a phenomenon that is my exclusive possession." I asked him to reconsider, but to no avail. Googling my name, he had discovered that it was at the Sorbonne that I would be speaking. That university, he wrote me on the fourth day, was the home of his greatest enemies. How could I have kept this from him?

That evening, he sent me yet another message. After accusing the Sorbonne of blackballing him for years, he lambasted the scholars who were intruding on his turf: "Not a single one among you knows the first thing about Nostradamus. And all of you spread inanities about him." One part of me understood the episode as a predictably testy encounter between two bodies of knowledge, one of them academic and the other one amateurish (in the descriptive sense of the word) or stigmatized. But I was also shaken by this scorching exchange with a live Nostradamian provider and by the high emotions that continue to surround the phenomenon. I never replied to his last e-mail.[20]

It was harder to make a break when tragedy struck within my home. I would not draw the reader into the vicissitudes of my personal life if this book had not been written under the shadow of a loss that hangs over every one of its pages. A few years ago, my family was involved in a rafting accident in which our younger son drowned. It happened in minutes—a boy snatched away deep in a canyon, twenty-four hours of numbness, and then the sudden awareness that sucks out the air.

I made my way to my office two weeks after the funeral. Back to Nostradamus. There was nothing else to do. But I did not bury my grief in work. It did not seem possible or advisable to muffle discordant sounds and retreat to a monastic abode in which repeated activity steadies the days, leaving only the nights unprotected. Minutes were now laden with the weight of years while months elapsed in what seemed like seconds. The outside world looked pretty much the same, and yet everything had changed. The foundation that had seemed so sturdy weeks earlier had cracked, along with reason and justice, visions of our son's future and our own as well, and even the possibility of moral order. As the boundaries that used to organize our lives collapsed, it became impossible to separate the personal and the professional. I attended a lecture in which a psychiatrist spoke about trauma and wondered whether I was there for research purposes or for myself. During the day, I read about people who engaged in magical thinking, others who debunked it, and psychological theories about the whole matter. In the evening, my wife and friends shared stories about signs of our son's presence: the sudden breeze during the funeral, the rabbit that came onto our lawn and allowed us to approach, the miniature rainbow around a sapling, and heart-shaped rocks—lots of those. My wife saw these signs, I did not, but everything seemed to blend together.

One evening, thunder resounded at the exact moment that I opened the front door. Freak storms are common in the Catskills during the summer, so I did not pay attention. But I sprained my ankle the following day and strange thoughts began to billow in my head as I lay on a couch with an ice pack. They brought me back to the aftermath of the accident, when a massive storm broke out while we searched for our son on the banks of the Green River in Utah. Someone is angry, a voice inside me said, a voice that I barely recognized but whose force I could not deny. During the following months, other injuries and ailments followed. It is easy now to recognize not post-traumatic stress disorder exactly but trauma lodging itself in the body. Whatever I understood then was too inchoate to silence the notion that Nostradamus was trying to stop or punish me. While the left side of my brain worked fine, it could not prevent this specter from burrowing itself in my psyche. I told myself that these were mind games; I did not have to play along. But on some days I ended up arguing it out against myself. Why would Nostredame come after me and prevent the completion of a book that seeks to understand the man and his posterity?

It was the strangest thing. Was I incurably superstitious? Had I succumbed to irrational fears? It took me a long time to go beyond such questions and their all-too-familiar frame and acknowledge that, not unlike Samuel Pepys after the Fire of London and others over the centuries, a part of me remained intrigued by the possibility of magical forces. My 1980s Nostradamus moment was no vertigo of teenage delusion. Nor was it necessarily behind me. I read at one point about an Israeli psychologist whose subjects could entertain magical thoughts, see them as irrational, and yet prove unable to push them away. It is one thing to hear about such behavior and trace the endurance of magical thinking in modern times. It is something else—equally powerful, though in a different way—to think these thoughts and encounter what we call Nostradamus in such close quarters.[21]

The boundary between my own self and the broader world was the last to go. The edge person Nostredame, the ambivalences of our late modernity, and my inner conflicts came together in ways I could not have foreseen. My personal situation does not a pattern make, of course. But perhaps it points toward something larger, something that the writer Rebecca West voiced with terse eloquence some years ago. She was writing about Yugoslavia, but her words—comments on a time and place and on human nature—are germane. "Only part of us is sane," she wrote. "The other half of us is nearly mad. . . . Neither part is commonly quite victorious, for we are divided against ourselves." The same is true of Nostradamus, ever so divided, ever so alluring, and ever so unsettling at the dawn of the third millennium.[22]

Notes

The following abbreviations are used in the notes:

AMS   Archives municipales de Salon-de-Provence.

AN   Archives Nationales (Paris).

BML   Bibliothèque municipale de Lyon.

Leoni   Edgar Leoni, *Nostradamus and His Prophecies* (Mineola: Dover, NY, 2000 [1961]).

Lettres   Michel Nostradamus, *Lettres inédites,* ed. Jean Dupèbe (Geneva: Droz, 1983). Translated from the original Latin by Peter Lemesurier and the Nostradamus Research Group, http://bit.ly/mNdCOK.

Présages   *Présages de Nostradamus,* ed. Bernard Chevignard (Paris: Seuil, 1999).

Prophecies   Nostradamus, *Prophecies,* ed. Stéphane Gerson and Richard Sieburth, trans. Richard Sieburth (New York: Penguin, 2012).

PREFACE

1   "Fire at the earth's core": quatrain 1.87, quoted in *Ottawa Citizen,* September 14, 2001. "This guy": Henry, "What Madness Prompts, Reason Writes," 286. The other quatrains in the e-mails were 6.97 and 10.72. See *Daily Telegraph,* October 3, 2001; Barkun, *A Culture of Conspiracy,* 160; and 2001 Year-End Google Zeitgeist, http://bit.ly/4VQ2wo.

2   "It's one of those": "Nostradamus Sales Shoot Straight Up," BBC News, September 14, 2001, http://bbc.in/lIzY0F. "We were even": *Straits Times,* September 16, 2001. See National Research Council (U.S.), *The Internet Under Crisis Conditions,* 43–44; *New York Times,* September 18, 2001; *The Times* (London), October 12, 2001; Joe McNally, "Spinning Nostradamus," *Fortean Times* 152 (2001): 17; and the Mail Archive, September 12–13, 2001, http://bit.ly/mL5s3N.

3 A picture of Norm Magnusson's scupture and this author note can be found on his Web site: www.funism.com/art/afterthe11th.html.

4 David Chase, "For All Debts Private and Public," *The Sopranos*, HBO, September 15, 2002.

INTRODUCTION

1 On the publications about Nostradamus: *Los Angeles Times,* August 2, 1966.

2 "The kooks": Brown, "Nostradamus Called It!" See Rachleff, *The Occult Conceit*, 139; *Time*, June 19, 1972; Jim Tester, *A History of Western Astrology* (New York: Ballantine, 1989), 215; and Minois, *Histoire de l'avenir, des prophètes à la prospective*, 321. There are few attentive studies of the phenomenon over time. See Sobel, "The Resurrection of Nostradamus"; Laroche, *Prophéties pour temps de crise*; Drévillon and Lagrange, *Nostradamus, l'éternel retour*; and Bellenger, "Nostradamus au fil du temps."

3 "Refuse of history": Walter Benjamin, *Das Passagen-Werk* (Frankfurt am Main, 1983), 575, quoted in Irving Wohlfarth, "Et Cetera? The Historian as Chiffonnier," in Beatrice Hanssen, ed., *Walter Benjamin and the Arcades Project* (New York: Continuum, 2006), 13. On the neglect of Nostradamus: Grafton's probing "Starry Messengers," 71–72; and Céard, "J. A. de Chavigny," 427–29. On disenchantment, Max Weber, "Science as a Vocation," in H. H. Gerth and C. Wright Mills, eds., *From Max Weber: Essays in Sociology* (New York: Oxford University Press, 1946), 129–56; as well as the recent statements in Walsham, "The Reformation and 'the Disenchantment of the World' Reassessed"; and Saler, "Modernity and Enchantment."

4 "Masterpiece": Thurston, *The War & the Prophets*, 164–65.

5 Charpak and Broch, *Debunked!* 3–4.

6 Tony Judt, "Edge People," *The Memory Chalet* (New York: Penguin, 2010), 201–08.

7 Koyré, *From the Closed World to the Infinite Universe.*

8 On collective memory, see Halbwachs, *On Collective Memory*; and Pierre Nora, ed., *Rethinking France: Les Lieux de mémoire*, 4 vols. (Chicago: University of Chicago Press, 1999–2010).

9 See, for instance, Gary J. McDonald, "Prophets of Doom," Huffington Post, February 21, 2011, http://huff.to/m4V594. On Nostradamus and 2012, see the afterword to Smoley, *The Essential Nostradamus.*

CHAPTER 1: A GOOD FRIEND IN RENAISSANCE EUROPE

1 Nostradamus, *Excellent & moult utile Opuscule, à tous nécessaire qui désirent avoir connoissance* (Lyon, 1556), www.propheties.it/nostradamus/1555opuscole/opuscole.html; Nostredame to Lorenz Tubbe, July 15, 1561, *Lettres*, 85–89; Nostradamus, *Almanach pour l'an M.D.LXVI . . . composé par Maistre Michel de Nostradame Docteur en médicine, Conseiller et Médecin ordinaire du Roy, de Salon de Craux en Provence* (Lyon, [1565]); and *Pronostico dell'anno M.D.LXIII. Composto & calculato par M. Michele Nostradamo, dottore in medicina di Salon di Craux in Provenza* (Rimini, [1562]). On Salon: Sabine Baring-Gould, *In Troubadour-land* (London W. H. Allen, 1891), 60; Robert Brun, *La ville de Salon au Moyen-Age* (Aix-en-Provence: Imprimerie universitaire de Provence, 1924); and Gimon, *Chroniques de la ville de Salon*, 277–78.

2 Lemesurier, *Nostradamus Encyclopedia*, 38; Knecht, *The French Renaissance Court*, 44, 259; Boutier, Dewerpe, and Nordman, *Un tour de France royal*; and Wilson, *Nostradamus*, 190.

3 "I pray to God": Catherine de Médicis, *Lettres de Catherine de Médicis, publiées par M. le*

comte Hector de La Ferrière (Paris: Imprimerie nationale, 1905), 10: 145; Gaufridi, *Histoire de Provence*, 2:526; César de Nostradamus, *L'histoire et la chronique de Provence de Caesar de Nostradamus*, 802; and Gimon, *Chroniques de la ville de Salon*, 198–99, 243–44.

4 "But one Nostradamus": Tubbe to Nostredame, December 1, 1560, *Lettres*, 63–66. See also Hans Rosenberger to Nostredame, March 11, 1561, *Lettres*, 67–72.

5 Leroy, *Nostradamus*, 27–28; and Rouvier, *Nostradamus et les de Nostredame*, 17. On Nostradamus as a humanist: Jean Dupèbe, "Nostradamus humaniste," in Chomarat et al., *Nostradamus ou le savoir transmis*, 28–43.

6 Regarding Nostradamus and his family: Lhez, "L'ascendance paternelle de Michel de Nostredame"; Louis Gimon, "Généalogie des Nostradamus," *La Provence poétique, historique et littéraire* 11 (1883): 1; and Chevignard, introduction to *Présages*, 21. On Provençal Jews: Danièle and Carol Iancu, *Les Juifs du Midi: une histoire millénaire* (Avignon: A. Barthélemy, 1995); and Venard, "L'Eglise d'Avignon au XVIᵉ siècle," 206–10.

7 Leroy, *Nostradamus*, 33–50; Drévillon and Lagrange, *Nostradamus*, 12; and Rouvier, *Nostradamus and les de Nostredame*, 22–25.

8 Bonnet, *La faculté de médecine de Montpellier*, 68–75; and Gouron, "Documents inédits sur l'Université de médecine de Montpellier," 374–75.

9 "Terrible evil": Nostradamus, *Excellent & moult utile Opuscule*, 99. On Renaissance physicians, see Brockliss and Jones, *The Medical World in Early Modern France*, 202; and Daston and Park's important *Wonders and the Order of Nature*, 172.

10 Brockliss and Jones, *Medical World*, 209–13; Jouanna, *La France du XVIᵉ siècle*, 9; and Knecht, *French Renaissance Court*, 43.

11 Crosby, *The Measure of Reality*, 90.

12 Brockliss and Jones, *Medical World*, 38–49, 67–69; Thomas, *Religion and the Decline of Magic*, 8–9; Delaunay, *La vie médicale aux XVIᵉ, XVIIᵉ et XVIIIᵉ siècles*, 264–66; and Lucenet, *Les grandes pestes en France*, 18, 30, 115–16, 156–63.

13 "Sins and wickedness": Nostradamus, *Excellent Tretise, Shewing Suche Perillous, and Contagious Infirmities* (London, [1559]), n.p. [5]. See Nostradamus, *Excellent & moult utile Opuscule*, 49–53; and *Forme et manière de vivre, très utile, pour éviter Au danger de Peste* 6–7. On understandings of the plague: Delumeau, *La peur en Occident*, 155–56.

14 On Nostradamus and public hygiene: Lemesurier, *Nostradamus Encyclopedia*, 53; and Allemand, "La présence lyonnaise de Nostradamus." On doctors and the plague: Park, *Doctors and Medicine in Early Renaissance Florence*, 34–35.

15 Leroy, *Nostradamus*, 28–29; and Greenblatt, *Will in the World*, 288–90. On bereaved parents at this time: Ginette Raimbault, *Lorsque l'enfant disparaît* (Paris: Odile Jacob, 1996), 13–25.

16 "When you receive": Nostredame to Tubbe, July 15, 1561, *Lettres*, 85–89. See the biographical sketch of Nostredame in Chavigny, *La Première face*.

17 Nostradamus, medical consultation of the cardinal Laurent Strozzi, in Visier, *Nostradamus au XVIᵉ siècle*. See Wilson, *Nostradamus*, 55; Christian Kert, *Salon-de-Provence en 1900* (Aix-en-Provence: Edisud, 1980), 23; and Delaunay, *Vie médicale*, 171–87.

18 Nostradamus, *Excellent Tretise*, [6–8]; and Nostradamus, *Excellent & moult utile Opuscule*, 3–4, 20–22.

19 There are many books on astrology. See, for instance, Thomas's classic *Religion and the Decline of Magic*; and Grafton's superb *Cardano's Cosmos*.

20 Roland H. Bainton, *Hunted Heretic: The Life and Death of Michael Servetus, 1511–1553* (Boston: Beacon Press, 1953), 113; and Pomian, "Astrology as a Naturalistic Theology of History," 32–33.

21 *Réimpression de l'almanach de Michel de Nostredame pour l'année 1563* (Mariebourg: Sub St Michaelis, 1905), 14. See Rouvier, *Nostradamus et les de Nostredame*, 35; and Brind'Amour, *Nostradamus astrophile*, 108–18.

22 "Our ill-fated": Rosenberger to Nostredame, December 15, 1561, *Lettres*, 109–15. See also Brind'Amour, *Nostradamus astrophile*, 210–45.

23 Lemesurier, *Nostradamus Encyclopedia*, 55; and Cunningham and Grell, *Four Horsemen*, 305.

24 "Many nights": Nostredame to Rosenberger, September 8, 1561, *Lettres*, 94–98. The key sources for our understanding of Nostradamus's practice are his correspondence and Brind'Amour, *Nostradamus astrophile*, esp. 123–25, 318–19.

25 "I await": Rosenberger to Nostredame, April 8, 1561, *Lettres*, 73–75. See Sigismund Woyssell to Nostredame, May 19, 1555, *Lettres*, 38.

26 "Your value": Nostredame to Lobbetius, July 7, 1565, *Lettres*, 154–55.

27 "The stars": Nostredame to Bérard, August 27, 1562, *Lettres*, 140–43. "Profit": Benoît de Flandria to Nostredame, May 1, 1564, *Lettres*, 151.

28 "Effort": Nostredame to Rosenberger, October 15, 1561, *Lettres*, 102–105. "Take care": Nostredame to Rosenberger, September 9, 1561, *Lettres*, 94–98. "I will continue": Rosenberger to Nostredame, June 17, 1561, *Lettres*, 82–84.

29 "I am one": Tubbe to Nostredame, August 9, 1561, *Lettres*, 91–93. See Pierre de Forlivio to Nostredame, November 1557, *Lettres*, 33.

30 There is growing interest in the history of friendship. See Marlow, "Friendship in Renaissance England"; Langer, *Perfect Friendship*, 22, 97; and Rey, "Communauté et individu," 618–19.

31 "I sympathized": Nostredame to Tubbe, July 15, 1561, *Lettres*, 85–89. "Deepest thoughts": Nostredame to Tubbe, May 13, 1562, *Lettres*, 131–37. "Venerated friend": François Bérard to Nostredame, [1562?], *Lettres*, 35. See Nostredame to Bérard, August 27, 1562, *Lettres*, 140–43; and Brind'Amour, *Nostradamus astrophile*, 105.

32 Knecht, *French Renaissance Court*, 71, 247. On Catherine's strategies: Crawford, *Perilous Performances*, chap. 2.

33 Knecht, *French Renaissance Court*, 220–23; and Solnon, *Catherine de Médicis*, 160–61, 335–37.

34 "Spectacle historique. Le siècle de Nostradamus," [1987], AMS box "Brochures touristiques."

35 On this episode, see Monluc, *Commentaires et lettres*, 2:287, quoted in Brind'Amour, *Nostradamus astrophile*, 33, 39–41; Defrance, *Catherine de Médicis*, 57–73; Knecht, *French Renaissance Court*, 17–21, 90, 241–42; and Solnon, *Catherine de Médicis*, 81–82. See also Sutherland, "Antoine de Bourbon, King of Navarre and the French Crisis of Authority, 1559–1562," in his *Princes, Politics and Religion*, 55.

36 Contemporaries may also have consulted Nostredame's 1557 almanac, which contained a line about a great loss for France two years hence. See Patrice Guinard, "Le décès du roi Henri II deux fois présagé par Nostradamus," Corpus Nostradamus 51, http://bit.ly/zhGz0v.

37 Larkey, "Astrology and Politics in the First Years of Elizabeth's Reign," 181; Capp, *Astrology and the Popular Press*, 60, 70; Monluc, *Commentaires et Lettres*, 2:287; and Rosenberger to Nostredame, December 15, 1561, *Lettres*, 109–15.

38 "Peace, love": Nostredame to Catherine de Médicis, December 22, 1565, trans. Lemesurier, http://bit.ly/kygW7K. "Success": Gabrielle Simeoni to Nostredame, February 1, 1556, *Lettres*, 29. See Don Frances de Alava to Philip II, April 4, 1565, in Alexandre Teulet, ed., *Relations politiques de la France et de l'Espagne avec l'Ecosse au XVIe siècle*, 5 vols. (Paris, 1862), 5:9; Brind'Amour, *Nostradamus astrophile*, 51–53, 435–37; and Jean-Patrice Boudet, "Les astrologues et le pouvoir sous le règne de Louis XI," in Ribémont, ed., *Observer, lire, écrire*, 43. On Renaissance professionals: Biow, *Doctors, Ambassadors, Secretaries*, 13.

CHAPTER 2: THE POWER OF WORDS

1 "I believe": Rosenbeger to Nostredame, December 15, 1561, *Lettres,* 109–15. "Admirable virtues": Rosenberger to Nostredame, March 11, 1561, *Lettres,* 69–72. "Coin of the realm": quatrain 6.23.

2 "General disposition": Nostradamus, *La Grand' Pronostication nouvelle avec portenteuse prediction, pour l'an MDLVII* (Paris, 1557). See Robert Benazra, "Les Pronostications et Almanachs de Michel Nostradamus," 2002, http://bit.ly/mmBTfd.

3 On the *Mirabilis Liber:* Britnell and Stubbs, "The *Mirabilis Liber.*"

4 I refer to publishers, although members of the book trade labeled themselves printers (*imprimeurs*) or booksellers (*libraires*) at this time. Many combined the two activities.

5 André Pelletier et al., *Histoire de Lyon des origines à nos jours* (Lyon: Editions lyonnaises d'art et d'histoire, 2007); and Allemand, "La présence lyonnaise de Nostradamus."

6 On Lyon and print: Febvre and Martin, *L'apparition du livre*; Davis, "Publisher Guillaume Rouillé, Businessman and Humanist"; and Alison Saunders, "Paris to Lyon and Back Again: Trends in Emblem Publishing in the Mid-Sixteenth Century in France," in Ford and Jondorf, eds., *Intellectual Life in Renaissance Lyon,* 67–74.

7 "Such is the fashion": Jean Brotot to Nostredame, September 20, 1557, *Lettres,* 31–32.

8 Mirella Conenna and Anna Firenze, "Les signes de Nostradamus: Sur les traductions italiennes des *Centuries,*" in Bracops, ed., *Nostradamus traducteur traduit,* 111–31; and Larkey, "Astrology and Politics," 179.

9 "Changed the appearance": Olivier de Serres, *Le théâtre d'agriculture,* 2 vols. (Grenoble: Dardelet, 1973 [1600]), 2:254. See Bertin and Audin, *Adam de Craponne et son canal,* esp. 117–18.

10 "I would like you": Nostredame to Rosenberger, September 9, 1561, *Lettres,* 94–98. On this media culture, see Thompson's stimulating *The Media and Modernity.*

11 Delaurenti, *La puissance des mots.*

12 On poetic furor: Thomas Sébillet, *Art poétique français,* 1548, in Francis Goyet, ed., *Traités de poétique et de rhétorique de la Renaissance* 52; and Claude-Gilbert Dubois, *La poésie du XVIe siècle* (Paris: Bordas, 1989), 55–57. Floyd Gray discusses the power of words in his *La Renaissance des mots,* 46.

13 On Nostradamus, kabbalah, and Judaism: Secret, *Les kabbalistes chrétiens de la Renaissance,* 319; and Pierre Béhar, "Nostradamus et la tradition de l'occultisme renaissant," talk given in Salon, August 23, 2003. On Judaism and books: Jean Baumgarten, *Le peuple des livres: Les ouvrages populaires dans la société ashkénaze, XVIe–XVIIIe siècle* (Paris: Albin Michel 2010), 13. On Nostredame as a poet: Crouzet, *Nostradamus*; Carlstedt, "La poésie oraculaire de Nostradamus"; and Bellenger, "Nostradamus prophète ou poète?" On Nostredame's poetics: Richard Sieburth, "The Poetics of Futurity," *Prophecies,* xxiii–xlii.

14 Royon, *Lyon l'humaniste*; McFarlane, *Renaissance France,* 148; and Richard Sieburth, introduction to Maurice Scève, *Emblems of Desire* (Philadelphia: University of Pennsylvania Press, 2003).

15 "Honor": Nostradamus, *Pronostication nouvelle, pour l'an mil cinq cens cinquante & huict* (Paris, 1557) [1]; and Gabrielle Simeoni to Nostredame, February 1, 1556, *Lettres,* 29. On Vauzelles, see Nostradamus, dedication to Vauzelles, *Pronostication nouvelle pour l'an mil cinq cens soixante deux. Composée par Maistre Michel Nostradamus Docteur en Médecine, de Salon de Craux en Provence* (Paris, [1561]); and Natalie Zemon Davis, *Society and Culture in Early Modern France* (Stanford: Stanford University Press, 1975), 29–30.

16 The original portent can be found in *Présages,* 132. I am adapting the translation from Leoni, 467. See Chevignard, annotations in *Présages,* 121, 174. On the quatrain in the sixteenth century: Baradié, "Pibrac et le genre du quatrain moralisateur au XVIe siècle."

17 "All dying": quatrain 3.84. See *Présages,* 132.
18 "I have written out": Nostredame to Johannes Lobbetius, July 7, 1565, *Lettres,* 154–55. See Lemesurier, *Nostradamus Encyclopedia,* 100.
19 "Adventures": *Réimpression de l'almanac de Michel de Nostredame pour l'année 1563,* 25. "Unusual": *Présages,* 279. See *La Grand' Pronostication nouvelle avec portenteuse prediction, pour l'an MDLVII,* [6, 11].
20 "Snow" and "many and various": *La Grand' Pronostication nouvelle avec portenteuse prediction, pour l'an MDLVII,* [17, 13]. "Beaten": Nostradamus, *Pronostication nouvelle, pour l'an mil cinq cens cinquante & huict,* [7]. "For forty": quatrain 1.17. On Nostredame's poetic style, see also Carlstedt, "Poésie oraculaire," 142–45, 162; and Dubois, *L'imaginaire de la Renaissance,* 39–40, 60.
21 "Us": Nostradamus, *Pronostication nouvelle, pour l'an mil cinq cens cinquante & huict,* [22]. See Cornelys Scute, *A Pronostication for the Yere of Our Lord God M.CCCCC.XLIIII* (London: R. Grafton, 1544); and Chevignard, introduction to *Présages,* 33–34. Debbagi Baranova discusses the politics of poetry in war-torn France in "Poésie officielle, poésie partisane pendant les guerres de religion."
22 "I gargle": interview of Blaise Cendrars by Michel Manoll.
23 On Nostradamus as cribber: Gilles Polizzi, "'Lac trasmenien portera tesmoignage ou de l'usage de l'histoire romaine dans les *Centuries,*" in Chomarat et al., *Nostradamus ou le savoir transmis,* 70–71.

CHAPTER 3: UNFATHOMABLE AFFLICTIONS

1 "I enjoy": interview of Cendrars by Michel Manoll. "Veiled terms": Haton, *Mémoires,* 1:39–40.
2 "If you could": François Bérard to Nostredame, [1562], *Lettres,* 35 "What is it": Tubbe to Nostredame, June 7, 1561, *Lettres,* 79–81. "Tears": quatrain 6.81.
3 Lemesurier, *Nostradamus Encyclopedia,* 89; Béhar, *Langues occultes de la Renaissance,* 291; and Chomarat, introduction to Michel de Nostradamus, *Les Prophéties: Lyon, 1568* (Lyon: Editions M. Chomarat, 2000), 18–20.
4 For these dates: quatrains 6.2, 6.54, 10.91, 1.49, 10.72, and Epistle to Henri II (June 27, 1558), in *Prophecies,* 203. See also Chomarat, "De quelques dates clairement exprimées par Michel Nostradamus dans ses 'Prophéties,'" 83–93.
5 "If I have made": Nostradamus, preface, *Prophecies,* 4–5.
6 "Natural instinct" and "nocturnal": Nostradamus, preface to Henri II, *Prophecies,* 196–97. See Nostredame to François Bérard, August 27, 1562, *Lettres,* 140–43. The best studies of Nostradamus as a prophet are Pot, "Prophétie et mélancolie," 217–21; and Béhar, *Langues occultes,* chap. 5.
7 Quatrains 4.14, 3.94, and 2.70; Brind'Amour, annotation in Nostradamus, *Premières centuries,* 125; and Dubois, "L'invention prédictive," 551–53.
8 "Par la puissance des trois rois temporelz, / En autre lieu sera mis le saint siege: / Où la substance de l'esprit corporel, / Sera remys & receu pour vray siege." There are references to the divine word in quatrains 2.27 and 3.2. See *Prophecies,* 322.
9 "Brothers & sisters": quatrain 2.20. "As a good": Nostradamus, Last Will and Testament, June 17, 1566, in Leoni, 773. See quatrain 2.8. On Nostradamus as a Protestant: Lhez, "Aperçu d'un fragment de la correspondance de Michel de Nostredame," 224; Dupèbe, introduction to *Lettres,* 20–21; and Chevignard, introduction to *Présages,* 22–25. On Nostradamus as a devout Catholic: Brind'Amour, *Nostradamus astrophile,* 101–02.
10 "Execrable": Nostradamus, preface, *Prophecies,* 5. "Atlas": Nostredame to Pope Pius IV, April 20, 1561, http://bit.ly/twlgRc. See Nostredame to Jean de Morel, November 30, 1561, *Bulletin de la Société de l'Histoire de France* 7 (1853): 117–20, http://cura.free

.fr/dico3/701Acour.html; Brind'Amour, *Nostradamus astrophile,* 103; quatrain 10.65; and *Réimpression de l'almanach de Michel de Nostredame pour l'année 1563,* 28.

11 Perrine Galand-Hallyn, "Les 'fureurs plus basses' de la Pléiade," *Cahiers V.-L. Saulnier* 15 (1998): 170.

12 *Présages,* 200; and Nostradamus, *La Grand' Pronostication nouvelle avec portenteuse prediction, pour l'an MDLVII,* [13].

13 "Dispatched": quatrain 1.5. The original line in quatrain 2.9 is "Pour luy grand peuple sans foy & loy mourra." I am quoting the translation in *Prophecies,* 41. See LeVert, *The Prophecies and Enigmas of Nostradamus,* 35–38.

14 Chevignard, introduction to *Présages,* 54; Lemesurier, *The Nostradamus Encyclopedia,* 122; and Brind'Amour, *Nostradamus astrophile,* 14–15.

15 These are quatrains 7.41 and 7.42. See Brind'Amour, introduction to Nostradamus, *Premières Centuries,* xxxi; von Klinckowstroem, "Die ältesten Ausgaben," 364; and Chomarat, introduction to Nostradamus, *Les Prophéties: Lyon, 1568,* 15.

16 Compare *Présages,* 114, and *An Almanac for the Yere MDLXII Made by Maister Michael Nostrodamus* (1562). See Chomarat, *Bibliographie Nostradamus,* 38.

17 On meter: Carlstedt, "La poésie oraculaire." On Nostredame's Provençal roots: Clébert, *Nostradamus mode d'emploi.* On Nostradamus as historian: Polizzi, " 'Lac trasmenien portera tesmoignage' ou de l'usage de l'histoire romaine dans les *Centuries,*" in Chomarat et al., *Nostradamus ou le savoir transmis,* 46–50; and Prévost, *Nostradamus, le mythe et la réalité,* 41.

18 Nostradamus's translation, an eighty-six-page manuscript, was itself lost and rediscovered in France's National Library in 1967. See Nostradamus, *Interprétation des hiéroglyphes de Horapollo;* and Nostradamus, dedication to Vauzelles, *Pronostication nouvelle pour l'an mil cinq cens soixante deux. Composée par Maistre Michel Nostradamus.* On hieroglyphs and symbolic expression during the Renaissance: Boas, ed., *The Hieroglyphics of Horapollo;* and Martin et al., *L'énigmatique à la Renaissance.*

19 "Cryptic sentences": Nostradamus, *Prophecies,* 123. "Will be discovered": *Présages,* 229. See Camden, "Elizabethan Almanacs and Prognostications," 88–90.

20 Nostradamus, *La Grand' Pronostication nouvelle avec portenteuse prediction, pour l'an MDLVII,* [13]. These poets included Jacques Peletier du Mans and Pontus de Tyard. See Peletier du Mans, *Art poétique,* 1555, in Goyet, *Traités de poétique,* esp. 272–82; and François Lecercle, "Enigme et poésie à Lyon au milieu du seizième siècle," in Ford and Jondorf, *Intellectual Life in Renaissance Lyon,* 166–68. On Renaissance poetry and obscurity: Dubois, "L'invention prédictive," 551; and Pantin, *La poésie du ciel en France,* 107. On Nostradamus and Scève: Saulnier, *Maurice Scève,* 141–45.

21 Quatrain 6.38; Marconville, *Recueil mémorable d'aucuns cas merveilleux advenuz de noz ans,* fol. 8 verso and 9 recto, quoted in Benazra, *Répertoire chronologique,* 63; Anon., *Remonstrances, to the Duke de Mayne,* 10; and Greenblatt, *Will in the World,* 85.

22 "Hunger": presage for July 1560, in Leoni, 473. "Everything": Nostradamus, *La Grand' Pronostication nouvelle avec portenteuse prediction, pour l'an MDLVII,* [3]. "Double doubt": quatrain 3.55. "Renovation": Nostradamus, *Pronostication nouvelle, pour l'an mil cinq cens cinquante & huict,* [12]. On Nostredame's references to darkness and lightness: Carlstedt, "Nostradamus mélancolique," 50.

23 "The good": 1558 portent, *Présages,* 288. See also *Présages,* 146; *La Grand' Pronostication nouvelle avec portenteuse prediction, pour l'an MDLVII,* [18]; and Carlstedt, "Poésie oraculaire," 115.

24 This paragraph and the next draw from Cunningham and Grell, *Four Horsemen,* 2, 14, 96–115, 206, and chap. 5; Rabb, *The Last Days of the Renaissance and the March to Modernity,*

42–44, 93–94; Jouanna, *La France du XVIe siècle,* 543–53, 620–21; and Lucenet, *Grandes pestes en France,* 109–10.

25 "Popular fury": Nostredame to Tubbe, May 13, 1562, *Lettres,* 131–37. See Venard, "L'Eglise d'Avignon," 517, 655–58, 1816–22; and Chevignard, introduction to *Présages,* 29–30.

26 Bernard McGinn presents these features in his *Visions of the End,* 10. See also his "The End Is Not Yet: Reflections on the State of Apocalyptic Studies," in Vauchez, ed., *L'attente des temps nouveaux,* 136.

27 On perceptions of Turks and the Ottoman Empire: Tinguely, *L'écriture du Levant à la Renaissance,* 15–18; Lestringant, "Guillaume Postel et l''obsession turque,'" in his *Ecrire le monde à la Renaissance,* 202–12; and Deny, "Les pseudo-prophéties concernant les Turcs au XVIe siècle," 204–10. I quote the King James Bible.

28 Claude Baecher, "Phénomène prophétique et schémas eschatologiques," 39–42; Weber, *Apocalypses,* 69; and Crouzet, *Guerriers de Dieu,* 1:109–30. Compare Venard, "L'Eglise d'Avignon," 262–68.

29 "Horrendous": *Li Presagi et Pronostici di M. Michele Nostradamo Francese* (1564). See *An Almanacke for the Yeare of Oure Lorde God, 1559. Composed by Mayster Mychael Nostradamus;* and Brind'Amour, *Nostradamus astrophile,* 32, 37.

30 *Présages,* 295; and *Réimpression de l'almanach de Michel de Nostredame pour l'année 1563,* 28, 34. See Béhar, *Langues occultes,* 153, 301; and McGinn, *Visions of the End,* xvii. On the tragic and comic plots of apocalyptic literature: O'Leary, *Arguing the Apocalypse,* esp. 72, 200–05.

31 "Help": Nostradamus, *Pronostication nouvelle, pour l'an mil cinq cens cinquante & huict,* [11]. See Chevignard, introduction to *Présages,* 80–83; and Crouzet, *Nostradamus: Une médecine des âmes à la Renaissance.*

32 "Transmutations": *Présages,* 232. "From good": *Présages,* 160. Nostradamus melded fortune with divine Providence to ward off suggestions that happenstance or the devil, rather than God, governed human destiny. See Chevignard, introduction to *Présages,* 76. On time and the Renaissance: Roubichou-Stretz, *La vision de l'histoire dans l'oeuvre de la Pléiade,* 12–15; la Garanderie, "La méditation philosophique sur le temps au XVIe siècle"; and Jones-Davies, "Les prognostications ou les destins artificiels au temps de la Renaissance anglaise," in Jones-Davies, *Devins et charlatans,* 66–67.

33 "It is not easy": Rosenberger to Nostredame, March 11, 1561, *Lettres,* 69–72. "Here is the month": Nostradamus, presage for October 1563, translated in Leoni, 485. "Venom": Nostradamus, presage for September 1557, in *Présages,* 125. On time, see Petey-Girard, introduction to Nostradamus, *Prophéties,* 28–29, 40. See also Dubois, "L'invention prédictive," 552.

34 "World explanations": Nostredame to Pope Pius IV, April 20, 1561, http://bit.ly/twlgRc. "France": quatrain 3.23. "Galllic monarch": *Présages,* 265. The statistics come from Leoni, 538–41.

35 Nostradamus, *La Grand' Pronostication nouvelle avec portenteuse prediction, pour l'an MDLVII,* [11]; *Présages,* 197; and Robert Bartlett, *The Making of Europe: Conquest, Colonization and Cultural Change, 950–1350* (Princeton: Princeton University Press, 1993), chap. 11. On European consciousness, compare J. R. Hale, *The Civilization of Europe in the Renaissance* (New York: Atheneum, 1994), 36–38; and Jean Balsamo, "'Voici venir d'Europe tout honneur': identité aristocratique et conscience européenne au XVIe siècle," in David Cowling, ed., *Conceptions of Europe in Renaissance France* (Amsterdam: Rodopi, 2006), 24–29.

36 "Folk": quatrain 3.43. "Topographies of sensation": Conley, *An Errant Eye,* 201. On Nostredame and guidebooks: Liaroutzos, "Les prophéties de Nostradamus."

37 "Literary nationalism": Hodges, *Urban Poetics in the French Renaissance*, 61. Hodges's view is close to the one articulated by Timothy Hampton in his *Literature and Nation in the Sixteenth Century*. Cf. Cohen, "Poets into Frenchmen," 173–202. On maps: Pelletier, *De Ptolémée à la Guillotière*, 36. My discussion benefited from exchanges with Paul Cohen.

38 On Nostradamus's literary structure: Shepheard, "Pour une poétique du genre oraculaire," 60.

39 On these genres, see Lever, "Introduction. Naissance du fait divers," in his *Canards sanglants*, 7–46; Séguin, *L'information en France avant le périodique;* and Biet, *Théâtre de la cruauté et récits sanglants en France*, esp. editor's introduction.

40 "Extraordinary": *Réimpression de l'almanach de Michel de Nostredame pour l'année 1563*, 21. See Arthur O. Lovejoy's classic *The Great Chain of Being: A Study of the History of an Idea* (Cambridge, MA: Harvard University Press, 1936).

41 "Life is more": *Excellent Treatise*, 1559, [4]. "The yearning": Nostradamus, *Présages*, 309.

42 "From all sides" and "for the great ones": presages for 1561, translated in Leoni, 475, 477.

43 Ernest B. Gilman, *Plague Writing in Early Modern England* (Chicago: University of Chicago Press, 2009), 123.

44 "A sinister age": quatrain 2.10.

45 Thompson, *Media and Modernity*, 32–35.

CHAPTER 4: FAME AND INFAMY

1 This holy day marked Mary's visit to her kin Elizabeth. "May God": Nostradamus, *Almanach pour l'an MDLXVI*, 82. See Nostredame to Johannes Lobbetius, December 13, 1565, *Lettres*, 163–65; and Nostradamus, Last Will and Testament, June 17, 1566, in Leoni, 773–79.

2 "With full pomp": Buget, "Etude sur Nostradamus" (1863), 462. See Gimon, *Chroniques de la ville de Salon*, 250; and Lhez, "Aperçu d'un fragment," 222.

3 On death during the Renaissance: Harding, *The Dead and the Living in Paris and London;* Chaunu, *La mort à Paris;* and Jean-Luc Laffont, ed., *Visages de la mort dans l'histoire du Midi toulousain IVᵉ–XIXᵉ siècles* (Aspet: Pyrégraph, 1999).

4 "The most famous": Garencières, *The True Prophecies or Prognostications*, [vii]. "One name alone": Sigismund Woyssell to Nostredame, May 19, 1559, *Lettres*, 38.

5 "Aware": Rosenberger to Nostredame, March 11, 1562, *Lettres*, 69–72.

6 "Almost divine": Benoît de Flandria to Nostredame, May 1, 1564, *Lettres*, 151. "Praised to the skies": Iocabus Securivagus to Nostredame, May 1, 1561, *Lettres*, 76–77.

7 Alexandre (?) de la Tourette to Nostredame, December 12, 1554, quoted in *Lettres*, 172; Thomas, *Religion and the Decline of Magic*, 332–33, 342; and François de Boivin, *Mémoires du Sieur François de Boivin*, 44. On Gouberville: Gouberville, *Un Sire de Gouberville*, 209–10; as well as the annotated passages in Guinard, "Dictionnaire Nostradamus," http://bit.ly/lgGzvQ.

8 Léon Ménard, *Histoire civile, ecclésiastique et littéraire de la ville de Nîmes*, 7 vols. (Paris: Chaubert & Herissant, 1744–1758), 4:223; Brind'Amour, *Nostradamus astrophile*, 34–41; and Estienne Pasquier to Airault, in Pasquier, *Lettres historiques pour les années 1556–1594*, 361. I am grateful to Alan Tulchin for the Nîmes reference.

9 Guglielmo Cavallo and Roger Chartier, introduction, and Paul Saenger, "Reading in the Later Middle Ages," in Cavallo and Chartier, eds., *A History of Reading in the West*, 27–36, 173–82; and Coleman, *Public Reading and the Reading Public*.

10 Chartier, "Publishing Strategies," 179; Gouberville, *Un Sire de Gouberville*, 210; and Grafton, *Cardano's Cosmos*, 225. On popular and elite cultures: Niccoli, *Prophecy and People in Renaissance Italy*, xi–xiii, 193.

11 "Reigned here": Fulke, *Antiprognosticon,* 12. See Rochemaillet, *Portraicts de plusieurs hommes illustres.*

12 "The beginning": Girolamo Cardano, quoted in Eamon, *Science and the Secrets of Nature,* 106. On reputation and fame: Leon Battista Alberti, "On the Family" (1432), in John W. Boyer et al., eds., *Readings in Western Civilization,* 9 vols. (Chicago: University of Chicago Press, 1986), 5:94–95, 103; Guenée, *Du Guesclin et Froissart,* 10, 29–42, 53; and Braudy, *The Frenzy of Renown,* 236, 282–84, 302–03.

13 "Sublime name": La Daguenière, *Monstre d'abus,* [7]. See Guenée, *Du Guesclin et Froissart,* 134.

14 "May the universe": Chevignard, introduction to *Présages,* 40. Stephen Greenblatt embraces this position in his classic *Renaissance Self-Fashioning.* See also Rigolot, *Poésie et Renaissance,* 72.

15 "Spirit of truth": *Réimpression de l'almanach de Michel de Nostredame pour l'année 1563,* 20. "A commiseration": Nostradamus, *The Prognostication for the Yeare 1559,* [46–47].

16 "Once captive": quatrain 3.87. "Western planets": Nostradamus, *Almanach pour l'an 1557,* [40].

17 "Infection": Coxe, *A Short Treatise,* [4]. "Calumniators": Nostradamus, epistle to Lord Birague, June 15, 1566, http://bit.ly/kPSN6Z. See Nostredame to Tubbe, July 15, 1561, *Lettres,* 85–89; and Bloch, *Les rois thaumaturges,* 421–26. My discussion of Nostradamus's detractors builds upon Brind'Amour, *Nostradamus astrophile;* Chevignard, introduction to *Présages;* and Millet, "Feux croisés."

18 Julius Scaliger, "In Nostradamum," *Poemata Farrago,* 1:22, discussed in Guinard, "Les trois épigrammes de Julius Caesar Scaliger contre Nostradamus," http://bit.ly/k0yrHe.

19 "Sorcerers": *Première invective du Seigneur Hercules,* [8]. "Foolish": Calvin, *Advertissement contre l'astrologie judiciaire,* 51. See Millet, "Feux croisés," 115–21; and John Lewis, "Les pronostications et la propagande évangélique," *Cahiers V.-L. Saulnier* 4 (1987): 76–82.

20 "Diabolical": Videl, *Déclaration des abus, ignorances et séditions,* [33]. "Judaic": Scaliger, "In Nostradamum," 1:222. The dinner and the attempted sack took place; Nostradamus's prediction is hearsay. See Saconay, *Généalogie et la fin des Huguenaux,* 96 recto and verso; and Guinard, "Une prédiction de Nostradamus attestée par Gabriel de Saconay," http://bit.ly/iABinM.

21 "Off the top": Nikolaus Prueckner, tract on comets of 1532, quoted in Green, *Printing and Prophecy,* 135. "Sweet": Coxe, *A Short Treatise,* [3–4]. See Videl, *Déclaration des abus,* [i, 2, 5, 19, 33]; Couillart, *Les contredits du seigneur du Pavillon les Lorriz en Gastinois,* 3a, 8a; and Brind'Amour, *Nostradamus astrophile,* 37.

22 "Hideous": *Première invective du Seigneur Hercules,* [10]; Daston and Park, *Wonders and the Order of Nature,* 66, 181, 192, 202, 209; and David Cressy, "Lamentable, Strange, and Wonderful: Headless Monsters in the English Revolution," in Knoppers and Landes, eds., *Monstrous Bodies/Political Monstrosities,* 47–48.

23 Burns, "The King's Two Monstrous Bodies," 189.

24 "Great liar": "Le fol s'y fie de Monstradabus," in Montaiglon, *Recueil de poésies françoises des XVᵉ et XVIᵉ siècles,* 4:294. "*Nostra damus*": This distich has been attributed to the poets Estienne Jodelle and Charles Utenhove and to the theologian Théodore Beza. Its author matters less than its wide circulation. The earliest reference I uncovered is a 1559 letter by the poet Joachim du Bellay, in his *Lettres,* 28–29. See Marconville, *Recueil mémorable d'aucuns cas merveilleux advenuz de noz ans,* fol. 9, quoted in Chevignard, introduction to *Présages,* 73.

25 "These incompetent": Tubbe to Nostredame, December 1, 1560, *Lettres,* 63–66. "Poor France": Ronsard, "Elegie à G. des Autels," 1560, in *Elégie de P. de Ronsard Vandomois,* 4

recto. "O crazed Ronsard": Anon., *Remonstrance à la Royne mère du Roy sur le discours de Pierre de Ronsard des misères de ce temps,* 1563, in Pineaux, *La polémique protestante contre Ronsard,* 180–81. On Ronsard, wonders, and Nostradamus, see Céard, *La nature et les prodiges,* 213–14. See also la Croix du Maine, *Premier volume de la bibliothèque,* 330.

26 "Let those": quatrain 6.100. On Renaissance personas: Greenblatt, *Renaissance Self-Fashioning,* 9; Nostradamus, dedication to Fabrice de Serbelloni, *Réimpression de l'almanach de Michel de Nostredame pour l'année 1563,* 16; and Nostradamus, epistle to Lord Birague, June 15, 1566.

27 "The Book": Gadbury, *Cardines Coeli,* 60. See "Petit abrégé de [la vie de] Nostradamus," undated seventeenth-century manuscript, xxxv, Bibliothèque de l'Institut de France, ms. 820; Marie-Claude Groshens, ed., *Héros populaires* (Paris: Réunion des Musées Nationaux, 2001); and Raglan, *The Hero,* 174–75.

28 "Wish for your money": *Thomas Jefferson's European Travel Diaries* (Ithaca: I. Stephanus, 1987), 35. "Has made Salon": Anon., *Relation divertissante d'un voyage fait en Provence,* 64. I have drawn from Louis Coulon, *L'Ulysse françois, ou le Voyage de France, de Flandre et de Savoye* (Paris: G. Clousier, 1643), 534–35; *Locke's Travels in France, 1675–1679,* ed. John Lough (Cambridge: Cambridge University Press, 1993), 72–73; *Journal d'un voyage aux environs de la Loire et de la Saône jusqu'à la mer Méditerranée,* ed. Henri Duranton and Christiane Lauvergnat-Gagnière (Saint-Etienne: Université de Saint-Etienne, 1993 [1772 and 1776]), 115; and Boyer, *Histoire de l'invention du tourisme,* 60–61.

29 "Michel": *Première invective du Seigneur Hercules,* [12]. "Exactly in his own": John Durant Breval, *Remarks on Several Parts of Europe, Relating Chiefly to Their Antiquities and History,* 2 vols. (London: Linton, 1738), 2:171.

30 "My death": Chavigny, *Première face,* 4. "Will be found": *Presages,* 189. See de La Porte, *Les epithètes,* 25, 220; and Charles de Basci and Léon Ménard, *Pièces fugitives pour servir à l'histoire de France,* 2 vols. (Paris, 1759), 1:82, in Brind'Amour, *Nostradamus astrophile,* 524.

CHAPTER 5: THE NOSTRADAMIAN UNDERWORLD

1 "Great Celtic Lion": François de Malherbe to Nicolas-Claude Fabri de Peiresc, December 11, 1609, in *Œuvres de Malherbe,* 3:121. "All that is new": Pierre de L'Estoile, entry of March 1606, *Registre-journal de Henri IV et de Louis XIII,* 395. "There are many": Naudé, *History of Magick,* 217. This account also rests on Belot, *Centuries Prophétiques;* Anon., *Procès, examen, confessions et négations du méchant & exécrable parricide François Ravaillac,* 2nd ed. (Paris: J. Richer, 1611), in *Supplément aux Mémoires de Condé,* part 3 (The Hague and Paris: Rallin fils, 1743?), 255–56; Mathieu, *The Heroyk Life and Deplorable Death of the Most Christian King Henry the Fourth,* 39; Pierre de l'Estoile, *Mémoires et journal depuis la mort de Henri III (1589) jusqu'en 1611* (Paris: Didier, 1854), 332–33; "Prophétie de Nostradamus," 40, undated manuscript, Bibliothèque Nationale de France, Dupuy 843 (p. 40); Yvonne Bellenger, ed., *Pierre de Larivey: Champenois, chanoine, traducteur, auteur de comédies et astrologue (1541–1619)* (Paris: Klincksieck, 1993); and Cassan, *La grande peur de 1610.*

2 La Perrière, *Les considerations des quatre mondes;* Kassell, *Medicine and Magic in Elizabethan London,* 159; Béhar, *Langues occultes;* Grafton, *Cardano's Cosmos;* and Russell, "Astrology as Popular Propaganda."

3 Pierre de Bourdeilles, lord of Brantôme, *Les vies des grands capitaines du siècle dernier,* in his *Oeuvres complètes,* 6:249, 304.

4 "Nostradamus is a planet": Chasles, "Nostradamus et ses commentateurs," 335.

5 Jean de Chevigny to Nostredame, September 1560, Nostredame to Rosenberger, November 9, 1561, and Chevigny to Nostredame, May 7, 1563, *Lettres,* 56–58, 97, 146–47; Chevigny,

L'Androgyn né à Paris le XXI juillet, MDLXX (Lyon: M. Jove, 1570), [4]. On Chavigny: Gautheret-Comboulot, *Les auteurs beaunois du XVIe au XIXe siècle,* 131–32; Brind'Amour, introduction to Nostradamus, *Premières centuries,* lxiii–lxiv; and the works listed in the following note.

6　The single-author hypothesis is articulated most forcefully by Bernard Chevignard in "L'énigme Chevigny/Chavigny," and "Jean-Aimé de Chavigny." For the multiple-author hypothesis, see Dupèbe, introduction to *Lettres,* 21–22; and Jacques Halbronn, "Contribution aux recherches biographiques sur Michel de Nostredame," http://bit.ly/mFFsqa. For an overview, see Barbier, "Jean de Chevigny et Jean-Aimé de Chavigny."

7　Fontenay, *Conjuncion magna de pronosticos, feliz ascendiente de la real sangre de Borbon y francesa monarchia* (Barcelona: J. Matevad, 1641), discussed in Halbronn, *Le texte prophétique en France,* 1211; L'Ancre, *L'incredulité et mescreance du sortilège pleinement convaincue,* 230; Chevignard, introduction to *Présages,* 12, 19, 43, 97; and Mirella Conenna and Anna Firenze, "Les signes de Nostradamus: Sur les traductions italiennes des *Centuries,*" in Bracops, ed., *Nostradamus traducteur traduit,* 113.

8　On changes in Nostredame's text: Brind'Amour, introduction to *Premières centuries,* xxv; and Chevignard, annotation in *Présages,* 117.

9　Gaufridi, *Histoire de Provence,* 2:526–27. On this prophetic enthusiasm: Drévillon, *Lire et écrire l'avenir,* 70.

10　Haton, *Mémoires,* 1: 39–40; *Nouvelles et curieuses Prédictions de Michel Nostradamus, pour sept ans, depuis l'année 1800, jusqu'à l'année 1806;* Brind'Amour, *Nostradamus astrophile,* 47, 56–58; and Wilson, *Nostradamus,* 182.

11　"I think": Hubert Languet to Camerarius, February 1, 1563, quoted in Guinard, "Les vignettes de Nostradamus," http://bit.ly/jyj3pV. See Rosenberger to Nostredame, December 15, 1561, *Lettres,* 109–15; Nostradamus, *Almanach pour l'an MDLXVI,* in *Cahiers Nostradamus* 5–6 (1987–88): 104; and Brind'Amour, *Nostradamus astrophile,* 47.

12　"Impetuous": L'Estoile, entry of March 1606, *Registre-journal de Henri IV,* 395. "Three times": Anon., *Centuries de Nostradamus avec l'interprétation* (n.p., 1627). See also Anon., "Quatrain rencontré dans les centuries de Nostradamus sur le siège de Sedan par le Roy," undated manuscript, Bibliothèque de l'Arsenal, ms. 3137, fol. 1; Benazra, *Répertoire chronologique,* 118–20, 157–60, 208–09; and Hawkins, "A Prognostication by Nostradamus in an Unpublished Letter of the Seventeenth Century," *Romanic Review* 7 (1916): 224–25.

13　On Seve: Advielle, *Document inédits,* 12–14; and Benazra, *Répertoire chronologique,* 162–64. On the editions of Nostradamus's *Prophecies:* Guinard, "Historique des éditions des *Prophécies* de Nostradamus."

14　"Epitre dédicatoire de Vincent Seve présentée à Henry IV, le 19 mars 1605," found in many seventeenth-century editions of the *Prophecies; Prophéties sur les affaires du temps présent et advenir;* and Athénosy family member, untitled interpretation of quatrains [1694?], Bibliothèque municipale d'Avignon, ms. 3194. On Nostradamus as author of the sixains: Lemesurier, *Nostradamus Encyclopedia,* 95–97. See also Halbronn, *Texte prophétique,* 970–71.

15　"I don't know": Jean de Nostradamus to Scipion Cibo, January 25, 1570, quoted in Guinard, "Les imposteurs et pièces apocryphes sur Nostradamus," http://bit.ly/iO5QCQ. "Ancestor": "Discours sur la véritable origine des Moulins à barbe," in Fournier, *Variétés historiques et littéraires,* 2:55. See also Nostradamus, *Almanach pour l'an M.D.LXVI,* in *Cahiers Nostradamus* 5–6 (1987–88): 102.

16　Nostradamus le Jeune, *Présages pour treize ans;* and Agrippa d'Aubigné, *Histoire universelle,* ed. André Thierry, 11 vols. (Geneva: Droz, 1981–2000), 4:234.

17 Filippo Nostradamus, *La Salutifera;* Crespin, *Prognostications avec ses Présages, pour l'an MDLXXI,* [8]; Anon., *Les triolets du temps, selon les visions d'un petit fils du grand Nostradamus;* and *L'ami de la religion et du roi,* November 14, 1827, 32.

18 "Good speculator": Chavigny, *Première face,* 21.

19 Ibid., 20–22, 31, 35; and Chavigny, "Vaticination fort ancienne, interprétée du très chréstien Henry IIII, roy de France et de Navarre, et conférée avec les oracles et présages de M. Michel de Nostredame," n.d., Bibliothèque Méjanes, ms. 451, fol. 395.

20 Chavigny, *Première face,* 35–38, 50, 110, 210; Chevignard, introduction to *Présages,* 87–90; and Céard, "J. A. de Chavigny," 441.

21 "Clearly": *Les vraies Centuries et Prophéties de Maistre Michael Nostradamus* (Amsterdam: J. Jansson, 1668), [i–ii]. See Anon., *Petit discours ou commentaire sur les Centuries de Maistre Michel Nostradamus;* and Calvet, "Les tours de Nostredame," 171.

22 "Peculiar Genius": Garencières, *The True Prophecies,* [ii]. See Le Roux, *La clef de Nostradamus,* xxxix, 314.

23 "Century's corruption": Chavigny, *Discours parénétique sur les choses turques,* [ii]. "Defining trait": Chavigny, *Première face,* 20–21, 40–42.

24 Marion, "Narratologie médiatique," 71.

25 "Of all the editions": "Observation sur les prophéties de M. Michel Nostradamus," *Les vraies Centuries et Prophéties de Maistre Michel Nostradamus* (Amsterdam: D. Winkermans, 1667), [i]. "Be the source": Chavigny, *Première face,* 279, trans. Steven Crumb.

26 The sociologist Daniel Gros discusses the appeal of astrology in his "Le paradoxe de l'astrologue," in Edgar Morin, ed., *La croyance astrologique moderne,* 192.

27 Le Roux, *Clef de Nostradamus,* 466.

28 "Wrapped in wrinkles": Hugh Latimer, quoted in Ferrell, *The Bible and the People,* 127. There is a vast literature on the history of the Bible. In addition to Ferrell's book, I have learned much from Armstrong, *The Bible: A Biography;* Daniell, *The Bible in English;* Hill, *The English Bible and the Seventeenth-Century Revolution;* and Sharpe, "Reading Revelations."

29 "Advertissement au lecteur," in Nostradamus le Jeune, *Présages pour treize ans,* 24; "De l'instruction de M. le Dauphin," in *Oeuvres de François de La Mothe Le Vayer,* 1:314; Buget, "Etude sur les prophéties de Nostradamus," 1702–06; and Hobbes, *Leviathan,* chap. 12.

CHAPTER 6: WONDER AND POLITICS AT THE COURT OF FRANCE

1 Undated manuscript describing the events, BML ms. 1336–37 (1212), in Tennevin, *François Michel,* 175.

2 The best source on Michel and the ghost is Tennevin's detailed *François Michel.* I have drawn from it copiously in the paragraphs that follow. I also consulted Saint-Simon, *Mémoires,* 6:222–27; articles from the *Gazette d'Amsterdam* (1697), ibid., 6:549; Palamède Tronc de Coudoulet, "Abrégé de l'histoire de Michel Nostradamus" [1701?], 52–64, AMS, copy in box "Nostradamus"; Sourches, *Mémoires,* 5:260; Callières, *Letters,* 260; and Achard, *Dictionnaire de la Provence,* 524–25. Two engravings of the blacksmith are held at the Bibliothèque Nationale de France, Département des Estampes, Hennin 6332 and 6333. On Nostredame's descendants in Salon: "Voyage fait en Provence 13 avril–18 juin 1671 d'après un manuscrit inédit," in Louise Godard de Donville, "Découverte de la Provence au XVIIᵉ siècle," *Marseille. Revue municipale trimestrielle* 120 (1980): 102.

3 "This man": Sourches, *Mémoires,* 260. The portents in the chapbook were from May and December 1555. See *François-Michel Placide, Marechal ferrant, natif de Salon en Provence* (n.p., [1697?]), [2].

4 On ghosts in early modern Europe: Mercier, *Leonarde's Ghost;* Maxwell-Stuart, *Ghosts;* Bruce Gordon and Peter Marshall, eds., *The Place of the Dead: Death and Remembrance in Late Medieval and Early Modern Europe* (New York: Cambridge University Press, 2000); and Davies, *The Haunted.*

5 Quevedo, *Visions;* Anon., *Description véritable d'un phantosme;* Anon., *Visions astrologiques de Michel Nostradamus;* and Hubert Carrier, *La presse de la Fronde (1648–1653): Les Mazarinades,* 2 vols. (Geneva: Droz, 1991), 1:299.

6 This discussion draws from Bynum, "Wonder," and Daston and Park, *Wonders and the Order of Nature.* I thank Chantal Liaroutzos for sharing her unpublished essay, "Les catastrophes naturelles dans les Antiquités de villes."

7 Burns, *An Age of Wonders;* and Friedman, *The Battle of the Frogs and Fairbord's Flies.*

8 "Numerous wonders": Nostredame to Rosenberger, September 9, 1561, *Lettres,* 94–98. "Many strange": *A Collection of Twenty-Three Prophecies and Predictions of the Famous Michael Nostrodamus.* See Chavigny, *Première face,* 18; Anon., *Discours merveilleux et mémorable,* in Lever, *Canards sanglants,* 253–55; Anon., *Bataille prodigieuse d'une grande quantité d'oyseaux;* and Madame de Sévigné to Madame de Grignan, March 11, 1676, in her *Correspondance,* 2:251–52.

9 "Something extraordinary": "Copie d'une lettre écrite de Salon en Provence," in Tennevin, *François Michel,* 160.

10 The statistics come from Richard S. Dunn, *The Age of Religious Wars, 1559–1715,* 2nd ed. (New York: Norton, 1979), 264–65. See John A. Lynn, *The Wars of Louis XIV: 1667–1714* (New York: Longman, 1999).

11 Anon., *Présages émerveillables pour XX ans;* Chavigny, "Vaticination fort ancienne," op.cit., [2–4]; Chavigny, *Première face,* 40, 50, 283; and *Les Pléiades du S. de Chavigny, Beaunois.* On political uses of Nostradamus in the late sixteenth century: Halbronn, "Les prophéties et la Ligue," 124–25. On Chavigny's politics: Céard, "J. A. De Chavigny," 436–42; and Poumarède, *Pour en finir avec la Croisade,* 113–17. On the Great Monarch: Haran, *Le lys et le globe.*

12 "Unfit": Anon., *L'horoscope de Jules Mazarin,* [1].

13 "These are days": Rabb, *Last Days of the Renaissance,* 103. This paragraph and the next draw from Thomas, *Religion and the Decline of Magic,* 142–43; Popkin, "Seventeenth-Century Millenarianism," 112–21; and Williamson, *Apocalypse Then,* 91–92.

14 Merlin Ambrosius, *The Lord Merlin's Prophecy Concerning the King of Scots,* 3–4; John Rogers, *Sagrir, or, Doomes-Day Drawing Nigh* (London: Hucklescot, 1654), 132; and Rusche, "Prophecies and Propaganda, 1641 to 1651," 767.

15 "Predictions, or prophecies": *A Collection of Twenty-Three Prophecies,* 3. On saints: Moshe Sluhovsky, "La mobilisation des saints dans la Fronde parisienne d'après les Mazarinades," *Annales,* 54, no. 2 (1999): 358.

16 Jean Berenger, *Léopold 1er, 1640–1705: fondateur de la puissance autrichienne* (Paris: Presses Universitaires de France, 2004), 241–42; van der Wall, "'Antichrist Stormed,'" 162; Faith Wigzell, *Reading Russian Fortunes: Print Culture, Gender and Divination in Russia from 1765* (New York: Cambridge University Press, 1998), 163; Anon., *Dr Martin Luther's Prophecies of the Destruction of Rome* (Edinburgh, 1679); Philalelos, *Good and Joyful News for England;* and Atwood, *The Wonderful Predictions of Nostradamus.*

17 Darryl Dee, *Expansion and Crisis in Louis XIV's France: Franche-Comté and Absolute Monarchy, 1674–1715* (Rochester: University of Rochester Press, 2009).

18 "Pleace and plenty": *A Collection of Twenty-Three Prophecies,* 7. "Spectacle of horror": "L'issue funeste du prince d'Orange prédite par Nostradamus," January 1, 1690, engraving

in the Bibliothèque Nationale de France, Département des Estampes. See *Les Vrayes Centuries et Prophéties de Maistre Michel Nostradamus* (1667); Massard, *Relation exacte, & curieuse des Malheurs extrêmes & prochains*; Le Noble, "Nostradamus, ou les oracles," 9:47; and Drévillon, *Lire et écrire l'avenir*, 203–05. On glory and propaganda: Moriceau, "Le Coq et l'Orange"; and Préaud, *Les effets du soleil*, 21–29.

19 "Famous *French* prophet": John Ray, *Observations Topographical, Moral, & Physiological Made in a Journey Through Part of the Low-Countries, Germany, Italy, and France* (London: J. Martyn, 1673), 465. "Prophet of their own": Anon., *The Fortune of France*, 16. "A triumphant reign": *Les Vrayes Centuries et Prophéties de Maistre Michel Nostradamus* (Rouen: B. Gyrin, 1710), quoted in Benazra, *Répertoire chronologique*, 29. "Indispensable": Espitalier, *Les Oracles secrets de Nostradamus*, 4–5.

20 "Is thought": "Copie d'une lettre écrite de Salon en Provence," in Tennevin, *François Michel*, 161.

21 "That is assured": "Chanson nouvelle" [1698], in Tennevin, *François Michel*, 164. See *François-Michel Placide, Marechal ferrant, natif de Salon en Provence*, [1]; and Henri Duclos, *Mademoiselle de La Vallière et Marie-Thérèse d'Autriche, femme de Louis XIV*, 2 vols. (Paris: Didier, 1870), 2:980.

22 "Good and joyful news": Philalelos, *Good and Joyful News for England*, 3. See Jean Bernier, "Jugements ou nouvelles observations sur les oeuvre grecques, latines, toscanes et françaises de maître François Rabelais," 1697, quoted in Tennevin, *François Michel*, 80–81; and *The Works of Sir William Temple*, 2:486–87. On the Maintenon plot: Achard, *Dictionnaire de la Provence*, 525.

23 Letter from Salon, published in *Gazette d'Amsterdam*, in Tennevin, *François Michel*, 158.

24 Jean-Baptiste Colbert to cardinal Mazarin, February 18, 1656, in Colbert, *Lettres, instructions et mémoires*, 1:239–40; and Gacon, *Le poète sans fard, contenant satires, épitres et épigrammes*. On official concerns: Anon., *Procès, examen, confessions et négations du méchant et exécrable parricide François Ravaillac*, 2nd ed. (Paris, 1611), in *Supplément aux Mémoires de Condé*, 3rd part (n.p., n.d.), 257; and unidentified article dated May 20, 1697, in Saint-Simon, *Mémoires*, 6:550. On taxation revolts: Yves-Marie Bercé, *History of Peasant Revolts: The Social Origins of Rebellion in Early Modern France*, trans. Amanda Whitmore (Ithaca: Cornell University Press, 1990).

25 His will and pawnshop records are reproduced in Tennevin, *François Michel*, 76–78, 211–12.

26 "The troops": William Perwich to Lord Arlington, July 29, 1670, in Perwich, *Despatches*, 104. See Isaac de Larrey, *Histoire de France sous le règne de Louis XIV*, 9 vols. (Rotterdam: M. Bohm, 1738), 2:443. On astrology's declining legitimacy: Davies, *Witchcraft, Magic and Culture*, 111–12, 126–27; and Drévillon, *Lire et écrire l'avenir*, 178, 224, 236. The monarchy's change of course owed much to the Affair of the Poisons (1679), in which the police uncovered a community of alchemists, fortune-tellers, and magicians who sold poisons and charms that some nobles had used against the king.

27 "Fodder": François de Callières to marquise d'Huxelles, April 22, 1697, Callières, *Letters*, 249. See Bayle, *Dictionnaire historique et critique*, 578; and article dated March 22, 1697, *Gazette d'Amsterdam*, in Saint-Simon, *Mémoires*, 6:547.

28 "Nostredame to the princes": Gimon, *Chroniques de la ville de Salon*, 564–65. On the 1701 visit to Salon: "Journal de toutes les affaires de la commune depuis l'année 1699 1700 1701," fol. 11, AM Salon BB19 bis; and Levantal, *La route des Princes*, 110. See also Villars, *Mémoires*, 141.

CHAPTER 7: AMAZING BONES

1 This paragraph and the next draw from Gimon, *Chroniques de la ville de Salon*, 708, 718–19; Claude Badet, *La Révolution en Provence* (Avignon: A. Barthélemy, 1989); Joseph Megy, "Notice sur Michel Nostradamus," February 7, 1818, Archives départementales des Bouches-du-Rhône, 6 M 1610; Buget, "Etude sur Nostradamus," 1863, 523; and Le Normand, *Souvenirs prophétiques d'une Sibylle*, 333.

2 See, for instance, the account given in Delumeau, *Le Catholicisme entre Luther et Voltaire* (Paris: Presses Universitaires de France, 1971).

3 "Erroneous": Belier de Saint-Brisson, *Accomplissement d'une prophétie de Nostradamus*, 2. See Belier de Saint-Brisson, *Epistre au Roy*, quoting sixain 48; Count Moszynski, *Voyage en Provence d'un Gentilhomme polonais (1784–1785)*, ed. Fernand Benoit (Marseille: Institut historique de Provence, 1930), 48–49; and Davies, *Witchcraft, Magic and Culture*, 146. On provincial censorship of the *Prophecies:* Mellot, *L'édition rouennaise et ses marchés*, 597.

4 "A great nation": Brun, "Nostradamus Centurie 53" [1721?], Bibliothèque municipale d'Avignon, ms. 3188, fol. 1. See *Journal des débats*, October 19, 1881; Dinet, "Les bibliothèques monastiques," 296; Pierre Goubert, *The Ancien Régime: French Society, 1600–1750*, trans. Steve Cox (New York: Harper, 1969), 172, 176; and Buvat, *Journal de la Régence*, 1:437.

5 "If the famed": entry dated March 1744 in Barbier, *Chronique de la régence et du règne de Louis XV*, 495. See Pluquet, *Dictionnaire des hérésies*, 2:848.

6 The best expression of this view is Walsham, "The Reformation and 'the Disenchantment of the World' Reassessed." See also Edelstein, *The Super-Enlightenment;* and Darnton's pioneering *Mesmerism and the End of the Enlightenment in France*.

7 For a thorough account of the king's flight and the panic that ensued: Timothy Tackett, *When the King Took Flight* (Cambridge, MA: Harvard University Press, 2003).

8 "All of Paris": *Journal de Paris*, May 1, 1790, quoted in Harvey, *Beyond Enlightenment*, 131. "The greatest": Rouy l'aîné, *Le magicien républicain*, 18. See Laroche, *Prophéties pour temps de crise*, 65; Anon., *L'astrologue patriote; Journal de la cour et de la ville* 45 (April 14, 1792): 359–60; and *The World*, February 22, 1790.

9 "Beginning": Epistle to Henri II, *Prophecies*, 203.

10 "Truth to triumph": *Nouveaux et vrais pronostics de Michel Nostradamus . . . Pour huit ans, à commencer en l'année 1793 jusqu'à l'année 1800 inclusivement*, 2. See Boussemart, *Grande arrivée de Nostradamus à Paris*, 2; Rouy l'aîné, *Le magicien républicain*, 77–78; *Journal historique et littéraire*, February 1, 1792, 233–34, quoted in Benazra, *Répertoire chronologique*, 336; and Weber, *Apocalypses*, 110–14.

11 Tronc de Coudoulet, *Abrégé de la vie et de l'histoire de Michel Nostradamus*, 44; and Claude Jordan, *Voyages historiques en France*, 8 vols. (Paris: P. Abouyn, 1693–1700), 1:17–18.

12 Haitze, *La vie de Michel Nostradamus*, 135–37; Chavigny, *Première face*, 5; Guynaud, *La concordance des Prophéties de Nostradamus*, 27; Garencières, *True Prophecies*, [vii]; and Paul Lucas, *Troisième voyage du sieur Paul Lucas dans le Levant: mai 1714–novembre 1717*, ed. Henri Duranton (Saint-Etienne: Presses Universitaires de Saint-Etienne, 2004), 25–26.

13 Pepys, *Diary*, 460; *Nouvelles et curieuses prédictions de Michel Nostradamus, pour sept ans, depuis l'année 1778, jusqu'à l'année 1785* (Salon: 1778), 5–6; and "New Prediction Said to Be Found at the Opening of the Tomb of Michael Nostradamus" [1713?], British Library, ms. Sloane 3722.

14 "Amazing bones": Anon., *Relation divertissante d'un voyage fait en Provence*, 65. See *Le Journal de la cour et de la ville*, January 9, 1792, 71; Knight, *Merlin*, 110; and Mauss, *A General Theory of Magic*, 51.

15 Peter McPhee, *Living the French Revolution, 1789–1799* (New York: Palgrave Macmillan, 2006), 144.

16 Gimon, *Chroniques de la ville de Salon,* 706; and Buget, "Etude sur Nostradamus," 1863, 523. On the National Guard: Serge Bianchi and Roger Dupuy, eds., *La garde nationale entre nation et peuple en armes* (Rennes: Presses Universitaires de Rennes, 2006); and Michael L. Kennedy, *The Jacobin Club of Marseilles, 1790–1794* (Ithaca: Cornell University Press, 1973), 82–95.

17 D'Odoucet, *Révolution française,* quotation on 9; and *Nouveaux et vrais pronostics de Michel Nostradamus Pour huit ans, à commencer en l'année 1793 jusqu'à l'année 1800 inclusivement.*

18 "This unjust": *Les vraies Centuries, présages et prédictions de Maistre Michel Nostradamus* (Antwerp: P. van Duren 1792), 271 (this quatrain was an imitation). "Let heaven": *Journal général de la cour et de la ville,* April 28 and July 1, 1790, quoted in Garrett, *Respectable Folly,* 45–46. See also Anon., *Prophétie de Nostradamus accomplie.*

19 "It will all go": Miller, *Memoir of the Rev. Charles Nisbet, D.D.,* 84, 222, 311–12. See Diesbach de Belleroche, commentary on "Prophétie de Nostradamus, publiée en 1790, par Durofoi," ms. 1790, traces-ecrites.com; and Proceedings of the French National Assembly, April 24, 1792, in Jérôme Madival and Emile Laurent, eds., *Archives parlementaires de 1787 à 1860,* 1st ser., 82 vols. (Paris: Dupont, 1862–96), 42:354–55.

20 "Modern Nostradamus": Olympe de Gouges, "Response to the Justification of Robespierre. Addressed to Jérôme Pétion. November 1792," in *Writings by Pre-Revolutionary French Women,* ed. Anne R. Larsen and Colette H. Winn (New York: Routledge, 1999), 567. "Imaginings": proceedings of the Convention, June 15, 1794, in Philippe Buchez and Pierre-Célestin Roux-Lavergne, eds., *Histoire parlementaire de la Révolution française,* 40 vols. (Paris: Paulin, 1834–38), 38:255.

21 "Step beyond": Edwards, *Cometomantia,* 230–31. See Menestrier, *Philosophie des images,* 385–89; and Drévillon, *Lire et écrire l'avenir,* 251.

22 "Fear of invisible": Jean-François de Saint-Lambert, *Catéchisme universel,* appended to Cadmus, *A, B, C, abécédairo nouveau, conforme au principe adopté par l'Institut national* (Paris: F. Bonneville, Year VII), 73. On early modern supersitition: Cambers, "Demonic Possession, Literacy and 'Superstition' in Early Modern England"; and Revel, "Forms of Expertise," 256–64.

23 "Owed their success": Abbé de Laporte, Abbé de Fontenai, and Louis Domairon, *Le voyageur françois, ou la connoissance de l'ancien et du nouveau monde,* 42 vols. (Paris: Moutard, 1765–96), 29:391.

24 "Old matrons": Gildon, *The Post-Boy Rob'd of his Mail,* 234–35. "So disdained": Gayot de Pitaval, *Bibliothèque de cour, de ville et de campagne,* 6:191. "Needed to terrorize": Joseph Lavallée, *Voyage dans les départements de la France* (Paris: Brion, 1792–1802), 27. See Achard, *Dictionnaire de la Provence,* 2:8–11.

25 On reason and magic, see Styers's rich *Making Magic.*

26 On the intermingling of elite and popular cultures: Goulemot, "Démons, merveilles et philosophie à l'âge classique." On enduring doubts: Brockliss and Jones, *Medical World,* 282–83.

27 Joseph Cérutti, *Les jardins de Betz. Poème accompagné de notes instructives. . . .* 2nd ed. (Paris: Desenne, 1792), 36.

28 Ariès, *The Hour of Our Death*; and Emmanuel Fureix, *La France des larmes: deuils politiques à l'âge romantique (1814–1840)* (Seyssel: Champ Vallon, 2009), 85–93.

29 "Rigid embrace": Edgar Allan Poe, "The Premature Burial," 1850. Bourke discusses this poem and these developments in *Fear,* 29–49. On these fears, see also Dickey, *Cranioklepty*; Bondeson, *Buried Alive;* and Martin Pernick, "Back from the Grave: Recurring Controversies Over Defining and Diagnosing Death in History," in Richard M. Zaner, ed., *Death: Beyond Whole-Brain Criteria* (Dordrecht: Kluwer, 1988), 17–74.

30 "I had promised": Anon., *Nouvelles Prophéties de Nostradamus ressucité, aux Parisiens,* 3. "The great secret": Martonne, "Etudes historiques: Nostradamus," 283–84.

31　On the early presence of Nostradamus in songs: Tourangeau, *Le second livre des chansons folastres et prologues,* 25. See also Taconet, "Nostradamus, Parodie de Zoroastre"; Collot d'Herbois, *Le nouveau Nostradamus, ou les Fêtes provencales;* André Tissier, *Les spectacles à Paris pendant la Revolution: répertoire analytique, chronologique et bibliographique,* 2 vols. (Geneva: Droz, 2002), 2:212–18; Alphonse Aulard, *Paris pendant la réaction thermidorienne et sous le Directoire,* 5 vols. (Paris: L. Cerf, 1898–1902), 1:88; and Nathalie Rizzoni, "De l'origine théâtrale de Gil Blas," *Revue d'histoire littéraire de la France* 103 (2003): 823–45.

32　"Resolutions of the fates": Le Sage and d'Orneval, *Le Tombeau de Nostradamus,* 1:173.

33　"All that people" and "commoners": Ménétra, *Journal of my Life,* 77. Thanks to Paul Cohen for this reference. On the domestication of the supernatural: Walsham, "Reformation and 'the Disenchantment of the World' Reassessed," 518–19; and Schmidt, "From Demon Possession to Magic Show," 304.

34　The anecdote about Henri IV, which the king himself reportedly told, circulated as early as 1589. Still, it may be apocryphal. See l'Estoile, August 1589, *Registre-journal de Henri IV,* 5; and Marguerite de Valois, *Mémoires,* 279–80.

35　Le Sage and d'Orneval, *Le Tombeau de Nostradamus,* 175; Christelle Bahier-Porte, *La poétique d'Alain-René Lesage* (Paris: H. Champion, 2006), 387–88; and Prothero, *American Jesus,* 72–78.

36　*Archives littéraires de l'Europe* 14 (1807?): 297; *Grey River Argus* 14 (January 15, 1874): 4; John Lorenz Mosheim, *An Ecclesiastic History, Ancient and Modern,* 6 vols. (London: Vernor & Hood, Poultry, 1803), 3:209; and Walter, *Merlin,* 172.

37　Jaulnay, *L'enfer burlesque,* 57.

38　"Tomb of the prophet": *The Wizard,* iii.

39　"By metaplasm": Ward, "Nostradamus," 609–10. See *Almanach pittoresque, comique & prophétique pour 1851,* 37.

40　This account rests on the proceedings of Salon's municipal council, September 29, and November 6, 1791, AM Salon I D 1/1 and I D 1/2; Moulin, *La propriété foncière,* 258–59; *Le tout-Salon: Revue annuelle* (Marseille, 1897): 48–55; and Gimon, *Chroniques de la ville de Salon,* 717–18. Nostradamus's new epitaph can be found in Millin, *Voyage dans les départemens du midi de la France,* 4:61–62. The original was restored two decades later, when the Bourbon dynasty returned to power.

41.　"Iron clasped": *The Wizard,* vii. "Picture of furor": *Journal des débats,* June 17, 1834. These tales come from *Almanach des gens de bien pour l'année 1795* (1794): 204; *Quarterly Review* 23 (1820): 357; Bonnelier, *Nostradamus, roman;* Berin, "Michel Nostradamus," 70; and Halévy, *La Mort de Nostradamus,* 20. On the Gothic: Jerrold E. Hogle, ed., *The Cambridge Companion to Gothic Fiction* (New York: Cambridge University Press, 2002), 3–8.

42　*Journal de Paris,* March 31, 1806.

CHAPTER 8: A WORLD OF ONE'S OWN

1　"Magnificient": Pasquier to Airault, in Pasquier, *Lettres historiques pour les années 1556–1594,* 362. "Stained and ragged": Anon., "My Grandmother's Books," *Atlantic Monthly* 472 (1897): 286. See Prion, *Pierre Prion, scribe,* 95–97.

2　Bynum, "Wonder," 14–15.

3　Smail, *On Deep History and the Brain,* esp. chap. 4.

4　"Meant to say": Anon., "Affaires des Turcs tant passées que présentes et futures depuis l'an 1555 jusques à l'avènement de l'Antechrist, selon ce qu'en a presagé Michel Nostredame dans ses dix centuries," BML ms. 992.

5　"When you read": William Drake, quoted in Sharpe, *Reading Revolutions,* 84. See Anon.,

"Livre d'astrologie par un noble vénitien" [sixteenth century?], Bibliothèque de l'Arsenal, ms. 8514, folio 86. On humanist reading: Grafton, "The Humanist as Reader," in Cavallo and Chartier, eds., *A History of Reading in the West,* 198–209; Jackson, *Marginalia;* and Blair, "Reading Strategies."

6 On marginalia in early modern Bibles: William H. Sherman, " 'The Book Thus Put in Every Vulgar Hand': Impressions of Readers in Early English Printed Bibles," in Saenger and Van Kampen, eds., *The Bible as Book,* 125–33.

7 "Interest of his work": Paul Valéry, "Homage to Marcel Proust," in his *Masters and Friends,* trans. Martin Turnell (Princeton: Bollingen Foundation, 1968), 298.

8 "More things": Nostradamus, *Almanach pour l'an M.D.LXVI,* in *Cahiers Nostradamus* 5–6 (1987–88): 102. See Grafton, *Cardano's Cosmos,* 201.

9 See the respective positions of Norbert Elias, *The Society of Individuals,* trans. Edmund Jephcott (Cambridge, MA: Blackwell, 1991), 78; Lillqvist and Lindeman, "Belief in Astrology as a Strategy for Self-Verification," 203–06; and Baecher, "Phénomène prophétique et schémas eschatologiques," 37.

10 On locus: Vyse, *Believing in Magic,* 50–57. On such journeys during the Renaissance: Cave, "The Mimesis of Reading in the Renaissance."

11 "Whoever will apply": *Les Vrayes Centuries et Prophéties de Maistre Michel Nostradamus* (Amsterdam, 1667), n.p. "I had rather": Garencières, *True Prophecies of Michael Nostradamus,* 81. Garencières did, however, restrict such interventions to learned readers, whom he expected to avoid the future and "business of state."

12 The prince to whom Denys II referred was Charles de Lorraine. Léon's travel journals also mention ghosts and demons. On Denys II: Anon., "De la comparaison des prédictions de Nostradamus, avec les prédictions de l'Abbé Joachim [de Flore], d'après les discours tenus par le P. Michaelis en son petit couvent du collège de Boissy près Saint André des Arts le 25 juillet 1612," Bibliothèque de l'Institut de France, Godefroy 15, fol. 223–24; and Anon., "Centurie sixième de Nostradamus, quatrain quarente trois," undated manuscript, Bibliothèque de l'Institut de France, Godefroy 329, fol. 43. Caroline R. Sherman contextualizes all of this in "The Genealogy of Knowledge," esp. 94, 239. I am grateful to her for sharing her unpublished notes on the Godefroy family and Nostradamus.

13 "Explanations": Anon., "Eclaircissements ou Explications des véritables quatrains de Maistre Michel Nostradamus . . . spécialement pour la connoissance des choses futures depuis MXCIVI jusques à MDCLXX," 1656, Bibliothèque Nationale de France, ms. NAF 11548. "Strange and extraordinary": Anon., "Prophéties de Michel Nostradamus sur les révolutions présentes d'Angleterre" [1694?], Bibliothèque municipale d'Avignon, ms. 3194. Annotations can be found in *Les Prophéties de. M. Michel Nostradamus* (Troyes, 1628), copy sold at the Swann Auction Galleries, November 8, 2007; and *Les Vrayes Centuries et Prophéties de Maistre Michel Nostradamus,* (Amsterdam: Winkermans, 1667), 36, copy of the BML. On Bonnie Prince Charlie: Joseph Forsyth, *Remarks on Antiquities, Arts and Letters* (Boston: Wells and Lilly, 1818), 401.

14 "Is it not": Mathieu Marais to Jean Bouhier, October 15, 1727, *Correspondance littéraire du président Bouhier.* 2:166. See Chartier, "Publishing Strategies," 152–58; Gouberville, *Un Sire de Gouberville,* 210; and John Newman to Abraham Hill, August 19, 1659, *The Monthly Review,* 1767, 446.

15 On this burden: Shepheard, "Pour une poétique du genre oraculaire," 63.

16 Henry Krystal, "Trauma and Aging: A Thirty-Year Follow-Up," in Caruth, ed., *Trauma,* 80; Adorno, *The Stars Down to Earth,* 49–52, 157; and Suzanne M. Miller, "Why Having Control Reduces Stress: If I Can Stop the Roller Coaster, I Don't Want to Get Off," in Garber and Seligman, eds., *Human Helplessness,* 86–89.

17 "Nature was not": Clark, "French Historians and Early Modern Popular Culture," 84. On pessimism as meaningful: Dienstag, *Pessimism.*

18 "It is above all": Anon., *Prophéties politiques de Michel Nostradamus sur les républicains rouges et les socialistes*, 99. "The only certain thing": Moré, *Mémoires,* 132.

19 "Saddest": Tomalin, *Samuel Pepys*, 225. "Apocalyptic and mysterious": John Booker, *New Almanack and Prognostication* (London, 1666), quoted in Tinniswood, *By Permission of Heaven*, 21. On Pepys and the Fire of London, see Minois, *Histoire de l'avenir,* 392; and Miller, *Popery and Politics in England,* 103–04.

20 "I have never lived" and "It is strange": Tomalin, *Samuel Pepys,* 168, 227. "Most horrid": Pepys, quoted in Daly, "Samuel Pepys and Post-Traumatic Stress Disorder," 65.

21 "Despise that stanza": Tenison, *The Creed of Mr. Hobbes*, 62. See Pepys, *Diary*, 460; Windham Sandys to a "lord," September 6, 1666, in *The Gentleman's Magazine* 51 (July 1831): 6; and Thomas Vincent, *God's Terrible Voice in the City of London* (Cambridge: S. Green, 1667), 25.

22 On magic, precedents, and conditioning: Vyse, *Believing in Magic*, 60, 75, 199.

23 "It is a strange thing": Pepys, *Diary*, 417. "Put a century": Marquis de Condorcet, "Sur l'instruction publique" (1791) quoted in Nelson, "The Weapon of Time," 233. On time and the French Revolution: Nelson, ibid., 3–7, 30–35, 233–43; Hunt, "The World We Have Gained," 4–6; and Hunt, *Measuring Time*, 69–71.

24 "It's odd": Hélène Berr, *Journal 1942–1944* (Paris: Tallendier, 2008), 182. Berr was not talking about Nostradamus. This distinction between fear and anxiety is drawn in Bourke, *Fear*, esp. 189–91.

25 "People feel worse": Daniel Gilbert, "What You Don't Know Makes You Nervous," *New York Times*, May 21, 2009. This paragraph and the following distill a wide body of research. See Gilbert, *Stumbling on Happiness,* chap. 1; Keinan, "The Effects of Stress and Desire for Control on Superstitious Behavior"; Langer, "The Illusion of Control"; Damisch et al., "Keep Your Fingers Crossed!"; and Taylor and Brown, "Illusions and Well-Being."

26 Gilbert, *Stumbling on Happiness*, 17.

27 "Listening": Diesbach de Belleroche, *Une éducation manquée*, 83, trans. Joshua Jordan. This Diesbach may be a descendant of the nobleman who consulted Nostradamus during the revolution (chapter 7). See Shelley E. Taylor, "Adjustment to Threatening Events: A Theory of Cognitive Adaptation," *American Psychologist* 38, no. 11 (November 1983): 1165; and Sonja Lyubomirsky, "Why We're Still Happy," *New York Times*, December 26, 2008.

28 On the Apocalypse and community: O'Leary, *Arguing the Apocalypse*, 6, 199; and Williamson, *Apocalypse Then*, 2–3.

29 Pierre François Chiflet to the baron de Saffre, November 5, 1659, in Morrison, *Collection of Autograph Letters and Historical Documents*, 2:201; and Anon., *Lettre d'un seigneur anglois à un seigneur irlandois*, 3–4.

30 "To pass the time": Cardinal Farnèse, quoted in Brind'Amour, *Nostradamus astrophile*, 33. "Jokers": Bachaumont, *Mémoires secrets,* 217. Nostradamus may have provided entertainment among the populace as well, but traces are once again elusive. See Guy Patin to Charles Spon, March 8, 1644, in Patin, *Lettres*, 1:378; and Bachaumont, *Mémoires secrets*, 340. On aristocratic entertainment: Drévillon, *Lire et écrire l'avenir*, 87–89; and Lilti, *Le monde des salons*, chap. 7.

31 "Nostradamus as you render him": Frederick the Great to the Count of Manteuffel, January 10, 1736, in *Oeuvres de Frédéric le Grand*, 25:408. See Menestrier, *Philosophie des images*, 387; and *Le Causeur: ambigu littéraire, critique, moral et philosophique 1* (Paris: Ferra jeune, 1817), 309–10.

32 "My pastime": Chanoine Penez to a lackey, February 26, 1694, in Advielle, *Documents inédits*, 11. See Abbé Lebeuf to Claude Prévost, June 28, 1722, in *Lettres de l'abbé Lebeuf*

(Aix-en-Provence: G. Perriquet, 1866–68), 316–17; and Anon., "Prophéties de Michel Nostradamus sur la Rochelle" [1718?], Bibliothèque municipale de La Rochelle, ms. 153.

33 Advielle, *Documents inédits,* 10; and *Catalogue des livres de la bibliothèque de M. Pierre-Antoine Bolongaro-Crevenna* (Amsterdam: D. J. Changuion, 1789).

34 "They are not": Anon., "Lettre écrite en réponse à un de mes amis, qui me demandait ce que je pensois de Nostradamus" (eighteenth century), Bibliothèque nationale de France, ms. français 12294.

35 This account rests on Rolland, *Journey Within,* 64–66; and Romain Baron, "Jean-Baptiste Boniard (1768–1843)," *Mémoires de la Société académique du Nivernais* 62 (1980): 23–38.

36 "Utter": *Le Causeur* (1817), 310. "Rare and curious": *Catalog of the Curious and Extensive Library of the Late James Bindley* (London: 1818). "Amusing book": *Catalog of a Library Constituting the Collections of the Late Peter Hastie and the Late Edward H. Tracy* (New York: 1877), 244. See Arthur Dinaux, annotation (1843) on the cover page of Guynaud, *Concordance des Prophéties,* personal collection of the author; *Catalogue des livres composant la bibliothèque poétique de M. Viollet le Duc* (Paris: Hachette, 1843), 241–43; and Daston and Park, *Wonders and the Order of Nature,* 218–31, 349.

37 Chavigny, *Première face,* 276; and *Catalogue de la partie réservée de la bibliothèque de feu Mr. J. Renard, de Lyon* (Paris: A. Claudin, 1884), 72. On the written work and pleasure: Coleman, *Public Reading and the Reading Public,* 171, 176; and Dubois, *L'imaginaire de la Renaissance,* 41–42.

38 "From time to time": Partridge, *Remarkable Predictions.*

39 "The hand" and "What to ascribe": *The Predictions of Nostradamus Before the Year 1558,* 8.

CHAPTER 9: WE ARE NOT NOSTRADAMITES!

1 "Can a serious person": *La Phalange* 10, no. 3 (1841): 324. "Below": *La Presse,* November 24, 1840. On this revival: Lucius, "La littérature visionnaire en France," 256–59; Edelman, *Histoire de la voyance et du paranomal,* 40–69; and Davies, *Witchcraft, Magic and Culture,* 245–47.

2 *Journal des débats,* August 31, 1815.

3 Bouys, *Nouvelles considérations;* and Chaillot, *Les vraies Centuries et prophéties de Maistre Michel Nostradamus.*

4 Auguste Villiers de L'Isle-Adam to Gustave Flaubert, 1864, in Villiers de L'Isle-Adam, *Correspondance,* ed. Joseph Bollery, 2 vols. (Paris: Mercure de France, 1962), 1:66–67; and Normand, *L'abbé Rigaux,* 5.

5 The best book on this transformation is Vaillant and Thérenty, *1836, l'an I de l'ère médiatique.*

6 "Most of the concierges": "French Almanacks," *All the Year Round* (February 9, 1878), 65. On Bareste, see the sketch in *Journal des arts, des sciences et des lettres,* January 12, 1859; and Mustafa, "Republican Socialism."

7 "To check": Perrot, *Lettres sur Nismes et le Midi,* 134–35. The anecdote about the crown prince comes from the reputed historian Auguste Geoffroy, "Des intérêts du Nord Scandinave dans la guerre d'Orient," *Revue des deux mondes,* 1856, 732. See Salgues, *Des erreurs et des préjugés,* 2:xi; and *Commercial Advertiser,* August 6, 1817. The translation of quatrain 8.57 is mine.

8 The most up-to-date survey on popular almanacs is Lüsebrink et al., *Lectures du peuple;* though Bollème's older *Almanachs populaires* remains valuable. See *Nouveaux et Vrais Pronostics de Michel Nostradamus, calculés & supputés très-exactement d'après les observations des Anciens, pour cinq ans, à commencer en l'année 1832, jusqu'à l'année 1836* (Avignon: n.p., [1831?]); and the inventory of books approved by the *préfecture* of the Vosges for November 1853, AN F18 554.

9   "Almanacs have undergone": Draft of a directive on grocers and haberdashers who sell al-
    manacs (1858?), AN F18 554. See Fournel, *Ce qu'on voit dans les rues de Paris,* 207; and
    Revue méridionale 4, no. 50 (1857): 1.
10 "If Europeans": *Almanach prophétique, pittoresque et utile pour 1842* (1841): 10–11.
11 "French society": *Le Mémorial d'Aix,* May 13, 1850. "Several old prophecies": Raikes, *A Por-
    tion of the Journal,* 4:47. See *Fraser's Magazine for Town and Country* 21 (1840): 737–38;
    Bareste, *Nostradamus,* 239; Bareste, *Prophéties;* and Buget, "Etude sur Nostradamus,"
    1863, 583–86.
12 "Mystery": Fournel, *Ce qu'on voit dans les rues de Paris,* 210–11, trans. Steven Crumb.
13 "They take on": *Le Patriote de l'Ain,* November 26, 1839. See Maistre, *Saint-Petersburg
    Dialogues,* 340; documents reproduced in *La Légitimité* 25 (1907): 226–29; prosecutor of
    Montpellier to the Minister of Justice, November 22, 1843, AN BB18 1417; *La Gazette de
    France,* March 5, 1839; and Girault, *Le passé, le présent et l'avenir,* 39–41.
14 Eugène Bareste, *A tous les citoyens: Du droit de réponse dans les journaux* (Paris: Lavigne,
    1841); Bareste, "Nécessité d'une politique nouvelle," *Almanach prophétique, pittoresque et
    utile pour 1848* (1847): 16–20; and Mustafa, "Republican Socialism," 18–19.
15 Paul Bénichou, *Le sacre de l'écrivain, 1750–1830: essai sur l'avènement d'un pouvoir spiri-
    tuel dans la France moderne* (Paris: J. Corti, 1973).
16 "I absolutely need": Bareste to L. Pommier, n.d., AN 454 AP 21. This discussion rests on
    three files on Bareste in the Archives Nationales: 454 AP 21, F17 2935/2, and F17 3114/2.
17 Inventory of books approved by the Bureau de l'estampillage in December 1867, AN F18
    555; and Hélène Landre, "Laurent-Antoine Pagnerre (1805–1854): le combat pour la Ré-
    publique d'un libraire éditeur oublié," *Trames* 10 (2002). On self-made individuals in this
    realm: Albanese, *A Republic of Mind & Spirit,* 235–37; Verter, "Dark Star Rising," 266–68;
    and Curry, *A Confusion of Prophets,* 48–60.
18 "Nostradamite" and "trash pamphlets": Bareste, *Nostradamus,* 31, ii. See *Memoirs Read
    Before the Anthropological Society of London* 1 (1863–64): 392.
19 "Fatal": *Almanach prophétique, pittoresque et utile pour 1844* (1843): 14. "Shivers": E.
    Brossard, "Centuries de Nostradamus mises en vers français nouveau style," undated man-
    uscript, consulted at the Swann Auction Galleries, New York City, November 8, 2007. See
    also Rosman, *Evangelicals and Culture,* 23–26.
20 "Everyone": Bareste, *Nostradamus,* i; also see, 251–52, 478.
21 "Before ending": *Almanach prophétique, pittoresque et utile pour 1841* (1840): 159.
22 "There is no point": Nau, *Le Nostradamus moderne,* [6]. On irony: Ten-Doesschate Chu,
    The Most Arrogant Man in France, 76; and Thérenty, *La littérature au quotidien,* 153–64. I
    am grateful to Judith Lyon-Caen for sharing her thoughts on this question.
23 "Superstitious dreamer": *Fraser's Magazine for Town and Country* 21 (1840): 737–38.
24 The journalist was the well-known Catholic Louis Veuillot. See *Minerva: Ein Journal histo-
    rischen und politischen Inhalts* 1 (1840); *Notes and Queries* 4 (1851): 140; Edmond Texier,
    Histoire des journaux, biographie des journalistes (Paris: Pagnerre, 1850), 152; *L'Ami de la
    religion* (December 10, 1842), 494; Flora Tristan, *Le tour de France: Journal inédit, 1843–
    1844,* ed. Jules L. Puech (Paris: Editions Têtes de Feuilles, 1973), 189; and Louis Veuillot to
    Eugène Veuillot, August 26, 1848, in Veuillot, *Correspondance,* 4:170.
25 "One can be": Leibniz, *Esprit de Leibniz,* 70. See Pasquier, *Lettres historiques pour les an-
    nées 1556–1594,* 376; and François de Callières to marquise d'Huxelles, April 22, 1697,
    Callières, *Letters,* 249. On the Enlightenment's ambivalence, see Walsham, "The Reforma-
    tion and 'the Disenchantment of the World,'" 526.
26 "For all the airs": Fournel, *Ce qu'on voit dans les rues de Paris,* 207, trans. Steven Crumb.
    "But secretly": *Atlanta Constitution,* June 1, 1941. See Moszynski, *Voyage en Provence d'un*

Gentilhomme Polonais, vii–viii; *Journal des débats,* August 31, 1815; Abbé Guillois, *Essai sur les superstitions* (Lille: L. Lefort, 1836), 35, quoted in Minois, *Histoire de l'avenir,* 470; and Seabrook, *Witchcraft,* 366.

27 Miller, *Memoir of the Rev. Charles Nisbet,* 222. This discussion is indebted to Campbell, "Half-Belief"; and Warner, *No Go the Bogeyman.* See also Lena Petrossian, "La croyance," in Morin, ed., *Croyance astrologique moderne,* 113–14. On self-mocking and the supernatural, see Bown ed., *The Victorian Supernatural,* 1.

28 "Thrill": Diesbach de Belleroche, *Une éducation manquée,* 82. On artful deception: Cook, *The Arts of Deception,* 16. For other thoughts on play and fear: Serge Moscovici, "La crainte du contact," in Paillard, *Peurs,* 39; and Bourke, *Fear,* 386.

29 "More than ever": *Almanach de l'ère nouvelle, historique et prophétique pour 1849,* 102.

30 *John Bull,* September 1, 1849, and March 9, 1850; Mustafa, "Republican Socialism," 16; and Peter McPhee, "*La République* (1848–1851)," in Edgar Leon Newman and Robert Lawrence Simpson, eds., *Historical Dictionary of France from the 1815 Restoration to the Second Empire,* 2 vols. (Westport, CT: Greenwood, 1987), 2:886–87.

31 "Eugène Bareste de Nostradamus": *Les coulisses,* December 24, 1840. See Bareste to Abel-François Villemain, January 21, 1843, AN F17 3114/2; *La Presse,* August 29, 1840; and Fortunatus, *Le Rivarol de 1842* (Paris, 1843), 20.

32 "Old friend": *New York Times,* April 15, 1872. "Let us essay": "Prophetic Fits," 162–64. "Let our readers": "Nostradamus," *Household Words* 12 (October 1855): 298. This paragraph also rests on *New York Times,* February 23, 1878; *La Presse,* July 6, 1883; *Pall Mall Magazine,* July 20, 1899; Charpentier, "Nostradamus et ses prophéties," 81; and *La Croix,* May 2, 1931.

33 "But there is": *Chicago Daily Tribune,* October 5, 1941. The *Daily Mail* said essentially the same thing decades later: "Believe what you like, Nostradamus still grasps the public imagination," June 10, 1995. See also Dominique Kalifa, *L'encre et le sang: récits de crimes* (Paris: Fayard, 1995), 294–95.

CHAPTER 10: FIN DE SIÈCLE MADNESS

1 Schivelbuch, *The Railway Journey,* 191.

2 This paragraph and the following draw from Timothée, "L'abbé Torné et le merveilleux," *L'Echo du merveilleux* 13 (October 1, 1909): 372–75; Multon, "Temps sont proches," 3:610–12; and Chevignard, introduction to *Présages,* 47.

3 Henri Torné-Chavigny, *Almanach du 'Grand Prophète' Nostradamus pour 1878,* 1877, 113. See Mayeur, "Monseigneur Dupanloup et Louis Veuillot," 194.

4 *Courrier des Etats-Unis,* September 29, 1861; *Wisconsin Patriot,* December 5, 1863; *The Crisis,* November 21, 1861; and *Daily True Delta,* October 20, 1861. This discussion has benefited from an exchange with Antonio Urias.

5 "The country fell": Suttner, *Lay Down Your Arms,* 411. See Bois, "Comment je suis devenu sceptique," 554–56; *New York Times,* April 15, 1872; and *Almanach des Prophéties,* 1871, 81. On the apocalyptic climate in France: Jonas, *France and the Cult of the Sacred Heart;* and Multon, "Temps sont proches," 1:22–25, 49–53.

6 "Hotheaded": Bois, "Comment je suis devenu sceptique," 556. See Torné-Chavigny, *Les Blancs & les Rouges,* 16; *Le Français,* July 20, 1874; Torné-Chavigny to Raoul de Tricqueville, June 7, 1879, in Nostradamus, *Les significations de l'Eclipse, qui sera le 16 septembre 1559* (Méricout, 1904), preamble; and Airiau, "Le Grand Monarque," 77.

7 "I will find him": Torné-Chavigny, *Ce qui sera!,* 20. "With a verse": Torné-Chavigny, *Réédition du livre des prophéties de Nostradamus publié en 1566* (Bordeaux: J. Dupuy, 1862), 6, trans. Steven Crumb.

8 "How strange": Torné-Chavigny, *Ce qui sera!*, 57. See Hugo, *Propos de table de Victor Hugo*, 104–05.

9 I draw my information on Zévaco from Demars, "Michel Zévaco et le roman feuilleton"; Sarah Mombert, "Profession: romancier populaire," in Artiaga, ed., *Le roman populaire*, 60–71; and Bastaire, "Pour saluer Zévaco," 151–52.

10 "Novel full of magic": *Le Matin*, April 5, 1907. On the mass press and *Le Matin*: Martin, *Médias et journalistes de la République*; and Palmer, *Des petits journaux aux grandes agences*. On popular novels: Thérenty, *Littérature au quotidien*, 51. See proceedings of the board of *Le Matin*, September 20, 1906, AN 1 AR 9.

11 "During your descent": Zévaco, *Nostradamus*, 109, trans. Steven Crumb.

12 Béraud and Valory, *Nostradamus*; Balzac, *About Catherine de Medici*, 241; and "Nostradamus, the Wizard of France," *Boys of England* (January 2, 1891): 44–46.

13 On this cultic milieu and Spiritualism (known as spiritism in France): Campbell, "The Cult, the Cultic Milieu and Secularization," 14–15; Albanese, *Republic of Mind*, 258–79; Treitel, *A Science for the Soul*, 86; Sharp, *Secular Spirituality*; and Monroe, *Laboratories of Faith*.

14 Demars, "Michel Zévaco," 76, 522; Horowitz, *Occult America*, 51–53; and Jean-Marcel Humbert, ed., *Egyptomania: Egypt in Western Art, 1730–1930* (Paris: Réunion des Musées Nationaux, 1994).

15 On theosophy and Nostradamus: Blavatsky, *Isis Unveiled*, 1:260; *Sphinx: Monatschift für die geschichtliche und experimentale Begründung der übersinnlichen Weltanschauung* 2 (1887): 91–111; and Banon, "Nostradamus." On the occult and magic: Dr. Grasset, *The Marvels Beyond Science* (New York: Funk & Wagnalls, 1907), 268–69; Verter, "Dark Star Rising," 206–26; and Albanese, *Republic of Mind*, 261.

16 Garrett, *Respectable Folly*, 228; Muray, *Le XIXe siècle à travers les âges*, 224–49; and Edelman, "Spiritisme et politique."

17 "Nostradamus's mystical poetry": interview of Marcel Janco in Henri Béhar and Catherine Dufour, eds., *Dada circuit total* (Lausanne: L'Age d'Homme, 2005), 167. See Guillaume Apollinaire to Louise de Coligny, January 19, 1915, in Apollinaire, *Lettres à Lou*, 125. On Dada's recovery of Nostradamus: Stéphane Gerson, "Nostradamus's Worlds," *Prophecies*, xviii; and Browning, "Tristan Tzara." More broadly, see Long, "Occultism, Anarchism, and Abstraction"; and Choucha, *Surrealism and the Occult*.

18 On magic: During, *Modern Enchantments*.

19 "American Nostradamus": Kellar, *A Magician's Tour Up and Down and Round About the Earth, Being the Life and Adventures of the American Nostradamus*. "Fantastic illusions": advertisement in *L'Orchestre: revue quotidienne des théâtres*, July 27–August 3, 1891. "Mystifying": *Los Angeles Times*, February 3, 1927. "Magic mirror": *The Complete Fortune-Teller*, 1–2. See *Lloyd's Weekly Newspaper*, July 16, 1865; and Jacques Malthête and Laurent Mannoni, *L'œuvre de Georges Méliès* (Paris: Editions de la Martinière, 2008), 73. On dream books: Weiss, *Oneirocritica Americana*, 10–16; and Britten, *Art Magic*, 421–23.

20 Proceedings of the board of *Le Matin*, December 24, 1906, AN 1 AR 10; and Caillot, "Le lancement du *Capitan*."

21 Robert Orsi speaks of devotional promoters in *Thank You, St. Jude*. See also Moore, *Selling God*.

22 *Milwaukee Sentinel*, March 17, 1860; and *Ogden Standard*, April 26, 1909.

23 "Peep": *Deseret News*, February 12, 1898, quoted in Pietruska, "Propheteering," 298. On the lure of the future, see Pietruska as well as Perkins, *The Reform of Time*.

24 "Dark kingdom": *Dimanche illustré*, December 29, 1935. See Weyman, *The Man in Black*, 29; *San Francisco Call*, March 19, 1899; *Journal des débats*, January 1, 1904; and "The Enchanted Book," *Washington Post*, August 7, 1904.

25 "The more I probe": Rouy l'aîné, *Le magicien républicain,* [3]. "No longer knows": Octave Mirbeau, "Le Tripot aux champs," in his *Lettres de ma chaumière* (Paris: A. Laurent, 1886), 11.

26 "End of everything": Emile Zola, quoted in Weber, *Apocalypses,* 20. See Boia, *La fin du monde,* 164; and *Hampshire Telegraph and Sussex Chronicle,* June 5, 1897.

27 "End of the World": *Otago Witness,* April 30, 1886. See Terrie Dopp Aamodt, *Righteous Armies, Holy Cause: Apocalyptical Imagery in the Civil War* (Macon, GA: Mercer University Press, 2002); Christopher McIntosh, *The Swan King: Ludwig II of Bavaria* (London: I. B. Taurus, 2003), 2, 193; Moore, *Society Recollections in Paris and Vienna,* 97; *Leeds Mercury,* April 24, 1886; and *Le Petit Journal,* June 25, 1886.

28 On this secularization of the apocalyptic, see Hall, *Apocalypse,* 7.

29 "Another authority": *British Colonist,* November 14, 1882.

30 "Old Nostradamus": Congreve, *The Way of the World,* 238. "Each *Nostradamus*": Dryden, *The Hind and the Panther,* 102. "Little is generally known": Holmes, "Nostradamus," 25. See Horace Walpole to George Montagu, July 20, 1752, in Walpole, *Private correspondence,* 1:254; and "Nostradamus," *Household Words* 12 (1855): 296.

31 "Magic!": *Le Matin,* April 10, 1907, trans. Steven Crumb; see also the issues of April 5, 6, and 7. On stock images: Kalifa, *Crime et Culture,* 39; and Marion, "Narratologie médiatique," 69–70.

32 Gabriel Nostradamus, *Consult the Oracle;* and *Les Annales,* October 27, 1912.

33 "Great popular storyteller": *Le Matin,* April 8, 1907. "*Luisant torné*": quatrain 8.5.

34 "That author of genius": Jean-Paul Sartre, *The Words,* trans. Bernard Fretchman (New York: Braziller, 1964), 132. See *Littell's Living Age,* April 5, 1879; *Daily Southern Cross,* August 12, 1873; Parisot, *Au 17 février 1874 Le Grand Avènement!!;* Torné-Chavigny, *Lo Que Sera;* Hohlenberg, *Michel de Nostredame;* and Demars, "Michel Zévaco," 147–49.

35 On mass media and emotions: Bodnar, "*Saving Private Ryan* and Postwar Memory in America," 809; and Singer, "Modernity, Hyperstimulus, and the Rise of Popular Sensationalism." On the modern media culture: Kalifa, "L'envers fantasmé du quotidien," in Kalifa et al., *Civilisation du journal,* 1329–54. On new experiences of time and space: Kern, *Culture of Time and Space.*

36 "Sorcerer abbot": *L'Evènement,* January 26, 1877. "Crotchety": Anon., "Nunquam Dormio," *Bell's Life in London* 3 (1885): 474. See also Louis Gimon, "Revue sommaire et chronologique des écrits les plus remarquables qui ont paru pour et contre Michel Nostradamus," *La Provence poétique, historique et littéraire* 8 (1883): 5–6.

37 "Even in this present": *Every Saturday,* May 23, 1874, 575. See Tristan, *Le tour de France,* 189–91; and Caston, *Les marchands de miracles.*

38 "Personal wants": John Burroughs, "Science and Theology," in *The Writings of John Burroughs,* 11: 19. On religion: *L'Univers,* April 4, 1874; Dupanloup, *On Contemporary Prophecies,* 4; Chabauty, *Lettre sur les Prophéties modernes,* 77; Chabauty, quoted in Torné-Chavigny, *Nostradamus éclairci,* 63; Mayeur, "Monseigneur Dupanloup et Louis Veuillot," 199–201; and Multon, "Temps sont proches," 2:285–423. On science: *La France nouvelle,* January 9, 1873, quoted in Torne-Chavigny, *Nostradamus éclairci,* 142; Advielle, *Documents inédits,* 57; and Winter, *Mesmerized.*

39 "Prophets of evil": Camille Flammarion, *Omega,* 147. "Mysterious": Anon., "Nunquam Dormio," *Bell's Life in London* 3 (May 13, 1885): 474. See "Centuries" and "Nostradamus," in Pierre Larousse, ed., *Grand Dictionnaire universel du XIXe siècle,* 17 vols. (Paris: Administration du grand Dictionnaire universel, 1866–90), 3:736, and 11, part 2: 1102–03; Dupanloup, *On Contemporary Prophecies,* 4, 19–24; Mauger, *Nostradamus, ou le physicien plaideur;* Lucien de la Hodde, *The Cradle of Rebellions: A History of the Secret Societies of France* (New York: J. Bradburn, 1864 [1850]), 338; and Théodar, *Nostradamus démasqué.*

40 "The best path": François-René de Chateaubriand, *Mémoires d'outre-tombe,* 4 vols. (Paris: Flammarion, 1948 [1848]), 4:415. On fame: Braudy, *Frenzy of Renown;* and Lilti, "The Writing of Paranoia," 55, 70. On these anxieties: Hahn, *Scenes of Parisian Modernity,* 90.

41 "Much too famous": "Chavigny (Jean-Aimé de)," in Joseph-François Michaud, *Biographie universelle, ancienne et moderne,* 52 vols. (Paris: Michaud, 1811–28), 8:312. "Taken advantage": Gimon, "Michel Nostradamus," 4. See Lecanu, *Histoire de Satan,* 322; and Anon., *Prophéties et documents prophétiques: Le danger de croire facilement aux Prophéties,* 47.

42 Hitchcock, *Frankenstein,* 106; and Pietruska, "Propheteering," 252–56.

43 Bois, "Comment je suis devenu sceptique," 556; Multon, "Temps sont proches," 3:612; and Elisée du Vignois, "Notre histoire et Nostradamus," *L'Echo du merveilleux* 13 (1909): 436, and 14 (1911): 420.

44 "Utterly eccentric": Le Pelletier, *Oracles de Michel de Nostredame,* 1:47. "That long chapter": "Nostradamus the Astrologer," *Every Saturday* (May 23, 1874): 575. See Larousse, *Grand dictionnaire,* 3:736; and John Delaware Lewis, *Our College. Leaves from an Undergraduate's Scribbling Book* (London: G. Earle, 1857), 404–05.

45 This discussion has benefited from conversations with Aude Fauvel and Dominique Martin. Torné-Chavigny appears in Brunet, *Les Fous littéraires*, and Tcherpakov, *Les fous littéraires.* See Benazra, *Répertoire chronologique,* 406–07; and Blavier, *Les fous littéraires.*

46 "Carries a dignity": quoted in Ferrell, *The Bible and the People,* 207. See *L'Echo du merveilleux* 9 (1905): 96, 11 (1907): 196–97, 455, 13 (1909): 373, and 14 (1910): 64–65; Normand, *L'abbé Rigaux,* 9; Jean-Pierre Laurant, *L'ésotérisme chrétien au XIXᵉ siècle* (Lausanne: L'Age d'Homme, 1992), 123, 199; and Willa Silverman, "Anti-Semitism and Occultism in Fin-de-Siècle France," in Barbara Cooper and Mary Donaldson-Evans, eds., *Modernity and Revolution in Late Nineteenth-Century France* (Newark: University of Delaware Press, 1992), 159.

47 *New York Times,* February 23, 1878; Emile Berr, "Nostradamus," 520–28; and *Los Angeles Times,* March 21, 1943.

CHAPTER 11: NOSTRADAMUS IS ADOLF HITLER

1 Jeffrey Meyers, *Modigliani: A Life* (Orlando: Harcourt, 2006), 132–34; and Le Naour, *Nostradamus s'en va-t-en guerre, 1914–1918.*

2 "Makes for fascinating": Ward, *Oracles of Nostradamus,* front jacket flap.

3 *Lectures pour tous,* December 1932, quoted in Panchasi, *Future Tense,* 39; Claude Fischler, "L'astrologie de masse," and Philippe Defrance, "Astrologie d'élite, astrologie bourgeoise," in Morin, ed., *Croyance astrologique moderne,* 44–45, 65–67.

4 "All we hear": Kepler, "1937, sous le signe des astres," *Sud-Magazine* 10 (January 1937): 28. "Great Jewish": Céline, *Bagatelles pour un Massacre,* 276. See *La Semaine à Paris,* December 8, 1933, 45; and *Le Petit Régional,* October 28, 1933.

5 Seabrook, *Witchcraft,* 366; *Paris-Midi,* October 24, 1939; autobiographical sketch by Marcel Mousset, in Jean-François Costes, *Hommes et femmes des impôts: récits autobiographiques, 1920–1990,* 2 vols. (Paris: Documentation française, 2004), 1:419; *New York Times,* January 4, 1942; and Liebling, "The Road Back from Paris," in *World War II Writings,* 38.

6 Mericourt, *Gesta Dei per Francos,* 66; Edouard, *Texte original et complet des Prophéties de Michel Nostradamus,* 189; Diesbach de Belleroche, *Une éducation manquée,* 82; and *Le Figaro,* August 18, 1939.

7 Ian Kershaw, *Hitler: 1936–1945: Nemesis* (New York: Norton, 2000), 297. On the exodus and its psychological effects: Diamond, *Fleeing Hitler.*

8 "France no longer": Green, *Fin d'un monde,* 11–12. On trauma: Hoffman, "The Trauma of 1940," 354–70; Henry Rousso, *Le syndrome de Vichy de 1944 à nos jours,* 2nd ed. (Paris: Seuil, 1990), 18; Crocq, *Les traumatismes psychiques de guerre,* 164; and Garland, "Thinking About Trauma," in Garland, ed., *Understanding Trauma,* 9–11.

9 "A kind of popular": Green, *Fin d'un monde,* 18. "Our disaster": Mus, *Le destin de l'Union française,* 202. "A spirit of mysticism": Kaplan, *Scroll of Agony,* 167. See *Le Petit Régional,* September 21, 1940; *Mexico City College Collegian,* September 3 and October 29, 1947, http://bit.ly /jSUS1B; and Elise Freinet to Célestin Freinet, July 15, 1940, Freinet, *Correspondance,* 174.

10 "Their shadowy, stupefying refuge": Aragon, "Ombres," in his *Le crève-coeur,* 61. "Nothing": Léon Werth, *33 jours* (Paris: V. Hamy, 1992), 43. See André Breton, interview by Charles-Henri Ford, August 1941, in *Entretiens,* 225–26; and *Le Petit Régional,* September 21, 1940.

11 "We put": Vallotton, *C'était au jour le jour,* 89. See Seurat, *1918–1948,* 129; and *Poughkeepsie New Yorker,* November 10, 1941.

12 "End of their misery": *Le Petit Provençal,* September 24, 1943. See Némirovsky, *Suite française,* 402–03; and Elisabeth Gille, *Le mirador: mémoires rêvés* (Paris: Presses de la Renaissance, 1992), 259.

13 "We firmly": Dutry-Soinne, *Les méconnus de Londres,* 2:174. "Bald eagle": *Life* (March 29, 1943): 102.

14 "The West": Privat, *1940, année de grandeur française,* 20, 28. On Privat and the ministry: Jacques Halbronn, *La vie astrologique: années 30–50, de Maurice Privat à Dom Néroman* (Paris: La Grande Conjonction, 1995); and Drévillon and Lagrange, *Nostradamus, l'éternel retour,* 84–85.

15 "Undesirables": Blocher-Saillens, *Témoin des années noires,* 149. See Ruir, *Le grand carnage;* Fontbrune, *Les Prophéties de Maistre Michel Nostradamus,* 26; Howe, *Urania's Children,* 186; Charles Nismes to the Couesland printers, November 13, 1940, in Fontbrune, *Ce que Nostradamus a vraiment dit,* 26; and "Liste Otto. Index par auteurs" [1941–43?], 26, Bibliothèque Nationale de France, reference room X.

16 "Prophet with a raging head": Loog, *Die Weissagungen des Nostradamus,* 68. On Loog and Hitler: Howe, *Urania's Children,* 162; and Ryback, *Hitler's Private Library,* xvi, 217–18.

17 "In the National Socialist State": Heinrich Himmler, quoted in Bobrick, *The Fated Sky,* 285. This discussion also rests on *Time,* September 25, 1939; Magida, *The Nazi Séance,* 166–67; Harvey, *Beyond Enlightenment,* 156–57; Howe, *Urania's Children,* 102–18, 193–98; and Schellenberg, *The Labyrinth,* 189.

18 Goebbels is quoted in Boelcke, *The Secret Conferences of Dr. Goebbels,* 6. For the first version: Howe, *Urania's Children,* 124, 159–66. For the second version: Boelcke, *Kriegspropaganda,* 223–24, translation by François Biver available at the BML; and van Berkel, "Nostradamus, Astrology, and the Bible. Substudy World War II," http://bit.ly/kivPGc. See also Clayton D. Laurie, *The Propaganda Warriors: America's Crusade Against Nazi Germany* (Lawrence: University of Kansas Press, 1996), 9.

19 Boelcke, *Secret Conferences of Dr. Goebbels,* 6, 42–45, 65–66; Boelcke, *Kriegspropaganda,* 242, 366, 383; Goebbels, *Diaries, 1939–1941,* 60, 89, 95; Howe, *Urania's Children,* 185; and de Launay, *La France de Pétain,* 12.

20 "Must once again": Goebbels, *Diaries, 1942–1943,* 220. See Boelcke, *Secret Conferences of Dr. Goebbels,* 69–70, 89; and *Les Prophéties de Nostradamus* (Paris, 1941). On Krafft, see his *Comment Nostradamus a-t-il entrevu l'avenir de l'Europe?;* and Howe, *Urania's Children,* 182–91, 220.

21 "The Americans": Goebbels, *Diaries, 1942–1943,* 220. See Doob, "Goebbels' Principles of Propaganda," 200, 210–12.

22 "I realized": Louis de Wohl, "Hitler and the Stars," *Palestine Post,* October 28, 1945. "Great gifts": W.T. Caufeild, memorandum (October 6, 1942), National Archives (U.K.), KV 2/2821. See Angus Calder, *The People's War,* 481; Howe, *Urania's Children,* 205–18; T.W.M. van Berkel, "Nostradamus Prophezeit der Kriegsverlauf," http://bit.ly/11LmhW; and Emma Garman, "The Inconvenient Astrologer of M15," The Awl, http://bit.ly/HCeBYi. This account also rests on de Wohl's security service personal file in the National Archives, KV 2/2821.

23 I am quoting the translation of quatrain 9.90 in the *Los Angeles Times,* May 15, 1941. On divination: *New York Times,* December 22, 1940; Weiss, *Oneirocritica Americana,* 3; and Richard Gerald Culleton, *The Prophets and Our Times* (Taft, CA: self-published, 1943), 140. On Nostradamus's appeal: *Washington Post,* June 5, 1942; and Seabrook, *Witchcraft,* 366.

24 "Background on the news": *Binghampton Press,* August 27, 1941. "We could all be Nostradamus": *Niagara Falls Gazette,* July 16, 1941. "Replaced *Mein Kampf*": *Washington Post,* April 9, 1941. See Neavill,"Publishing in Wartime," 590.

25 "U.S. cinema star": *Time,* May 5, 1941. See Jacques Portes, "Les Etats-Unis, terre de naissance d'une culture de masse moderne," in Mollier et al., *Culture de masse et culture médiatique,* 91.

26 "The great psychic": Norse, *Memoirs of a Bastard Angel,* 50. See *Nostradamus,* June 8, 1911, Gaumont script held at the Bibliothèque Nationale de France, Arts du Spectacle. Norse made this remark while recalling his feverish readings of quatrains in the late 1930s. It is not clear that Gaumont ever produced this script.

27 "Educate the public": *Brooklyn Daily Eagle,* April 14, 1937. On documentaries and shorts: Jack C. Ellis and Betsy A. McLane, *A New History of Documentary Film* (New York: Continuum, 2005); Schatz, *Boom and Bust,* 47–49; and Neal Gabler, *An Empire of Their Own: How the Jews Invented Hollywood* (New York: Crown, 1999), 210–11. On Wilson and the shorts: Carey Wilson oral history (1959), Columbia University Oral History Collection; *Poughkeepsie Eagle-News,* February 3, 1927; *Niagara Falls Gazette,* August 30, 1927; *New York Times,* June 1, 1941; Fujiwara, *Jacques Tourneur,* 43–52; and Vieira, *Irving Thalberg,* 41, 70.

28 "Riddling": *Motion Picture Herald* 133 (October 22, 1938): 48. See script of *What Do You Think? (Nostradamus),* July 7, 1938, 3, Margaret Herrick Library, Academy of Motion Picture Arts and Sciences, MGM Shorts Dept. scripts, box 4.

29 "New and even more": script of *More About Nostradamus,* September 4, 1940, 5, Margaret Herrick Library, MGM Shorts Dept. scripts, box 4. "Stellar road map": Nona Howard, *Follow Your Lucky Stars: A Handbook for Student Astrologers* (Cleveland: World, 1943), 13. See Carey Wilson oral history, 203; Richard Goldstone oral history (1991–92), Margaret Herrick Library, 235–39; and *Time,* September 25, 1939. On Manly Hall: Horowitz, *Occult America,* 147–58; Sahagun, *Master of the Mysteries*; Manly Hall, "The Inward Look and the Outward" and "Nostradamus," *Horizon* 2 (1942): 1–2, 14–15; and Hall, "Nostradamus Translations" (February 20, 1943), University of Southern California, MGM Collection, box 582.

30 "Now, we're digging": *Niagara Falls Gazette,* February 19, 1943. See Hall, quoted in Sahagun, *Master of the Mysteries,* 83; and *MGM's Short Story* (July–September 1938): 15.

31 "Read the fateful": Ward, *Oracles of Nostradamus,* front cover; See E. P. Summerson, Jr., letter to the editor, *Life* (April 21, 1941): 8; and Anderson, *Seven Years That Changed the World,* 45–47.

32 "A certain doctrinaire": Goldstone oral history, 342. See Schatz, *Boom and Bust,* 139–41; May, *The Big Tomorrow,* 143; and Koppes and Black, *Hollywood Goes to War,* 63, 141.

33 "The United States will be": script for *More About Nostradamus,* 16. See Hall, "Nostradamus Translations."

34 "Make a given verse": Goldstone oral history, 242; see also 21–42, 342–47. See Wilson oral history, 203. On American wartime propaganda and Hollywood: Fox, "Propaganda and the Flight of Rudolf Hess," 89; Eyman, *Lion of Hollywood,* 277; and Hay, *MGM,* 192–93.

35 "Psychology": *The Lion's Roar* 10 (1942). "You have to seek out": Sidney Carroll, "Nostradamus Up to Date," *Coronet* 13 (December 1942): 172. See J. A. Hammerton, *Other Things Than War* (London: MacDonald, 1943), 114; *MGM's Short Story* (July–September 1938): 15; and Goldstone oral history, 237–38.

36 "New generations," *Time,* May 5, 1941. See Hodgson, *Winning My Wings,* 219.

37 "Divert the great streams": Schellenberg, *Labyrinth,* 105. "Energetic movie scholar": *Niagara Falls Gazette,* February 19, 1943. "A whole army": Sidney Carroll, "Nostradamus Up to Date," *Coronet* 13 (December 1942): 172. See *Films for Classroom Use: Handbook of Information on Films Selected and Classified by the Advisory Committee on the Use of Motion Pictures in Education* (New York: Teaching Films Custodians, 1941), 205–06; *Tulsa Sunday World,* May 3, 1942; and *The Lion's Roar* 9 (1942): 58.

38 "Occultist propaganda": Goebbels, *Diaries, 1942–1943,* 220. "Who Is Nostradamus?": quotation in Wulff, *Zodiac and Swastika,* 96. "Ally on the propaganda front": *New York Times,* January 4, 1942. "*Mein Kampf*": *Poughkeepsie New Yorker,* November 10, 1941. See Breton, interview by Charles-Henri Ford, August 1941, in Breton, *Entretiens,* 225–26.

39 "Silly rubbish": Goebbels, November 22, 1939, quoted in Boelcke, *Secret Conferences,* 6. "This superstitious philosophy": Goldstone oral history, 237. On American perceptions of propaganda: Ralph D. Casey, *What Is Propaganda? War Department Education Manual* (1944); Mark Crispin Miller, introduction to Edward Bernays, *Propaganda* (Brooklyn: Ig Publishing, 2005 [1928]), 9–14; and Koppes and Black, *Hollywood Goes to War,* 66–67.

40 "It was an anti-English": Vercors, *La bataille du silence: souvenirs de minuit* (Paris: Presses de la cité, 1992), 325. See Wulff, *Zodiac and Swastika,* 95–96; Simonin, *Les Editions de Minuit,* 192–93; and Jean Sasson, *Mayada, Daughter of Iraq: One Woman's Survival Under Saddam Hussein* (New York: Penguin, 2003), 53.

41 "Possibly": R. De Witt Miller, *Forgotten Mysteries* (Chicago: Cloud, 1947), 164. "Enough": *Atlanta Constitution,* August 18, 1945. "Amidst the jubilation": *Herald-Mail* (Fairport, NY), May 17, 1945.

CHAPTER 12: APOCALYPSE NOW?

1 "Nostradamus superstar": *Le Provençal,* August 19, 1981. "This fall": *Bonne soirée,* September 25–October 1, 1981.

2 Fontbrune's real name was Pigeard. This account draws from Fontbrune, *Nostradamus: Countdown to Apocalypse; Le Régional,* September 17, 1981; Roger Sandell, "Apocalypse When?," *Magonia,* January 18, 1985; *Le Provençal,* April 14, 1989; Bessard-Banquy, *La vie du livre contemporain,* 135–36; and Dumézil, *The Riddle of Nostradamus.*

3 "The Shape of Tomorrow," *The Economist,* January 23, 1982; *Chicago Tribune,* August 23, 1981; and Conrad, *Orson Welles,* 101–02.

4 "It is difficult": Henri Peyre, *History in Modern Culture* (New York: French Historical Society, 1950), 18. On this cold war climate: Arthur M. Schlesinger, Jr., *The Vital Center* (Boston: Houghton Mifflin, 1949); Boyer, *By the Bomb's Early Light;* and Graebner, *The Age of Doubt.*

5 "A war": Beye, *120 Charles Street,* 224. "Like to know": Gary Lee Horton, "Nostradamus— Historian of the Future," *Fantastic Adventures,* July 1947.

6 "With terrifying": Roberts, *The Complete Prophecies of Nostradamus,* 292. "Short": John Kobler, "Yrs. Truly, A. Lincoln," *New Yorker,* February 25, 1956, http://nyr.kr/lJQSLg. See *New York Times,* January 25, 1966.

7 *Chicago Tribune,* February 21, 1963. This is the original version of quatrain 1.26:

Le grand du fouldre tumbe d'heure diurne,
Mal est predict par porteur postulaire :
Suivant presaige tumbe d'heure nocturne,
Conflit Reims, Londres, Etrusque pestifere.

8 Susan Emmanuel, *The Day After,* Museum of Broadcast Communications, http://bit.ly/2SmjCL; and Samuel, *Future,* 12–14.

9 "The press is just full": Tony Benn, quoted in Francis Wheen, *Strange Days Indeed,* 309. On these changes: Boyer, *By the Bomb's Early Light,* 223, 359–61; Tony Judt, *Postwar: A History of Europe Since 1945* (New York: Penguin, 2005), chap. 14; and Gardner, *The Science of Fear,* 300.

10 *Time,* June 19, 1972; and Rodgers, *Age of Fracture,* 49, 88. The transformation of the religious landscape is discussed in Roof et al., *The Post-War Generation and Establishment Religion;* Bréchon, "L'évolution du religieux"; and Hervieu-Léger, *Le pèlerin et le converti.* For a recent statistical analysis of the United States, see Charles M. Blow, "Paranormal Flexibility," *New York Times,* December 12, 2009.

11 On the supernatural and modern media: Claude Fischler, preface to Morin, ed., *Croyance astrologique moderne,* 12–13; and Augé, *Non-Places,* xi. See also *Ici-Paris,* May 4–10, 1948.

12 On Nostradamus's global presence: George Packer, *The Assassins' Gate: America in Iraq* (New York: Farrar, Straus and Giroux, 2005), 171; *Time,* December 26, 1994; and Xiaoying Zhang, "Nostradamus's Effect in China," research paper, New York University, May 2010.

13 "A kind of Ayatollah": *Bonne soirée,* September 25–October 1, 1981. "The star": *Sunday Times,* July 4, 1999. "From Heaven": Garencières, *The True Prophecies,* 433. See the note in *Prophecies,* 372.

14 "Day of judgment": "Nostradamus," *Littell's Living Age,* April 5, 1879. "Cataclysm": *Manti Messenger,* October 11, 1940. "Nostradamus prophesied": Aldous Huxley, quoted in Sybille Bedford, *Aldous Huxley: A Biography* (Chicago: Ivan R. Dee, 2002), 608. See Torné-Chavigny, *Concordance des prophéties de Nostradamus,* 156.

15 "The confrontation": *Paris-Match,* June 8, 1995. "All Japanese": Hidetoshi Tahahashi, interview in Murakami, *Underground,* 349. See Fontbrune, *Nostradamus: Countdown to Apocalypse,* 315; and Kingston, *Japan's Quiet Transformation,* chap. 1.

16 "More to this enduring figure": *Daily Mail,* May 14, 1999. See Paulus, *Nostradamus 1999; Guardian,* July 1, 1999; *Le Régional,* April 8–14, 1999; and *Telegraph,* December 10, 2010.

17 "If we don't wake up": José Argüelles, "The Mayan Factor: Path Beyond Technology," in Braden, *The Mystery of 2012,* 77. See Chris Mooney, "Surprising Nostradamus," *American Prospect,* February 12, 2001, http://bit.ly/sAw7AD.

18 "Modernity": Hall, *Apocalypse,* 206. On the turn of the millennium: *Newsweek,* October 24, 1999; Airiau, *L'Eglise et l'Apocalypse,* 77, 125; Weber, *Apocalypses,* 199–211; Guyatt, *Have a Nice Doomsday,* 6–7; and Barkun, *Culture of Conspiracy.*

19 "Sadistic": Fontbrune, *L'étrange XXe siècle vu par Nostradamus,* 155. "Acute": *Le Régional,* February 5, 1981. "Final Shit Rain": Hunter S. Thompson, *Kingdom of Fear: Loathsome Secrets of a Star-Crossed Child in the Final Days of the American Century* (New York: Simon & Schuster 2003), 332. See *Ici-Paris,* November 5–11, 1952; Ragusa, *The Skin Between Us,* 52; and Fontbrune, interviews in *Le Matin de Paris,* August 18, 1981, *Paris-Match,* August 21, 1981, and *Le Régional,* August 27, 1981.

20 For such views on the Bible, see Armstrong, *The Bible,* 226–29; and Gutjahr, *An American Bible,* 173.

21 "To cash in": Roger W. Straus to Matthew Evans, April 14, 1982, Farrar, Straus and Giroux

records, New York Public Library, Series VII, box 570. "Morbid": Fontbrune, *Nostradamus: Countdown to Apocalypse,* 441. See *Paris-Match,* August 21, 1981.

22 "You will live" and subsequent posts: http://amzn.to/mmXho2. "The sense": Tahahashi, interview in Murakami, *Underground,* 348. See *New York Times,* April 8, 1988; Wheen, *Idiot Proof,* 118; and *Broadcasting & Cable,* January 7, 2009.

23 "Rising spiral": *Sun,* December 31, 2002. See Adorno, *Stars Down to Earth;* Hall et al., *Policing the Crisis;* and Glassner, *The Culture of Fear,* 201, 206. On media and short-term alarm: Cusset, *Décennie,* 227–28.

24 "Something": Abramsky, "The New Fear," B6. See Joel Aschenbach, "The Century of Disasters," *Slate,* May 13, 2011, http://slate.me/kLhJFD. Within the growing literature on the culture of fear, I have learned most from Bourke, *Fear;* Beck, *Risk Society;* Giddens, *Modernity and Self-Identity;* and Frank Füredi, "Toward a Sociology of Fear," in Kate Hebblethwaite and Eliza McCarthy, eds., *Fear: Essays on the Meaning and Experience of Fear* (Portland, OR: Four Courts Press, 2007), 23–26. Web sites linking Nostradamus to cataclysms in 2012 include Nostradamus Predictions, http://bit.ly/tJBcZc, and nostradamus.org, http://bit.ly/sHRcCj.

25 On the 2003 heat wave and vulnerability: Michel Kokoreff and Jacques Rodriguez, "Une société de l'incertitude," *Sciences humaines* 50 (2005), http://bit.ly/km8X8G.

26 Kaplan, and Marshal, *The Cult at the End of the World;* Reader, "Violent Millenarianism," 239–40; Kogo, "Aum Shinrikyo and Spiritual Emergency," 82–101; and Kisala, "Nostradamus and the Apocalypse in Japan."

27 "Shocking Nostradamus Cover-Up," *Sun,* October 18, 2004. See Hofstadter, *The Paranoid Style in American Politics,* 3–40; Abramsky, "New Fear," B6; John Evan-Jones, *The Nostradamus Conspiracy* (Bloomington, IN: Xlibris, 2001); Barkun, *Culture of Conspiracy,* 20; Taguieff, *L'imaginaire du complot mondial;* as well as www.911truth.org/images/ZogbyPoll2007 .pdf and www.fourwinds10.com/siterun_data/government/war/news.php?q=1300727277.

28 This view can be found in Füredi, *Politics of Fear.* On Aum: Murakami, *Underground,* 274–76, 318; and Lifton, *Destroying the World to Save It,* 50–51, 128–29. On astrology's appeal among vulnerable people: Wuthnow, *Experimentation in American Religion,* chap. 2; and Boy and Michelat, "Croyances aux parasciences." On our melancholy modernity: Charle, *Discordance des temps.*

29 On myths and fate, I am drawing from Buck-Morss, *The Dialectics of Seeing,* 79.

30 Nostradamus syndrome and "this is about": Boia, *Fin du monde,* 233. See *Time,* September 7, 1981; *Le Point,* August 24–30, 1981; *Le Figaro Magazine,* June 12, 1999; *The Scotsman,* October 20, 2001; and Luis Prada, "The 6 Best 2012 Apocalypse Theories (Are All Bullshit)," cracked.com, http://bit.ly/bDAfgF.

31 See Hobbes, *Leviathan,* 76; Boyer, *By the Bomb's Early Light,* 21, 238, 282–87; and Etienne Gilson, "Les terreurs de l'an 2000," *Ecclesia* 14 (1950): 10.

32 "Shreds": *The Times,* October 12, 2001. "In response": Boia, *Fin du monde,* 233. See Esquerre, *La manipulation mentale;* Louise Samways, *Dangerous Persuaders* (New York: Penguin, 1994); and Fenech, *Face aux sectes,* ii, 5.

33 "When faith": *Guardian,* July 2, 1999. "Nattering": *Daily Telegraph,* October 17, 2001. See Guilhaume, *Nostradamus,* 237.

34 *L'Evènement* (June 10–16, 1999): 59; *Washington Post,* February 17, 1953; Fenech, *Face aux sectes,* 166–67; and Pagels, *Revelations,* 174.

35 *Le Régional,* November 24, 1983; Brooks, *Letters to My Husband,* 106; and John Tierney, "Will You Be E-Mailing This Column? It's Awesome," *New York Times,* February 9, 2010.

36 On apocalypticism today: Michael Moyer, "Eternal Fascinations with the End," *Scientific American,* September 2010, http://bit.ly/ckk9gs.

37 "A name": Henry Miller, "A Few Chaotic Recollections," *From Your Capricorn Friend,* 36. See Miller, aphorism in *The Henry Miller Reader,* 365.

38 "Strife": Miller, "A Few Chaotic Recollections," 38. See Vrebos, *Henry Miller,* 74.

39 "Smash-up": Miller, *Conversations with Henry Miller,* 97. "Vast multitude": Miller, foreword to Omarr, *Henry Miller,* 19–20. See Max Ernst, "Nostradamus, Blanche de Castille et le petit Saint-Louis," *Révolution surréaliste* 12 (December 15, 1929): 49; and Miller to Fontbrune, April 28, 1951, November 13, 1951, and January 7, 1954, Fontbrune, *Henry Miller et Nostradamus,* 81, 92, 100. Thank you to Denis Hollier for directing me toward Ernst's collage.

40 "Fundamentally": 1969 interview of Henry Miller, quoted in Wallace Fowlie, "Henry Miller as Visionary," in Gottesman, ed., *Critical Essays on Henry Miller,* 187. On Miller's religiosity and Greenwich Village: Nesbit, *Henry Miller and Religion,* 29–30, 126.

41 Spangler, *Emergence,* 17–19; and Yun-Shik, *Korea Confronts Globalization,* 222. On the New Age and syncretic spirituality: Horowitz, *Occult America,* 257. On the transformation of religion: Roof et al., *The Post-War Generation;* and James A. Beckford, "Social Movements as Free-Floating Religious Phenomena," in Fenn, ed., *Blackwell Companion to Sociology of Religion,* 232–35.

42 Scholars have shown that, in France at least, belief in astrology or fortune-tellers has served as a complement to mainstream religion rather than a substitution. But it also feeds off dissatisfaction with traditional religious institutions. See, for instance, Bréchon, "Les attitudes religieuses en France," 24. On the transformations of spirituality: Robert Wuthnow, "Spirituality and Spiritual Practice," in Fenn, ed., *Blackwell Companion to Sociology of Religion,* 306–12.

43 "Scaremongering": *The Times,* October 12, 2001. Jonathan Kay places much of the blame for recent conspiracy theories on the Internet in his *Among the Truthers: A Journey Through America's Growing Conspiracist Underground* (New York: Harper, 2011). On the Internet: Roger Chartier, "L'écrit et l'écran, une révolution en marche," *Le Monde,* October 13, 2007.

44 Rodgers, *Age of Fracture.*

45 "Symbol": Lévi-Strauss, *Introduction to the Work of Marcel Mauss,* 64. This discussion benefited from a conversation with Jacques Revel.

46 "Don't even see": Adorno, *Stars Down to Earth,* 57. On the current enthusiasm for geniuses: Garber, "Our Genius Problem," 65–72.

47 This portrait of late modernity is in conversation with Giddens, *Modernity and Self-Identity,* 27; Augé, *Non-Places,* xxii; and Lenoir, *Les métamorphoses de Dieu,* 223.

48 "Uncertain": Miller, quoted in Vrebos, *Henry Miller,* 35–36.

EPILOGUE: TIMES FOR NOSTRADAMUS

1 I interviewed François Wyss-Mercier in person on November 25, 2003, and by phone on January 21, 2004. See *Le Régional,* September 29, 1983.

2 "Nothing interesting": Joseph François Megy, "Notice sur Michel Nostradamus," February 7, 1818, Archives départementales des Bouches-du-Rhône, 6M 1610. See Garcin, *Dictionnaire historique et topographique de la Provence,* 1:84–85; Frédéric Mistral, "Avans-prepaus," *La Bresco d'Antoni-Blasi Crouisillat,* iii; *Le tout-Salon: Revue annuelle* (Marseille, 1897): 41; and Audier, *Salon: capitale des huiles.*

3 "Engineers": *Le Régional,* January 13, 1950. See the mayor's speech at the inauguration of the Craponne monument, October 22, 1854, AMS DD 126, fol. 216–18.

4 Francou, *Salon et son devenir; Salon de Provence. Etudes des perspectives de développement de la ville. Rapport no. 1: perspectives démographiques et économiques* (Paris: Omnium technique d'études urbaines, 1965); Jacques Van Migom, "Plan d'urbanisme directeur des quartiers de L'Empéri et de Craponne," February 26, 1964, Archives départementales des

Bouches-du-Rhône, O 12 2320; and D'Agostino, "Les extensions récentes de Salon-de-Provence."

5 "What's the reason": Miller to Braissaï, November 25, 1964, in Brassaï, *Henry Miller, Happy Rock,* 7. "Salon the tourist center": Frédéric Alquier, "Programme en faveur du tourisme salonais," *Le Régional,* February 26, 1954. "Century of speed": *Le Régional,* June 13–19, 1960. See *Salon de Provence. Guide officiel de tourisme 1956* (Béziers: Sodier, [1956]); and Young, "La Vieille France as Object of Bourgeois Desire."

6 "Kasbah": collective letter by twenty-one small business owners to Francou, June 14, 1974, AMS 3 T 7. "Impose their rule": *Le Régional,* September 27, 1984. "Is no longer": *Le Régional,* February 28, 1980.

7 "Reconquest": *Le Régional,* March 9, 1989. See *Le Régional,* August 14, 1980, and March 21, 1985. On postwar urban planning, heritage, and tourism: Kirshenblatt-Gimblett, *Destination Culture;* Castells, *The Informational City;* and Wakeman, *Modernizing the Provincial City.*

8 "Everything has been": press kit for the inauguration of the Maison Nostradamus, February 22, 1992, AMS 231 W 53. Among other sources, I relied on *Le Régional,* April 8, 1982; *Salon mensuel* 10 (1991): 12; and my interview with Jacqueline Allemand in Salon, March 30, 2004.

9 On these summer festivals: Crivello, "Du passé, faisons un spectacle!"

10 "Mecca": clipping of Jacques Bouisset, "Sur les pas de Nostradamus," *Paris-Match Provence,* [1979?], AMS 7 M 6/2. "Super-genius": *Le Régional,* May 9, 1985. "Cultural versatility": press kit for the *Journés Nostradamus* [April–May 1985], AMS 7M 6/2.

11 "Nostradamian year": program for *Les Nostradamiques de Salon-de-Provence,* 1999, [1]. "We were in the city": Colette (pseud.), interview by the author, Salon, January 13, 2004. Christian Kert, interview by the author, Paris, March 31, 2004. See Françoise Wyss-Mercier, memorandum to Francou, May 1985, AMS 7 M 6/2; and the interview of Christian Kert in *Salon Centre: bulletin du comité d'intérêts du quartier centre ville* 9 (September 1987): 2.

12 "Dreams": dossier presenting the 1991 historical pageant of Salon, AMS 166 W 14/4. I am also drawing from my telephone interview with Jo Stofati, January 19, 2004.

13 For seminal statements about all of this, see Pierre Nora, "The Reasons for the Current Upsurge in Memory," *Transit* 22 (2002): 1–6, repr. in *Eurozine,* April 19, 2002, http://bit.ly/jhIhyl; and Hartog, *Régimes d'historicité,* 125–26.

14 "Nostradamus jostles": *Reconstitution historique. Salon de Provence. 10ᵉ édition* 1995, 8. See *Le Régional,* March 21, 1985; and Jean-Louis Kamoun, "Le chant des étoiles," 1999, private collection of Françoise Wyss-Mercier.

15 "Times of Nostradamus": *Le Provençal,* March 29, 1989. "People were saying": Georges (pseud.), interview by the author, Salon, November 25, 2003.

16 "Flesh him out": Christian Kert interview. See *Le Régional,* April 8–14, 1999; and Orsi, *Thank You, St. Jude,* 16–19.

17 "The business of fear": press kit for the 1999 Nostradamiques, AMS 312 W 4. "Less than scrupulous": Jacqueline Allemand, quoted in *Le Provençal,* June 13, 1996. See *Le Provençal,* July 8, 1991.

18 "As linked": Gimon, "Michel Nostradamus": 4.

19 "We don't get": *The Times,* June 26, 1999.

20 On stigmatized knowledge, see Barkun, *Culture of Conspiracy.*

21 Benedict Carey, "Do You Believe in Magic?," *New York Times,* January 23, 2007.

22 "Only part of us": Rebecca West, *Black Lamb and Grey Falcon: A Journey Through Yugoslavia* (New York: Penguin, 2007 [1941]), 1102.

Bibliography

꙳꙳꙳

The indispensable road map to the Nostradamian universe (at least, for French publications) is Robert Benazra, *Répertoire chronologique nostradamique: 1545–1989* (Paris: La Grande Conjonction, 1990). The key complements are Patrice Guinard, "Historique des éditions des *Prophéties* de Nostradamus (1555–1615)," *Revue française d'histoire du livre* 129 (2009): 7–142; Michel Chomarat with Jean-Paul Laroche, *Bibliographie Nostradamus: XVIᵉ–XVIIᵉ–XVIIIᵉ siècles* (Baden-Baden: V. Koerner, 1989); Chomarat, "Nouvelles recherches sur les 'Prophéties' de Michel Nostradamus," *Revue française d'histoire du livre*, new ser., 48, no. 22 (1979): 123–31; Chomarat, *Supplément à la Bibliographie lyonnaise des Nostradamus* (Lyon: Centre Culturel de Buenc, 1976); De Rg., "De quelques ouvrages contenant des prédictions," *Le bibliophile belge* 5 (1848): 91–113; and Graf Carl von Klinckowstroem, "Die ältesten Ausgaben der 'Prophéties' des Nostradamus: Ein Beitrag zur Nostradamus-Bibliographie," *Zeitschrift für Bücherfreunde,* March 1913, 361–72. The catalogs of the early printed books sales held at the Swann Auction Galleries on April 23 and November 8, 2007, also contain valuable information.

While many of Nostredame's almanacs, prognostications, and pamphlets have vanished, a fair number have survived. For the real thing, readers should visit the Bibliothèque Nationale de France (Paris) and the Bibliothèque municipale de Lyon, whose Fonds Chomarat contains more than fifteen hundred texts and images by or about Nostredame and his prophecies. Some of these publications have been digitized on gallica.bnf.fr, the Early English Books online database (a trove for the early modern period at http://eebo.chadwyck.com/home), the Maison Nostradamus' e-corpus, http://www.e-corpus.org/sclon-nostradamus.html; and the Répertoire chronologique Nostradamus (www.propheties.it/bibliotheque/index.html). This Web site also provides many documents about Nostradamus across the centuries. Bernard Chevignard has collated all of Nostredame's presages in his *Présages de Nostradamus* (Paris: Seuil, 1999). The book also contains Nostredame's *La Grand' Pronostication nouvelle avec portenteuse prédiction, pour l'an MDLVII* (Paris: J. Kerver, 1557); *Pronostication nouvelle, pour l'an mil cinq cens cinquante & huict* (Paris: G. le Noir, [1557?]); and *Les significations de l'Eclipse, qui sera le 16 Septembre 1559* (Paris: G. le Noir, [1559?]).

Other publications by Nostredame include (in rough chronological order):

Interprétation des hiéroglyphes de Horapollo. Edited by Pierre Rollet. Raphèlè-lès-Arles: M. Petit, 1993.

Forme et manière de vivre, très utile, pour éviter Au danger de Peste. Paris: R. Ruelle, n.d.

Excellent & moult utile Opuscule à tous necessaire, qui desirent avoir cognoissance de plusieurs exquises Receptes, divisé en deux parties. Lyon: A. Volant, 1556. Partial translation available at www.propheties.it/nostradamus/1555opuscole/opuscole.html.

Almanach pour l'An 1557. Composé par Maistre Michel Nostradamus. Docteur en Medecine, de Salon de Craux en Provence. Paris: Jacques Kerver, [1556].

The Prognostication for the Yeare 1559. Amsterdam: Theatrum Orbis Terrarum, 1558. Reprint, New York: Da Capo, 1969.

An Excellent Tretise, Shewing Suche Perillous, and Contagious Infirmities, as Shall Insue. 1559. and .1566. With the Signes, Causes, Accidentes, and Curatio, for the Health of Such as Inhabit the. 7.8. and. 9. Climat. Compiled by Maister Michael Nostrodamus, Doctor in Phisicke. London: J. Daye, [1559?].

An Almanacke Made By The Notable And Worthie Clerke Michael Nostradamus, Doctor in Physicke, For The Yere, From The Birth Of Our Saviour Jesu Christ, 1559. [London?, 1559?].

An Almanacke for the Yeare of Oure Lorde God, 1559. Composed by Mayster Mychael Nostradamus, Doctour of Physike. London: H. Sutton, 1559.

Pronostication nouvelle pour l'an mil cinq cens soixante deux. Composée par Maistre Michel Nostradamus Docteur en Médecine, de Salon de Craux en Provence. Paris: Veuve B. Regnault, [1561?].

An Almanach for the Yere MDLXII Made by Maister Michael Nostrodamus Doctour of Phisike, of Salon of Craux in Provance. N.p.: W. Powell, 1562.

Pronostico dell'anno M.D. LXIII. Composto & calculato par M. Michele Nostradamo, dottore in medicina di Salon di Craux in Provenza. Rimini, [1562?].

Réimpression de l'almanach de Michel de Nostredame pour l'année 1563. Mariebourg: Sub St Michaelis, 1905.

Li Presagi et pronostici di M. Michele Nostradamo Francese. N.p., 1564.

Almanach: Ende Pronosticatie vanden Iare M.D.LXVI. Ghemaect deur. M. Michiel Nostradamus, Docteur Inder Medicine van Salon vâ Craux in Provence, Medicin van de Conincliche Maiestey. Campen: B. Petersen, [1565?].

Almanach pour l'an M.D.LXVI. avec les amples significations & explications, composé par Maistre Michel de Nostradame Docteur en medicine, Conseiller et Médecin ordinaire du Roy, de Salon de Craux en Provence. Lyon: A. Volant & P. Broton, [1565?]. Reprint, *Cahiers Nostradamus* 5–6 (1987–88): 69–104.

Des Weitberumbten hocherfarnen philosophi, astrologi und medici. Augsburg: M. Manger, 1572.

Nostredame was a prolific letter writer. Fifty-one missives from and to him are collected in his *Lettres inédites,* edited by Jean Dupèbe (Geneva: Droz, 1983). They are in Latin, with French summaries. English translations may be found on www.propheties.it/nostradamus /inedites/inedites1.htm. Other letters and documents by Nostredame are contained in *Nostradamus au XVIᵉ siècle: dix fac-similés,* edited by Eric Visier (Verna: Les 7 Fontaines, 1995); and Edgar Leoni, *Nostradamus and His Prophecies* (Mineola, NY: Dover, 2000). See also E.-P.-E. Lhez, "Aperçu d'un fragment de la correspondance de Michel de Nostredame," *Provence historique* 11 (1961): 117–42, 205–29.

The first edition of Nostredame's *Prophecies* (1555) has been reissued with a scholarly apparatus: *Les premières centuries ou Prophéties,* edited by Pierre Brind'Amour (Geneva: Droz, 1996). For the second and third editions (1557 and 1568), see Nostradamus, *Les Prophéties,* ed.

Bruno Petey-Girard (Paris: Garnier-Flammarion, 2003); and *Les Prophéties: Lyon, 1568* (Lyon: Michel Chomarat, 1993).

While Nostredame left few handwritten traces, there are manuscript sources regarding his readers and his posterity. The Bibliothèque Nationale de France holds relevant letters, interpretations, prophecies, and poems (ms. français 12294, 20863, and 22566, NAF 11548, Clairambault 379 and 530, and Dupuy 661, 843, and 951). I found other such documents at the Bibliothèque de l'Arsenal in Paris (ms. 3137 [1] and ms. 8514); the Bibliothèque Méjanes in Aix-en-Provence (ms. 451 [395] and 526 [647]); the Bibliothèque municipale d'Avignon (ms. 3188 and 3194); the Bibliothèque municipale de Blois (ms. 291); the Bibliothèque municipale de Lyon (ms. 992 and 994); the Bibliothèque municipale de La Rochelle (ms. 153 and 673); and the Institut de France (Godefroy 15 and 329, and ms. 820). The British Library contains a few English and Italian documents of the kind, from the seventeenth and eighteenth centuries (Add. 8344, 61360, and 61479, and Sloane 3722). The Archives Nationales (Paris) hold dossiers about the Nostradamian editor Eugène Bareste (454 AP 21, F17 2935/2, and F17 3114/2).

Sources on Nostradamus's presence in Salon and Provence are found in the Archives départementales des Bouches-du-Rhône in Marseille (esp. 6 M 1610 and O 12 2320); the Médiathèque de l'architecture et du patrimoine in Paris (81/13/76 and 81/13/77); and especially the Archives municipales de Salon. The latter contain dozens of cartons regarding municipal affairs (BB19 bis, 1 D 1, and DD 126), Nostradamus's statue (7 M 6/1 and 7 M 6/2), museums (7 R series), festivities (15 R series), urban renovation (3 T 6 and 3 T 7), as well as tourism and historical pageants (W series). Salon's Maison Nostradamus holds rare sixteenth-century publications and a copious file of twentieth-century clippings.

The two largest repositories for iconography are the Bibliothèque Nationale de France's Département des Estampes and the Musée des Civilisations de l'Europe et de la Méditerranée in Marseille. Leading American libraries all have pertinent holdings regarding Nostradamus's presence in the United States. The New York Public Library also holds a file on the publication of Lee McCann's *Nostradamus* in 1982 (Farrar, Straus and Giroux records, series VII, box 570, folder 9). Scripts and promotional material for MGM's Nostradamus shorts (1938–53) can be found at the Margaret Herrick Library of the Motion Picture Arts and Sciences in Los Angeles (MGM Shorts department, scripts, boxes 1, 4, and 11). The library also holds Richard Goldstone's rich oral history (OH 119), which must be completed by Carey Wilson's own oral history (Columbia University Oral History Collection) and the dossier on *Nostradamus IV* in the USC Cinematic Arts Library (MGM Collection, box 582).

Almanacs constituted one of the foundations of the Nostradamus phenomenon until the mid-twentieth century. There are troves in the Bibliothèque de l'Arsenal and the Musée des Civilisations de l'Europe et de la Méditerranée. I provide a significant but nonexhaustive selection below (in rough chronological order) and then list the key primary and secondary sources I have consulted. This bibliography does not include the countless newspapers, periodicals, dictionaries, encyclopedias, auction catalogs, travel accounts, and publications about Salon-de-Provence that contain mentions—or else revealing silences—about Nostradamus. Readers will find those references in the notes.

Almanach historial pour l'an de grâce mil six cens septante et quatre. Exactement supputé par Me M. Nostredamus, Grand Astrologue & Mathématicien. Paris: A. Raffle, [1673?].
Almanach journalier pour l'an de grâce bisextil mil six cents septente-six diligemment supputé & calculé par les plus doctes mathématiciens, par Michel Nostradamus, grand astrologue et mathématicien. Lyon: Claude-la-Rue, [1675?].
Almanach pour l'an de grâce mil six cens quatre-vingts trois. Par Michel Nostradamus Astrologue. Rouen: J. Ourseil, [1682?].

Générales prédictions pour douze ans, commençant en l'année mil six cens quatre-vingt trois, & finissant en l'année mil six cens quatre-vingt quatorze . . . tiré des anciens manuscrits de Maistre Michel Nostradamus; & nouvellement supputé suivant le calcul de Ticho-Brahé, maistre Petit Lyonnois. Troyes: N. Oudot, [1682?].

Almanach bissextil et historial pour l'an de grâce, mil six cent quatre-vingt douze . . . . Tiré des anciens manuscrits de Maistre Michel Nostradamus. Troyes: J. Oudot, [1691?].

Le véritable almanach journalier, historial et prophétique de Pierre de Larrivey extrait de quelques mémoires manuscrits de Michel Nostradamus pour l'an de grâce 1711. Marseille: C. Garcin, [1710?].

The Prophecies of Michael Nostradamus Concerning the Fate of all the Kings and Queens of Great Britain Since the Reformation, and the Wonderful Fulfillings Thereof. London: J. Roberts, 1715.

Almanach du Palais pour l'an de Grâce 1741, dans lequel on observera les divers changemens que les Astres produisent icy-bas, tiré des anciens manuscrits de Maître Michel Nostradamus. Troyes: Veuve P. Garnier, [1741?].

Prophéties ou prédictions perpétuelles, composées par Pitagoras, Joseph le Juste, Daniel le Prophète, Michel Nostradamus & plusieurs autres Philosophes. Salon en Provence: A. Florion, [18th century].

Prophéties générales, nouvelles et curieuses . . . depuis l'An 1760, jusqu'en l'An 1767. Tirées des anciens Manuscrits de Me. Michel Nostradamus. Troyes: J. Garnier, [1760?].

Nouvelles et curieuses prédictions de Michel Nostradamus, pour sept ans: depuis l'année 1776 jusqu'à l'année 1782 inclusivement, augmentées de l'ouverture du tombeau de Nostradamus. Salon en Provence, 1775.

Almanach journalier pour l'année de Grâce 1783, contenant les prédictions des douze mois de l'année, et les différens changemens de tems . . . Le tout fidellement recueilli des écrits de Me Michel Nostradamus, grand astrologue. Brussels: J. Basile, [1782?].

Nostradamus, J. B. *Lovenschen Almanach oft Tydt-Verkonder voor het Jaer ons Heere Jesu-Christi 1787 Op den Horizond van Braband en d'Omliggende Plaestsen, door J.B Nostradamus.* Loven: J. Jacobs, [1786?].

Nostradamus moderne, ou almanach prophétique des grands évènements pour l'année 1791. Chambéri, [1790?].

Almanach royaliste, ou la contre-révolution prédite par Me Michel Nostradamus pour l'année bissexte 1792. Petersbourg [*sic*]: Presses impériales, [1791?].

Nouveaux et vrais pronostics de Michel Nostradamus, calculés et supputés très exactement d'après les observations des Anciens. Pour huit ans, à commencer en l'année 1793 jusqu'à l'année 1800 inclusivement. Avec l'ouverture de son tombeau et un abrégé de sa vie. Salon en Provence, 1793.

Rouy l'aîné. *Le magicien républicain, ou Oracles des évènemens dont l'Europe, et particulièrement la France, sera le théâtre en 1793.* Paris: published by the author, [1792?].

Nouvelles et curieuses Prédictions de Michel Nostradamus, pour sept ans, depuis l'année 1800, jusqu'à l'année 1806. Augmentées de l'ouverture du Tombeau de Nostradamus. Lausanne: Frères Associés, [1799?].

L'Incroyable pour 1807. Almanach des curieux: petit livre très-intéressant, contenant les principales Prédictions de Nostradamus et du Mirabilis Liber. Chalons-sur-Marne: Martin, [1806?].

Prophéties perpétuelles, très-anciennes et très-certaines, de Nostradamus, Grand Astronome et Philosophe. Epinal: Pellerin, [1812?].

Prophéties perpétuelles très-anciennes et très-certaines de Nostradamus, astronome, prophète, et philosophe. Avignon: Offray aîné, [1815?].

Nouveaux et Vrais Pronostics de Michel Nostradamus, calculés & supputés très-exactement d'après les observations des Anciens, pour cinq ans, à commencer en l'année 1817, jusqu'à l'année 1821 inclusivement. Avec l'ouverture de son tombeau & un abrégé de sa vie. Avignon: Chaillot aîné, 1816.

Prophéties nouvelles de Michel Nostradamus, trouvées dans sa tombe, Au moment de l'Ouverture, dans l'Eglise des Cordeliers de Salon, pour 1816, 1817, 1818, 1819 et 1820. Reims: Pierard, 1817.

Abrégé du cabinet d'éloquence: augmenté des Centuries et Prophéties de Thomas-Joseph Moult et de Michel Nostradamus, les deux plus célèbres Astrologues et Philosophes du siècle passé. Noyon: Leméni-Devin, 1820.

Almanach prophétique, pittoresque et utile . . . publié par l'auteur de "Nostradamus." Paris: Aubert and Pagnerre, 1841–95.

Nouvelles et curieuses Prédictions de Michel Nostradamus, pour sept ans, depuis l'année 1844, jusqu'à l'année 1850 inclusivement. Augmentées de la vie de Nostradamus. Salon en Provence, 1844.

Almanach de l'ère nouvelle, historique et prophétique pour 1849. Paris: P.-J. Camus, [1849?].

Nostradamus lillois, nouvel almanach instructif, récréatif et prophétique, pour l'an de grâce 1850. Lille, L. Danel, [1849?].

Le neveu du grand homme. Almanach pour 1850 par Michel Nostradamus. Paris, [1849?].

Le diable rouge: almanach cabalistique. Paris: Aubert, 1850.

Almanach historique, littéraire et biographique de la Provence. Marseille: Au Bureau du Plutarque Provençal, 1856–75.

Almanach-guide de Marseille et du département des Bouches-du-Rhône pour l'année 1870, 1871, 1872. Marseille: H. Seren, [1870–72?].

Nouvelles et curieuses Prédictions de Michel Nostradamus, pour sept ans, depuis l'année 1871 jusqu'à l'année 1877 inclusivement. Grenoble: Baratier, [1871?].

PRIMARY LITERATURE

??? Par Nostradamus. Lorsque Chambord nous reviendra. Paris: L. Hugonis, [1873?].

Achard, Claude-François. *Dictionnaire de la Provence et du Comté-Venaissin.* 2 vols. Marseille: Jean Mossy, 1786–87.

Advielle, Victor. *Documents inédits sur les prophéties de Nostradamus et sur Vincent Seve, son continuateur.* Bruges: Daveloy and Aubry, 1878.

Anderson, Wing. *Seven Years That Changed the World, 1941–48.* Los Angeles: Kosmon, 1940.

Apollinaire, Guillaume. *Lettres à Lou.* Edited by Michel Décaudin. Paris: Gallimard, 1969.

Aragon, Louis. *Le crève-coeur.* [1941?] Reprint, Paris: Gallimard, 1956.

Ashe, Ken. "Nostradamus: 2012." DVD. Directed by Andy Pickard. New York: A&E Television Networks, 2008.

L'astrologue patriote, ou Récit curieux de différents prodiges, vus par un descendant de Nostradamus. N.p., 1789.

Astruc, Jean. *Mémoires pour servir à l'histoire de la faculté de médecine de Montpellier.* Paris: P. G. Cavelier, 1767.

"Attention Called to a Prophecy of a Very Serious Import, Written by the Celebrated Nostradamus." *The Straggling Astrologer* 8 (1824): 122–24.

Atwood, William. *The Wonderful Predictions of Nostredamus, Grebner, David Pareus, and Antonius Torquatus: Wherein the Grandeur of Their Present Majesties, the Happiness of England, and Downfall of France and Rome, Are Plainly Delineated.* London: J. Robinson, 1689.

Audier, Vincent. *Salon: capitale des huiles.* Salon: L. Eyriez, 1911.

Bachaumont, Louis Petit de. *Mémoires secrets de Bachaumont.* Edited by P.-L. Jacob. Paris: Garnier, 1883.

Balzac, Honoré de. 1841. *About Catherine de Medici.* Translated by Clara Bell. London: J. M. Dent, 1901.

Banon, A. T. "Nostradamus." *The Theosophist* 19 (1898): 287–89.

Barbier, Edmond. *Chronique de la Régence et du règne de Louis XV (1718–1763) ou Journal de Barbier.* Paris: Charpentier, 1858.

Bareste, Eugène. *Nostradamus.* Paris: Maillet, 1840.

———. *Prophéties: la fin des temps.* Paris: Lavigne, 1840.

———. "Nostradamus et Napoléon." *L'Echo des feuilletons* 1 (1841): 69–71.

Barsy, Carlotta de. *The Gates of the Future Drawn Open: Dreams and Omens from the Ancient Manuscripts of Nostradamus, Albertus Magnus and Other Famous Sorcerers.* Chicago: Laird & Lee, 1899.

Bataille prodigieuse d'une grande quantité d'oyseaux, arrivée en Franche Comté proche Dole veriffié par Nostradamus. N.p., 1668.

Bayle, Pierre. *Dictionnaire historique et critique de Pierre Bayle.* Paris: Desoer, 1820.

Belier de Saint-Brisson. *Epistre au Roy, présentée à Sa Majesté le vingt-sept avril 1716, qui contient une application d'une prophétie de Nostradamus à Louis XV.* Paris: P. Prault, 1716.

———. *Accomplissement d'une prophétie de Nostradamus, en la personne de Louis XV, roi de France et de Navarre, à qui elle fut appliquée & présentée dès l'Année 1716.* Paris: P. Prault, 1744.

Bellaud, François. *Napoléon, premier Empereur des français, prédit par Nostradamus, ou nouvelle concordance des prophéties de Nostradamus, avec l'Histoire.* Paris: Desenne, 1806.

Belot, Jean. *Centuries Prophétiques révélées par sacrée Théurgie & secrette Astrologie à M. Jean Belot Curé de Mil-monts, professeur ès Mathematiques Divines & Celestes.* Paris: A. Champenois, 1621.

Béranger, Pierre-Jean de. "Prédiction de Nostradamus pour l'an deux mil." In vol. 4 of *Oeuvres complètes de P. J. de Béranger.* Paris: Perrotin, 1834.

Béraud, Antony, and Valory [Jean Joseph Charles Mourier]. *Nostradamus. Drame en trois actes et en six parties.* Paris: J.-N. Barba, 1829.

Berin, Charles. "Michel Nostradamus." *Mosaïque du Midi* 3 (1839): 65–70.

Berr, Emile. "Nostradamus." *Journal de l'Université des Annales* 7 (1913): 516–29.

Bertin, J.-B., and V. Audin. *Adam de Craponne et son canal.* Salon-de-Provence: L. Eyriez, 1904.

Beye, Holly. *120 Charles Street, the Village: Journals and Writings, 1949–1950.* Huron, OH: Bottom Dog, 2006.

Bichat, Félix. *Prédictions sensationnelles de Nostradamus.* Paris: Administration, [1940?].

Blanchard, Jean. *Le Vieux Salon: monographie des rues et monuments de la ville.* Salon-de-Provence: Imprimerie régionale, 1926.

Blanchard, Jean, and Charles Reynaud-Plense. *La vie et l'oeuvre de Michel Nostradamus.* Salon-de-Provence: L. Guillaumichon, 1933.

Blavatsky, Helena P. *Isis Unveiled: A Master Key to the Mysteries of Ancient and Modern Science and Theology.* New York: J. W. Bouton, 1877.

Blocher-Saillens, Madeleine. *Témoin des années noires: journal d'une femme pasteur, 1938–1945.* Edited by Jacques-E. Blocher. Paris: Editions de Paris, 1998.

Boelcke, Willi A. *Kriegspropaganda 1939–1941: Geheime Ministerkonferenzen im Reischspropagandaministerium.* Stuttgart: Deutsche Verlags-Anstalt, 1966.

———, ed. *The Secret Conferences of Dr. Goebbels: The Nazi Propaganda War, 1939–43.* New York: Dutton, 1970.

Bois, Georges. "Comment je suis devenu sceptique." *Revue du monde invisible* 4 (1902): 554–56.

Boivin, François de. *Mémoires du sieur François de Boivin.* Vol. 36 of *Collection universelle des mémoires particuliers relatifs à l'histoire de France.* Edited by J. A. Roucher, Antoine Perrin, and Louis d'Ussieux. Paris: Cuchet, 1787.

Bonnelier, Hippolyte. *Nostradamus, roman.* 2 vols. Paris: A. Ledoux, 1833.

Bouhier, Jean. *Correspondence littéraire du président Bouhier.* 8 vols. Saint-Etienne: Université de Saint-Etienne, 1980–88.

Boussemart, Charles. *Grande arrivée de Nostradamus à Paris, introduit dans la tour du Temple, par Charles libre, devant M. Louis Capet l'esclave.* Paris: C.-F. Cagnion, 1792.

Bouys, Théodore. *Nouvelles considérations puisées dans la clairvoyance instinctive de l'homme, sur les oracles, les sibylles et les prophéties, et particulièrement sur Nostradamus.* Paris: Desenne, 1806.

Brantôme, Pierre de Bourdeilles, lord of. *Les vies des grands capitaines du siècle dernier.* Vol. 6 of *Oeuvres complètes de Pierre de Bourdeilles.* Edited by André de Bourdeilles, Louis Lacour, and Prosper Mérimée. Paris: P. Jannet, 1858–95.

Breton, André. *Entretiens (1913–1952).* 1952. New edition, Paris: Gallimard, 1969.

Britten, William. *Art Magic; or, Mundane, Sub-Mundane and Super-Mundane Spiritism; A Treatise in Three Parts and Twenty-Three Sections . . .* New York: published by the author, 1876.

Brooks, Fern Field. *Letters to My Husband.* Franklin Lakes, NJ: Career, 1995.

Brown, Janelle. "Nostradamus Called It! Internet Conspiracy Theorists Are Having a Field Day After the Attacks." Salon.com. September 17, 2001, www.salon.com/2001/09/17/kooks_2/.

Brunet, Gustave. *Les Fous littéraires: essai bibliographique sur la littérature excentrique, les illuminés, visionnaires, etc.* Brussels: Gay et Doucé, 1880.

Buget, François. "Etude sur les prophéties de Nostradamus." *Bulletin du bibliophile et du bibliothécaire,* 1860, 1699–1721.

———. "Etude sur Nostradamus." *Bulletin du bibliophile et du bibliothécaire,* 1861, 68–94, 241–68, 383–421, 657–91.

———. "Etude sur Nostradamus." *Bulletin du bibliophile et du bibliothécaire,* 1862, 761–85.

———. "Etude sur Nostradamus." *Bulletin du bibliophile et du bibliothécaire,* 1863, 449–73, 513–30, 577–88.

Burroughs, John. *The Writings of John Burroughs.* 20 vols. Boston: Houghton Mifflin, 1904–19.

Buvat, Jean. *Journal de la Régence (1715–1723).* 2 vols. Edited by Emile Campardon. Paris: Plon, 1865.

Callières, François de. *Letters (1694–1700) of François de Callières to the Marquise d'Huxelles.* Edited by Laurence Pope with William S. Brooks. Lewiston, NY: Edwin Mellen, 2004.

Calvin, Jean. *Advertissement contre l'astrologie judiciaire.* Edited by Olivier Millet. Geneva: Droz, 1985.

Caston, Alfred de. *Les marchands de miracles: histoire de la superstition humaine.* Paris: E. Dentu, 1864.

Céline, Louis-Ferdinand. *Bagatelles pour un massacre.* Paris: Denoël, [1937?].

Cendrars, Blaise. Interview with Michel Manoll. *Paris Review* 37, Spring 1966, www.theparis review.org/interviews/4388/the-art-of-fiction-no-38-blaise-cendrars.

Centurie de Nostradamus, déterrée par un savant antiquaire du Club d'Alençon, et présentée par un comité de dames citoyennes, à très-gros et très-puissant Fessier, Evêque de l'Orne. Le jour de son installation. N.p., 1791.

Chabauty, Abbé E. A. *Lettre sur les Prophéties modernes et concordance de toutes les prédictions jusqu'au règne de Henri V inclusivement.* 2nd ed. Poitiers: H. Oudin, 1872.

Chaillot, Pierre. *Les vraies Centuries et prophéties de Maistre Michel Nostradamus interprétées pour le passé, le présent et l'avenir et corrigées d'après les plus anciennes éditions.* Avignon: P. Chaillot jeune, 1839.

Charpentier, Léon. "Nostradamus et ses prophéties." *Revue hebdomadaire* 11 (1902): 75–81.

Chasles, Philarète. "Nostradamus et ses commentateurs." In his *Études sur le seizième siècle en France, précédées d'une histoire de la littérature,* 317–35. 1848. Paris: G. Charpentier, 1876.

Chavigny, Jean-Aimé de. *La Première face du Janus françois, contenant sommairement les troubles, guerres civiles et autres choses mémorables advenues en la France et ailleurs, dès l'an de salut M.D.XXXIII jusques à l'an M.D.LXXXIX, fin de la maison Valésienne, extraite et colligée des centuries et autres commentaires de M. Michel de Nostredame.* Lyon: héritiers de P. Roussin, 1594.

———. *Commentaires du Sr de Chavigny Beaunois sur les Centuries et Pronostications de feu M. Michel de Nostradamus.* Paris: A. du Breuil, 1596.

———. *Les Pléiades du S. de Chavigny, Beaunois: divisées en VII livres.* 1603. Lyon: P. Rigaud, 1606.

———. *Discours parénétique sur les choses turques . . . : où est proposé s'il est expédient et utile à la République chrestienne de prendre les armes par communes forces . . . contre ce . . . pernicieux ennemi du nom chrestien . . .* Lyon: P. Rigaud, 1606.

Colbert, Jean-Baptiste. *Lettres, instructions et mémoires de Colbert.* 7 vols. Edited by Pierre Clément. Paris: Imprimerie impériale, 1861–82.

Collin de Plancy, Jacques-Albin-Simon. *Dictionnaire infernal, ou Recherches et anecdotes sur les démons, etc.* Paris: Mongie, 1818.

Collot d'Herbois, Jean-Marie. *Le Nouveau Nostradamus, ou Les Fêtes Provençales, comédie en un acte et en prose.* Avignon: Bonnet frères, 1777.

The Complete Fortune Teller, Being the Magic Mirror of Nostradamus. London: Lawrence & Bullen, 1899.

Congreve, William. *The Way of the World and Other Plays.* Edited by Eric S. Rump. London: Penguin, 2006.

Cottin, Louis. *Un homme . . . une vie.* Aubagne: Imprimerie nouvelle d'Aubagne, 1977.

Couillart, Antoine. *Les contredicts du seigneur du Pavillon, les Lorriz, en Gastinois, aux faulses & abbusifves prophéties de Nostradamus, & aultres astrologues.* Paris: C. l'Angelier, 1560.

Coxe, Francis. *A Short Treatise Declaringe the Detestable Wickednesse, of Magicall Sciences: as Necromancie, Conjurations of Spirites, Curiouse Astrologie and Such Lyke.* London: I. Alde, 1561.

Crespin, Anthoine dit Nostradamus. *Prognostication avec ses Présages pour l'an MDLXXI, composée & calculée par tout les neuf climats de la terre. . . .* Paris: R. Colombel, [1570?].

———. *Pronostication, et prédiction des quatre temps pour l'an bisextil 1572.* Lyon: M. Arnoullet, 1572.

———. *Prophéties par l'astrologue du très chrestien Roy de France & de Madame la Duchesse de Savoye, dédiées à la puissance Divine & à la nation Françoise.* Lyon: F. Arnoullet, 1572.

———. *Epistre dédiée au très-hault et très chrestien, Charles IX, Roy de France.* Paris: Martin le Jeune, [1583?].

Crousillat, Antoine-Blaise. *La Bresco d'Antoni-Blasi Crousillat (1837–1864).* Avignon: J. Roumanille, 1865.

Des Brosses, Marie-Thérèse. "Plus loin avec Nostradamus." *Paris-Match*, August 21, 1981.

Description véritable d'un phantosme qui s'est apparu dans le cabinet de la reine. [Paris?], 1649.

Die neue Dreieinigkeit: ein Nachtrag zu der Monarchenzusammenkunft in Paris. Von Nostradamus. 2nd ed. Hamburg: Richter, 1867.

Diesbach de Belleroche, Ghislain de. *Une éducation manquée: souvenirs, 1931–1949.* Paris: Perrin, 2000.

Discours merveilleux et mémorable, d'une isle qui apparut nageante en la mer Méditerranée, au mois de décembre dernier. Ensemble la docte & subtille explication d'une Prophétie de Nostradamus sur le mesme subject. Paris: F. Bourriquant, 1606.

D'Odoucet, Melchior-Montmignon. *Révolution française, les évènements qui l'ont provoquée, accompagnée, & ceux qui la suivront, pronostiquées par les prophétiques Centuries de M. Michel Nostradamus. . . .* [Paris?], 1790.

Dryden, John. *The Hind and the Panther: A Poem, in Three Parts.* London: J. Tonson, 1687.

Du Bellay, Joachim. *Lettres.* Edited by Pierre de Nolhac, 1883. Reprint, Geneva: Slatkine, 1974.

Dumézil, Georges. *The Riddle of Nostradamus: A Critical Dialogue.* 1985. Translated by Betsy Wing. Baltimore: Johns Hopkins University Press, 1999.

Dupanloup, Félix. *On Contemporary Prophecies: A Letter Addressed by the Bishop of Orleans to the Clergy of His Diocese.* Translated by Edward Redmond. London: R. Washbourne, 1874.

Dutry-Soinne, Tinou. *Les méconnus de Londres: journal de guerre d'une Belge, 1940–1945.* 2 vols. Brussels: Racine, 2006.

Du Verdier, Antoine. *La bibliothèque d'Antoine Du Verdier.* Lyon: B. Honorat, 1585.

Edouard, P. *Texte original et complet des Prophéties de Michel Nostradamus.* Paris: Les Belles Editions, [1939?].

Edwards, John. *Cometomantia, A Discourse Of Comets: Shewing their Original, Substance, Place, Time, Magnitude, Motion, Number, Colour, Figure, Kinds, Names, and, More Especially, Their Prognosticks, Significations and Presages.* London: B. Aylmer, 1684.

Espitalier, Jean. *Les Oracles secrets de Nostradamus sur l'auguste règne de Louis le Grand.* Chartres: Veuve E. Massot, 1698.

Fabri, Claude. *Paradoxes de la cure de peste par une méthode succincte, contre l'opinion de ceux qui ont escrit et pratiqué au passé.* Paris: N. Chesneau, 1568.

Fenech, Georges. *Face aux sectes: politique, justice, Etat.* Paris: Presses Universitaires de France, 1999.

Flammarion, Camille. *Omega: The Last Days of the World.* Lincoln: University of Nebraska Press, 1999.

Fontbrune, Jean-Charles de. *Nostradamus, historien et prophète. Les prophéties de 1555 à l'an 2000.* Monaco: Rocher, 1980.

———. *Nostradamus: Countdown to Apocalypse.* Translated by Alexis Lykiard. New York: Holt, 1983.

———. *Henry Miller et Nostradamus: entretiens sur la fin d'un monde.* Monaco: Rocher, 1994.

Fontbrune, Max de. *Les Prophéties de Maistre Michel Nostradamus expliquées et commentées.* Sarlat: Michelet, 1939.

———. *L'étrange XXe siècle vu par Nostradamus.* Sarlat: Michelet, 1950.

———. *Ce que Nostradamus a vraiment dit.* Paris: Stock, 1976.

The Fortune of France, From the Prophetical Predictions of Mr. Truswell, the Recorder of Lincoln, and Michael Nostradamus. London: J. Edwin, 1678.

Fournel, Victor. *Ce qu'on voit dans les rues de Paris.* Paris: E. Dentu, 1867.

Fournier, Edouard, ed. *Variétés historiques et littéraires: recueil de pièces volantes rares et curieuses en prose et en vers.* 10 vols. Paris: P. Jannet, 1855–63.

Francou, Jean. *Salon et son devenir.* Salon: n.p., [1959?].

Frederick the Great. *Oeuvres de Frédéric le Grand.* 31 vols. Berlin: Decker, 1846–57.

Freinet, Elise, and Célestin Freinet. *Elise et Célestin Freinet: correspondance, 21 mars 1940–28 octobre 1941.* Edited by Madeleine Freinet. Paris: Presses Universitaires de France, 2004.

Fulke, William. *Antiprognosticon That Is To Saye, an Invective Agaynst the Vayne and Unprofitable Predictions of the Astrologians as Nostrodame. . . .* London: H. Sutton, 1560.

Gacon, François. *Le poète sans fard, contenant satires, épitres et épigrames, sur toutes sortes de sujets.* Libreville: Paul, 1698.

Gadbury, John. *Cardines Coeli, or, An Appeal to the Learned and Experienced Observers of Sublunars and Their Vicissitudes Whether the Cardinal Signs of Heaven Are Most Influential Upon Men and Things. . . .* London: M. G., 1685.

Garcin, E. *Dictionnaire historique et topographique de la Provence ancienne et moderne.* 2 vols. 2nd edition. Draguignan: published by the author, 1835.

Garencières, Theophilus de. *The True Prophecies or Prognostications of Michael Nostradamus, Physician to Henry II, Francis II and Charles IX.* . . . London: Ratcliffe and Thompson, 1672.

Gaufridi, Jean-François de. *Histoire de Provence.* 2 vols. Aix: C. David, 1646.

Gayot de Pitaval, François. *Bibliothèque de cour, de ville et de campagne.* . . . 7 vols. Paris: T. Le Gras, 1746.

Gildon, Charles. *The Post-Boy Rob'd of His Mail, or, The Pacquet Broke Open: Consisting of Five Hundred Letters to Persons of Several Qualities and Conditions.* London: J. Dunton, 1692.

Gimon, Louis. *Chroniques de la ville de Salon depuis son origine jusqu'en 1792, adaptées à l'histoire.* Aix: Veuve Remondet-Aubin, 1882.

———. "Michel Nostradamus." *La Provence poétique, historique et littéraire* 6 (1883): 1–4.

Girault, Francis. *Le passé, le présent et l'avenir, ou prédictions, vérifications et explications de quelques prophéties remarquables de Michel Nostradamus.* Paris: Hivert, 1839.

Godwin, William. *Lives of the Necromancers; or, An Account of the Most Eminent Persons in Successive Ages, Who Have Claimed for Themselves, or to Whom Has Been Imputed By Others, the Exercise of Magical Power.* London: F. J. Mason, 1834.

Goebbels, Joseph. *The Goebbels Diaries: 1939–1941.* Translated and edited by Fred Taylor. New York: Putnam, 1983.

———. *The Goebbels Diaries, 1942–1943.* Translated and edited by Louis P. Lochner. Westport, CT: Greenwood, 1970.

Gouberville, Sire de. *Un Sire de Gouberville, gentilhomme campagnard au Cotentin de 1553 à 1562.* Edited by Abbé A. Tollemer, 1879. Paris: Mouton, 1972.

Goyet, Francis, ed. *Traités de poétique et de rhétorique de la Renaissance.* Paris: Librairie générale française, 1990.

Les grandes prédictions du grand Nostradamus, trouvées dans la grande culotte de peau de messire Honoré Barnave. N.p., [1793?].

Gratien de Semur. *Traité des erreurs et des préjugés.* Paris: A. Levavasseur, 1843.

Green, Julien. *La fin d'un monde: juin 1940.* Paris: Seuil, 1992.

Guichardan, Roger. *La chasse aux prophéties.* Limoges: La Bonne Presse, 1941.

Guilhaume, Pierre. *Nostradamus: l'exploitation seculaire d'un fonds de commerce.* Monte Carlo: RMC, 1987.

Guynaud, Balthazar. *La concordance des Prophéties de Nostradamus avec l'histoire depuis Henri II, jusqu'à Louis le Grand, la vie & l'apologie de cet auteur.* 1693. New edition, Paris: Veuve Jacques Morel, 1712.

Haitze, Pierre-Joseph. *La vie de Michel Nostradamus.* Aix: Veuve C. David, 1712.

Halévy, Léon. *La mort de Nostradamus: drame historique en un acte et en vers (d'après des documents inédits).* Paris: M. Lévy frères, 1875.

Hall, Manly. "Nostradamus." *Horizon* 2 (1942): 12–19.

Hammer, Charles. "The 'Prophetic Centuries': The Incredible Verses of Nostradamus, the Man Who Could Foretell the Future." *Coronet* 3 (1937): 185–90.

Haton, Claude: *Mémoires de Claude Haton, 1553–82.* 4 vols. Edited by Laurent Bourquin. Paris: Comité des travaux historiques et scientifiques, 2001–07.

Henry, Jeanne. "What Madness Prompts, Reason Writes: New York City September 11–October 2, 2001." *Anthropology & Education Quarterly* 33, no. 3 (2002): 283–96.

Hobbes, Thomas. *Leviathan.* 1651. Edited by Richard Tuck. Cambridge: Cambridge University Press, 1996.

Hodgson, Marion Stegeman. *Winning My Wings: A Woman Airforce Service Pilot in World War II.* Annapolis, MD: Naval Institute Press, 2005.

Hohlenberg, Johannes E. *Michel de Nostredame, Kaldet Nostradamus.* Copenhagen: Nyt Nord. Forl., 1918.

Holmes, George Frederick. "Nostradamus." *Southern Magazine* 16 (1875): 24–38.

Holmes, Oliver Wendell. "The Medical Profession in Massachusetts." In vol. 9 of *The Works of Oliver Wendell Holmes,* 312–69. Boston: Houghton Mifflin, 1892.

L'horoscope de Jules Mazarin, naifvement & fidellement expliquée des Centuries de M. Nostradamus. Tant du passé, present qu'advenir. Paris, 1649.

Hugo, Victor. *Propos de table de Victor Hugo.* Edited by Richard Lesclide. Paris: E. Dentu, 1885.

Jant, Jacques de. *Explication des Prédictions tirées des Centuries de Nostradamus, sur la présente guerre de France avec la Hollande.* Lyon: M. Gautherin, 1672.

Jaulnay, Charles. *L'enfer burlesque.* 1668. New edition, Cologne: J. Le Blanc, 1677.

Kaplan, Chaim A. *Scroll of Agony: The Warsaw Diary of Chaim A. Kaplan.* Translated and edited by Abraham I. Katsh. Bloomington: Indiana University Press, 1999.

Kellar, Harry. *A Magician's Tour Up and Down and Round About the Earth, Being the Life and Adventures of the American Nostradamus.* Chicago: R. R. Donnelley, 1886.

Kert, Christian. *Nostradamus: le mage de Salon.* Salon-de-Provence: Les Centuries, 1984.

Krafft, Karl. *Comment Nostradamus a-t-il entrevu l'avenir de l'Europe?* Brussels: Snellew, 1941.

La Croix du Maine, François Grudé, sieur de. *Premier volume de la bibliothèque du sieur de la Croix du Maine.* Paris: A. l'Angelier, 1584.

La Daguenière, Jean de. *Le monstre d'abus.* Paris: B. Regnault, 1558.

Lamont, André. *Nostradamus Sees All: Detailed Predictions Regarding America, Hitler, Mussolini, Franco, Pétain, Stalin, Churchill, the Jews, etc.* 2nd edition. Philadelphia: W. Foulsham, 1942.

La Mothe Le Vayer, François de. "De l'instruction de M. le Dauphin." Vol. 1 of *Oeuvres de François de La Mothe Le Vayer.* 14 vols. Dresden: M. Groell, 1756.

L'Ancre, Pierre de. *L'incrédulité et mescréance du sortilège plainement convaincue.* Paris: N. Buon, 1622.

La Perrière, Guillaume de. *Les considérations des quatre mondes, à savoir est: divin, angélique, céleste, & sensible: Comprinses en quatre Centuries de quatrains, contenans la cresme de divine & humaine philosophie.* Lyon: M. Bonhomme, 1552.

La Porte, Maurice de. *Les épithètes de M. de la Porte parisien.* Paris: G. Buon, 1571.

Lecanu, Abbé. *Histoire de Satan.* Paris: Parent-Desbornes, 1861.

Leibniz, Gottfried Wilhem. *Esprit de Leibniz, ou recueil de pensées choisies.* Edited by Abbé Emery. Lyon: Bruyset, 1772.

Le Noble, Eustache. "Nostradamus, ou les oracles." Vol. 9 of *Les oeuvres de M. Le Noble.* 19 vols. The Hague: P. L'Attentif, 1692.

Le Normand, M. A. *Les souvenirs prophétiques d'une sibylle, sur les causes secrètes de son arrestation.* Paris: published by the author, 1814.

Le Pelletier, Anatole. *Les oracles de Michel de Nostredame dit Nostradamus.* 2 vols. Paris: J. de Bonnot, 1867.

Le Roux, Jean. *La clef de Nostradamus, isagoge ou introduction au véritable sens des Prophéties de ce fameux Auteur.* Paris: P. Giffart, 1710.

Le Sage, Alain-René, and Jacques Philippe d'Orneval. *Le Tombeau de Nostradamus.* Vol. 1 of *Le théâtre de la foire, ou l'opéra comique; contenant les meilleures pièces qui ont été représentées aux foires de S. Germain et de S. Laurent.* 10 vols. 1737. Reprint, Geneva: Slatkine, 1968.

L'Estoile, Pierre de. *Registres-journaux de Pierre de l'Estoile sur le règne de Louis XIII depuis le 15 mai 1610 jusqu'au 15 mai 1611.* Edited by Claude-Bernard Petitot. Paris: Foucault, 1826.

———. *Registre-journal de Henri IV et de Louis XIII.* Edited by Aimé-Louis Champollion-Figeac and Aimé Champollion fils. In *Nouvelle collection des mémoires pour servir à l'histoire de*

France depuis le XIIIe siècle jusqu'à la fin du XVIIIe. Edited by Joseph-François Michaud and Jean-Joseph Poujoulat. Paris: Chez l'éditeur du Commentaire analytique du Code civil, 1837.

"Lettre critique sur la personne & sur les écrits de Michel Nostradamus." *Mercure de France,* August 1724, 1730–49, 2363–86.

Lettre d'un seigneur anglois à un seigneur irlandois touchant quelques évènements prédits par Nostradamus. N.p., [1760?].

Liebling A. J. *World War II Writings.* Edited by Pete Hamill. New York: Library of America, 2008.

Loog, Carl. *Die Weissagungen des Nostradamus.* Pfullingen: J. Baum, 1921.

Mackay, Charles. *Memoirs of Extraordinary Popular Delusions and the Madness of Crowds.* Philadelphia: Lindsay and Blakiston, 1850.

Maistre, Joseph de. *Saint-Petersburg Dialogues.* Edited and translated by Richard A. Lebrun. Montreal: McGill–Queen's University Press, 1993.

Malherbe, François de. *Lettres à Peiresc.* Vol. 3. of *Oeuvres de Malherbe.* 5 vols. Edited by M. L. Lalanne. Paris: Hachette, 1862.

Marais, Mathieu. *Journal de Paris.* 2 vols. Edited by Henri Duranton and Robert Granderoute. Saint-Etienne: Publications de l'Université de Saint-Etienne, 2004.

Marconville, Guillaume de. *Recueil mémorable d'aucuns cas merveilleux advenuz de noz ans, et d'aucunes choses estranges & monstrueuses advenues en siecles passez.* Paris: J. Dallier, 1564.

Marguerite de Valois. *Mémoires de Marguerite de Valois.* Edited by Ludovic Lalanne. Paris: P. Jannet, 1858.

Martonne, Alfred de. "Etudes historiques: Nostradamus." *Musée des familles* 14 (1847): 281–85.

Massard, Jacques. *Relation exacte, & curieuse des Malheurs extrêmes, & prochains, tant de Louis XIV, que de toute la France prédits par Nostradamus.* Amsterdam: printed for the author, 1693.

Mathieu, Pierre. *The Heroyk Life and Deplorable Death of the Most Christian King Henry the Fourth.* Translated by Edward Grimeston. London: G. Eld, 1612.

Mauger, Dom Etienne. *Nostradamus, ou le physicien plaideur, comédie en un acte & en vers.* Leyden, 1779.

McCann, Lee. *Nostradamus: The Man Who Saw Through Time.* New York: Creative Age Press, 1941 Reprint, New York: Farrar, Straus and Giroux, 1982.

Menestrier, Claude-François. *La philosophie des images énigmatiques.* Lyon: J. Lions, 1694.

Ménétra, Jacques-Louis. *Journal of My Life.* Edited by Daniel Roche. Translated by Arthur Goldhammer. New York: Columbia University Press, 1986.

Mengau, Jacques. *Avertissement à Messieurs les prevosts des marchands et eschevin de Paris: Sur la fuite, & le retour funeste du Cardinal Mazarin. Predict par Michel Nostradamus.* Paris: J. Boucher, 1651.

———. *Advertissement aux bons François sur ce qui doit arriver devant la ville d'Estempes, prédit par Michel Nostradamus. Huictiesme partie.* Paris: F. Huart, 1652.

Mericourt, M. J. de. *Gesta Dei Per Francos. Le Miracle au pays de France d'après un prophète méconnu.* Paris: Les Oeuvres Françaises, 1937.

Merlin Ambrosius. *The Lord Merlin's Prophecy Concerning the King of Scots: Foretelling the Strange and Wonderfull Things That Shall Befall Him in England. . . .* London: G. Horton, 1651.

Miller, Henry. *The Henry Miller Reader.* Edited by Lawrence Durrell. New York: New Directions, 1969.

———. *From Your Capricorn Friend: Henry Miller and the "Stroker," 1978–1980.* Edited by Irving Stettner. New York: New Directions, 1984.

———. *Conversations with Henry Miller.* Edited by Frank L. Kersnowski and Alice Hughes. Jackson, MS: University Press of Mississippi, 1994.

Miller, Samuel. *Memoir of the Rev. Charles Nisbet, D.D., Late President of Dickinson College, Carlisle.* New York: R. Carter, 1840.

Millin, Aubin-Louis. *Voyage dans les départemens du midi de la France.* 4 vols. Paris: Imprimerie impériale, 1807–11.

Monluc, Blaise de. *Commentaires et lettres de Blaise de Monluc, maréchal de France.* 5 vols. Edited by Alphonse de Ruble. Paris: Veuve J. Renouard, 1864–72.

Montaiglon, Anatole de, ed. *Recueil de poésies françoises des XVᵉ et XVIᵉ siècles.* 13 vols. Paris: P. Daffis, 1855–78.

[Moore, Greville G.] *Society Recollections in Paris and Vienna 1879–1904 by an English Officer.* London: J. Long, 1907.

Moré, Comte de. *Mémoires du comte de Moré (1728–1837).* 1827. Edited by Geoffroy de Grandmaison and the Count of Pontgibaud. New edition, Paris: A. Picard, 1898.

Morrison, Alfred. *The Collection of Autograph Letters and Historical Documents of Alfred Morrison.* Edited by Alphonse Wyatt Thibaudeau. 3 vols. London: printed for private circulation, 1883–97.

Moura, Jean, and Paul Louvet. *La vie de Nostradamus.* Paris: Gallimard, 1930.

Mus, Paul. *Le destin de l'Union française de l'Indochine à l'Afrique.* Paris: Seuil, 1954.

Nau, François. *Le Nostradamus moderne, ou les oracles chantants.* Paris: Duchesne, [1757?].

Naudé, Gabriel. *History of Magick By Way of Apology, For all the Wise Men Who Have Unjustly Been Reputed Magicians, from the Creation, to the Present Age.* Translated by John Davies. London: J. Streater, 1657.

Némirovsky, Irène. *Suite française.* Paris: Denoël, 2004.

Normand, N. *L'abbe Rigaux, curé d'Argoeuves, interprète de Nostradamus.* Amiens: Yvert, 1930.

Norse, Harold. *Memoirs of a Bastard Angel: A Fifty-Year Literary and Erotic Odyssey.* New York: Morrow, 1989.

Nostradamus, César de. *L'histoire et la chronique de Provence de Caesar de Nostradamus, gentilhomme provencal.* Lyon: S. Rigaud, 1614.

Nostradamus, Filippo. *La Salutifera. Fatica dell'eccell. Astrolago M. Filippo Nostradamus.* Bologna: A. Benacci, 1573.

Nostradamus, Gabriel. *Consult the Oracle; or, How to Read the Future. A Guide to the Interpretation of Dreams and to Other Matters Magical and Mysterious. . . .* London: C. A. Pearson, 1899.

Nostradamus, Michel de. *A Collection of Twenty-Three Prophecies and Predictions of the Famous Michael Nostrodamus, the Learned Astrologer of France.* London: R. Taylor, 1690.

———. *Nouvelles Prophéties de Nostradamus ressucité, aux Parisiens.* N.p., [1792?].

Nostradamus, Mi[chel] de. *Prognostication ou Révolution, avec les Presages, Pour l'an Mil cinq cens Soixante-cinq.* Lyon: B. Rigaud, [1564?].

———. *Prophétie, ou révolution, merveilleuse, des quatre saisons de l'an . . . qui pourront advenir depuis l'an présent jusques en l'an de grande mortalité 1568, An de Bissexte.* Lyon: M. Jove, 1567.

———. *Les Vrayes Centuries et Prophéties de Maistre Michel Nostradamus.* Amsterdam: D. Winkeermans, 1667.

Nostradamus le Jeune, Michel de. *Prédictions des choses plus mémorables qui sont à advenir, depuis cette présente Année, jusques à l'An mil cinq cens quatre vingt & cinq. . . .* Troyes: C. Garnier, 1571.

———. *Présages pour treize ans, continuant d'an en an jusques à celuy de mil cinq cens vingts trois . . . recueillies de divers autheurs, & trouvées en la bibliothèque de defunct maistre Michel de Nostre Dame.* Paris: N. du Mont, 1573.

Omarr, Sidney. *Henry Miller: His World of Urania.* London: Villiers, 1960.

Parisot, F. *Au 17 février 1874 Le Grand Avènement!! précédé d'un Grand Prodige!!!* Bar-le-Duc: Imprimerie des Célestins, 1873.

Partridge, John. *Remarkable Predictions of the Great Prophet Michael Nostradamus Concerning the Ruin and Downfall of the French, the Pope of Rome, by his Highness the Prince of Orange.* N.p., 1689.

Pasquier, Estienne. *Lettres historiques pour les années 1556-1594.* Edited by D. Thickett. Geneva: Droz, 1966.

Patin, Gui. *Lettres de Gui Patin.* Edited by Paul Triaire. Paris: Champion, 1907.

Paulus, Stefan. *Nostradamus 1999: Who Will Survive?* St. Paul, MN: Llewellyn, 1999.

Pepys, Samuel. *Diary of Samuel Pepys.* 1825. Edited by G. Gregory Smith. London: Macmillan, 1905.

Perrot, J.-F.-A. *Lettres sur Nismes et le Midi.* Nîmes: published by the author, 1840.

Perwich, William. *The Despatches of William Perwich, English Agent in Paris, 1669-1677.* Edited by Minnie Beryl Curran. London: Royal Historical Society, 1903.

Petit discours ou commentaire sur les Centuries de Maistre Michel Nostradamus. N.p., 1620.

Le petit Nostradamus, ou prédiction pour l'an de grâce 1789 et suivans. N.p., 1789.

Philalelos, J. B. *Good and Joyful News for England: or, The Prophecy of the Renowned Michael Nostradamus That Charles the II. of Great Britain, France and Ireland King, Defender of the Faith, &c. Shall Have a Son of his Own Body Lawfully Begotten. . . .* London: A. Banks, 1681.

Pineaux, Jacques, ed. *La polémique protestante contre Ronsard.* Paris: M. Didier, 1973.

Pissot, Louis. *Les véritables prophéties de Michel Nostradamus, en concordance avec les événemens de la révolution, pendant les années 1789, 1790 et suivantes, jusques et compris le retour de S. M. Louis XVIII.* 2 vols. Paris: Lesné jeune, 1816.

Pluquet, Abbé François. *Dictionnaire des hérésies, des erreurs et des schismes.* 1762. 2 vols. New edition, Paris: J. Migne, 1863.

[Poyntz, Albany]. *A World of Wonders, With Anecdotes and Opinions Concerning Popular Superstitions.* London: R. Bentley, 1853.

The Predictions of Nostradamus, Before the Year 1558. Foretelling the Trial and Death of Charles I. The Parliamentary and Protectorian Government. The Burning of London in Sixty Six . . . Considered in a Letter to a Friend. London: J. Crossand, 1691.

La Première Invective du Seigneur Hercules le François, contre Monstradamus. Paris: S. Calvarin, 1558.

Présages émerveillables pour XX ans. Aportez de l'autre monde en celuy-ciy par le Sieur Godard, gentil homme poictevin, grand Astronome, Disciple de Nostradamus, surnommé passe par tout, le dernier septembre 1611. N.p., [1611?].

Prion, Pierre. *Pierre Prion, scribe: mémoires d'un écrivain de campagne au XVIIIᵉ siècle.* Edited by Emmanuel Le Roy Ladurie and Orest A. Ranum. Paris: Gallimard-Julliard, 1985.

Privat, Maurice. *1940, année de grandeur française.* Paris: Médicis, 1939.

Pronostication perpetuelle Recueillie de plusieurs Autheurs, par Maistre Michel Nostradamus. Avec les signes preservatifz contre la Peste, & le gouvernement des quatre saisons de l'An, pour soy garder des maladies qui adviennent, selon les astres, & Cours des lunes. Paris: J. Bonfons, [1543?].

Le prophète politique, ou entretiens sur les affaires du tems. Paris: Champigny, [1790?].

"Prophetic Fits—and Misfits." *All the Year Round* 15 (1866): 160-64.

Prophetical Extracts. No. V. Relative to the Revolution in France, and the Decline of the Papal Power in the World. London: G. Terry, 1794.

Prophétie de Nostradamus accomplie. L'ordre, la marche, et l'entrée des princes et autres émigrants à Paris. 2nd edition. N.p., 1792.

Prophéties de Michel Nostradamus: prix quatre sous. Salon-de-Provence: Danielle, [1806?].

"Prophéties de Nostradamus sur les années présentes 1848–1852." *Almanach pittoresque, comique & prophétique pour 1851* (1850), 35–43.

Les Prophéties de Nostradamus. Paris, Editions universelles, 1941.

Prophéties et documents prophétiques: le danger de croire facilement aux prophéties, aux extases, aux stigmates et aux révélations. Brussels: H. Goemaere, 1872.

Prophéties politiques de Michel Nostradamus sur les républicains rouges et les socialistes. Paris: Lévy, [1848?].

Prophéties sur les affaires du temps présent et advenir. Tirée de la Centurie II. Prop. 34. 35. de M. Nostradamus. Et ce que dit Kepler pour la présente année 1649. Paris, 1649.

Quevedo, Francisco de. *The Visions of Dom Francisco de Quevedo Villegas, Knight of the Order of St. James.* Translated by Sir Roger L'Estrange. London: H. Herringman, 1667.

Rachleff, Owen. *The Occult Conceit: A New Look at Astrology, Witchcraft & Sorcery.* Chicago: Cowles, 1971.

Ragusa, Kym. *The Skin Between Us: A Memoir of Race, Beauty, and Belonging.* New York: Norton, 2006.

Raikes, Thomas. *A Portion of the Journal Kept by Thomas Raikes, Esq., From 1813 to 1847.* 4 vols. London: Longman, 1856–58.

Relation divertissante d'un voyage fait en Provence, envoyé à Madame la duchesse de Chaunes Villeroy. Paris: C. de Sercy, 1667.

Remonstrances, To the Duke de Mayne: Lieutenaunt Generall of the Estate and Crowne of France. Translated by Anthony Chute. London: J. Wolfe, 1593.

Reynaud-Plense, Charles. *Les vraies centuries et prophéties de Michel Nostradamus.* Salon: Imprimerie régionale, 1939.

Roberts, Henry C. *The Complete Prophecies of Nostradamus.* New York: Crown, 1947.

Rochemaillet, Gabriel Michel de la. *Portraicts de plusieurs hommes illustres, qui ont flory en France depuis l'an 1500 jusques à present.* Paris: J. Le Clerc, [1600?].

Rolland, Romain. *Journey Within.* 1942. Translated by Elsie Estelle Pell. New York: Philosophical Library, 1947.

Ronsard, Pierre de. *Elégie de P. de Ronsard Vandomois sur les troubles d'Amboise, 1560.* Paris: G. Buon, 1563.

Rouvier, Camille. *Nostradamus et les de Nostredame.* Marseille: La Savoisienne, 1964.

La ruine et submergement de la ville d'Amsterdam en Hollande . . . Ensemble la prophétie de Nostradamus, & l'explication d'icelle sur ce sujet. N.p., 1649.

Ruir, Emile. *Le grand carnage d'après les prophéties de "Nostradamus" de 1938 à 1947.* Paris: Médicis, 1938.

Saconay, Gabriel de. *Généalogie et la fin des Huguenaux, & descouverte du Calvinisme.* Lyon: B. Rigaud, 1573.

Saint-Simon, Louis de Rouvroy, duc de. *Mémoires de Saint-Simon.* 43 vols. Edited by A. de Boislisle. Paris: Hachette, 1879–1928.

Salgues, Jacques-Barthélémy. *Des erreurs et des préjugés répandus dans les diverses classes.* 3 vols. Paris: F. Buisson, 1811.

Schellenberg, Walter. *The Labyrinth: Memoirs of Walter Schellenberg, Hitler's Chief of Counter-intelligence.* Translated by Louis Hagen. Boulder, CO: Da Capo, 2000.

Seabrook, William. *Witchcraft: Its Power in the World Today.* New York: Harcourt, 1940.

Seurat, Silvère. *1918–1948: Souvenirs de paix et de guerre.* Paris: Publibook, 2008.

Sévigné, Madame de. *Correspondance.* 1725. 3 vols. Edited by Roger Duchêne. Paris: Gallimard, 1972–78.

Sourches, Marquis de. *Mémoires sur le règne de Louis XIV.* 9 vols. Paris: Hachette, 1885.

Stockton, Frank. *Round-About Rambles in Lands of Fact and Fancy.* 1872. Reprint, New York: Scribner, Amstrong & Co., 1910.

Suffert, Georges. "Nostradamus: le marché de la peur." *Le Point,* August 24, 1981.

Suttner, Bertha von. *Lay Down Your Arms: The Autobiography of Martha von Tilling.* Translated by T. Holmes. London: Longmans, 1914.

Taconet, Toussaint-Gaspar. "Nostradamus, Parodie de Zoroastre." In *Suite de nouveau choix de pièces, ou Théâtre comique de province.* Edited by Léonard Cuissart. Paris: Cuissart, 1758.

Tcherpakov, Avgoust Ivanovitch. *Les fous littéraires: rectifications et additions à l'Essai bibliographique sur la littérature excentrique, les illuminés, visionnaires, etc., de Philomneste junior.* Moscow: W. G. Gautier, 1883.

Temple, William. *The Works of Sir William Temple.* 4 vols. London: Rivington, 1814.

Tenison, Thomas. *The Creed of Mr. Hobbes Examined in a Feigned Conference Between Him and a Student in Divinity.* London: F. Tyton, 1671.

Théodar, Just. *Nostradamus démasqué: prédiction de l'avènement de Gambetta.* Mirande: Farré le Garé, 1872.

Thurston, Herbert. *The War & the Prophets: Notes on Certain Popular Predictions Current in This Latter Age.* London: Burns & Oates, 1915.

Torné-Chavigny, Abbé Henri. *Nostradamus écrit L'Histoire prédite et jugée, comprenant toute l'histoire de France et les grands faits de l'histoire de l'Eglise et des peuples étrangers.* Bordeaux: Poirier, 1862.

——. *Les Blancs & les Rouges, nouvelle lettre du Grand Prophète d'après l'Histoire prédite et jugée par Nostradamus.* Saint-Denis-du-Pin: published by the author, 1872.

——. *Concordance des Prophéties de Nostradamus avec l'Apocalypse, ou l'Apocalypse interprétée par Nostradamus.* Bordeaux: J. Dupuy, 1872.

——. *Nostradamus éclairci, ou Nostradamus devant Mgr. Dupanloup, M. L. Veuillot et nos interprètes de prophéties modernes: nouvelles lettres du grand prophète.* Saint-Denis-du-Pin: N. Texier, 1874.

——. *Ce qui sera! d'après le 'Grand Prophète' Nostradamus commenté par l'abbé H. Torné-Chavigny.* Paris: Imprimerie des apprentis catholiques, 1877.

——. *Lo Que Sera. Profecia del Gran Profeta Nostradamus.* Translated by Victor Rosello. Barcelona: Libreria Religiosa y Cientifica, 1877.

Tourangeau, Estienne Bellonne. *Le second livre des chansons folastres et prologues.* Rouen: J. Petit, 1612.

Les triolets du temps, selon les visions d'un petit fils du grand Nostradamus. Paris: D. Langlois, 1649.

Tronc de Coudoulet, Palamède. *Abrégé de la vie et de l'histoire de Michel Nostradamus: imprimé et manuscrit du XVIIIᵉ siècle.* Edited by Robert Benazra. 1712. Feyzin: Ramkat, 2001.

Tzara, Tristan. *Oeuvres complètes.* 6 vols. Edited by Henri Béhar. Paris: Flammarion, 1975–91.

Vallelly, Paul. "It's the End of the World as We Know It." *The Independent,* July 1, 1999.

Vallotton, Gritou, and Annie Vallotton. *C'était au jour le jour: carnets (1939–1944).* Paris: Payot, 1995.

Veuillot, Louis. *Correspondance de Louis Veuillot.* 6 vols. Paris: Société générale de librairie catholique, 1883–85.

Videl, Laurent. *Déclaration des abus, ignorances et séditions de Michel Nostradamus, de Salon de Craux en Provence.* Avignon: P. Roux and J. Tramblay, 1558.

La vie et le testament de Michel Nostradamus, Docteur en médecine, Astrophile, Conseiller-médecin ordinaire du roi. Paris: Gattey, 1789.

Vignois, Elisée du. "Notre histoire et Nostradamus." *L'Echo du merveilleux* 13 (1899): 435–37.

Villars, Claude Louis Hector de. *Mémoires du Maréchal de Villars.* Vol. 69 of *Collection des mémoires relatifs à l'histoire de France.* Paris: Foucault, 1828.

Visions astrologiques de Michel Nostradamus sur toutes les affaires de ce temps, et la confusion de Mazarin: en vers burlesques. Paris: Veuve A. Musnier, 1649.

Vrebos, Pascal. *Henry Miller: ultimes entretiens.* Brussels: Le Cri, 1991.

Walpole, Horace. *Private Correspondence of Horace Walpole, Earl of Orford.* 4 vols. London: Rodwell and Martin, 1820.

Ward, Charles A. "Nostradamus." *The Gentleman's Magazine* 269 (1890): 601–14.

——. *Oracles of Nostradamus.* London: Leadenhall, [1891]. Reprint, New York: Modern Library, 1940.

Weiss, Harry B. *Oneirocritica Americana*: *The Story of American Dream Books.* New York: New York Public Library, 1944.

Weyman, Stanley. *The Man in Black.* London: Longmans, 1901.

The Wizard; or, the Whole Art of Divining Dreams, and of Foretelling Events from Various Prognostics; by the Help of Which Persons May Interpret for Themselves on the Principles of the Great Nostradamus. Derby, 1816.

Wolper, David L. "The Man Who Saw Tomorrow." VHS. Directed by Robert Guenette. Burbank, CA: Warner Bros., 1981.

Zévaco, Michel. *Nostradamus.* Edited by Aline Demars. Paris: Robert Laffont, 2000.

Secondary Literature

Abramsky, Sasha. "The New Fear: It's Not Just About 9/11." *Chronicle Review* 55, no. 9 (2008): B6–B10.

Adorno, Theodor W. *The Stars Down to Earth and Other Essays on the Irrational in Culture.* Edited by Stephen Crook. New York: Routledge, 1994.

Airiau, Paul. "Le Grand Monarque dans le catholicisme français (XIXe–XXe siècles)." *Politica hermetica* 14 (2000): 66–95.

——. *L'Eglise et l'Apocalypse: du XIXe siècle à nos jours.* Paris: Berg International, 2000.

Albanese, Catharine. *A Republic of Mind & Spirit: A Cultural History of American Metaphysical Religion.* New Haven: Yale University Press, 2007.

Allemand, Jacqueline. "La présence lyonnaise de Nostradamus." *Espace Nostradamus* (2004). http://nostredame.chez-alice.fr/njall.html.

Ariès, Philippe. *The Hour of Our Death.* 1981. Translated by Helen Weaver. New York: Barnes & Noble, 2000.

Armstrong, Karen. *The Bible: A Biography.* New York: Atlantic Monthly Press, 2007.

Artiaga, Loïc, ed. *Le roman populaire: des premiers feuilletons aux adaptations télévisuelles, 1836–1960.* Paris: Autrement, 2008.

Augé, Marc. *Non-Places: An Introduction to Supermodernity.* 1995. Translated by John Howe. London: Verso, 2008.

Baecher, Claude. "Phénomène prophétique et schémas eschatologiques." *Cahiers V.-L. Saulnier* 15 (1998): 29–63.

Baradié, Mouna. "Pibrac et le genre du quatrain moralisateur au XVIe siècle." PhD diss., Université Stendhal–Grenoble III, 1999.

Barbier, Jean-Paul. "Jean de Chevigny et Jean-Aimé de Chavigny." *Bibliothèque d'Humanisme et Renaissance* 63 (2001): 297–304.

Barkun, Michael. *A Culture of Conspiracy: Apocalyptic Visions in Contemporary America.* Berkeley: University of California Press, 2003.

Bastaire, Jean. "Pour Saluer Zévaco." *La Nouvelle Revue Française* 426–27 (1988): 150–59.

Beck, Ulrich. *Risk Society: Towards a New Modernity.* London: Sage, 1992.

Béhar, Pierre. *Les langues occultes de la Renaissance: essai sur la crise intellectuelle de l'Europe au XVIᵉ siècle.* Paris: Desjonquères, 1996.

Bellenger, Yvonne. "Nostradamus prophète ou poète?" In *Devins et charlatans au temps de la Renaissance,* edited by M. T. Jones-Davies, 83–100.

——. "Sur la poétique de Nostradamus." In *Poétique et narration: mélanges offerts à Guy De-merson,* edited by François Marotin and Jacques-Philippe Saint-Gérand, 177–90. Paris: Champion, 1993.

——. "Nostradamus au fil du temps." In *La postérité de la Renaissance,* edited by Fiona McIntosh-Varjabédian and Véronique Gély, 115–27. Lille: Editions du conseil scientifique de l'Université Charles-de-Gaulle-Lille 3, 2007.

Bessard-Banquy, Olivier. *La vie du livre contemporain: étude sur l'édition littéraire, 1975–2005.* Pessac: Presses Universitaires de Bordeaux, 2009.

Biet, Christian, ed. *Théâtre de la cruauté et récits sanglants en France (XVIᵉ–XVIIᵉ siècle).* Paris: Laffont-Bouquins, 2006.

Biow, Douglas. *Doctors, Ambassadors, Secretaries: Humanism and Professions in Renaissance Italy.* Chicago: University of Chicago Press, 2002.

Blair, Ann. "Reading Strategies for Coping with Information Overload, ca. 1550–1700." *Journal of the History of Ideas* 64, no. 1 (2003): 11–28.

Blavier, André. *Les fous littéraires.* Alençon: Henri Veyrier, 1982.

Bloch, Marc. *Les rois thaumaturges: étude sur le caractère surnaturel attribué à la puissance royale particulièrement en France et en Angleterre.* 1924. Reprint, Paris: Gallimard, 1983.

Boas, George, ed. and trans. *The Hieroglyphics of Horapollo.* Princeton: Princeton University Press, 1993.

Bobrick, Benson. *The Fated Sky: Astrology in History.* New York: Simon & Schuster, 2005.

Bodnar, John. "*Saving Private Ryan* and Postwar Memory in America." *American Historical Review* 106, no. 3 (2001): 805–17.

Boia, Lucian. *La fin du monde: une histoire sans fin.* Paris: La Découverte, 1989.

Bollème, Geneviève. *Les almanachs populaires aux XVIIe et XVIIIe siècle. Essai d'histoire sociale.* Paris: Mouton, 1969.

Bondeson, Jan. *Buried Alive: The Terrifying History of Our Most Primal Fear.* New York: Norton, 2001.

Bonnet, Hubert. *La faculté de médecine de Montpellier: huit siècles d'histoire et d'éclat.* Montpellier: Sauramps médical, 1992.

Bourke, Joanna. *Fear: A Cultural History.* Emeryville, CA: Shoemaker & Hoard, 2006.

Boutier, Jean, Alain Dewerpe, and Daniel Nordman. *Un tour de France royal: le voyage de Charles IX (1564–1566).* Paris: Aubier, 1984.

Bown, Nicola, Carolyn Burdett, and Pamela Thurschwell. *The Victorian Supernatural.* Cambridge: Cambridge University Press, 2004.

Boy, Daniel, and Guy Michelat. "Croyances aux parasciences: dimensions sociales et culturelles." *Revue française de sociologie* 27 (1986): 175–204.

Boyer, Marc. *Histoire de l'invention du tourisme XVIᵉ–XIXᵉ siècles: origines et développement du tourisme dans le Sud-Est de la France.* La Tour-d'Aigues: Editions de l'Aube, 2000.

Boyer, Paul S. *By the Bomb's Early Light: American Thought and Culture at the Dawn of the Atomic Age.* 1985. New edition, Chapel Hill: University of North Carolina Press, 1994.

Bracops, Martine, ed. *Nostradamus traducteur traduit: actes du colloque international de traductologie. . . .* Brussels: Editions du Hazard, 2000.

Braden, Gregg, et al. *The Mystery of 2012: Predictions, Prophecies & Possibilities.* Boulder, CO: Sounds True, 2007.

Brassaï. *Henry Miller, Happy Rock*. 1978. Translated by Jane Marie Todd. Chicago: University of Chicago Press, 2002.

Braudy, Leo. *The Frenzy of Renown: Fame and Its History*. 1986. New York: Vintage, 1997.

Bréchon, Pierre. "Les attitudes religieuses en France: quelles recompositions en cours?" *Archives de sciences sociales des religions* 109 (2000): 11–30.

———. "L'évolution du religieux." *Futuribles* 260 (2001): 39–48.

Brind'Amour, Pierre. *Nostradamus astrophile: les astres et l'astrologie dans la vie et l'oeuvre de Nostradamus*. Ottawa: Presses de l'Université d'Ottawa, 1993.

Britnell, Jennifer, and Derek Stubbs. "The *Mirabilis Liber:* Its Compilation and Influence." *Journal of the Warburg and Courtauld Institutes* 49 (1986): 126–49.

Brockliss, Laurence, and Colin Jones. *The Medical World in Early Modern France*. Oxford: Oxford University Press, 1997.

Browning, Gordon. "Tristan Tzara: 'La grande complainte de mon obscurité.'" *Europe* 555–56 (1975): 202–13.

Buck-Morss, Susan. *The Dialectics of Seeing: Walter Benjamin and the Arcades Project*. Cambridge, MA: MIT Press, 1991.

Burns, William E. "The King's Two Monstrous Bodies: John Bulwer and the English Revolution." In *Wonders, Marvels, and Monsters in Early Modern Culture*, edited by Peter G. Platt, 187–202. Newark, NJ: University of Delaware Press, 1999.

———. *An Age of Wonders: Prodigies, Politics, and Providence in England, 1657–1727*. Manchester: Manchester University Press, 2002.

Bynum, Caroline Walker. "Wonder." *American Historical Review* 102, no. 1 (1997): 1–26.

Caillot, Patrice. "Le lancement du *Capitan:* février–mars 1906." *Le masque noir* 1 (1979): 19–31.

Calder, Angus. *The People's War: Britain, 1939–1945*. New York: Pantheon, 1969.

Calvet, Louis-Jean. "Les tours de Nostredame." In *Hommage à Pierre Guiraud*, 163–74. Nice: Annales de la Faculté des lettres et sciences humaines de Nice, 1985.

Cambers, Andrew. "Demonic Possession, Literacy and 'Superstition' in Early Modern England." *Past & Present* 202, no. 1 (2009): 3–35.

Camden, Carroll, Jr. "Elizabethan Almanacs and Prognostications." *The Library*, 4th ser., 12, no. 1 (1931): 83–108, 194–207.

Campbell, Colin. "Half-Belief and the Paradox of Ritual Instrumental Activism: A Theory of Modern Superstition." *British Journal of Sociology* 47, no. 1 (1996): 151–66.

———. "The Cult, the Cultic Milieu and Secularization." In *The Cultic Milieu: Oppositional Subcultures in an Age of Globalization*, edited by Jeffrey Kaplan and Heléne Lööw, 12–25. Walnut Creek, CA: AltaMira Press, 2002.

Capp, Bernard. *Astrology and the Popular Press: English Almanacs 1500–1800*. London: Faber & Faber, 1979.

Carlstedt, Anna. "Nostradamus mélancolique: un poète déguisé en prophète?" *Nouvelle revue du seizième siècle* 22, no. 2 (2004): 41–55.

———. "La poésie oraculaire de Nostradamus: langue, style et genre des Centuries." Ph.D. diss., University of Stockholm, 2005.

Caruth, Cathy, ed. *Trauma: Explorations in Memory*. Baltimore: Johns Hopkins University Press, 1995.

Cassan, Michel. *La grande peur de 1610: les Français et l'assassinat d'Henri IV*. Seyssel: Champ Vallon, 2010.

Castells, Manuel. *The Informational City: Information Technology, Economic Restructuring, and the Urban-Regional Process*. Oxford: Blackwell, 1989.

Cavallo, Guglielmo, and Roger Chartier, eds. *A History of Reading in the West*. Translated by Lydia G. Cochrane. Amherst: University of Massachusetts Press, 1999.

Cave, Terence. "The Mimesis of Reading in the Renaissance." In *Mimesis: From Mirror to Method, Augustine to Descartes,* edited by John D. Lyons and Stephen G. Nichols, Jr., 149–65. Hanover, NH: University Press of New England, 1982.

Céard, Jean. *La nature et les prodiges: l'insolite au XVIᵉ siècle, en France.* Geneva: Droz, 1977.

———. "J. A. de Chavigny: le premier commentateur de Nostradamus." In *Scienze, credenze occulte, livelli di cultura,* edited by Giancarlo Garfagnini, 427–42. Florence: Leo S. Olschki, 1982.

Charle, Christophe. *Discordance des temps. Une brève histoire de la modernité.* Paris: Armand Colin, 2011.

Charpak, Georges, and Henri Broch. *Debunked! ESP, Telekinesis, and Other Pseudoscience.* Translated by Bart K. Holland. Baltimore: Johns Hopkins University Press, 2004.

Chartier, Roger. "Publishing Strategies and What the People Read, 1530–1660." In Chartier, *The Cultural Uses of Print in Early Modern France,* 145–82. Trans. Lydia G. Cochrane. Princeton: Princeton University Press, 1987.

Chaunu, Pierre. *La mort à Paris. XVIᵉ, XVIIᵉ et XVIIIᵉ siècles.* Paris: Fayard, 1978.

Chevignard, Bernard. "Jean-Aimé de Chavigny: son identité, ses origines familiales." *Bibliothèque d'Humanisme et Renaissance* 58 (1996): 419–25.

———. "L'énigme Chevigny/Chavigny: les pièces du dossier." *Bibliothèque d'Humanisme et Renaissance* 67 (2005): 353–71.

Chomarat, Michel. "De quelques dates clairement exprimées par Michel Nostradamus dans ses 'Prophéties.'" *Cahiers V.-L. Saulnier* 15 (1998): 83–93.

Chomarat, Michel, Jean Dupèbe, and Gilles Polizzi. *Nostradamus ou le savoir transmis.* Lyon: Michel Chomarat, 1997.

Choucha, Nadia. *Surrealism and the Occult: Shamanism, Magic, Alchemy, and the Birth of an Artistic Movement.* Rochester, VT: Destiny Books, 1992.

Clark, Stuart. "French Historians and Early Modern Popular Culture." *Past & Present* 100, no. 1 (1983): 62–99.

Clébert, Jean-Paul. *Nostradamus, mode d'emploi: la clé des prophéties.* Paris: J.-C. Lattès, 1981.

Cohen, Paul. "Poets into Frenchmen: Timothy Hampton on Literature and National Sentiment in Renaissance France." *Shakespeare Studies* 33 (2005): 173–204.

Coleman, Joyce. *Public Reading and the Reading Public in Late Medieval England and France.* Cambridge: Cambridge University Press, 1996.

Conley, Tom. *An Errant Eye: Poetry and Topography in Early Modern France.* Minneapolis: University of Minnesota Press, 2011.

Conrad, Peter. *Orson Welles: The Stories of His Life.* London: Faber & Faber, 2003.

Cook, James W. *The Arts of Deception: Playing with Fraud in the Age of Barnum.* Cambridge, MA: Harvard University Press, 2001.

Crawford, Katherine. *Perilous Performances: Gender and Regency in Early Modern France.* Cambridge, MA: Harvard University Press, 2004.

Crivello, Maryline. "Du passé, faisons un spectacle! Généalogies des reconstitutions historiques de Salon et Grans en Provence (XIXᵉ–XXᵉ siècles)." *Sociétés et représentations* 12 (2001): 225–34.

Crocq, Louis. *Les traumatismes psychiques de guerre.* Paris: Odile Jacob, 1999.

Crosby, Alfred W. *The Measure of Reality: Quantification and Western Society, 1250–1600.* Cambridge: Cambridge University Press, 1997.

Crouzet, Denis. *Les guerriers de Dieu: la violence au temps des troubles de religion (vers 1525–vers 1610).* 2 vols. Seyssel: Champ Vallon, 1990.

———. *Nostradamus: une médecine des âmes à la Renaissance.* Paris: Payot & Rivages, 2011.

Crouzet, François. *Nostradamus, poète français.* Paris: Julliard, 1973.

Cunningham, Andrew, and Ole Peter Grell. *The Four Horsemen of the Apocalypse: Religion, War, Famine, and Death in Reformation Europe.* Cambridge: Cambridge University Press, 2000.

Curry, Patrick. *A Confusion of Prophets: Victorian and Edwardian Astrology.* London: Collins & Brown, 1992.

Cusset, François. *La décennie: le grand cauchemar des années 1980.* Paris: La Découverte, 2006.

D'Agostino, Denise. "Les extensions récentes de Salon-de-Provence." Master's thesis, Faculté des lettres et sciences humaines d'Aix-en-Provence, 1966.

Daly, R. J. "Samuel Pepys and Post-Traumatic Stress Disorder." *British Journal of Psychiatry* 143 (1983): 64–68.

Damisch, Lysann, Barbara Stoberock, and Thomas Mussweiler. "Keep Your Fingers Crossed! How Superstition Improves Performance." *Psychological Science* 21, no. 7 (2010): 1014–20.

Daniell, David. *The Bible in English: Its History and Influence.* New Haven: Yale University Press, 2003.

Darnton, Robert. *Mesmerism and the End of the Enlightenment in France.* Cambridge, MA: Harvard University Press, 1968.

Daston, Lorraine, and Katharine Park. *Wonders and the Order of Nature, 1150–1750.* New York: Zone Books, 2001.

Davies, Owen. *Witchcraft, Magic and Culture, 1736–1951.* Manchester: Manchester University Press, 1999.

———. *The Haunted: A Social History of Ghosts.* New York: Palgrave Macmillan, 2007.

Davis, Natalie Zemon. "Publisher Guillaume Rouillé, Businessman and Humanist." In *Editing Sixteenth-Century Texts,* edited by Richard J. Schoeck, 72–112. Toronto: University of Toronto Press, 1966.

Debbagi Baranova, Tatiana. "Poésie officielle, poésie partisane pendant les guerres de Religion." *Terrain* 41 (2003): 15–34.

Defrance, Eugène. *Catherine de Médicis, ses astrologues et ses magiciens-envoûteurs.* Paris: Mercure de France, 1911.

De Launay, Jacques. *La France de Pétain.* Paris: Editions du Trident, 1990.

Delaunay, Paul. *La vie médicale aux XVIᵉ, XVIIᵉ et XVIIIᵉ siècles.* 1935. Reprint, Geneva: Slatkine, 2001.

Delaurenti, Béatrice. *La puissance des mots: vitus verborum: débats doctrinaux sur le pouvoir des incantations au Moyen Age.* Paris: Cerf, 2007.

Delumeau, Jean. *La peur en Occident (XIVᵉ–XVIIIᵉ siècles): une cité assiégée.* Paris: Fayard, 1978.

Demars, Aline. "Michel Zévaco et le roman feuilleton." PhD diss., University of Paris–IV, 1986.

Deny, Jean. "Les pseudo-prophéties concernant les Turcs au XVIᵉ siècle." *Revue des études islamiques* 10 (1936): 201–20.

Diamond, Hanna. *Fleeing Hitler: France 1940.* Oxford: Oxford University Press, 2007.

Dickey, Colin. *Cranioklepty: Grave Robbing and the Search for Genius.* Denver: Unbridled Books, 2009.

Dienstag, Joshua Foa. *Pessimism: Philosophy, Ethic, Spirit.* Princeton: Princeton University Press, 2006.

Dinet, Dominique. "Les bibliothèques monastiques de Bourgogne et de Champagne au XVIIIᵉ siècle." *Histoire, économie et société* 2 (1983): 281–302.

Doob, Leonard W. "Goebbels' Principles of Propaganda." In *Propaganda,* edited by Robert Jackall, 190–216. New York: New York University Press, 1995 [1950].

Drévillon, Hervé. *Lire et écrire l'avenir: l'astrologie dans la France du Grand Siècle, 1610–1715.* Seyssel: Champ Vallon, 1996.

Drévillon, Hervé, and Pierre Lagrange. *Nostradamus, l'éternel retour.* Paris: Découvertes Galli-
    mard, 2003.

Dubois, Claude-Gilbert. *L'imaginaire de la Renaissance.* Paris: Presses Universitaires de France,
    1985.

———. "L'invention prédictive dans les *Prophéties* de Nostradamus." In *Ésotérisme, gnoses et
    imaginaire symbolique: mélanges offerts à Antoine Faivre,* edited by Richard Caron et al.,
    547–57. Leuven: Peeters, 2001.

———. "Un imaginaire de la catastrophe: Nostradamus, témoin du présent et visionnaire du fu-
    tur." *Eidôlon* 58 (2001): 69–82.

During, Simon. *Modern Enchantments: The Cultural Power of Secular Magic.* Cambridge, MA:
    Harvard University Press, 2004.

Eamon, William. *Science and the Secrets of Nature: Books of Secrets in Medieval and Early Mod-
    ern Culture.* Princeton: Princeton University Press, 1994.

Edelman, Nicole. "Spiritisme et politique." *Revue d'histoire du XIXe siècle* 28 (2004): 149–61.

———. *Histoire de la voyance et du paranomal du XVIIIe siècle à nos jours.* Paris: Seuil, 2006.

Edelstein, Dan, ed. *The Super-Enlightenment: Daring to Know Too Much.* Oxford: Voltaire Foun-
    dation, 2010.

Esquerre, Arnaud. *La manipulation mentale: sociologie des sectes en France.* Paris: Fayard, 2009.

Eyman, Scott. *Lion of Hollywood: The Life and Legend of Louis B. Mayer.* New York: Simon &
    Schuster, 2005.

Febvre, Lucien, and Henri-Jean Martin. 1958. *L'apparition du livre.* Paris: Albin Michel, 1971.

Fenn, Richard K., ed. *The Blackwell Companion to Sociology of Religion.* Oxford: Blackwell,
    2001.

Ferrell, Lori Anne. *The Bible and the People.* New Haven: Yale University Press, 2008.

Ford, Philip, and Gillian Jondorf, eds. *Intellectual Life in Renaissance Lyon: Proceedings of the
    Cambridge Lyon Colloquim, 14–16 April 1991.* Cambridge: Cambridge French Colloquia,
    1993.

Fox, Jo. "Propaganda and the Flight of Rudolf Hess, 1941–45." *Journal of Modern History* 83,
    no. 1 (2011): 78–110.

Friedman, Jerome. *The Battle of the Frogs and Fairford's Flies: Miracles and the Pulp Press Dur-
    ing the English Revolution.* New York: St. Martin's Press, 1993.

Fujiwara, Chris. *Jacques Tourneur: The Cinema of Nightfall.* Baltimore: Johns Hopkins Univer-
    sity Press, 2001.

Füredi, Frank. *Politics of Fear: Beyond Left and Right.* New York: Continuum, 2005.

Garber, Judy, and Martin E. P. Seligman, eds. *Human Helplessness: Theory and Applications.*
    London: Academic Press, 1980.

Garber, Marjorie. "Our Genius Problem." *Atlantic* 290, no. 5 (2002): 64–72.

Gardner, Daniel. *The Science of Fear: Why We Fear the Things We Shouldn't—and Put Ourselves
    in Greater Danger.* New York: Dutton, 2008.

Garland, Caroline, ed. *Understanding Trauma: A Psychoanalytical Approach.* New York: Rout-
    ledge, 1998.

Garrett, Clarke. *Respectable Folly: Millenarians and the French Revolution in France and En-
    gland.* Baltimore: Johns Hopkins University Press, 1975.

Gautheret-Comboulot, Simon. *Les auteurs beaunois du XVIe au XIXe siècle.* 1893. Reprint, Ge-
    neva: Slatkine, 1971.

Gerson, Stéphane. "Searching for Nostradamus: Tracking the Man, the Legend, and the Name
    Across Five Centuries." *Esopus* 13 (2009): 135–48.

———. "Five Hundred Years of Reading Nostradamus." In Nostradamus, *Prophecies.* Edited by
    Gerson and Richard Sieburth, translated by Sieburth, 297–314. New York: Penguin, 2012.

Giddens, Anthony. *Modernity and Self-Identity: Self and Society in the Late Modern Age.* Stanford, CA: Stanford University Press, 1991.

Gilbert, Daniel Todd. *Stumbling on Happiness.* New York: Vintage, 2007.

Glassner, Barry. *The Culture of Fear: Why Americans Are Afraid of the Wrong Things.* New York: Basic Books, 1999.

Gottesman, Ronald, ed. *Critical Essays on Henry Miller.* New York: G. K. Hall, 1992.

Goulemot, Jean-Marie. "Démons, merveilles et philosophie à l'âge classique." *Annales* 35, no. 6 (1980): 1223–50.

Gouron, Marcel. "Documents inédits sur l'Université de médecine de Montpellier." *Montpellier médical,* 3rd ser., 99, no. 50 (1956): 372–77.

Graebner, William. *The Age of Doubt: American Thought and Culture in the 1940s.* Long Grove, IL: Waveland, 1991.

Grafton, Anthony. *Cardano's Cosmos: The Worlds and Works of a Renaissance Astrologer.* Cambridge, MA: Harvard University Press, 1999.

———. "Starry Messengers: Recent Work in the History of Western Astrology." *Perspectives on Science* 8, no. 1 (2000): 70–83.

Gray, Floyd. *La Renaissance des mots: de Jean Lemaire de Belges à Agrippa d'Aubigné.* Paris: Champion, 2008.

Green, Jonathan. *Printing and Prophecy: Prognostication and Media Change, 1540–1550.* Ann Arbor: University of Michigan Press, 2012.

Greenblatt, Stephen. *Renaissance Self-Fashioning: From More to Shakespeare.* 1980. Chicago: University of Chicago Press, 2005.

———. *Will in the World: How Shakespeare Became Shakespeare.* New York: Norton, 2004.

Gruber, Elmar R. *Nostradamus: Sein Leben, sein Werk und die wahre Bedeutung seiner Prophezeiungen.* Bern: Scherz, 2003.

Guenée, Bernard. *Du Guesclin et Froissart: la fabrication de la renommée.* Paris: Tallandier, 2008.

Guinard, Patrice. Corpus Nostradamus. http//: cura.free.fr.

Gutjahr, Paul C. *An American Bible: A History of the Good Book in the United States, 1777–1880.* Stanford, CA: Stanford University Press, 1999.

Guyatt, Nicholas. *Have a Nice Doomsday: Why Millions of Americans Are Looking Forward to the End of the World.* New York: Harper, 2007.

Hahn, H. Hazel. *Scenes of Parisian Modernity: Culture and Consumption in the Nineteenth Century.* New York: Palgrave Macmillan, 2009.

Halbronn, Jacques. "Les prophéties et la Ligue." *Cahiers V.-L. Saulnier* 15 (1998): 95–133.

———. *Le texte prophétique en France: formation et fortune.* Villeneuve d'Ascq: Presses du Septentrion, 1999.

Halbwachs, Maurice. *On Collective Memory.* Edited and translated by Lewis A. Coser. Chicago: University of Chicago Press, 1992.

Hall, John R. *Apocalypse: From Antiquity to the Empire of Modernity.* Cambridge: Polity, 2009.

Hall, Stuart, et al. *Policing the Crisis: Mugging, the State, and Law and Order.* London: Macmillan, 1978.

Hampton, Timothy. *Literature and Nation in the Sixteenth Century: Inventing Renaissance France.* Ithaca, NY: Cornell University Press, 2001.

Haran, Alexandre Y. *Le lys et le globe: messianisme dynastique et rêve impérial en France à l'aube des temps modernes.* Seyssel: Champ Vallon, 2000.

Harding, Vanessa. *The Dead and the Living in Paris and London, 1500–1670.* Cambridge: Cambridge University Press, 2002

Hartog, François. *Régimes d'historicité: présentisme et expériences du temps.* Paris: Seuil, 2003.

Harvey, David Allen. *Beyond Enlightenment: Occultism and Politics in Modern France.* DeKalb: Northern Illinois University Press, 2005.

Hawkins, R. L. "A Prognostication by Nostradamus in an Unpublished Letter of the Seventeenth Century." *Romanic Review* 7 (1916): 224–25.

Hay, Peter. *MGM: When the Lion Roars.* Atlanta: Turner, 1991.

Hervieu-Léger, Danièle. *Le pèlerin et le converti: la religion en mouvement.* Paris: Flammarion, 1999.

Hill, Christopher. *The English Bible and the Seventeenth-Century Revolution.* London: Allen Lane, 1993.

Hitchcock, Susan Tyler. *Frankenstein: A Cultural History.* New York: Norton, 2007.

Hodges, Elisabeth. *Urban Poetics in the French Renaissance.* Aldershot: Ashgate, 2008.

Hoffmann, Stanley. "The Trauma of 1940: A Disaster and Its Traces." In *The French Defeat of 1940: Reassessments,* edited by Joel Blatt, 354–70. Providence, RI: Berghahn Books, 1998.

Hofstadter, Richard. *The Paranoid Style in American Politics, and Other Essays.* 1965. New York: Vintage, 2008.

Horowitz, Mitch. *Occult America: The Secret History of How Mysticism Shaped Our Nation.* New York: Bantam, 2009.

Howe, Ellic. *Urania's Children: The Strange World of the Astrologers.* London: Kimber, 1967.

Hunt, Lynn. "The World We Have Gained: The Future of the French Revolution." *American Historical Review* 108, no. 1 (2003): 1–19.

———. *Measuring Time, Making History.* Budapest: Central European University Press, 2008.

Jackson, H. J. *Marginalia: Readers Writing in Books.* New Haven: Yale University Press, 2001.

Jonas, Raymond. *France and the Cult of the Sacred Heart: An Epic Tale for Modern Times.* Berkeley: University of California Press, 2000.

Jones-Davies, M.T., ed. *Devins et charlatans au temps de la Renaissance.* Paris: Université de Paris-Sorbonne, 1979.

Jouanna, Arlette. *La France du XVIe siècle, 1483–1598.* 2nd ed. Paris: Presses Universitaires de France, 1997.

Kalifa, Dominique, Philippe Régnier, Marie-Eve Thérenty, and Alain Vaillant, eds. *La civilisation du journal: histoire culturelle et littéraire de la presse française au XIXe siècle.* Paris: Nouveau Monde, 2011.

Kalifa, Dominique. *Crime et Culture au XIXe siècle.* Paris: Perrin, 2005.

Kaplan, David E., and Andrew Marshal. *The Cult at the End of the World: The Incredible Story of the Aum Doomsday Cult, from the Subways of Tokyo to the Nuclear Arsenals of Russia.* New York: Crown, 1996.

Kassell, Lauren. *Medicine and Magic in Elizabethan London: Simon Forman, Astrologer, Alchemist, and Physician.* Oxford: Clarendon Press, 2005.

Keinan, Giora. "The Effects of Stress and Desire for Control on Superstitious Behavior." *Personality and Social Psychology Bulletin* 28 (2002): 102–08.

Kern, Stephen. *The Culture of Time and Space, 1880–1918.* Cambridge, MA.: Harvard University Press, 1983.

Kingston, Jeff. *Japan's Quiet Transformation: Social Change and Civil Society in the Twenty-First Century.* New York: Routledge, 2004.

Kirshenblatt-Gimblett, Barbara. *Destination Culture: Tourism, Museums, and Heritage.* Berkeley: University of California Press, 1998.

Kisala, Robert. "Nostradamus and the Apocalypse in Japan." *Inter-Religio* 32 (1997): 47–62.

Knecht, Robert J. *The French Renaissance Court, 1483–1589.* New Haven: Yale University Press, 2008.

Knight, Stephen. *Merlin: Knowledge and Power Through the Ages.* Ithaca, NY: Cornell University Press, 2009.

Knoppers, Laura Lunger, and Joan B. Landes, eds. *Monstrous Bodies/Political Monstrosities in Early Modern Europe.* Ithaca, NY: Cornell University Press, 2004.

Kogo, Yoshiyuki. "Aum Shinrikyo and Spiritual Emergency." *Journal of Humanistic Psychology* 42, no. 4 (2002): 82–101.

Koppes, Clayton R., and Gregory D. Black. *Hollywood Goes to War: How Politics, Profits, and Propaganda Shaped World War II Movies.* New York: Free Press, 1987.

Koyré, Alexandre. *From the Closed World to the Infinite Universe.* Baltimore: Johns Hopkins University Press, 1957.

La Garanderie, Marie-Madeleine de. "La méditation philosophique sur le temps au XVIᵉ siècle: Budé, Montaigne." In *Le temps et la durée dans la littérature au Moyen Age et à la Renaissance,* edited by Yvonne Bellenger, 193–209. Paris: A.-G. Nizet, 1986.

Langer, Ellen J. "The Illusion of Control." *Journal of Personality and Social Psychology* 32, no. 2 (1975): 311–28.

Langer, Ulrich. *Perfect Friendship: Studies in Literature and Moral Philosophy from Boccaccio to Corneille.* Geneva: Droz, 1994.

Larkey, Sanford V. "Astrology and Politics in the First Years of Elizabeth's Reign." *Bulletin of the Institute of the History of Medicine* 3, no. 3 (1935): 171–86.

Laroche, Jean-Paul. *Prophéties pour temps de crise: interprétations de Nostradamus au fil des siècles.* Lyon: Michel Chomarat, 2003.

Lemesurier, Peter. *The Nostradamus Encyclopedia: The Definitive Reference Guide to the Work and the World of Nostradamus.* New York: St. Martin's Press, 1997.

Le Naour, Jean-Yves. *Nostradamus s'en va-t-en guerre, 1914–1918.* Paris: Hachette, 2008.

Lenoir, Frédéric. *Les métamorphoses de Dieu: la nouvelle spiritualité occidentale.* Paris: Plon, 2003.

Leroy, Edgar. *Nostradamus: ses origines, sa vie, son oeuvre.* 1972. Marseille: Laffitte, 1993.

Lestringant, Frank. *Ecrire le monde à la Renaissance: quinze études sur Rabelais, Postel, Bodin et la littérature géographique.* Caen: Paradigme, 1993.

Levantal, Christophe. *La route des Princes: le voyage des ducs de Bourgogne et de Berry, de la frontière espagnole jusqu'à Versailles (1701) d'après le "Mercure Galant."* Paris: Sicre, 2001.

Lever, Maurice, ed. *Canards sanglants: naissance du fait divers.* Paris: Fayard, 1993.

LeVert, Liberté E. *The Prophecies and Enigmas of Nostradamus.* Glen Rock, NJ: Firebell Books, 1979.

Lévi-Strauss, Claude. *Introduction to the Work of Marcel Mauss.* 1950. Translated by Felicity Baker. New York: Routledge, 1987.

Lhez, E.-P.-E. "L'ascendance paternelle de Michel de Nostredame." *Provence historique* 18, no. 74 (1968): 385–424.

Liaroutzos, Chantal. "Les prophéties de Nostradamus: suivez la Guide." *Réforme, Humanisme, Renaissance* 12, no. 23 (1986): 35–40.

Lifton, Robert Jay. *Destroying the World to Save It: Aum Shinrikyō, Apocalyptic Violence, and the New Global Terrorism.* New York: Henry Holt, 2000.

Lillqvist, Outi, and Marjaana Lindeman. "Belief in Astrology as a Strategy for Self-Verification and Coping with Negative Life-Events." *European Psychologist* 3, no. 3 (1998): 202–08.

Lilti, Antoine. *Le monde des salons: sociabilité et mondanité à Paris au XVIIIᵉ siècle.* Paris: Fayard, 2005.

——. "The Writing of Paranoia: Jean-Jacques Rousseau and the Paradoxes of Celebrity." *Representations* 103, no.1 (2008): 53–83.

Long, Rose-Carol Washton. "Occultism, Anarchism, and Abstraction: Kandinsky's Art of the Future." *Art Journal* 46, no. 1 (1987): 38–45.

Lucenet, Monique. *Les grandes pestes en France.* Paris: Aubier, 1985.

Lucius, Henriette. "La littérature visionnaire en France du début du XVIᵉ au début du XIXᵉ siècle." PhD diss., University of Basel, 1970.

Lüsebrink, Hans-Jürgen, York-Gothart Mix, Jean-Yves Mollier, and Patricia Sorel, eds. *Les lectures du peuple en Europe et dans les Amériques (XVIIe au XXe siècle).* Brussels: Complexe, 2003.

Magida, Arthur J. *The Nazi Séance: The Strange Story of the Jewish Psychic in Hitler's Circle.* New York: Palgrave Macmillan, 2011.

Marion, Philippe. "Narratologie médiatique et médiagénie des récits." *Recherches en communication* 7 (1997): 61–87.

Marlow, Christopher. "Friendship in Renaissance England." *Literature Compass* 1 (2003): 1–10.

Martin, Daniel R., Pierre Servet, and André Tournon, eds. *L'énigmatique à la Renaissance: formes, significations, esthétiques.* Paris: Champion, 2008.

Martin, Marc. *Médias et journalistes de la République.* Paris: Odile Jacob, 1997.

Mauss, Marcel. *A General Theory of Magic.* Translated by Robert Brain. 1902. New edition, London: Routledge, 1972.

Maxwell-Stuart, P. G. *Ghosts: A History of Phantoms, Ghouls & Other Spirits of the Dead.* Stroud: Tempus, 2006.

May, Lary. *The Big Tomorrow: Hollywood and the Politics of the American Way.* Chicago: University of Chicago Press, 2000.

Mayeur, Jean-Marie. "Monseigneur Dupanloup et Louis Veuillot devant les prophéties contemporaines en 1874." *Revue d'histoire de la spiritualité* 48 (1972): 193–204.

McFarlane, Ian Dalrymple. *Renaissance France, 1470–1589.* London: Benn, 1974.

McGinn, Bernard. *Visions of the End: Apocalyptic Traditions in the Middle Ages.* 2nd ed. New York: Columbia University Press, 1998.

Mellot, Jean-Dominique. *L'édition rouennaise et ses marchés (vers 1600–vers 1730): dynamisme provincial et centralisme parisien.* Paris: Ecole Nationale des Chartes, 1998.

Mercier, Christophe. *Leonarde's Ghost: Popular Piety and "The Appearance of a Spirit" in 1628.* Edited and translated by Katherine A. Edwards and Susie Speakman Sutch. Kirksville, MO: Truman State University Press, 2008.

Miller, John. *Popery and Politics in England, 1660–1688.* Cambridge: Cambridge University Press, 1973.

Millet, Olivier. "Feux croisés sur Nostradamus au XVIᵉ siècle." *Cahiers V.-L. Saulnier* 4 (1987): 103–21.

Minois, Georges. *Histoire de l'avenir, des prophètes à la prospective.* Paris: Fayard, 1996.

Mollier, Jean-Yves, Jean-François Sirinelli, and François Vallotton, eds. *Culture de masse et culture médiatique en Europe et dans les Amériques: 1860–1940.* Paris: Presses Universitaires de France, 2006.

Monroe, John Warne. *Laboratories of Faith: Mesmerism, Spiritism, and Occultism in Modern France.* Ithaca, NY: Cornell University Press, 2008.

Moore, R. Laurence. *Selling God: American Religion in the Marketplace of Culture.* Oxford: Oxford University Press, 1994.

Moriceau, Lucie. "Le Coq et l'Orange: récit d'une guerre métallique entre Louis XIV et Guillaume III." *Revue historique des armées* 253 (2008): 22–29.

Morin, Edgar, ed. *La croyance astrologique moderne: diagnostic sociologique.* 1981. New edition, in collaboration with Claude Fischler, Philippe Defrance, and Lena Petrossian. Lausanne: L'Age d'Homme, 1982.

Moulin, Paul. *La propriété foncière et la vente des biens nationaux à Salon.* Aix-en-Provence: B. Niel, 1906.

Multon, Hilaire. "Les temps sont proches: prophétisme politique et culture apocalyptique dans le catholicisme français et italien (1859–1878)." 3 vols. PhD diss., University of Paris–XII, 2002.

Murakami, Haruki. *Underground: The Tokyo Gas Attack and the Japanese Psyche.* Translated by Alfred Birnbaum and Philip Gabriel. New York: Vintage, 2001.

Muray, Philippe. *Le XIXe siècle à travers les âges.* Paris: Denoël, 1999.

Mustafa, Kathleen Edna. "Republican Socialism and Revolution in France: *La République* of Eugène Bareste, 1848–1851." PhD diss., University of Melbourne, 1999.

National Research Council (U.S.). *The Internet Under Crisis Conditions: Learning from September 11.* Washington, DC: National Academies Press, 2003.

Neavill, Gordon B. "Publishing in Wartime: The Modern Library Series During the Second World War." *Library Trends* 55, no. 3 (2007): 583–96.

Nelson, William Max. "The Weapon of Time: Constructing the Future in France, 1750 to Year I." PhD diss., UCLA, 2006.

Nesbit, Thomas. *Henry Miller and Religion.* New York: Routledge, 2007.

Niccoli, Ottavia. *Prophecy and People in Renaissance Italy.* 1987. Translated by Lydia G. Cochrane. Princeton: Princeton University Press, 1990.

Nora, Pierre. "The Reasons for the Current Upsurge in Memory." *Transit* 22 (2002): 1–6.

O'Leary, Stephen D. *Arguing the Apocalypse: A Theory of Millennial Rhetoric.* New York: Oxford University Press, 1994.

Orsi, Robert. *Thank You, St. Jude: Women's Devotion to the Patron Saint of Hopeless Causes.* New Haven: Yale University Press, 1996.

Pagels, Elaine H. *Revelations: Visions, Prophecy, and Politics in the Book of Revelation.* New York: Viking, 2012.

Paillard, Bernard, ed. *Peurs.* Paris: Seuil, 1993.

Palmer, Michael Beaussenat. *Des petits journaux aux grandes agences: naissance du journalisme moderne, 1863–1914.* Paris: Aubier, 1983.

Panchasi, Roxanne. *Future Tense: The Culture of Anticipation in France Between the Wars.* Ithaca, NY: Cornell University Press, 2009.

Pantin, Isabelle. *La poésie du ciel en France dans la seconde moitié du seizième siècle.* Geneva: Droz, 1995.

Park, Katharine. *Doctors and Medicine in Early Renaissance Florence.* Princeton: Princeton University Press, 1985.

Pelletier, Monique. *De Ptolémée à la Guillotière (XVe–XVIe siècle): des cartes pour la France pourquoi, comment?* Paris: Comité des travaux historiques et scientifiques, 2009.

Perkins, Maureen. *The Reform of Time: Magic and Modernity.* London: Pluto Press, 2001.

Pietruska, Jamie L. "Propheteering: A Cultural History of Prediction in the Gilded Age." Ph.D. diss., MIT, 2009.

Pomian, Krzysztof. "Astrology as a Naturalistic Theology of History." In *"Astrologi Hallucinati": Stars and the End of the World in Luther's Time,* edited by Paola Zambelli, 29–43. Berlin: de Gruyter, 1986.

Popkin, Richard. "Seventeenth-Century Millenarianism." In *Apocalypse Theory and the Ends of the World,* edited by Malcolm Bull, 112–34. Oxford: Blackwell, 1995.

Pot, Olivier. "Prophétie et mélancolie: la querelle entre Ronsard et les Protestants (1562–1565)." *Cahiers V.-L. Saulnier* 15 (1998): 189–229.

Poumarède, Géraud. *Pour en finir avec la Croisade: mythes et réalités de la lutte contre les Turcs aux XVIe et XVIIe siècles.* Paris: Presses Universitaires de France, 2004.

Préaud, Maxime. *Les effets du soleil: almanachs du règne de Louis XIV.* Paris: Réunion des musées nationaux, 1995.

Prévost, Roger. *Nostradamus, le mythe et la réalité: un historien au temps des astrologues*. Paris: Laffont, 1999.

Prothero, Stephen R. *American Jesus: How the Son of God Became a National Icon*. New York: Farrar, Straus and Giroux, 2003.

Rabb, Theodore K. *The Last Days of the Renaissance and the March to Modernity*. New York: Basic Books, 2006.

Raglan, Lord. *The Hero: A Study in Tradition, Myth and Drama*. 1936. Mineola, NY: Dover, 2003.

Reader, Ian. "Violent Millenarianism with a Christian Touch: Syncretic Themes in the Millennial Perspective of Aum Shinrikyo." In *Christian Millenarianism: From the Early Church to Waco*, edited by Stephen Hunt, 239–54. Bloomington: Indiana University Press, 2001.

Revel, Jacques. "Forms of Expertise: Intellectuals and 'Popular' Culture in France (1650–1800)." In *Understanding Popular Culture: Europe from the Middle Ages to the Nineteenth Century*, edited by Steven L. Kaplan, 255–73. Berlin: Mouton, 1984.

Rey, Michel. "Communauté et individu: l'amitié comme lien social à la Renaissance." *Revue d'histoire moderne et contemporaine* 38, no. 4 (1991): 617–25.

Ribémont, Bernard, ed. *Observer, lire, écrire le ciel au Moyen Age*. Paris: Klincksieck, 1991.

Rigolot, François. *Poésie et Renaissance*. Paris: Seuil, 2002.

Rodgers, Daniel T. *Age of Fracture*. Cambridge, MA.: Belknap Press, 2011.

Roof, Wade Clark, Jackson W. Carroll, and David A. Roozen, eds. *The Post-War Generation and Establishment Religion*. Boulder, CO: Westview Press, 1995.

Rose, Marie-Eugénie. "Les écrits prophétiques de Nostradamus: contribution à l'étude du langage et de ses implications historiques." PhD diss., Faculté des lettres et civilisations, University of Lyon III, 1988.

Rosman, Doreen M. *Evangelicals and Culture*. London: Croom Helm, 1984.

Roubichou-Stretz, Antoinette. *La vision de l'histoire dans l'oeuvre de la Pléiade: thèmes et structures*. Paris: A.-G. Nizet, 1973.

Royon, Claude, ed. *Lyon l'humaniste: depuis toujours, ville de foi et de révoltes*. Paris: Autrement, 2004.

Rusche, Harry. "Prophecies and Propaganda, 1641 to 1651." *English Historical Review* 84, no. 333 (1969): 752–70.

Russell, Paul Albert. "Astrology as Popular Propaganda: Expectations of the End in the German Pamphlets of Joseph Grünpeck." In *Forme e destinazione del messaggio religioso: aspetti della propaganda religiosa nel Cinquecento*, edited by Antonio Rotondò, 165–95. Florence: L. S. Olschki, 1991.

Ryback, Timothy W. *Hitler's Private Library: The Books That Shaped His Life*. New York: Knopf, 2008.

Saenger, Paul Henry, and Kimberly Van Kampen, eds. *The Bible as Book: The First Printed Editions*. New Castle, DE: Oak Knoll Press, 1999.

Sahagun, Louis. *Master of the Mysteries: The Life of Manly Palmer Hall*. Los Angeles: Process, 2008.

Saler, Michael. "Modernity and Enchantment: A Historiographic Review." *American Historical Review* 111, no. 3 (2006): 692–716.

Samuel, Lawrence R. *Future: A Recent History*. Austin: University of Texas Press, 2009.

Saulnier, Verdun-Léon. *Maurice Scève*. 1948–49. 2 vols. Geneva: Klincksieck, 1981.

Schatz, Thomas. *Boom and Bust: American Cinema in the 1940s*. New York: Scribner, 1997.

Schivelbusch, Wolfgang. *The Railway Journey: The Industrialization of Time and Space in the Nineteenth Century*. Berkeley: University of California Press, 1986.

Schmidt, Leigh Eric. "From Demon Possession to Magic Show: Ventriloquism, Religion, and the Enlightenment." *Church History* 67, no. 2 (1998): 274–304.

Secret, François. *Les kabbalistes chrétiens de la Renaissance.* Paris: Dunod, 1964.

Séguin, Jean-Pierre. *L'information en France avant le périodique.* Paris: G.-P. Maisonneuve et Larose, 1964.

Sharp, Lynn L. *Secular Spirituality: Reincarnation and Spiritism in Nineteenth-Century France.* Lanham, MD: Lexington Books, 2006.

Sharpe, Kevin. *Reading Revolutions: The Politics of Reading in Early Modern England.* New Haven: Yale University Press, 2000.

——. "Reading Revelations: Prophecy, Hermeneutics and Politics in Early Modern Britain." In *Reading, Society and Politics in Early Modern England,* edited by Kevin Sharpe and Steven N. Zwicker, 122–63. Cambridge: Cambridge University Press, 2003.

Shepheard, David. "Pour une poétique du genre oraculaire: à propos de Nostradamus." *Revue de littérature comparée* 60, no. 237 (1986): 59–65.

Sherman, Caroline R. "The Genealogy of Knowledge: The Godefroy Family, Erudition, and Legal-Historical Service to the State." PhD diss., Princeton University, 2008.

Simonin, Anne. *Les Editions de Minuit, 1942–1955: le devoir d'insoumission.* Paris: IMEC, 1994.

Singer, Ben. "Modernity, Hyperstimulus, and the Rise of Popular Sensationalism." In *Cinema and the Invention of Modern Life,* edited by Leo Charney and Vanessa R. Schwartz, 72–99. Berkeley: University of California Press, 1995.

Smail, Daniel Lord. *On Deep History and the Brain.* Berkeley: University of California Press, 2008.

Smoley, Richard. *The Essential Nostradamus: Literal Translation, Historical Commentary, and Biography.* 2006. 2nd ed. New York: J. P. Tarcher, 2010.

Sobel, Dava. "The Resurrection of Nostradamus." *Omni* 16, no. 3 (1993): 42–51.

Solnon, Jean-François. *Catherine de Médicis.* Paris: Perrin, 2003.

Spangler, David. *Emergence: The Rebirth of the Sacred.* New York: Dell, 1984.

Styers, Randall. *Making Magic: Religion, Magic, and Science in the Modern World.* Oxford: Oxford University Press, 2003.

Sutherland, N. M. *Princes, Politics and Religion, 1547–1589.* London: Hambledon Press, 1984.

Taguieff, Pierre-André. *L'imaginaire du complot mondial: aspects d'un mythe moderne.* Paris: Mille et une nuits, 2006.

Taylor, Shelley E., and Jonathon D. Brown. "Illusions and Well-Being: A Social Psychological Perspective on Mental Health." *Psychological Bulletin* 103, no. 2 (1988): 193–210.

Ten-Doesschate Chu, Petra. *The Most Arrogant Man in France: Gustave Courbet and the Nineteenth-Century Media Culture.* Princeton: Princeton University Press, 2007.

Tennevin, Jean-Pierre. *François Michel de Salon de Provence: le maréchal ferrant reçu par Louis XIV.* Raphèle-lès-Arles: Petit, 1990.

Thérenty, Marie-Eve. *La littérature au quotidien: poétiques journalistiques au XIXᵉ siècle.* Paris: Seuil, 2007.

Thomas, Keith. *Religion and the Decline of Magic: Studies in Popular Beliefs in Sixteenth- and Seventeenth-Century England.* 1971. New edition, New York: Oxford University Press, 1997.

Thompson, John B. *The Media and Modernity: A Social Theory of the Media.* Stanford, CA: Stanford University Press, 1995.

Tinguely, Frédéric. *L'écriture du Levant à la Renaissance: enquête sur les voyageurs français dans l'empire de Soliman le Magnifique.* Geneva: Droz, 2000.

Tinniswood, Adrian. *By Permission of Heaven: The True Story of the Great Fire of London.* New York: Riverhead Books, 2004.

Tomalin, Claire. *Samuel Pepys: The Unequalled Self.* New York: Knopf, 2002.

Treitel, Corinna. *A Science for the Soul: Occultism and the Genesis of the German Modern.* Baltimore: Johns Hopkins University Press, 2004.

Vaillant, Alain, and Marie-Eve Thérenty. *1836, l'an I de l'ère médiatique: étude littéraire et historique du journal 'La Presse,' d'Emile de Girardin.* Paris: Nouveau Monde, 2001.

van Berkel, T. W. M. "Nostradamus, Astrology, and the Bible." www.nostradamusresearch.org/en/home/00.htm.

van der Wall, Ernestine. " 'Antichrist Stormed': The Glorious Revolution and the Dutch Prophetic Tradition." In *The World of William and Mary: Anglo-Dutch Perspectives on the Revolution of 1688–89,* edited by Dale Hoak and Mordechai Feingold, 152–64. Stanford, CA: Stanford University Press, 1996.

Vauchez, André, ed. *L'attente des temps nouveaux: eschatologie, millénarismes et visions du futur, du Moyen Age au XXe siècle.* Turnhout: Brépols, 2002.

Venard, Marc. "L'Eglise d'Avignon au XVIe siècle." PhD diss., University of Paris IV, 1980.

Verter, Bradford J. M. "Dark Star Rising: The Emergence of Modern Occultism, 1800–1950." PhD diss., Princeton University, 1998.

Vieira, Mark A. *Irving Thalberg: Boy Wonder to Producer Prince.* Berkeley: University of California Press, 2009.

Vyse, Stuart A. *Believing in Magic: The Psychology of Superstition.* Oxford: Oxford University Press, 1997.

Wakeman, Rosemary. *Modernizing the Provincial City: Toulouse, 1945–1975.* Cambridge, MA: Harvard University Press, 1997.

Walsham, Alexandra. "The Reformation and 'the Disenchantment of the World' Reassessed." *The Historical Journal* 51, no. 2 (2008): 497–528.

Walter, Philippe. *Merlin ou le savoir du monde.* Paris: Imago, 2000.

Warner, Marina. *No Go the Bogeyman: Scaring, Lulling, and Making Mock.* New York: Farrar, Straus and Giroux, 1999.

Weber, Eugen. *Apocalypses: Prophecies, Cults, and Millennial Beliefs Through the Ages.* Cambridge, MA: Harvard University Press, 1999.

Wheen, Francis. *Idiot Proof: Deluded Celebrities, Irrational Power Brokers, Media Morons, and the Erosion of Common Sense.* New York: PublicAffairs, 2004.

———. *Strange Days Indeed: The 1970s: The Golden Age of Paranoia.* New York: PublicAffairs, 2010.

Williamson, Arthur H. *Apocalypse Then: Prophecy and the Making of the Modern World.* Westport, CT: Praeger, 2008.

Wilson, Ian. *Nostradamus: The Man Behind the Prophecies.* New York: St. Martin's Press, 2003.

Winter, Alison. *Mesmerized: Powers of Mind in Victorian Britain.* Chicago: University of Chicago Press, 1998.

Wulff, Wilhelm. *Zodiac and Swastika: How Astrology Guided Hitler's Germany.* New York: Coward, McCann, 1973.

Wuthnow, Robert. *Experimentation in American Religion: The New Mysticisms and Their Implications for the Churches.* Berkeley: University of California Press, 1978.

Young, Patrick. "La Vieille France as Object of Bourgeois Desire: The Touring Club de France and the French Regions, 1890–1918." In *Histories of Leisure,* edited by Rudy Koshar, 169–89. New York: Berg, 2002.

Yun-Shik, Chang, Hyun-Ho Seok, and Donald L. Baker, eds. *Korea Confronts Globalization.* New York: Routledge, 2008.

Illustration Credits

1

Michel Nostradamus, *Les significations de l'Eclipse, qui sera le 16 Septembre 1559* (Paris, ca. 1559). Bibliothèque Nationale de France, département des estampes, Paris [BNF].

2

Pierre Woeiriot, "Michel Nostradamus, médecin et astrologue à 58 ans" (1562). BNF.

3

"Salon. Vue générale." Undated postcard (ca. 1900). BNF.

4

Almanach historial pour l'an de grâce mil six cens septante & quatre. Exactement supputé par Me M. Nostredamus, Grand Astrologue & Mathématicien (Troyes, ca. 1673). Bibliothèque de l'Arsenal, Paris.

5

Balthasar Guynaud, *La concordance des prophéties de Nostradamus avec l'histoire* (Paris, 1712 [1693]). Collection of the author.

6

"François Michel Maréchal Ferrant Natif de Salon en Provence" (Paris, ca. 1697). BNF.

7

"Une femme consultant Nostrodamus [*sic*] sur les evenements il lui presente une Table de Marbre . . ." (France, late eighteenth century). BNF.

8

M.Z. [after Christian Dietrich], "Nostradamus" (Paris, eighteenth century). BNF.

9

The Wizard; or, the Whole Art of Divining Dreams, and of Foretelling Events from Various Prognostics; by the Help of Which Persons May Interpret for Themselves on the Principles of the Great Nostradamus (Derby, 1816). British Library, London.

10

"Almanach prophétique, pittoresque et utile pour 1841" (Paris, ca. 1840). Réunion des Musées Nationaux/Art Resource, NY.

11

"Portrait de Michel Nostradamus, Astronome célèbre" (Epinal, 1860s). Réunion des Musées Nationaux/Art Resource, NY.

12

Henri Torné-Chavigny, "Nostradamus écrit l'Histoire prédite et jugée, comprenant toute l'histoire de France et les grands faits de l'histoire de l'Eglise et des peuples étrangers" (Bordeaux, ca. 1862). Fonds Michel Chomarat, Bibliothèque municipale de Lyon.

13

Promotional poster for Michel Zévaco's *Nostradamus, Le Matin* (Paris, 1907). Réunion des Musées Nationaux/Art Resource, NY.

14

"Les farces de la lune et les mésaventures de Nostradamus" (Paris, 1891). Collection of Timothy H. Moore, D.D.S.

15

"Les prédictions de Nostradamus," board game cover (Paris, early twentieth century). Réunion des Musées Nationaux/Art Resource, NY.

16

Nostradamus IV (MGM, 1944). Margaret Herrick Library, Academy of Motion Picture Arts and Sciences, Los Angeles.

17

"Reconstitution historique. Salon-de-Provence" (ca. 1990). Collection of the author.

18

Advertisement for Jameson whiskey (2006). © Pernod Ricard USA, all rights reserved.

19

Sun (New York, May 18, 2009). Collection of the author.

Index